Studies in Early Medieval Britain

General Editor: Nicholas Brooks

About the series:

The early Middle Ages, between the withdrawal of Roman authority at the start of the fifth century and the establishment of French-speaking aristocracies in the eleventh and twelfth centuries, was a key period in the history of the island of Britain. For it was then that the English, Welsh and Scots defined and distinguished themselves in language, customs and territory; it was then that successive conquests and settlements lent distinctive Irish, Anglo-Saxon, Scandinavian and Norman elements to the British ethnic mix; it was then that royal dynasties were established, that most of the surviving rural and urban settlements of Britain were created and named, and the landscape took a form that can still be recognised today; it was then too that Christian churches were established with lasting consequences for our cultural, moral, legal and intellectual perspectives.

The *Studies in Early Medieval Britain* will illuminate the history of Britain during this defining period and reveal its roots. Books in the series will be written, individually or in collaboration, by historians, archaeologists, philologists and literary and cultural scholars and are aimed at a wide readership of scholars, students and lay people.

About this volume:

There is no published account of the history of religious women in England before the Norman Conquest. Yet, female saints and abbesses, such as Hild of Whitby or Edith of Wilton, are among the most celebrated women recorded in Anglo-Saxon sources and their stories are of popular interest. This book offers the first general and critical assessment of female religious communities in early medieval England. It transforms our understanding of the different modes of religious vocation and institutional provision and thereby gives early medieval women's history a new foundation.

About the author/editor:

Sarah Foot is Lecturer in medieval history at the Department of History, University of Sheffield.

Nicholas Brooks is the Professor and Head of the Department of Medieval History, University of Birmingham.

Forthcoming titles in the series will include:

Carolingian Connections: England and Francia, 750–870
Joanna Story

Alfred the Great and his World
edited by Timothy Reuter

Vikings and the Danelaw
edited by J. Jesch, J. Graham-Campbell, R. Hall and D. Parsons

Veiled Women
I

For Matthew

Veiled Women
I

The Disappearance of Nuns from Anglo-Saxon England

Sarah Foot

Ashgate

Aldershot • Burlington USA • Singapore • Sydney

Published by

Ashgate Publishing Limited
Gower House, Croft Road
Aldershot, Hants
GU11 3HR
England

Ashgate Publishing Company
131 Main Street
Burlington
Vermont 05401–5600
USA

Ashgate website: http://www.ashgate.com

British Library CIP Data
Foot, Sarah, 1961–
    Veiled Women. Vol. I: The Disappearance of Nuns from
    Anglo-Saxon England.(Studies in Early Medieval Britain).
    1. Monasticism and religious orders for women–England–
    History–Middle Ages, 600–1500. 2. Women and religion–
    England–History.
    I. Title.
    255. 9' 00942' 0902

US Library of Congress CIP Data
Library of Congress Card Number: 99–054083

ISBN 0 7546 0043 2

This book is printed on acid free paper

Printed and bound in Great Britain by MPG Books Ltd, Bodmin, Cornwall

STUDIES IN EARLY MEDIEVAL BRITAIN – 1

Contents

Foreword

In times of rapid change in the publishing industry, it is a privilege to inaugurate a new scholarly series devoted to the study of early medieval Britain. The *Studies in Early Medieval Britain* have been designed to illuminate all parts of the island of Britain from the collapse of Roman authority at the start of the fifth century to the establishment of French-speaking aristocracies in different parts of the island in the eleventh and twelfth centuries. The series will be a focus for interdisciplinary collaboration between historians, archaeologist, philologists and literary or cultural scholars. It will respect the differences between their disciplines, but facilitate communication between them. A very substantial body of evidence survives from the early middle Ages, but much of it is difficult to understand and to analyse. The task of early medievalists is to master the necessary technical skills without weakening the fascination of their subject. There is a large public, lay and academic, whose interest in the origins of our society and culture, and of our political, administrative and ecclesiastical institutions, has been first whetted at school, college or university, by local studies in adult education or by television programmes. The *Studies in Early Medieval Britain* will therefore seek to reach this public by eschewing inaccessible jargon and by explaining the early medieval past with the help of good illustrations and diagrams. The objective is to maintain the highest standards of scholarship, but also of exposition. It will therefore be open both to works of general synthesis and to monographs by specialists in particular disciplines attempting to reach a wider readership. It will also include collaborative studies by expert specialists gathered to advance understanding by pooling their intellectual resources.

Dr Sarah Foot's two-part study, *Veiled Women*, provides a splendid inauguration for the new series. It makes major contributions both to early medieval gender studies and to Anglo-Saxon monastic history. It provides the first convincing explanation for the evanescence of so many of the institutions of female religious in the early Middle Ages. Her careful attention to the language and the dating of the sources enables her to clarify the fundamental distinction between the rare communities of cloistered nuns and the more widespread groupings of devout 'vowesses', mostly aristocratic widows who chose to devote their later years to a publicly acknowledged regime of piety, in part at least in order to avoid the pressure to remarry. She relates this fundamental distinction very clearly to the wider history of European female religious devotion since late antiquity and thus brings the world of the Anglo-Saxon nun into the continental mainstream. The brief flourishing of Anglo-Saxon double monasteries ruled by royal abbesses in the late seventh and early eighth centuries, here well recounted, becomes less surprising given the later demise of the kingdoms and dynasties that sustained them. All this helps Dr Foot to offer a convincing assessment of the impact of the Viking activity of the ninth century on female religious vocations. Here and throughout this study, her judgments rest securely upon a consistent analysis in part II of every known site where Anglo-Saxon female religious have been recorded or conjectured. Local historians may in time come to emend her interpretation of some particular houses as new evidence appears or the old is reinterpreted. But until her assembling and analysis of the body of the evidence, they had had no hope of interpreting isolated references within a convincing critical context. Part II therefore provides both a *catalogue raisonée* and a springboard for future research. It is a great honour to welcome to the series a work which transforms our understanding of Anglo-Saxon women's religious devotion so fundamentally in the context of the political society of the age and which sets out so clearly the scholarship which underpins it.

NICHOLAS BROOKS

University of Birmingham
May 1999

Preface

It has been axiomatic in gender studies of the medieval world that women are under-represented in the extant sources for the European early middle ages. That religious women may have attracted more attention from contemporary chroniclers than their lay sisters might be anticipated (a feature as much of their predominantly noble and royal social status as of any distinctively religious role that they performed within society). However, a demonstration that nuns were, in fact, also neglected by the authors of the primary sources, while occasioning some disappointment, would probably excite little surprise. What is more remarkable about the sources for the female religious life in later pre-Conquest England is their deficiency in comparison not only with the extant materials for male monasticism, but also in relation to the evidence for English nunneries of the pre-Viking Age. Fewer religious houses for women are described in contemporary sources for the period 900–1066 than are known from equivalent materials for the years before 900. A trawl of tenth- and eleventh-century texts reveals more communities inhabited during the later Anglo-Saxon period by monks than by nuns. (It is possible, of course, that during these centuries men deliberately obliterated any evidence relating to the female expression of religious devotion, but if so, why did they leave the texts relating to nuns of the pre-Viking Age while exercising their partiality exclusively in relation to their own times?)

Women religious of the English monastic revolution and its aftermath are veiled not so much in the mists of time, or in the deliberate obfuscations of male (often monastic) historians, as muffled by the near silence – or at best the infrequent whisperings – of the surviving sources. This is the paradox that lies at the heart of this book. It seeks to explain the social forces – or historical imperatives – that appear to have removed from the record of the tenth and eleventh centuries a significant body of professed religious (that defined solely by its gender) and rendered it insubstantial behind an historical veil. Ingenuity, persistence and a disregard for the evidential criteria of modern historical criticism permit the identification of many more female communities than the small sample reported in the extant literature of the period, but the very inadequacy of the evidence on which much of the ensuing argument depends is in itself indicative of the problems this issue presents. This book thus represents as much a critical reading of the nature of historical evidence for a given period as a study of the particular case exemplified: that of the materials relating to religious women in later Anglo-Saxon England.

The form of this book – a discursive exploration of the history of female religious observance in England before the Norman Conquest followed by an analytical survey of individual communities of women after the First Viking Age – is better understood when its genesis is explained. It grew originally from a commission to investigate and describe the evidence for women's religious houses in England between *c*. 940 and 1066, a task designed as part of a collaborative project exploring the female experience of reformed monasticism in tenth-century England under the direction of David Dumville. The function of that paper, it was imagined, was to summarize the sources for the West Saxon 'royal' nunneries which have been seen as central to the Benedictine revival and to explore the extant contemporary literature in search of other female houses, less familiar from the secondary writing on the period. A brief discussion of any notable issues raised by the surviving material was to be followed by a short catalogue, listing the two dozen or so nunneries for which sources are extant; this would have provided a clear evidential framework into which to set the other papers in the volume. In the event, this scheme could not be realized. Female religious houses, or to be more precise, places at which women religious appear to have lived (which are not entirely the same thing) have proved to be far more numerous than was at first imagined, while the sources in which they are described are infinitely less satisfactory than preliminary excursions into the secondary literature suggested. The book that has resulted from this project both illustrates the problems presented by the extant materials (and provides a detailed analysis of the particular evidence pertaining to each separate place where women religious are attested in the later Anglo-Saxon period) and further advances an explanation to account for the apparent poverty of the sources for tenth- and eleventh-century English nunneries.

The argumentative chapters preceding the survey of places where religious women lived analyse the history of the female religious experience in England before the Conquest, concentrating on the problems of the sources, particularly their diminution across the First Viking Age. The first chapter addresses the nature of the evidence and the later historiography, setting the framework for all that is to follow. Since an argument is being advanced about difference in the endowment of women's religious houses during the pre-Conquest period, it has been necessary to say something about the nature of nunneries in the pre-Viking Age and the place of religious women outside the cloister in that period; this constitutes chapter two. Consideration is given in the next chapter to the overlapping contexts in which an explanation must be sought for the apparent disappearance of the early Anglo-Saxon nun across the First Viking Age, namely the demise of the double house, the influence of Carolingian ecclesiastical reforms, and Danish military activity. The effect of the monastic revolution on women's religious observance is explored in chapter four and detailed attention is paid there to the distinctions made in the vernacular vocabulary between cloistered women and vowesses. Chapter five investigates the position of widows in the pre- and post-viking periods, and at the liturgy for their consecration which, at least in Archbishop Wulfstan's environment, shows some modification in the later tenth century. The case is made here that language can explain the problems over the categorisation of religious women with which previous historians have struggled. The rest of this study provides a detailed analysis of all the written evidence for women's collective religious observance between the accession of King Alfred and the Norman Conquest. In order to make some sense of this mass of material, the sixth chapter in this volume looks at different ways of grouping women's communities together, either according to some common feature of their history or evidentially, in relation to the sort of text in which their activities were first recorded. The afterword summarises the conclusions advanced earlier and draws attention to the similarities between English and continental practice. Part II considers, in alphabetical sequence, each of the sixty-one places at which a congregation of women religious has been attested to have been active in this period, providing the analysis of the primary evidence out of which the argument already advanced has evolved.

This book is aimed at several readerships: those interested in women in the Anglo-Saxon Church; those concerned with the tenth-century monastic revolution in general, and female involvement in the movement in particular; or scholars pursuing the particular histories of individual nunneries (or of specific geographical areas of England). It will have relevance also to students of early medieval women and of the role of gender issues in shaping the extant historical record.

I have incurred a number of debts during the long period when I have worked on these nunneries. My greatest gratitude must be to my colleagues in Sheffield, who have endured interminable conversations about the invisibility of religious women in the literature and have supplied much helpful bibliography, particularly for periods and places beyond my expertise. The University of Sheffield generously paid for the maps. The manuscript was largely completed during a period as a visiting bye-fellow at Newnham College, Cambridge and I am extremely grateful to the Principal and Fellows for their support and intellectual stimulation. Papers working towards the articulation of the overall argument of the book were given during 1997 to the Early Medieval Research Group in Edinburgh, to the graduate research seminar in medieval history at the University of Birmingham, to the women's studies graduate seminar in the English Department of York University, Toronto, and at a conference on the Laws and the Prophets in the Middle Ages at the University of Western Ontario. Questions relating to the language of the religious life were first aired in a session sponsored by the Dictionary of Old English at the meeting of the Medieval Academy of America in Toronto in April 1997. I am grateful to the participants on each of those occasions for some fruitful discussions, especially over the points where my own thinking then remained muddled. Considerable advice on general and specific points has been provided by Lesley Abrams, Michael Bentley, Michelle Brown,

Patrick Conner, David Ganz, Brian Golding, Dawn Hadley, Joanna Innes, Sarah Larratt Keefer, Susan Kelly, Simon Keynes, Simon Loseby, Chris Loveluck, Kathryn Lowe, Rosamond McKitterick, Katherine O'Brien O'Keeffe, Patricia Skinner, Robert Shoemaker, Julia Smith, Jane Stevenson, Gillian Sutherland, Liesbeth van Houts, Mary Vincent, and Teresa Webber. John Blair has read and commented helpfully on the whole manuscript as well as clarifying numerous points of detail; Julia Crick has with equal generosity discussed many aspects of the argument, notably those relating to widows, and has kindly allowed me to read several of her unpublished papers. Without David Dumville's continuing encouragement I would certainly have abandoned this task many times. My husband, Geoffrey, has endured much to make the research and writing possible, particularly in sharing the care of our son, to whom the book is dedicated.

Feast of St Matthew, 1997

Despite the long delay between the completion of this manuscript and its appearance, the bibliography has not substantially been updated since September 1997. Brief mention was, however, inserted at proof stage of three important articles about Anglo-Saxon nunneries all of which have now appeared; I am grateful to Julia Crick for drawing these to my attention. The maps were most kindly drawn for me by Michael Frankland of the Humber Archaeological Partnership; I am most grateful to him and to Chris Loveluck for their help in designing these. Above all I must thank my editor Nicholas Brooks, not only for his meticulous reading of the text (and his generosity in constructive criticism), but for his enduring confidence in this project. I am proud to have had the opportunity of launching his new series *Studies in Early Medieval Britain*.

University of Sheffield
May 1999

A note on language

One of the difficulties faced by the historian of female religious institutions in pre-Conquest England is that of the vocabulary of the religious life. There is no gender-specific noun in Latin or Old English that means a convent of devout women; their houses are, like those occupied by monks and secular clergy, consistently described as *monasteria* (Old English *mynster*) throughout the pre-Conquest period, sometimes but not universally qualified as the habitations of nuns (*sanctimoniales*) or virgins. In discussion of the English Church in the pre-Viking Age I have chosen not to describe these institutions as nunneries (which conjures up anachronistic images of enclosed regular observance) but rather to use the more neutral minster or female religious house. After the monastic revolution of Edgar's reign it may be reasonable to use the word nunnery to denote those all-women houses (all in southern England, most in Wessex) that might have been brought within the scope of Æthelwold's reform and so placed under the Rule of St Benedict. It remains inappropriate to use this noun of the larger number of other female religious congregations found scattered more widely through England south of the Humber and I have not done so.

The choice of language to describe religious women presents as many difficulties, but here the problem lies not in the imprecision of the contemporary texts but in the translation of their language into modern English. Pre-Viking-Age writers used a variety of nouns apparently synonymously to describe women living the religious life, drawing distinctions only according to whether or not a woman made her choice as a virgin. I discuss these terms in chapter 2. All might equally be translated as 'nun' (if that were not thought to signify 'a woman living under a specific monastic rule'), but I have generally preferred the less specific 'religious woman'. After the monastic revolution, however, two separate nouns were used at least in the vernacular normative texts to distinguish two sorts of devout woman. A *mynecenu* was the female equivalent of a *munuc*, an occupant of a regular, enclosed monastic house, while a *nunne* was a religious woman (possibly, but by no means inevitably, a widow), who had retained her property and continued to live in the world after taking vows. Groups of *nunnan* might be found living communally together, but they were not strictly cloistered. Since the referent of the modern 'nun' is different from that of the Old English *nunne*, its use in relation to tenth- and eleventh-century circumstances can only lead to confusion. As is explained in chapter 4, *mynecenu* is here translated as 'cloistered woman' and *nunne* as 'vowess'; both terms have been used to describe religious women only in the period after King Edgar's reign, since they would be anachronistic if applied to the earlier period. Although admittedly somewhat inelegant, these terms have the merit of being unambiguous and do not presuppose among my readers a prior familiarity with the Old English language.

Abbreviations

ASE	*Anglo-Saxon England*
BCS	W. de Gray Birch, *Cartularium Saxonicum* (3 vols., 1885–93)
CCSL	Corpus Christianorum. Series latina
EETS	Early English Text Society
EHD	D. Whitelock, ed., *English Historical Documents I, c. 500–1042* (2nd edn, 1979)
EHR	*English Historical Review*
GP	William of Malmesbury, *De gestis pontificum Anglorum*, ed. N. E. S. A. Hamilton, Rolls series 52 (1870)
GR	William of Malmesbury, *De gestis regum Anglorum I*, ed. and trans. R. A. B. Mynors, R. M. Thomson and M. Winterbottom (1998)
HE	Bede, *Historia ecclesiastica gentis Anglorum*, in *Bede's Ecclesiastical History of the English People*, ed. B. Colgrave and R. A. B. Mynors (1969)
Harmer, *ASWrits*	*Anglo-Saxon Writs* (1952)
Harmer, *SEHD*	*Select English Historical Documents*, ed. F. E. Harmer (1914)
Robertson, *ASCharters*	*Anglo-Saxon Charters*, ed. A.J. Robertson (2nd edn, 1959)
MGH	Monumenta Germaniae Historica
PL	*Patrologia latina*, ed. J. P. Migne, 221 vols. (Paris, 1844–64)
S	P. H. Sawyer, *Anglo-Saxon Charters. An Annotated List and Biblography* (1968)
TRHS	*Transactions of the Royal Historical Society*
VCH	Victoria County History
Whitelock, *ASWills*	*Anglo-Saxon Wills* (1930)
Whitelock, *Councils and Synods*	*Councils and Synods with Other Documents relating to the English Church*, ed. D. Whitelock, M. Brett and C.N.L. Brooke (2 vols., 1981)

List of maps

Chapter 1

Evidential and historiographical problems

And she grants to Ceolthryth whichever she prefers of her black
tunics and her best holy veil and her best headband.

Will of Wynflæd, c. 950.[1]

(...) and Edwin the priest is to be freed, and he is to have the church
for his lifetime on condition that he keep it in repair, and he is to be
given a man. (...) and Ælfwaru, the daughter of Wulfric the
huntsman, is to be freed on condition that she sing four psalters every
week within thirty days and a psalter a week every week within
twelve months and Leofrun is to be freed on the same conditions and
Æthelflæd.

Will of Æthelgifu, c. 990.[2]

[By Ælfflæd, King Edward had six daughters] the first and third took
a vow of virginity and spurned the pleasures of earthly marriage,
Eadflæd taking the veil and Æthelhild in lay attire; both lie at Wilton,
buried next to their mother. (...) He also had by a third wife called
Eadgifu (...) two daughters Eadburh and Eadgifu. Eadburh became a
nun and lies at Winchester.

William of Malmesbury, *De gestis regum Anglorum.*[3]

In the middle years of the tenth century in England the boundary between the
secular and the religious way of life for women appears less sharply defined than
at other times in the pre-Conquest era. Female spiritual devotion found fluid and
diverse modes of expression in this period — whether as a reflection of the
perceived inadequacy of conventional, institutional forms, or as a mark of
innovative experimentation on the part of a few energetic women — to the extent
that it can be difficult to determine to which status certain pious women belonged.
Several female congregations were apparently organised on regular, possibly

---

[1]   Whitelock, *ASWills*, no. 3 (S 1539).
[2]   *The Will of Æthelgifu. A Tenth-Century Anglo-Saxon Manuscript*, ed. D. Whitelock
et al. (1968), pp. 8–9, lines 15–16 and pp. 12–13, lines 50–2 (S 1497).
[3]   William of Malmesbury, *GR*, I, 126 (ed. and trans. R. A. B. Mynors *et al.* (1998),
I, 199–201): 'prima et tertia celibatum Deo uouentes, Edfleda in sacrato, Ethelhida in laico
tegmine, terrenarum nuptiarum uoluptatem fastidiere; iacent ambae Wiltoniae iusta matrem
tumulatae. (...) Suscepit etiam ex tertia uxore Edgiua (...) filias duas, Edburgam et Edgiuam.
Edburga, sacrata Christo uirgo, Wintoniae quiescit'.

Benedictine, lines, mirroring the activities of the male houses prominent in the reorganisation of monasticism during King Edgar's reign. Some nunneries were rich, well-endowed, and patronised by the West Saxon royal house; a few housed women of that family, or cared for the relics of its dead. Three of the eight daughters of Edward the Elder were said to have adopted the religious life, one at Wilton, another at the Nunnaminster in Winchester, and the third apparently remaining within the world,[4] but there may have been little to distinguish the lifestyle of the lay vowess, Æthelhild, from that of her professed sisters Eadflæd and Eadburh. The more prominent occupants and close associates of women's monastic houses such as Wulfthryth and her daughter, St Edith of Wilton, Wynflæd (grandmother of King Edgar, who was somehow connected with Shaftesbury), or Ælfthryth, Edgar's queen (who ejected the abbess of Barking and took direct control of the community in her stead) are depicted in the sources leading lives far removed from the ideals espoused by St Benedict.

Furthermore, beside these few notable convents with prominent aristocratic and royal members was found a larger number of smaller, poorer houses with few lands; short-lived congregations, sustaining a community for only one or two generations before fading from the record; older foundations established before the Viking Age when Benedictine observance was rare, whose way of life — if it proved sustainable in the new climate — was not necessarily dramatically divergent from that followed by the earlier community. Although no genuinely double houses are recorded beyond *c.* 870, there were groups of female religious who lived in the shadow and under the protection of male houses; various single, devout women whose institutional affiliation (if any) cannot be determined are also mentioned in the sources for the tenth and eleventh centuries. This apparent diversity in the female expression of the religious life might point to a vibrant and imaginative generation of aspiring nuns whose devotion inspired the invention of novel, conventual and solitary lifestyles not bound by the Benedictine ideal and seemingly specific to their gender.[5] Yet the overwhelming emphasis on the rich and royally patronised houses found in both the contemporary literature and the subsequent historiography of the monastic life in this period has had the effect of obscuring the range of forms of the religious life open to women in this period. While efforts have been made by historians to redress that gender imbalance in recent years,[6] none has started with the very simple questions that underlie this study: what sorts of female religious communities were there in England in the tenth and eleventh centuries? Where were houses for women located? What is the evidence for their foundation,

---

[4]   Ibid., quoted at the head of the chapter.
[5]   P. Halpin, 'Women religious in late Anglo-Saxon England', *Haskins Society Journal*, 6 (1994), 97–110, at p. 107.
[6]   The neglect of the female contribution to the reform was noted by F. M. Stenton, *Anglo-Saxon England* (3rd edn, 1971), p. 445; recent work on the subject is discussed below.

endowment, female occupancy, and subsequent pre-Conquest history? The normative literature of the period espoused regular uniformity and thus deliberately obscures difference from our view. But it is relevant to question how varied may have been the rules or other systems employed for the internal organisation of women's convents, and indeed whether there were any congregations of religious women not following a recognised rule. Meaningful discussion about the place of women within the structures of the Church in the later Anglo-Saxon period must be grounded in a clear and defined evidential context. This book is designed to supply that need, yet the identification of the female religious houses of the late pre-Conquest period is not a wholly straightforward exercise.

The problem

To start with the veiled women themselves, the instances quoted at the head of this chapter may be seen as paradigmatic of the problems presented by the extant sources. These examples provide an apt entry to the difficulty of categorising female status and of identifying and locating congregations of religious women in the later pre-Conquest period. When William of Malmesbury stated that the Edward the Elder's third daughter, Æthelhild, lived in the 'lay habit' (*in laico tegmine*), he offered no clues as to how she should be distinguished from her elder sister Eadflæd who was said to have lived as a monastic (*in sacrata tegmine*), or her younger half-sister, Eadburh, whom he called a 'virgin dedicated to Christ' (*sacrata Christo uirgo*).[7] Wynflæd (whose will has survived as a single-sheet — possibly a stray from Shaftesbury's archive — dating from the mid-tenth century) is generally held to have had a close association with the abbey at Shaftesbury, although whether as a professed member of the congregation is unclear.[8] Æthelgifu had no obvious connection with any known religious community, yet the terms of her will (also a single-sheet, from the turn of the tenth century) suggest an interest in the religious life beyond the piety to be expected of a secular noblewoman.[9] Wynflæd's bequests included her 'nun's clothing' (*hyre nunscrude*) and veil, plus gifts made 'to the refectory', while Æthelgifu not only bequeathed garments that might be thought appropriate to a religious woman, but had, among the slaves whom she intended to manumit on her death, more than one woman

---

[7] William of Malmesbury, *GR*, I, 126 (ed. and trans. Mynors *et al.*, I, 200–1). Eadburh was a nun at Winchester, whose life was written in the twelfth century by Osbert of Clare: S. Ridyard, *The Royal Saints of Anglo-Saxon England. A Study of West Saxon and East Anglian Cults* (1988), pp. 96–139.

[8] Whitelock, *ASWills*, no. 3 (S 1539); see Kelly, *Charters of Shaftesbury*, p. 56.

[9] Whitelock, *The Will of Æthelgifu* (S 1497).

apparently capable of reciting the Psalter as well as a priest.[10] These two wills raise questions about the status of these female testators: neither appears to have been living a wholly secular life, yet both are equally hard to place within the institutionalised world of organised monasticism. Would William of Malmesbury have considered them, like Æthelhild, to have been celibates in lay habits, or did their position as widows afford them a different status?

The search for the female expression of religious devotion might be made more effectively if it were pursued via the institutions that housed religious women together; however, as will become apparent, the identification of later Anglo-Saxon nunneries is hampered by the paucity of extant contemporaneous sources relating to their activities. Further, beyond the difficulty of determining women's religious status, there is an equal confusion among historians as to what does and does not constitute a 'nunnery' in this period. This can be illustrated from the example of the early history of the female community at Wherwell. Frank Barlow has argued that Wherwell already housed a congregation of religious women a generation before its supposed 'foundation' by Ælfthryth as part of her penance for her alleged involvement in the murder of Edward the Martyr.[11] Barlow's supposition was based on his reading of the life of St Wulfhild, a nun of Wilton who in fleeing the unwanted advances of the youthful King Edgar escaped to her aunt, a woman called Wenflæd, living at Wherwell. At her aunt's house, however, instead of finding the safety she expected, the young nun found the king invited to dine; so she escaped through an underground passage and returned to Wilton, where the relics at the altar of the abbey church provided her with a secure sanctuary.[12] As I argue in detail in my discussion of the evidence for Wherwell in part II, the language used of the aunt's dwelling at Wherwell in the Latin Life of St Wulfhild strongly suggests that it is more probably the dwelling of a private noblewoman than a convent of religious women, but the very fact that Barlow's

---

[10]   Æthelgifu's ownership of an enslaved priest raises a number of problems; while it is possible that his presence among her slaves was related to Æthelgifu's own religious status, he may also have been an ordinary manorial priest. The slaves in Æthelgifu's will have been discussed by D. A. E. Pelteret, *Slavery in Early Mediaeval England* (1995), pp. 112–19, for Edwin see pp. 114–15 and 118.

[11]   William of Malmesbury, *GP*, §§78 and 87 (ed. Hamilton, pp. 175 and 188); see F. Barlow, ed., *The Life of King Edward the Confessor* (1962), p. 96.

[12]   Goscelin, *Vita S Wulfhilde*, ch. 2 (ed. M. Esposito, 'La vie de Sainte Vulfhilde par Goscelin de Cantorbéry', *Analecta Bollandiana*, 32 [1913], 10–26 at pp. 14–16). Attention was first drawn to this tale by Barlow, *The Life*, p. 96. It has also been narrated by D. H. Farmer, '*Regularis Concordia*: Millennium Conference', *Ampleforth Journal*, 76 (1971), 30–53 at pp. 52–3, and 'The progress of the monastic revival', in *Tenth-Century Studies*, ed. D. Parsons (1975), 10–19 at p. 14. See now also P. Stafford, *Queen Emma and Queen Edith* (1997), pp. 140–1 and J. Crick, 'The wealth, patronage, and connections of women's houses in late Anglo-Saxon England', *Revue bénédictine*, 109 (1999), 154–85, at pp. 172–3.

reading should have proved persuasive suggests that these boundaries are not easily drawn in the mid-tenth century.[13]

Even where it does appear that a group of women was living a religious life of some sort in common, it is remarkably difficult to draw distinctions between congregations of professed nuns and other groups of women religious: communities of secular canonesses, or vowesses and widows who may have chosen to join with other women in a similar position.[14] If one were to take a strict definition of a nunnery as being an exclusively female community of enclosed religious who, following a recognised rule of monastic organisation, were united in their acceptance of chastity and individual poverty, it would be hard to identify more than perhaps nine or ten such places in England around the year 1000. All these 'nunneries' lay in the south of the country, the majority in an even more tightly confined geographical area in southern Wessex; all but one had close connections with the West Saxon royal house.[15] A looser definition of a nunnery which takes the term to denote any group of women living together in the name of religion, perhaps in a distinctive habit and vowed to celibacy but without having forsworn personal property, permits the identification of many further places as the sites of congregations of this nature. But, as will be demonstrated repeatedly during the course of this study, the evidence for these establishments is markedly inferior both in quality and quantity to that available for the West Saxon royal nunneries. At first sight, both this sharp dichotomy between regular nunneries and less formal communities, and the wide disparity in the sources available for the two sorts of house appears to represent a significant change in comparison with female monasticism in pre-Viking-Age England. These issues have not fully been explored by historians of the later Anglo-Saxon Church.[16]

The historiography of later Anglo-Saxon religious houses for women

It is unsurprising that scholars of the role of women in the tenth-century English Church have tended to devote their energies to the cluster of nunneries for which

---

[13] For a full discussion of Wherwell's foundation see part II, *s. n.* Wherwell.

[14] Dagmar Schneider has argued (not wholly persuasively) for the use of a rule for canonesses in later tenth-century England: 'Anglo-Saxon women in the religious life: a study of the status and position of women in an early mediaeval society' (PhD thesis, University of Cambridge, 1985), pp. 85–6. The issue is addressed further below in chapter 4, pp. 107–10.

[15] Pauline Stafford has now commented on this distribution, and the association of each of this group of nunneries with the West Saxon royal family: 'Queens, nunneries and reforming churchmen: Gender, religious status and reform in tenth- and eleventh-century England', *Past and Present*, 163 (1999), 3–35. See further Crick, 'The wealth', pp. 179–81.

[16] The poverty of the evidence for West Saxon nunneries has been discussed, if not explained, by B. Yorke, '"Sisters under the skin?" Anglo-Saxon nuns and nunneries in southern England', in *Medieval Women in Southern England*, ed. K. Bate *et al.* (1989), 95–117, at pp. 97–8.

the fullest records have survived. Yet, it can be shown that the historiographical
focus on this small, and arguably unrepresentative, collection of nunneries has
served to construct a misleading picture of women's religious observance in the
two centuries before the Conquest. The surviving sources relating to women's
religious houses in England between the start of Alfred's reign and the Norman
Conquest concern predominantly the small group of nine or ten nunneries from
southern England already mentioned. Eight of these houses lay in Wessex
(Amesbury, Horton, Romsey, Shaftesbury and its cell at Bradford-on-Avon,
Wherwell, Wilton, and the Nunnaminster at Winchester), all of which, if not
founded by a member of the ruling royal house, were closely associated with
members of that family. In respect of source-survival there may be added to this
list the communities at Barking in Essex (in which King Edgar and his wife
Ælfthryth may have taken an interest) and Chatteris in Cambridgeshire (a non-
royal foundation of the early eleventh century and the poorest of the ten at the
Conquest).[17] On the face of it, there would appear to be a direct correlation
between the association of nine of these nunneries with the West Saxon royal
house, their consequent material prosperity and their dominance of the surviving
literature. Indeed Barbara Yorke has argued that it is because Anglo-Saxon
nunneries were peculiarly royal institutions that they appear most frequently in the
extant sources in context of their relationship with the ruling royal family.[18] Such
modern historical discussion as there has been of women's involvement in the
tenth-century monastic revolution and female religious activity in general in the
later pre-Conquest period has tended to focus on precisely these institutions and
on the more celebrated of the women who lived within them.[19] Nunneries have,
however, remained at the margins of research into tenth-century ecclesiastical
history.[20] It is striking how little space has been devoted to the female experience

---

[17]   Concentration on this group of houses was Marc Meyer's stated intention in his
paper, 'Patronage of West Saxon royal nunneries in late Anglo-Saxon England', *Revue
bénédictine*, 91 (1981), 332–58; compare also Crick, 'The wealth', especially pp. 170–1 for
discussion of Chatteris.

[18]   Yorke, '"Sisters under the skin?"', pp. 110–11.

[19]   See, for example, D. Knowles, *The Monastic Order in England* (2nd edn, 1963),
pp. 48–52. In his edition of the central normative text of the tenth-century monastic revolution, the
Regularis concordia, Thomas Symons listed the principal houses of nuns restored before the close
of the century as Berkeley, Exeter, Horton, Reading, Romsey, Shaftesbury, St Mildred's Thanet,
Wareham, Wherwell, Wilton and the Nunnaminster at Winchester: *Regularis concordia* (1953),
p. xxiii. The sources for each of these houses are analysed in detail in part II; few of these can in
fact be shown to have been reorganised under the reform, and other more likely candidates are
missing from Symons's list.

[20]   Michel Parisse has pointed to a similar concentration on the male experience in the
historiography of the Lotharingian reform: 'Der Anteil der Lothringischen Benediktinerinnen an
der monastischen Bewegung des 10. und 11. Jahrhunderts', *Religiöse Frauenbewegung und
mystische Frömmigkeit im Mittelalter*, ed. P. Dinzelbacher and D. R. Bauer (Cologne and Vienna,
1988), pp. 83–97.

of the monastic revolution in any of the three recently published volumes celebrating the leading reformers, Æthelwold, Dunstan, and Oswald, which together claim to offer a re-evaluation of the significance and achievement of the tenth-century monastic revolution.[21]

In recent years some scholars have begun to devote more attention to religious women in Anglo-Saxon England than to female monastic institutions. Dagmar Schneider's doctoral thesis for the University of Cambridge constitutes the most rigorous analysis of the widest range of literary and documentary evidence for the activities of English women in the religious life throughout the pre-Conquest period and covers many of the issues that will be explored here.[22] Stephanie Hollis's account of Anglo-Saxon women and the Church is narrower both chronologically and in the scope of the evidence surveyed;[23] more valuable for our purposes is Barbara Yorke's short essay comparing the female religious experience in England before and after the First Viking Age, which pays particular attention to the role of royal families in fostering monasteries for women but also looks at other modes of religious expression beyond these familiar West Saxon cloisters.[24] Having identified the lack of attention previously paid to women in the tenth-century Church, Marc Meyer has done much to increase our knowledge of the activities of pious women in the later Anglo-Saxon period by accumulating examples of women who expressed devotion other than within the convents associated with the West Saxon royal house, and by exploring the patronage of the female religious life.[25] From the basis laid by Meyer, Patricia Halpin has gone further and systematically combed a range of sources, many dating from the later medieval period, in order to identify the largest possible number of small groups of religious women or instances of solitary devout women, many of whom she has located in the immediate vicinity of male religious foundations.[26] Roberta Gilchrist's contribution to this field has been to bridge the gap between the institutional focus of the older literature and the concentration on women rather than female religious houses in more recent studies. With recourse to archaeology, architecture and place-names as well as to written evidence, Gilchrist has mapped more than thirty later Anglo-Saxon nunneries distributed over England south of

---

[21]   B. Yorke, ed., *Bishop Æthelwold. His Career and Influence* (1988); N. Ramsay, M. Sparkes and T. Tatton-Brown, ed., *St Dunstan. His Life, Times and Cult* (1992); N. Brooks and C. Cubitt, ed., *St Oswald of Worcester. Life and Influence* (1996). Reviewing these volumes, Catherine Cubitt has seen women's involvement with the reform as one of the undercurrents that runs through all three, but has noted the need for scholars to address a number of questions in this area: 'The tenth-century Benedictine reform in England', *Early Medieval Europe*, 6 (1997), 77–94, at p. 87.

[22]   Schneider, 'Anglo-Saxon women'.

[23]   S. Hollis, *Anglo-Saxon Women and the Church* (1992).

[24]   Yorke, '"Sisters under the skin?"'.

[25]   M. Meyer, 'Women and the tenth century English monastic reform', *Revue bénédictine*, 87 (1977), 34–61, and his 'Patronage'.

[26]   Halpin, 'Women'.

the Wash. She has drawn attention to the contrasts between the royal houses and the 'considerable number of nunneries which are less formally defined', which she has in part accounted for by reference to the two classes of religious woman defined in early eleventh-century law-codes.[27] The latest study of nunneries in later Anglo-Saxon England forms part of a wider, and more ambitious study by Bruce Venarde into women's monasticism and medieval society in England and France between 890 and 1215;[28] England in the tenth and eleventh centuries is discussed only by way of introduction to Venarde's main argument which is that a growth in female monasticism is witnessed in western Europe from about 1080. Venarde has followed Gilchrist in stressing the diversity of female vocations in the late Anglo-Saxon period and the opportunities available to women outside the cloister, and he has looked at individual *religiosae feminae* in the middle years of the tenth century.[29] However, his discussion of specific nunneries is not grounded in familiarity with the problems of the sources for England before the Conquest and his study does not offer a new, critical reading of the evidence for later Anglo-Saxon women's religious houses that goes beyond that supplied by the works just cited.[30]

The justification for my undertaking this project, and for addressing the subject of veiled women at length is that, although our understanding of the opportunities open to religious women in tenth- and eleventh-century England has been substantially enhanced in recent years, notably thanks to the work of Gilchrist and Halpin, the picture painted remains a partial one. No historian has attempted to search all the extant evidence with a view to illustrating as fully as possible where religious women found collective outlet for their spiritual

---

[27]   R. Gilchrist, *Gender and Material Culture* (1994); see fig. 3, p. 27, and for the nomenclature of the female religious life pp. 33–4. The question of language is explored at length in chapter 4 below.

[28]   I was unable to obtain a copy of Dr Venarde's book — *Women's Monasticism and Medieval Society* (Ithaca, New York and London, 1997) — until my manuscript had reached the final stages of completion, but despite the apparent similarities between our projects there is in fact little overlap between them. Of the sixty-one places I survey in part II (some of which are shown not, in fact, to have been the sites of female congregations during this period), only thirteen are listed in the Repertory of monastic foundations 900–1300 which constitutes Venarde's Appendix A: Amesbury, Barking, Canterbury, Chatteris, Chichester, Exeter, Leominster, Polesworth, Reading, Romsey, Wherwell, Wilton and Winchester (to these should be added Shaftesbury, discussed in Venarde's text but omitted from his database).

[29]   Venarde, *Women's Monasticism*, p. 24 and n. 27, and p. 47.

[30]   Venarde has supported his identification of pre-Conquest women's religious houses with citation of some pre-Conquest charters, together with the Anglo-Saxon Chronicle, and William of Malmesbury's *De gestis pontificum Anglorum*. However, from the references he has given in his Appendix A it is clear that Dr Venarde has placed the greatest reliance on D. Knowles and R. N. Hadcock's *Medieval Religious Houses* (2nd edn, 1971) in identifying the sites of later Anglo-Saxon nunneries, supplemented with the relevant volumes of the *Victoria County History*. For the limitations of such an approach, see below, chapter 3, pp. 79–81.

aspirations after the accession of King Alfred and before the Norman Conquest.[31] But this is not simply an exercise in data-collection. It asks not just 'what is the evidence?', but more significantly, what factors have conditioned and shaped that evidence and its survival in order to produce this particular image of these women's past? No other study has addressed that question other than tangentially.[32] Nor has anyone tried to look for patterns within the broad frame by asking whether houses of a particular type, those founded in similar circumstances, or those defined by geographical location are all similarly represented in the extant evidence, or indeed whether discrete types of source present distinctive images of women's religious experience. The purpose of this study is thus to place our understanding of female devotion in this period on a better footing, challenging the assumptions that have conditioned much previous thinking on the subject by posing some different questions and addressing the sources more critically. At issue is not why the royally-patronised nunneries have dominated the literature since the tenth century, but how women could satisfy a spiritual vocation other than by entering a Benedictine cloister, and how those non-standard forms of religious expression are represented in the sources. Veiled women are not invisible in our period, they will, however, only be exposed to view once their nature has fully been comprehended and the right questions have been asked of the evidence.

The significance of the approach adopted here can only be appreciated if the reader is taken through some of the more conventional interpretations and shown how these have proved inadequate for explaining the status of religious women in the tenth and eleventh centuries. This chapter begins by retracing what will to many be the familiar ground of the inadequacy of the contemporary sources, drawing out the contrast in the survival of evidence between the later and earlier Anglo-Saxon periods. Since this study is primarily concerned with women religious after the First Viking Age, the evidence for later Anglo-Saxon female communities will be addressed first and its limitations analysed, before the contrastingly more abundant sources for the early period are considered. The choice of a reverse chronology is deliberate: it accentuates the diminution in extant material across the pre-Conquest period, which runs counter to expectation and to

---

[31]   There is one sense in which all such projects are destined to be incomplete. Even were it possible to catalogue a substantial proportion of the places where groups of women lived as religious, it cannot be imagined that every devout widow or unmarried woman who contrived to use a portion of her own inheritance to support her (with or without a companion or two) in a life of devotion will have found a place in the written or material record. One purpose of this study is to draw attention to the frequency with which such arrangements may have been made; there are certainly other women who might be placed in this category other than those whom I have identified here.

[32]   Roberta Gilchrist has again come closest to so doing, incorporating her ideas about Anglo-Saxon nunneries into a wider argument about the gendering of the historical record (*Gender*, pp. 22–5), with which, however, I cannot entirely agree; see further below.

the general pattern of source-survival.[33] However, there is more that distinguishes the early and late periods than the survival of contemporaneous records and in the second chapter we will take a more extended detour into the pre-Viking Age, exploring the nature of female monasticism during that period before, in the third chapter, we ask what happened to the nuns of early Anglo-Saxon England in the ninth century. Only then will it be possible to revert to the substantive argument which underpins the study as a whole and explore against that informed background the available information for women religious in the last two centuries before the Conquest. Chapter four considers in detail what can be discovered about the involvement of women in the tenth-century monastic revolution, drawing attention to the language used to describe female religious in the normative literature. The status of consecrated widows in the Church and the position of devout women living outside the cloister are addressed in chapter five, where the question as to how most appropriately one might categorise the three women with whom this study began is answered. A final chapter investigates alternative ways of handling the different kinds of evidence that witness to the activities of veiled women during our period and links the material together into a variety of illustrative patterns by way of introduction to the analytical survey found in part II of the sources for each individual place where a congregation of religious women is thought to have lived in the later pre-Conquest period. Thus each of the chapters is designed to answer a specific question or series of questions; the result is a volume of uneven balance, but — it is hoped — of focussed clarity.

The nature of the evidence

The gulf separating the royal nunneries and the forty or so other places assembled in part II at which women religious are thought to have lived at some point between 871 and 1066 has previously been noted. It is, however, brought into sharper relief when the disparity between the sources available for each group is quantified. There is a clear correspondence between the demonstrable material wealth of a female religious house and the survival of documentary and historical evidence pertaining to its history (particularly where that wealth was acquired via royal patronage).[34] Recognition of the disproportion in the historical record is not,

---

[33]   Dagmar Baltrusch-Schneider has drawn attention to the discrepancy between the sixty-five female houses she has identified in sources as active before the tenth century and the thirteen for which she was able to find evidence in the later pre-Conquest period: 'Klosterleben als alternative Lebensform zur Ehe?', in *Weibliche Lebensgestaltung im frühen Mittelalter*, ed. H.-W. Goetz (Cologne and Vienna, 1991), pp. 45–64, at 45–6.

[34]   This material has recently been explored by Julia Crick, 'The wealth'. I am grateful to Dr Crick for letting me read this paper before its publication.

however, in itself an explanation for the relative silence of the sources about the activities of female religious in general during this period. The issues at stake here may be seen more clearly if a summary is given of the sorts of evidence to which recourse has been made in order to draw the fullest possible picture of the places at which women collectively fulfilled their vocations to the religious life. The evidence for the privileged ten, largely West Saxon houses, is discussed separately, before attention is turned to the larger, but less visible, body of other nunneries.

Sources for the 'royal' nunneries

Contemporary (or supposedly contemporaneous) diplomas recording royal grants of land in their favour survive for all but two of the richer group of nunneries.[35] There are no extant charters for Chatteris, but there is evidence that a diploma for Amesbury from this period has been lost.[36] The Nunnaminster at Winchester and Shaftesbury nunnery were both remembered in the two royal wills that survive from this period, those of King Eadred and of the ætheling Æthelstan, and the former made a bequest also to the house at Wilton.[37] Several of the same houses attracted noble patronage, receiving bequests of land, money or moveable wealth which are recorded in extant pre-Conquest wills.[38] If the survival of record of grants and bequests of land may be taken as indicative of the extent and proportion of donations originally made, these ten houses might be thought to have been the best, or among the best endowed female congregations in the tenth and eleventh centuries. The abbesses of eight of the ten abbeys are recorded as independent landholders in Domesday Book; the exceptions are Bradford-on-Avon (listed among the possessions of Shaftesbury) and Horton, the only one of these

---

[35]   See Crick, 'The wealth', pp. 164–71, for analysis of the landed benefaction of royally founded nunneries.

[36]   A fifteenth-century record of an exchequer suit brought by the then abbess of Amesbury makes reference to a diploma of King Æthelred's which can be partially reconstructed: H. P. R. Finberg, *The Early Charters of Wessex* (1964), 103–4.

[37]   Harmer, *SEHD*, no. 21 (S 1515); Whitelock, *ASWills*, no. 20 (S 1503).

[38]   For bequests to Barking see the wills of: Ælfgar (Whitelock, *ASWills*, no. 2, S 1483); Ælfflæd (Whitelock, *ASWills*, no. 15, S 1486); Thurstan (Whitelock, *ASWills*, no. 31, S 1531). For Romsey: Æthelmær (Whitelock, *ASWills*, no. 10, S 1498); Ælfgifu (Whitelock, *ASWills*, no. 8, S 1484). Shaftesbury: Æthelmær (Whitelock, *ASWills*, no. 10, S 1498); Wynflæd (Whitelock, *ASWills*, no. 3, S 1539). Wilton: Bishop Ælfwold (Whitelock *et al.*, *Councils and Synods*, no. 51, S 1492); Æthelmær (Whitelock, *ASWills*, no. 10, S 1498); Wynflæd (Whitelock, *ASWills*, no. 3, S 1539). The Nunnaminster at Winchester: Ælfgifu (Whitelock, *ASWills*, no. 8, S 1484); Æthelmær (Whitelock, *ASWills*, no. 10, S 1498). Summaries of wills relating to Chatteris were preserved in the Ramsey Chronicle and in the *Liber Eliensis*, ed. E. O. Blake (1962); see part II, *s.n.* Chatteris. A wider-ranging discussion of noble patronage of female religious houses may be found in Crick, 'The wealth', pp. 164–78.

nunneries no longer housing women at the Conquest.[39] An account of the foundation of a women's house at Shaftesbury for King Alfred's ailing daughter Æthelgifu was contained in the life of that king conventionally held to have been written in the 890s and attributed to the authorship of Asser, monk of St David's and later bishop of Sherborne.[40]

In the sources other than those relating to landed endowment these same houses are also the most prominent, although here the discrepancies between the extant evidence for female and male religious becomes more marked. It is generally presumed that all these nunneries played a significant part in the tenth-century monastic revolution, since women's communities were included by Bishop Æthelwold in his rhetorical statements about the need for a radical reorganisation of the religious life in King Edgar's reign.[41] There are, however, no contemporaneous accounts of the ejection of unreformed religious women from their convents and their replacement with regular Benedictine nuns equivalent to the accounts of the reform of male houses; indeed only one tenth-century text described — very briefly — the institution of nuns in any nunnery.[42] Pre-Conquest *Vitae* have survived for all three of the leading male proponents of reformed monasticism, but no woman associated with this movement is commemorated in surviving hagiographical literature from the Anglo-Saxon period. (Mention was made in the Life of St Dunstan of a noble widow, Æthelflæd, who lived a religious life in a house to the west of the abbey at Glastonbury;[43] she was clearly not living as an enclosed Benedictine and most probably was living alone.) It is only in the writings of the late-eleventh-century hagiographer Goscelin that the deeds of saints Edith of Wilton and Wulfhild of Barking found record and in the twelfth

---

39   Crick, 'The wealth', pp. 161–3, lists the Domesday holdings of all these nunneries. The holdings of the male house which succeeded the nunnery at Horton were listed in Domesday Book, discussed in part II, *s.n.* Horton.

40   Asser, Life of Alfred, ch. 98 (ed. W. H. Stevenson, *Asser's Life of King Alfred* [1904], p. 85; trans. S. Keynes and M. Lapidge, *Alfred the Great* [1983], p. 105). Doubt has recently been cast on the authorship of this life by Alfred Smyth, *King Alfred the Great* (1997), but I am unpersuaded by his argument that this incomplete text was 'forged' in the later tenth century at Ramsey or a reformed monastery with Ramsey associations. For the purposes of this study, I have presumed the life of the king genuinely to date from the late ninth century and to bear witness to attitudes towards monasticism current at that time. See further R. Abels, *Alfred the Great* (1998), pp. 318–26 and the critical reviews of Smyth cited there.

41   Compare Æthelwold, 'An account of King Edgar's establishment of monasteries' (ed. and trans. Whitelock *et al.*, *Councils and Synods,* I, 142–54, at p. 150, no. 33) and *Regularis concordia*, proem, ch. 4 (ed. and trans. Symons, pp. 2–3). For the presumption that women's houses, too, were reformed during Edgar's reign see Knowles, *The Monastic Order*, pp. 48–52.

42   Wulfstan, *Vita sancti Æthelwoldi*, ch. 22 (ed. and trans. M. Lapidge and M. Winterbottom, *Wulfstan of Winchester, The Life of St Æthelwold* [1991], pp. 36–9). Comparison is made between the rhetoric surrounding the reform and contemporary reference to its actual implementation in the case of women's houses below, chapter 4, pp. 89–94.

43   'B', *Vita sancti Dunstani*, chs. 10–11 (ed. W. Stubbs, *Memorials of St Dunstan*, Rolls Series 63 [1874], 250–324, at pp. 17–19).

century that the monks of Pershore turned to Osbert of Clare for a Life of St Eadburh whose relics they claimed.[44] It is, of course, possible that Goscelin at least was able to draw on written as well as oral memories of these saints but that such hagiographical material as was composed in eleventh-century nunneries has not survived.[45]

The identification of abbesses in the tenth and eleventh centuries is frequently difficult, but better information is available for the heads of the group of houses already discussed than for most other late Anglo-Saxon female communities. Obits of one abbess of Shaftesbury and one of Wherwell were recorded in the Anglo-Saxon Chronicle, and abbesses of Horton, Romsey, Shaftesbury and Wilton were among those notable women commemorated in the *Liber Vitae* of Hyde Abbey. Other heads of these houses were named in contemporary charters and saints' lives.[46] As the custodians of significant relics several of these nunneries achieved further fame. The early eleventh-century list of saints' resting-places mentioned the early saints lying at Amesbury and at Barking, and four consecutive entries in that list record the names of those saints whose relics were claimed by the Nunnaminster at Winchester, Romsey, Shaftesbury and Wilton.[47]

Beyond the Conquest similarly disproportionate attention was paid to the same few communities in the written record. Eight were mentioned as landowners in Domesday Book, and — perhaps more significantly — these eight are the only independent female communities mentioned in that survey.[48] Several of the royal nunneries were described by William of Malmesbury in his *De gestis pontificum Anglorum*, although he did not mention the house at Chatteris, and described only the later male congregation at Horton.[49] The Chronicle of John of Worcester also

[44] A. Wilmart, 'La légende de Ste Edithe en prose et vers par le moine Goscelin', *Analecta Bollandiana*, 56 (1938), 5–101 and 265–307; Esposito, 'La vie de sainte Vulfhilde'; Goscelin's writings and his methods as a hagiographer have been analysed by C. H. Talbot, 'The *Liber confortatorius* of Goscelin of St Bertin', *Studia Anselmiana*, 37 (1955), 1–117, at pp. 5–22. The *Vita Edburgae* has been edited by Ridyard, *The Royal Saints*, pp. 259–308.
[45] Stephanie Hollis has suggested that the Wilton nuns could have composed Lives of their saintly predecessors: *Anglo-Saxon Women*, p. 250, n. 41.
[46] ASC, *s.a.* 982, 1048; *Liber Vitae*, ed. W. Birch (1892), pp. 57–9, see *The Liber Vitae of the New Minster and Hyde Abbey Winchester*, ed. S. Keynes (Copenhagen, 1996), pp. 94–5. The available information has conveniently been tabulated by Crick, 'The wealth', table III, pp. 171–2.
[47] *Die heiligen Englands*, II, 51, II, 23, II, 33–36 (ed. F. Liebermann [Hannover, 1889], pp. 20, 13, 15–17).
[48] The exceptions are Horton and Bradford on Avon. There are other references to women religious in Domesday Book, but these are mostly instances of women who had in some manner affiliated themselves to male communities; see further below, chapter 6, §e.
[49] William of Malmesbury, *GP*, §§75 and 78 (ed. Hamilton, pp. 167 and 174): the Nunnaminster at Winchester; §78 (pp. 174–5): Romsey and Wherwell; §§84 and 86 (pp. 184 and 186–7): Shaftesbury; §87 (pp. 188–91): Amesbury, Wherwell and Wilton; only the pre-Viking age nunnery at Barking was described: §73 (pp. 143–4). Some of these houses were also discussed by

supplements the evidence provided by surviving versions of the Anglo-Saxon Chronicle.[50] Further information about prominent members of these communities is to be found in post-Conquest hagiographical materials, particularly the Lives written by Goscelin.[51] It is difficult to escape the conclusion that it is their landed wealth, and the surviving record of those possessions, that distinguished these houses to post-Conquest historians from the other places where religious women are thought to have lived at various times during the period under review. Even so, it should be noted that it is frequently far from easy to reconstruct the pre-Conquest history of these establishments, even where recourse has been made to the additional information supplied by Anglo-Norman and antiquarian writers. In almost every case it has also proved impossible to determine the direct involvement of each separate institution in the broader movement for the reorganisation of monasticism which reached its peak in Edgar's reign, even though this is the aspect of the tenth-century Church which has attracted the most attention from modern scholars.

Sources for other religious houses for women

The remainder of places at which religious women may be located at various times between 871 and 1066 have similarly been ignored in medieval and modern accounts of the progress of the tenth-century monastic revolution, but the silence of contemporary and later witnesses is here more readily understood. The sources for these female houses are much less plentiful than for the group already discussed, and the histories of these institutions in the two centuries before the Conquest more difficult to disentangle. Anglo-Saxon charters supply information about the presence of women in the late ninth century at two further congregations (Cheddar and Wenlock) and possibly in a third at Winchcombe;[52] a woman described as a *nunne* witnessed an early tenth-century manumission made in the presence of 'all the servants of God' at Bedwyn and recorded in a Gospel Book from that church.[53] A charter of King Eadred's relating to land near Canterbury referred to the boundary of the community of St Mildrith; this congregation may

William of Malmesbury *GR*, II, 122, 163 and 219 (ed. and trans. Mynors *et al.*, I, 190–1 and 266–9, 404–5): Shaftesbury; *GR*, II, 162 (pp. 266–7): Wherwell; *GR*, II, 126 and 218 (pp. 200–1, 402–5): Wilton.

[50]   John of Worcester, *Chronicon, s.a.* 1043 (ed. and transl. Darlington *et al.* [1995], II, 538–9): Amesbury; *s.a.* 967 and 971 (pp. 416–7, 420–1): Romsey; *s.a.* 880, 887, 979, 982, 1043 (pp. 314–15, 328–9, 430–1, 432–3, 538–9): Shaftesbury; *s.a.* 1051 (pp. 562–3): Wherwell; *s.a.* 970, 1043 (pp. 420–1, 538–9): Wilton; *s.a.* 905 (pp. 360–1): the Nunnaminster, Winchester.

[51]   Talbot, 'The *Liber confortatorius*', pp. 5–22.

[52]   Cheddar: Robertson, *ASCharters*, no. 45 (S 806); Wenlock: BCS 587 (S 221); Winchcombe: BCS 575 (S 1442).

[53]   H. Merritt, 'Old English entries in a manuscript at Bern', *Journal of English and Germanic Philology*, 33 (1934), 343–51, at pp. 346–7.

have been related to the minster for women formerly found on Thanet, which had perhaps by 948 left its island home for a more secure inland site.[54] It may also be thought that the widow Æthelgifu, whose will has survived as a single-sheet dating from the end of the tenth century, was living as a vowess with a small congregation (consisting at least of the three unfree women capable of reciting the psalter who were to be manumitted on her death, and clearly served by a priest); this community may have lived on the widow's estate at Standon in Hertfordshire.[55] Rather more uncertain charter evidence could be adduced to support the presence of women at Abingdon, St Paul's, London, Glastonbury, Westminster and the Old Minster at Winchester during the tenth and eleventh centuries.[56] There are no extant charters for any other women's religious house during our period.

Some female communities are thought to have been active at this time because references to communities or their abbesses were made in the Anglo-Saxon Chronicle: a *nunne*, apparently from Wimborne, is mentioned in the Chronicle entry for 900; the obit of an abbess of Wareham was reported in 982; an abbess of St Mildrith's community was captured by the Danes at Canterbury in 1011; and an abbess of Leominster was mentioned in 1046. As well as the references to Shaftesbury in Asser's Life of King Alfred, there is an allusion in that text to a monastic house for women at Wareham.[57] The existence of other houses at Reading and Berkeley is known because their abbesses were mentioned in the *Liber Vitae* of Hyde Abbey.[58] The impact that a community's possession of the relics of a notable saint might have had on its prominence within contemporary documentary or later historical literature is hard to measure. Various places thought to have housed congregations of religious women are named in the earliest of the surviving lists of saints resting-places, that preserved with the manuscript of the *Liber Vitae* of Hyde Abbey.[59] That a site was reputed to hold the relics of

---

[54]   BCS 869 (S 535); compare also BCS 791 (S 497).

[55]   Whitelock, *The Will of Æthelgifu*, pp. 33–4 (S 1497).

[56]   Abingdon: BCS 743 (S 448), BCS 759 (S 460), BCS 778 (S 482). St Paul's: M. Gibbs, *Early Charters of the Cathedral Church of St Paul, London* (1939), J. 12 (S 1793); Glastonbury: BCS 664 (S 399), BCS 768 (S 474), BCS 903 (S 563); Westminster: Harmer, *ASWrits*, 79 (S 1123); Winchester: BCS 734 (S 449), BCS 787 (S 487). Each case is discussed in detail below.

[57]   Asser, Life of King Alfred, ch. 49 (ed. Stevenson, *Asser*, p. 36, trans. Keynes and Lapidge, *Alfred the Great*, p. 82).

[58]   *Liber Vitae*, ed. Birch, p. 58. The abbess Leofrun who witnessed Robertson, *ASCharters*, no. 66, datable to 990x992 (S 1454), is usually taken to have been abbess of Reading.

[59]   Omitting the largely male houses to which religious women may have been in some fashion affiliated for a part of our period, the presence of relics is recorded at the following places, all thought to have housed religious women at some time 871x1066: Amesbury (*Die Heiligen Englands*, II, 51), Polesworth (ibid. II, 18), Romsey (ibid., II, 34), Shaftesbury (ibid., II, 36), Wenlock (ibid., II, 15), Wilton (ibid., II, 35), Wimborne (ibid., II, 45), Winchcombe (ibid., II, 44), the Nunnaminster at Winchester (ibid., II, 33). All but four of these houses have already been discussed as members of that group of nunneries patronised by the West Saxon royal house.

a given saint is of course no indication that there was a community resident at that place to care for the saint's cult at the time this list was compiled (before *c.* 1031); however, a congregation claiming to have charge of some famous relics might well find it easier to attract wealth and patronage than other nearby houses unable to make such claim.[60] Allusions to nuns (*moniales*) in Domesday Book permit the identification of a small number of additional sites as places that housed nuns in 1066 or 1086, even if these were not the sites of regularly constituted nunneries;[61] mention of single, named nuns in the same survey must be treated with greater caution, since these women need not have belonged to organised communities.[62] The witness of historians and hagiographers of the post-Conquest period can permit the identification of a few additional religious houses for women in the later Anglo-Saxon period at Chester, Chichester, Exeter, Polesworth, St Albans and Southampton. None appears to have been particularly well endowed, and the history of several is far from certain.[63] Further, there are places where it would not be thought religious women had lived in the tenth or eleventh centuries were it not that antiquaries such as Leland or Tanner reported that they had housed nunneries; putative female congregations at Bodmin, Boxwell, Castor, Coventry, Eltisley, Lincoln, Pershore, Southwark, Stone, Warwick, and Woodchester fall into this category.[64]

The problems presented by the extant sources

This larger body of women's religious houses that were less well endowed and lacked close links with the royal house were also markedly less well evidenced in the sources. The comparative paucity of the sources may be a reasonable reflection of, for example, the relative poverty of the institutions concerned. Certainly of those that were still active in 1066 none beyond the group addressed separately had landed endowments of sufficient size to warrant individual entry in Domesday Book. (The two issues are, as Julia Crick has shown, inextricably linked. The sources that support the most secure identification of women's religious houses are those that relate to the land-holdings of these establishments yet, inevitably, there is an element of pre-selection here: only those houses that have landed

---

[60]   This issue will be further confounded by the point raised above, namely the impact of royal and noble patronage on the making and preservation of written sources for nunneries.

[61]   These are discussed together as a group in the introduction to part II, §b. The language used by the Domesday commissioners to describe religious women is discussed in chapter 4, pp. 103–4.

[62]   See the wider analysis of single vowesses, chapter 6, §f.

[63]   This group of houses is analysed together in the introduction to part II, §c. Roberta Gilchrist has handled this material differently, arguing from an example taken from Domesday Book, 'the naming of religious women within the sources implies communities where none have previously been known to have existed': *Gender*, p. 34.

[64]   Discussed in the introduction to part II, §d.

endowments will be represented in the surviving corpus of pre-Conquest charters, or mentioned as landholders in Domesday Book.[65]) A lack of extant documentary references might in some instances be a sign of a house with a particularly short history, a community that flourished so briefly during our period that its occupants had insufficient time or motivation to create documents recording their transitory occupation of the site. Later owners of a former convent's lands might also have preferred to acquire (or forge) for themselves charters giving them direct title to the estates in question and so have failed to preserve any original charters issued in favour of the first congregation. It is notable that the few women's houses of the later Anglo-Saxon period which were located on the sites of pre-Viking-Age female communities are no differently represented in sources relating to the tenth and eleventh centuries from those convents which appear to be new foundations of the post-Viking Age. The reoccupation by veiled women of a site with a prior religious history was no guarantee that contemporary or post-Conquest historians would take any greater an interest in its affairs between 900 and 1066 than these writers did in the activities of more recently created congregations.[66] It may, however, be of relevance to note here that only one of the female houses apparently active at the Conquest could claim to have first been founded before A.D. 900, and even in that case — Barking Abbey — a continuous and unbroken history cannot be demonstrated.

The geographical distribution of tenth- and eleventh-century female religious houses for which sources have survived makes interesting comparison with the spread of those newly founded after the Conquest; compare maps 1 and 2 overleaf.[67] For the period between 871 and 1066, as has already been noted, the best and most plentiful evidence relates predominantly to a small group of nunneries lying in central Wessex. More partial and non-contemporaneous materials provide information about a larger collection of female houses, a handful in Greater Wessex, but the majority lying in the midlands and East Anglia. Few houses from this period can even tentatively be located in northern England, none is convincingly witnessed in pre-Conquest texts.[68] In marked contrast to this

---

[65]   Crick, 'The wealth', pp. 158–60.

[66]   Those houses found in our period at the sites of pre-Viking-Age nunneries are considered together below, chapter 6, §a.

[67]   It is otiose to note that dots on maps can mislead; compare J. L. Nelson, 'Kommentar', in *Frauen in Spätantike und Frühmittelalter*, ed. W. Affeldt (Sigmarinen, 1990), pp. 325–32, at p. 329.

[68]   The northernmost female community found during our period is that tenuously attested at Corbridge: Warner of Rouen, *Moriuht*, lines 78–141 (ed. and trans. C. J. McDonough [Toronto, 1995], pp. 76–81); there may possibly have been religious women at Durham also: *De obsessione Dunelmi*, ch. 3 (ed. T. Arnold, *Symeonis monachi opera omnia* [2 vols., 1882–5], I, 215–20, at p. 217). Otherwise none are known further north than Chester and Lincoln.

Map 1   Female religious communities in England, 871–1066

Map 2   The distribution of communities of women religious in England,
1066–1200 (after S. Thompson, *Women Religious*, 1991)

Anglo-Saxon pattern, the places at which new women's religious houses were founded after the Conquest lie largely north of the Thames but are otherwise distributed over most of England south of Hadrian's Wall, with only the north west and extreme north of the country remaining uncovered; see map 2. The scarcity of new nunneries in the south (particularly in Hampshire, Dorset and southern Wiltshire) is so marked as to invite explanation.[69] The most obvious is that this area was already, as a consequence of the generosity of the tenth-century kings of Wessex, deemed to be sufficiently provided with places for the pursuit of the female vocation such that further new foundations were not only redundant, but unlikely to flourish in competition with the royal houses. The midlands and even more obviously the north were much less well provided; one prime motive behind the location of houses in those areas may have been to remedy that deficiency. It is further possible that lay patrons preferred to direct their generosity towards houses with which they might sustain a close and personal relationship (in life and then in death), rather than towards those known to promote royal cults. The prior existence of local male communities which might offer veiled women some protection was also frequently, as Thompson has shown, a factor influencing the location of new houses in the twelfth century, but this does not account for the absence of new foundations in southern England during that period.[70] The sharp contrast between the locations of pre- and post-Conquest foundations does suggest that the survival of sources for both these groups of houses reflects accurately the distribution of women's religious houses in each period, and is not an indication of some geographical aberration determining the unequal survival of evidence by region.

That female religious houses are seemingly disadvantaged in comparison with their male counterparts in the quality and quantity of the extant historical record is not a peculiarity of the circumstances in later Anglo-Saxon England. Historians of other periods and places have noted a similar relative neglect of female religious houses among both contemporary and modern writers.[71] In England the apparent neglect of the female experience, as Sally Thompson has observed, was not a later pre-Conquest phenomenon but persisted in historical texts dating from the twelfth and thirteenth centuries. Rejecting as inherently implausible the notion that female religious were more vulnerable than their male

---

[69]   This point is illustrated vividly by Thompson's map which omits the seven pre-Conquest foundations still flourishing within her period (Barking, Chatteris, Romsey, Shaftesbury, Wherwell, Wilton, and the Nunnaminster at Winchester).

[70]   Thompson, *Women*, pp. 54–7.

[71]   See, for example, the general remarks about the historical invisibility of nuns made in a medieval context by Henrietta Leyser, *Medieval Women* (1995), pp. 189–90, and by Bruce Venarde, *Women's Monasticism*, pp. xi–xii and 6–7; and in a modern one by Susan O'Brien, 'Terra incognita: the nun in nineteenth-century England', *Past and Present*, 121 (1988), 110–40, at p. 118, together with the wide secondary literature on female religious cited in the latter's footnotes.

contemporaries to the loss of their muniments through misfortunes such as fire or flood, Thompson has suggested a number of possible reasons for the apparent failure of these institutions to create, or to have created for them, an historical record of their origins and endowments.[72] Several of the houses Thompson has examined appear to have evolved in diverse circumstances, whether from the accretion of sisters around an anchoress, or the addition of nuns to a hospital, or the creation of a female congregation out of a former double house, none of which arrangements would necessarily have led to the creation of a foundation charter for the new nunnery. The poverty of many of the institutions Thompson has studied is also a significant factor; it is not just that their endowments were often meagre and consisted of grants of relatively small portions of land from a number of separate donors, but also that lack of resources might preclude the commissioning of the making of documents by nuns who lacked the linguistic and palaeographical skills to create their own.[73] Poor and often ephemeral houses were, furthermore, those least likely to have whatever documents they had accumulated preserved within the archives of larger religious institutions or the later owners (secular or religious) of their lands. These are pertinent factors for a number of the institutions considered here and raise some difficult questions as to why the historical record is so silent about the majority of women religious in the period immediately before and after the Norman Conquest. It is even more striking that this discrepancy is not observable in the extant sources relating to women religious in the pre-Viking Age in England, when women's communities are at least as well represented in the historical record as are those for men.[74] One further point should perhaps be made at this point: of the hundreds of small unreformed minsters active in England in the later tenth and early eleventh centuries only a few provide explicit evidence for male communities, although certainly those congregations that are recorded are overwhelmingly male. To this extent, at least, the lacuna in the sources is not specific to women.[75]

The sources for pre-Viking-Age women's religious houses

Women religious individually and collectively are visible, active, and significant players in texts relating to the early Anglo-Saxon Church. This is not the place at which to enter into a detailed analysis of the extant sources for the history of pre-

---

[72]   S. Thompson, 'Why English nunneries had no history: a study of the problems of the English nunneries founded after the Conquest', in *Distant Echoes*, ed. Nichols and Shank (Kalamazoo, Michigan, 1984), pp. 131–49, at pp. 132–3.

[73]   Ibid., pp. 141, 133, 136–7.

[74]   This point was made by Patrick Wormald in a lecture for the centenary symposium at St Hilda's College in Oxford in 1993 ('St Hilda, saint and scholar (614–80)', in *The St Hilda's College Centenary Symposium*, ed. J. Mellanby (1993), pp. 93–103, at p. 102), but has not as yet acquired a wider currency. I am grateful to Lesley Abrams for drawing this paper to my attention.

[75]   I am grateful to John Blair for drawing this detail to my attention.

Viking Age minsters for women which have been widely explored elsewhere, but merely to point to the contrast between these and the materials available for the study of female monasticism in tenth- and eleventh-century England.[76] Extremely important to later medieval and modern perceptions of the Church in this period are obviously the historical writings of Bede, whose willingness to accord equal attention to female as to male religious has done much to bring these women to the attention of later generations of scholars.[77] His method in his History was to point to examples of the best practice and offer models of ideal behaviour to which his reader might aspire; almost one third of the chapters in the fourth book of the Ecclesiastical History relate to female religious and their houses, notably Barking, Ely and Whitby.[78] Bede's predilection for the unmarried state and his unequivocal advocacy of the highest standards of religious observance were not gender-specific attitudes but applicable to all Christians, just as his disapproval of the debauchery into which the mixed community at Coldingham was supposed to have descended was directed at all the congregation, men and women alike.[79] Similarly, in condemning pseudo-minsters in the letter which he wrote towards the end of his life to Ecgbert, bishop of York, Bede criticised the shamelessness of thegns who procured places for constructing minsters for their wives who 'with equal foolishness, seeing that they are lay-women, allow themselves to be mistresses of the handmaids of Christ'.[80]

The prominence of religious women in Bede's History is mirrored in other sources relating to the seventh and eighth centuries. Bede was able to draw on an earlier *liber* or *libellus* telling the life of St Æthelburh of Barking, and he was probably also able to use an early Ely Life of St Æthelthryth as well as possibly similar materials from Whitby about St Hild.[81] Leoba, a nun at Wimborne before

---

[76]   Various literary sources for women in the early Anglo-Saxon Church have been considered by Stephanie Hollis, *Anglo-Saxon Women*; a more rigorous analysis of the full extent of the surviving evidence for pre-Conquest religious women has been made by Dagmar Schneider in her, lamentably unpublished, doctoral thesis, 'Anglo-Saxon women'.

[77]   Stephanie Hollis has put a rather different gloss on this material, arguing that in fact religious women were a good deal more prominent within the seventh-century Church than is suggested by the deliberate muting of their achievements in Bede's writings; see, for example, her analysis of the changes in the representation of women made by Bede to the anonymous Life of Cuthbert: *Anglo-Saxon Women*, pp. 242–70.

[78]   Bede, *HE*, IV, 6–10 (Barking); IV, 19–20 (Æthelthryth and Ely); IV, 23–24 (Hild and Whitby); IV, 25 (Coldingham). See Wormald, 'St Hilda', p. 94.

[79]   Compare Bede's rather muted comments about marriage in his letter to Ecgbert *Epistola ad Ecgberhtum*, §15, ed. Plummer, *Venerabilis Baedae Opera* (1896), I, 405–23, at pp. 418–19; Coldingham's history was described by Bede, *HE*, IV, 25 (ed. and trans. B. Colgrave and R. A. B. Mynors [1969], pp. 424–7).

[80]   Bede, *Epistola ad Ecgbertum*, §12 (ed. Plummer, I, 416; trans. Whitelock, *EHD*, p. 806, no. 170).

[81]   For Bede's sources for Æthelburh see J. M. Wallace-Hadrill, *Bede's Ecclesiastical History of the English People. A Historical Commentary* (1988), pp. 146–7 and Hollis, *Anglo-Saxon Women*, pp. 79 and 111–12; for Æthelthryth see Wallace-Hadrill, *Commentary*, pp. 159–60;

joining Boniface's mission in Germany and becoming abbess of Bishofsheim, was commemorated in an extant *vita* written by a monk of Fulda in the early ninth century,[82] and there are further various surviving later medieval versions of early legends associated with St Mildrith of Thanet, St Mildburg of Wenlock, and St Frideswide of Oxford.[83] Women religious, particularly abbesses, also played significant roles in the lives of male saints such as Cuthbert, Wilfrid and Guthlac; the hagiographers of these saints portrayed such women as active figures, not merely as the providers of hospitality or passive witnesses to the saint's holiness.[84] Female saints figured prominently in both portions of the earliest extant list of saints' resting-places from Anglo-Saxon England, the first part of which (beginning with the words 'Her cyð ymbe þa halgan þe on Angelcynne restað') contains a version of the Mildrith legend which probably originated in Kent at some time between the death of King Wihtred (725) and the translation of Wihtburg's remains to Ely in 974.[85] All this contrasts markedly with the absence of extant contemporaneous hagiographical material relating to women active in the later Anglo-Saxon Church beyond those whose resting-places were noted in the second part of the list recorded with the *Liber Vitae* of Hyde Abbey and compiled around 1031.[86] The Lindisfarne *Liber Vitae*, an early ninth-century

---

Ridyard, *The Royal Saints*, pp. 53–6; Hollis, *Anglo-Saxon Women*, pp. 247–8; for Hild see Wallace-Hadrill, *Commentary*, pp. 163–7; Hollis, *Anglo-Saxon Women*, pp. 253–8 and 261–70 and C. Fell, 'Hild, abbess of Streonæshalch', in *Hagiography and Medieval Literature*, ed. H. Bekker-Nielsen *et al.* (Odense, 1981), pp. 76–99

[82]   Rudolf of Fulda's *Vita S Leobae* was edited by G. Waitz, *MGH, SS*, XV.I, pp. 118–31, and translated by C. H. Talbot, *The Anglo-Saxon Missionaries in Germany* (2nd edn., 1981), pp. 205–26. It has been discussed by Hollis, *Anglo-Saxon Women*, ch. 9.

[83]   The various versions of the so-called Mildrith Legend have been analysed by David Rollason, *The Mildrith Legend. A Study in Early Medieval Hagiography in England* (1982). A Life of St Mildburg of Wenlock was written after the Conquest by Goscelin of Saint-Bertin in which he included an autobiographical statement supposedly composed by the saint herself, which he called her *testamentum*: H. P. R. Finberg, *The Early Charters of the West Midlands* (2nd edn., 1972), pp. 197–216. The legend of St Frideswide is now known only from sources post-dating the refoundation of her house as an Augustinian priory in the 1120s, but these may have drawn on earlier materials since lost: J. Blair, *Anglo-Saxon Oxfordshire* (1994), pp. 52–4; and his 'Saint Frideswide reconsidered', *Oxoniensia*, 52 (1987), 71–127, at pp. 79–82.

[84]   The portrayal of women in Stephen's Life of Wilfrid has been analysed by Hollis, *Anglo-Saxon Women*, pp. 151–78 and 180–5 and the contrast between the representations of women in the anonymous Life of Cuthbert and Bede's Life of that saint ibid., pp. 185–207. Guthlac began his monastic career at the double house at Repton, where he received the tonsure at the hands of Abbess Ælfthryth and spent two years in learning the monastic discipline before he adopted the life of the solitary: Felix, *Vita sancti Guthlaci*, chs. 20–23 (ed. and trans. B. Colgrave, *Felix's Life of St Guthlac* [1956], pp. 84–7).

[85]   *Die Heiligen Englands*, ed. Liebermann, pp. 1–9; Rollason, *The Mildrith Legend*, p. 28.

[86]   *Die Heiligen Englands*, ed. Liebermann, pp. 9–20; the later Anglo-Saxon female saints whose resting-places are listed here are mentioned above, p. 15. It is of course possible, that

confraternity book continued after the community of St Cuthbert left their island home first at Chester-le-Street and later at Durham, recorded the names of 198 queens and abbesses, pointing once more to the vitality of women in the the early Northumbrian Church (as well as to their close royal connections).[87]

Religious women were prominent among the correspondents of Boniface and Alcuin, whose letters to devout women and abbesses offer plentiful advice about appropriate monastic behaviour as well as spiritual guidance; no later Anglo-Saxon or continental clerics addressed advisory letters to religious Englishwomen.[88] Insights into the level of Latin learning attained by some female religious are afforded by the letters from women preserved in the Boniface collection,[89] and from those writings of Aldhelm of Malmesbury that were dedicated to women: the prose treatise *De Virginitate* and its verse counterpart the *Carmen de Virginitate* which were both meant for the female community at Barking, and the verse titulus he wrote for a church of St Mary built by Bugga, daughter of Centwine of Wessex.[90] Although not recorded among the participants at Church councils in the early Anglo-Saxon period (either in the general lists of those present which often preface the canons of councils, or other than rarely among the witnesses to documents issued on such occasions[91]), abbesses may often have been present at such meetings and participated in their deliberations.[92]

---

later Anglo-Saxon nunneries did collect hagiographical material relating to their more prominent or saintly sisters but that these have not survived; Hollis, *Anglo-Saxon Women*, p. 250, n. 41.

[87]   *Liber Vitae ecclesiae Dunelmensis*, ed. J. Stevenson, Surtees Society 8 (1841), pp. 3–5 (London, British Library, Cotton MS Domitian vii, fos 13r–14v). See Schneider, 'Anglo-Saxon women', pp. 83–4.

[88]   Boniface's correspondence with women has been discussed by Hollis, *Anglo-Saxon Women*, ch. 4; now see also B. Yorke, 'The Bonifacian mission and female religious in Wessex', *Early Medieval Europe*, 7 (1998), 145–72. Patrick Wormald noted that one-sixth of the 150 letters preserved as Boniface's correspondence were to or from religious women: 'St Hilda', p. 96. Dagmar Schneider has considered Boniface's female correspondents ('Anglo-Saxon women', pp. 201–7) and has explored Alcuin's relationship with women as seen through his letters (ibid., pp. 207–12); she drew attention further (pp. 216–18) to the somewhat distanced attitude taken by later generations of English clergy, notably Wulfstan and Ælfric, to their female contemporaries. Compare here also Wormald, 'St Hilda', p. 102.

[89]   For example Boniface, *Epistolae*, nos. 8, 13–15 and 29 (ed. M. Tangl, *Die Briefe des Heiligen Bonifatius und Lullus*, MGH, Epistolae selectae I [Berlin, 1916], *Die Briefe*, pp. 3–4, 18–28, 52–3); the last of these includes a sample of Leoba's attempts at writing verse.

[90]   Lapidge and Herren have discussed the audience intended for the prose *De Virginitate*: M. Lapidge and M. Herren, trans., *Aldhelm. The Prose Works* (1979), pp. 51–7. Its verse counterpart and the third of Aldhelm's *Carmina ecclesiastica*, that for Bugga, have been examined by Michael Lapidge in M. Lapidge and J. Rosier, trans., *Aldhelm. The Poetic Works* (1985), pp. 40–1 and 97–101.

[91]   The exceptions are those cases where religious women were involved in disputes brought to an assembly for settlement; see Schneider, 'Anglo-Saxon women', pp. 297–9 and nn. 123 and 129.

[92]   The participation of early Anglo-Saxon abbesses in politics and their attendance at Church councils have been explored by Schneider, 'Anglo-Saxon women', pp. 286–301. She has

Hild certainly had considerable influence over the outcome of the synod held at her minster at Whitby in 664 and her successor Ælfflæd was a key player in the 706 synod on the river Nidd which settled Wilfrid's Northumbrian affairs.[93] Concerns relevant to religious women were debated at various of the Church councils in the eighth and early ninth centuries, which sought to legislate for the correct behaviour of monastic women and abbesses as well as for monks and their superiors.[94] At *Clofesho* in 747, for example, an attempt was made to define what the houses of nuns (*domicilia sanctimonialium*) should be like; not places of lewd talk, partying, drunkenness, and luxury they should be the dwellings of those who live in continence and sobriety, who read and sing psalms, not those who weave themselves elaborate party-dresses.[95]

The impression given by the literary and prescriptive sources of the centrality of women's monastic communities within the early Anglo-Saxon Church is reinforced by the evidence for female religious as landholders. Women received gifts of land both for the endowment of new houses and for the further support of existing ones; many of these were sizeable donations of substantial quantities of land making their abbesses lords of some significance in their locality. Diplomas purportedly issued in the period before 900 have survived in favour of religious communities apparently including women at Barking, Bath, Bradfield, Castor, Cookham, Fladbury, Folkestone, Gloucester, Hanbury, Hoo, Inkberrow (*Penitanham*), Lyminge, Minster-in-Sheppey, Minster-in-Thanet, *Nasyngum*, *Pectanege*, Tetbury, Twining, Westbury-on-Trym, Wirksworth, and Withington. Although these are not all authentic documents, as a group they show lay patronage to have been directed as much towards female as to male congregations at least in the seventh and early eighth centuries, and indeed illustrate the extent to which the

---

cited just one occasion on which five abbesses were listed together among the witnesses to a council supposedly held at Bapchild 699x716 and recorded as BCS 91 (S 22), but this text was forged early in the ninth century: Brooks, *The Early History*, pp. 191–7.

[93]   Stephen, *Vita sancti Wilfridi*, ch. 10 (ed. and trans. B. Colgrave, *The Life of Bishop Wilfrid by Eddius Stephanus* [1927], pp. 20–3); *HE*, III, 25 (pp. 298–9) synod on the Nidd: *Vita sancti Wilfridi*, ch. 60 (pp. 128–33). See Schneider, 'Anglo-Saxon women', pp. 275–6, 290–1 and 295–6; C. Cubitt, *Anglo-Saxon Church Councils c. 650–c. 850* (1995), pp. 88–91, 289–90. It seems likely, as Schneider has suggested ('Anglo-Saxon women', pp. 286–7), that since it was Ælfflæd who asked Cuthbert if he would be willing to assume episcopal office that she was present at the synod in 684 at *Adtuifyrdi* when he was elected: anon, *Vita sancti Cuthberti*, III, 6 and IV, 1; Bede, *Vita sancti Cuthberti*, ch. 24 (ed. and trans. B. Colgrave, *Two Lives of Saint Cuthbert* [1940], at pp. 104–5, 110–13, 234–9).

[94]   Council of *Clofesho*, A.D. 747, chs. 4, 19–20, 28–9 (ed. A. W. Haddan and W. Stubbs, *Councils and Ecclesiastical Documents Relating to Great Britain and Ireland* [3 vols., 1869–78], III, 360–85, at pp. 364, 368–9, 374–5); legatine synods, A.D. 786, chs. 4–5 (ed. E. Dümmler, *Epistolae Karolini Aevi*, II, MGH Epistolae IV [Berlin, 1885], 19–29, at p. 22, no. 3); council of Chelsea, A.D. 816, chs. 4, 7–8 (ed. Haddan and Stubbs, *Councils*, III, 579–85, at pp. 580–2).

[95]   Council of *Clofesho*, ch. 20 (Haddan and Stubbs, *Councils*, III, 369).

convent came to play a role in royal and aristocratic family politics.[96] That women's houses were as well endowed as male probably gave them an economic significance that does much to account for their visibility in the literature. Occasional examples are mentioned in the Anglo-Saxon Chronicle, for example the statement under the year 718 after the obituary notice for Ingild, brother of Ine, that his sister Cuthburg, divorced wife of Aldfrith of Northumbria, had founded the minster at Wimborne.[97] There are no extant pre-Viking Age Northumbrian charters for any beneficiaries (religious or lay, male or female) but the overwhelmingly Southumbrian bias of the documentary evidence is balanced by the northern interests of Bede and the Northumbrian saints' lives. Consequently the picture of female monasticism that can be constructed from the sources for the period before 900 is one of a vibrant dynamic institution of economic and spiritual significance whose protagonists were evenly spread over most of the Anglo-Saxon areas of Britain.[98] The contrast with the last Anglo-Saxon centuries is marked.

Language

The focus of this study (in common with that of much of the recent historiography) will be directed more towards the female religious devotee than to the institution that housed her, as has already been explained. Much of the argument that is to be defended here as explanation for the evidential problem just defined will turn on the language employed of religious women in late tenth- and eleventh-century English sources.[99] In order to provide a context for that analysis (which is found in chapter four), it is worth saying something here about the vocabulary used in contemporary sources to denote female religious in the first Christian centuries in England.

Before the middle years of the tenth century there is little discernible precision in the vocabulary employed in Latin or vernacular texts to describe female religious, and no sign that distinctions were drawn between women of different status inside minsters with one exception. It does seem that those who

---

[96]   The treatment of monastic property by religious women and their male relatives has been explored by Schneider, 'Anglo-Saxon women', pp. 255–70. Wormald has pointed out ('St Hilda', p. 95) that the number of charters for women's foundations has already become very scarce in the second half of the eighth century, long before their virtual cessation in the tenth and eleventh centuries.

[97]   ASC 718.

[98]   See the map 3, p. 38.

[99]   I have defended the value of language as a tool in historical explanation in my 'Language and method: the Dictionary of Old English and the historian', in *The Dictionary of Old English*, ed. M. J. Toswell, Old English Newsletter, Subsidia 26 (1998), 73–87. See also N. Partner, 'Making up lost time: Writing on the writing of History', *Speculum*, 61 (1986), 90–117, at pp. 94–8; and G. Spiegel, 'History, historicism and the social logic of the text', *Speculum*, 65 (1990), 59–86, p. 60.

joined the cloister as virgins were marked out within their communities from the other women (widowed and separated) who had previously been married.[100] Particular spiritual rewards were anticipated for those who retained their virginity untarnished: 'Virginity, which preserves chaste flesh without fault, defeats all other celebrations of virtue in glory. ... just as the stars yield to the extraordinary light of the sun ..., outshining all the stars of the upper skies — so likewise renowned Virginity, which adorns the saints, excels in providing all the rewards of saints'.[101] The collection of penitential canons attributed to Archbishop Theodore reported the Roman custom that virgin and widow (*uirgo* and *uidua*) should not be veiled together,[102] and used the term *sacra uirgo* on one occasion as the female equivalent of *monachus*.[103] However, more commonly Theodore wrote of *mulieres* when he meant to describe the female sex in general, subdividing that group into *sanctimoniales* (religious women) and the *laicae*, the laity from whom they were distinct.[104] That the Latin nouns other than *uirgo* used in texts pre-dating the tenth century for religious women — *ancilla Dei, Deo deuota, famula Christi, monacha, nonna, nunnona, [sancti]monialis, soror, femina* (or *nonna*) *consecrata* — were intended to be seen other than as synonymous labels for the same condition is far from clear. The chapters of Bede's Ecclesiastical History devoted to the minster at Barking reveal how fluid was his use of terms to describe religious women, for he appears to have sought only to differentiate the virgins from the other women dedicated to God within the minster.[105] In his letter to King Æthelbald of Mercia written 746/7, Boniface made a number of references to religious women employing, apparently as synonyms, the terms *sanctimonialis, sacra uirgo, nonna uelata et consecrata*, and *femina uelata et consecrata*.[106] The canons of the 747 Council of *Clofesho* paired

[100] See below, p. 41, and Schneider, 'Anglo-Saxon women', pp. 49–50.
[101] Aldhelm, *Carmen de uirginitate*, lines 145–6, and 183–4 (ed. R. Ehwald, *Aldhelmi Opera Omnia*, MGH, AA, XV [Berlin, 1919], 350–471, at pp. 359–60; trans. Lapidge and Rosier, *Aldhelm*, pp. 106–7).
[102] Theodore, penitential, II, iii, 7 (ed. P. W. Finsterwalder, *Die Canones Theodori Cantuariensis und ihre Überlieferungsformen* [Weimar, 1929], pp. 285–334, at p. 316).
[103] Ibid., I, viii, 6 (p. 301). Compare also ibid., I, xiv, 11: *puella Dei* and II, vii, 1: *Christi famulae* (pp. 308 and 322).
[104] Theodore, penitential, I, xiv, 17 (ed. Finsterwalder, *Die Canones*, p. 308): 'Mulieres autem menstruo tempore non intrent in ecclesiam neque communicent nec sanctemoniales nec laicae si praesumant tribus ebdomadibus ieiunent'. Consider also I, ix, 3 (p. 302): 'Nec mulier meruit uelari multo magis ut non dominaret in ecclesia'. This chapter relates to the female sex the injunctions of the preceding clause which concerned the treatment of one who had once been vowed to God but then adopted the secular habit, stipulating that a woman who had renounced her vows ought similarly not to come to prominence in the Church.
[105] *HE*, IV, 6 (p. 356): *Deo deuotae feminae; caterua ancellarum Dei. HE*, IV, 7 (p. 356): *conuentus sororum, famulae Christi. HE*, IV, 8 (p. 358): *uirgo Deo dedicata, consecratae Christo uirgines, ancellae Dei, puella.*
[106] Epistola 73 (ed. Tangl, *Die Briefe*, pp. 148–9).

nunnones with *monachi* and wrote coterminously of *monasteria nunnorum* and *sanctimonialium domicilia*; similarly the canons agreed at the legatine councils of 786 referred to *monachae*, *ancillae Dei*, and *sanctimoniales*.[107]

By contrast for male religious it can be shown from texts dating before the tenth-century monastic revolution that, while all the tonsured were differentiated by that outward sign from the mass of the laity, monks (*monachi*) were distinguished both from the ranks of the ordained clergy (priests and deacons) and from other religious not in orders (usually termed *clerici* or *ecclesiastici*) by virtue of the higher level of commitment they had made through their vows to a life of devotion.[108] *Monachi* were distinguished from the rest of the non-ordained *clerici* in the canons of the 672/3 council of Hertford, and clear differentiation was drawn between clerical ranks in the Dialogues attributed to Archbishop Ecgbert of York (?732–766).[109] The 747 Council of *Clofesho* distinguished *monachi* from *clerici*, and *ecclesiastici* from *monasteriales*, whilst the 786 legatine synods (here reflecting Frankish influence), directed that *canonici* were to live canonically and *monachi seu monachae* to conduct themselves regularly both in food and in dress so that there might be clear distinction between secular, canon and monk.[110] Higher penalties were often applied to the ordained clergy and professed monks than to other religious. The clearest indication that the distinction drawn between the two groups is one of spiritual status is found in the so-called Constitutions of Archbishop Oda, which date from the 940s; there *presbyteri* were instructed to set a good example to the people of God entrusted to them, *clerici* were directed to live canonically (*canonice*), while *monachi* and 'all those who have vowed an oath to God' were enjoined to struggle night and day to fulfil their vows, remaining in the fear of God in the churches where they bound themselves by vow, despising the example of *vagabundi* and *girovagi*.[111] Whether this last chapter was intended to encompass women who had taken vows is not explicitly made clear; the only reference Oda made to female religious was in the chapter of his Constitutions forbidding men from making illicit marriages with their relations and with nuns (*moniales*).[112]

---

[107]   Council of *Clofesho*, chs. 19–20 (ed. Haddan and Stubbs, *Councils*, III, 368–9). Legatine councils, 786, chs. 4, 15 and 16 (ed. Dümmler, pp. 22 and 25, no. 3). This issue has also been discussed by Schneider, 'Anglo-Saxon women', p. 82, and n. 5.

[108]   I have defended this argument in detail in my 'Language and method', pp. 76–7.

[109]   Council of Hertford, chs. 4 and 5 (*HE*, IV, 5, pp. 348–52). Ecgberht's *Dialogi*, *responsiones* 3, 7, 12 and 14 (ed. Haddan and Stubbs, *Councils*, III, 405–6, 408–9).

[110]   Council of *Clofesho*, A.D. 747, chs. 4–5, 7, 8–12, 28–9 (ed. Haddan and Stubbs, *Councils*, III, 403–13, at pp. 364–7, 374) and ibid., chs. 15, 17, 21–2 (pp. 367–70). Legatine synods, A.D. 786, ch. 4 (ed. Dümmler, p. 22, no. 3).

[111]   The 'Constitutions' of Archbishop Oda, chs. 4, 5 and 6 (ed. Whitelock *et al.*, *Councils and Synods*, I, 67–74, at pp. 71–2, no. 20).

[112]   Ibid., ch. 7 (p. 72); this chapter is reminiscent of the 786 legatine councils, ch. 15 (ed. Dümmler, p. 25, no. 3).

While it is highly likely that during the early Christian centuries in England there were women living inside minsters, wearing religious dress but without having taken the vows of full monastic profession (equivalent to the men generally called *clerici*), the profusion of Latin nouns and phrases available to describe religious women in this period makes it difficult to demonstrate whether or not such non-professed women were consistently differentiated linguistically from nuns under full vows. Nor is there any sign that the former were perceived to differ significantly from those women who adopted some of the trappings of the religious life while retaining their own property and living in the world. Distinctions between the canonical and the regular life were not drawn in the pre-Viking Age, and those features taken to be distinctive of the life of canonesses rather than 'nuns' can be seen to have characterised some female religious observance as represented in sources from the seventh and eighth centuries.[113] There is only one text supposedly from this period (the prologue to the penitential attributed to Ecgbert) that hints at the existence of discrete categories of religious woman by differentiating between *uirgo, femina canonica uel sanctimonialis*; however the prologue is, as Dagmar Schneider has argued, apparently of continental not Anglo-Saxon origin and so does not reflect English usage.[114] This negates Roberta Gilchrist's suggestion that the two types of professed religious distinguished in this text, '*canonica* (woman living under a rule) and *sanctimonialis* (nun), may imply the vocations appropriate to minsters and monasteries'.[115]

Vernacular texts offer little help here either, not least because of the paucity of surviving examples of Old English dating from before the tenth century. The noun most commonly used of religious women was *nunne*, a loan word from the late Latin *nonna*, which denoted no particular style of religious living. It appears only to have been from the second half of the tenth century that noun *mynecenu* was used of female religious.[116] If it could be argued that Bede had drawn a distinction between nuns who remained virgins and other religious women, this was not sustained by his ninth-century Mercian translator, who sometimes preferred the single noun *nunne* to translate both *femina sanctimonialis* and *uirgo* from the original Latin.[117] The sole mention of a religious woman in the

---

[113] For discussion of the characteristics of the canonical life M. Parisse, 'Les chanoinesses dans l'empire germanique (ixe–xie siècles)', *Francia*, 6 (1978), 107–26, at p. 109.

[114] Schneider, 'Anglo-Saxon women', p. 82, n. 5.

[115] Gilchrist, *Gender*, pp. 26–7.

[116] *A Microfiche Concordance to Old English,* A. DiPaolo Healey and R. L. Venezky, (Toronto, 1982), *s.v. mynecena* etc. The texts cited are predominantly the Old English Rule of St Benedict (and Æthelwold's introductory account of the reform), the vernacular gloss to the *Regularis concordia*, Ælfric's Homilies and Lives of the Saints. This point is discussed in detail in chapter 4.

[117] *The Old English Version of Bede's Ecclesiastical History of the English People*, IV, 11 and IV, 24 (ed. and trans. T. Miller, 2 vols., EETS orig. ser. 95–6 and 110–11 [1890], pp. 288

pre-tenth-century Chronicle relates to the woman said to have been consecrated as a *nunne* whom the ætheling Æthelwold abducted from Wimborne in 900.[118] In seeking to protect the chastity of religious women, the laws of King Alfred prohibited the taking of a *nunne* out of a minster and declared illegitimate any child born to a former religious woman.[119] In the next chapter we will see that the religious life for women in England before the First Viking Age was characterised by a diversity in which no single model of the 'right' rule of life prevailed. The evidence of the language used of religious women in the early period points to the same conclusion since it implies that the most significant criterion by which religious women were differentiated one from another was according to the extent of their previous sexual experience, not according to the vows they had taken or whether they lived within a community or outside in the world.

Accounting for the discrepancy in the sources across the First Viking Age

It is unclear to what extent there is anything uniquely English about the nature of the surviving record of religious houses for women, since it is hard in the absence of readily available comparative material to determine whether the pattern observed in the evidence for England is mirrored in other parts of the early medieval West. The expression of female devotion took markedly different forms in much of the Celtic world; there were no nunneries for which any evidence has survived in Brittany, Cornwall, or Scotland before the eleventh century, and only a few nuns are known from Wales in the early middle ages.[120] There are more attested examples of nuns from Ireland in this period, but few certain instances of

---

and 340) rendered as *nunne* and *haligu nunne* the *femina sanctimonialis* of the original (*HE* IV, 9 and IV, 23, pp. 360, 412). In the vernacular version of V, 3 (pp. 390–2) *nunne* was given to translate *uirgo* and *nunmynstre* for *monasterium uirginum* (*HE*, V, 3, p. 460).

[118] Anglo-Saxon Chronicle, *s.a.* 900 A (ed. Bately, *ASC A*, p. 62): 'forðon ðe heo wæs ær to nunnan gehalgod'.

[119] Laws of Alfred, chs. 8–8.3 (ed. F. Liebermann, *Die Gesetze der Angelsachsen*, [3 vols., Halle, 1903–16], I, 54); in the earliest of the versions of Alfred's code (Cambridge, Corpus Christi College, MS. 173) in chapter 8 the noun *munuc* was also used, clearly with reference to the *nunne* already described (in decreeing that compensation was to be paid either to the bishop or to the 'lord of the church in whose charge the nun is', *þære cirican hlaforde, ðe ðonne munuc age*), but later manuscripts altered this reading to *mynecenna* or *ða nunnan*. Christine Fell discussed the language of this clause, noting the masculine forms of both *hlaford* and *munuc* in a context where they must clearly relate to abbess and consecrated woman: *Women in Anglo-Saxon England and the Impact of 1066* (1984), p. 124. Compare also I Edmund, ch. 4 (ed. Liebermann, *Die Gesetze*, I, 184).

[120] W. Davies, 'Celtic women in the early middle ages', in *Images of Women in Antiquity*, ed. A. Cameron and A. Kuhrt (1993), pp. 145–66, at pp. 157–8. The only evidence for the presence of nuns in Cornwall is the allusion to their dwelling at Bodmin made by Leland, which cannot be dated; see further part II, *s.n.* Bodmin.

named women's religious communities, a situation that seems to correlate more closely with English conditions in the tenth and eleventh centuries but not with the position before the First Viking Age. Kathleen Hughes sought to find an explanation for this phenomenon in Irish laws of inheritance, which prevented women from acquiring more than a life interest in the land they inherited; suggesting that many Irish monasteries were set up on family lands, Hughes thought it likely that the pious women who appear in the sources supported religious communities only during their lifetimes, congregations that were broken up on the woman's death when her kin recovered the land.[121] The pattern of the sources for northern Francia resembles the Anglo-Saxon evidence in showing considerable interest in female monastic foundations in the seventh century but a marked decline from the ninth century with the disappearance of many houses from the historical record and revival of interest in and patronage of women's houses only in the eleventh.[122] The position of nunneries in Saxony stands out from the rest of western Europe for it is in precisely the period when nunneries are least well evidenced in England and Francia, namely the tenth century, that the sources witness to the foundation of considerable numbers of women's houses, established apparently in preference to male institutions.[123] To some extent, as Karl Leyser noted, Saxon society was here following the patterns of endowment in the period immediately after the conversion to Christianity seen earlier in both Francia and England, but for this period the peculiar German interest in houses for nuns is unparalleled.[124] The political fate of Italy during the early middle ages was so different from that of northern Europe that one would expect the sources to

---

[121] K. Hughes, *Early Christian Ireland. Introduction to the Sources* (1972), pp. 234–5. See further below, chapter 2. I am grateful to Tom Clancy for discussion of the Irish material.

[122] M. Skinner, 'Benedictine life for women in central France, 850–1100: a feminist revival', in *Medieval Religious Women I: Distant Echoes*, ed. Nichols and Shanks (1984), pp. 87–113. Jean Verdon's studies of the sources for female nunneries in France pointed to two periods — the seventh and eleventh centuries — when sources are relatively plentiful and many new nunneries founded, separated by three centuries when fewer new institutions were established; 'Recherches sur les monastères féminins dans la France du Sud aux ixe–xie siècles', *Annales du Midi*, 88 (1976), 118–38 and 'Recherches sur les monastères féminins dans la France du Nord aux ixe–xie siècles' *Revue Mabillon*, 59 (1976), 49–96. I owe these references to Julia Smith. See also Wormald, 'St Hilda', pp. 101–2; Venarde, *Women's Monasticism*, pp. 28–40.

[123] I cannot agree with Bruce Venarde's argument (*Women's Monasticism*, p. 27) that 'the character of female monasticism in England in the tenth and early eleventh centuries bears considerable resemblance to that of Ottonian Saxony'. Venarde has considered 'the prominence of religious women in late Anglo-Saxon England to be reminiscent of the high position accorded to nuns and their communities in early Anglo-Saxon England' and the 'golden age of female monasticism'. This opinion fails to take account of the relative decline in women's houses in England after *c.* 750 and of the relationship between the wealth (and the corresponding evidence for) royally-patronised male houses in the same period. Nor has Venarde allowed for the fact that the nine southern nunneries on which he has based his conclusions stand apart from all the other places that housed religious women in the last century before the Conquest.

[124] K. J. Leyser, *Rule and Conflict in an Early Medieval Society* (1979), p. 64.

present a rather different picture of the history of Italian nunneries. Evidence collected by Suzanne Wemple argues for a good deal of continuity across the period (notably in the ninth and tenth centuries, despite the disruptions of Saracen and Magyar raids) without the extremes of achievement and decay experienced elsewhere; as well as receiving the patronage of Lombard, Carolingian and Ottonian rulers, Italian nunneries were supported by the local nobility and may have owed some of their success to their willingness to be placed under the direct control of male abbeys or bishops.[125] From such comparative material as is available it does seem that the English pattern of source survival (relative abundance before the mid-eighth century, a gradual decline in the later eighth and ninth centuries followed by near silence for all but a handful of institutions from a geographically and socially restricted milieu) is not exactly replicated elsewhere in early medieval Europe.

Assuming that the extant sources reflect only a small proportion of those originally written, why do materials for women's houses in England in the tenth and eleventh centuries appear to survive not only less well than those relating to male congregations, but also, seemingly, in relatively smaller proportion than do the sources for pre-Viking-Age minsters for women? That all female houses in the later period were deliberately ignored by contemporary writers and later historians is demonstrably untrue: a small but significant group of houses has been singled out as dominating the contemporary and subsequent literature, several of which, far from being insignificant and impoverished, were in the tenth century and beyond among the richest and most prominent religious houses in medieval England. Yet these are less well attested in the literature than contemporary male establishments. The larger group of women's minsters, as has been shown, is even less visible, and here the contrast with the situation before 900 is still more marked. The inadequacy of the written evidence cannot be assumed to reflect the relative social, economic or spiritual unimportance or lack of success of all the women's religious houses identifiable during the tenth and eleventh centuries (although some, indubitably, had only a transitory existence, perhaps attributable to the meagreness of their resources): it requires some explanation.

That gender has had a role to play in shaping the historiography of medieval nunneries has recently been argued;[126] whether the bias thereby imputed is attributable to social attitudes (among early medieval authors or modern scholars) or is rather an accurate reflection of the impoverishment and ephemeral nature of the institutions to which women belonged is an important issue. Before adopting the conclusion that there was a genuine gender dichotomy between male and female experience in the post-Viking Age it is necessary to ask what it is that

---

[125] S. Wemple, 'Female monasticism in Italy and its comparison with France and Germany from the ninth through the eleventh century', in *Frauen in Spätantike und Frühmittelalter*, ed. W. Affeldt (Sigmaringen, 1990), pp. 291–310, at pp. 291–9.

[126] Gilchrist, *Gender*, pp. 22–5.

the surviving sources, which appear to show this marked difference, are in fact reflecting. It could be argued that male religious, dominating the construction of written records, deliberately suppressed the evidence for female religious (an 'androcentrism', to quote Roberta Gilchrist, then perpetuated by later generations of frequently male scholars). This would be to argue that there were substantial numbers of female religious to be found in this period if only historians could get behind the deceptive obfuscations practised by the male authors of our sources. Alternatively it might be, as Gilchrist has suggested, that the female religious experience was different from that of their male contemporaries, rather than less successful;[127] on this reading it becomes inappropriate to judge women's houses by the standards applied to those occupied by men, for women are thought to have expressed their devotion via different means that happen not to have found permanent place in the written record. It is certainly possible to identify a number of devout women during this period in addition to the three cited at the head of this chapter (Æthelhild, Wynflæd and Æthelgifu), whose vocation was fulfilled in the world, not in the cloister and this may well have been a more common practice than the surviving sources now suggest.[128]

A different response to the problem of the availability of the evidence is to seek its origins in tenth-century conditions. One such interpretation would be to see the apparent dearth of sources for women's religious houses in the tenth and eleventh centuries as reflecting a general social shift in attitudes to women after the First Viking Age; this might be thought to have induced a reluctance on the part of (generally male) writers to record any kind of female activity, secular as much as religious. If women religious were thought to have been viewed differently by seculars during this period, the nobility might consequently have proved less willing to patronise their activities with the result that female houses would be less well endowed than male monasteries. Inevitably this would mean that women's communities would not be in a position to act in the economic sphere in ways that directly paralleled the activities of their male counterparts. The tendency of the sources towards silence would thus further be exacerbated, since few female institutions would have possessed sufficient wealth or economic power to guarantee them a place in the written record. According to this analysis, the institutions that housed devout women have been rendered invisible by their failure, or inability, to acquire permanent landed endowments recorded in extant charters, rather than that their communities have deliberately been ignored or written out of the literature from later Anglo-Saxon England. One difficulty with this explanation is that the apparent tailing off in the landed endowment of female religious houses (as witnessed by the extant charters) long predates the First Viking Age, being manifest from the second half of the eighth century.[129] It may

---

[127] Ibid., p. 191.

[128] See further below, chapter 5

[129] Wormald, 'St Hilda', p. 95.

be less that tenth-century ecclesiastics suddenly cultivated a misogyny unknown
to their eighth-century counterparts, but that forms of religious life that were
before the First Viking Age open equally to both genders (and materially as well
rewarded) later fell into disfavour and were replaced by more diverse (but at the
same time more rigidly regulated) single-sex alternatives.

Before looking more closely at the female expression of religious devotion
in the period after *c.* 900 and exploring how it is that religious women have come
to be more prominent in the extant sources than the establishments that housed
them, it is necessary to say something further about pre-Viking Age minsters for
women. A contrast with the situation pertaining in the early period can only be
sustained once it is clear with what conditions the circumstances of later Anglo-
Saxon religious women are being compared.

Chapter 2

Religious women in England before the First Viking Age

> ... you flowers of the Church, monastic sisters, scholarly pupils, pearls of Christ, jewels of Paradise, and participants in the celestial homeland!
>
> Aldhelm, *De uirginitate*.[1]

> All who knew Hild, the handmaiden of Christ and abbess, used to call her mother because of her outstanding devotion and grace. She was not only an example of holy life to all who were in the minster but she also provided an opportunity for salvation and repentance to many who lived far away and heard the happy story of her industry and virtue.
>
> Bede, *Historia ecclesiastica*.[2]

> Among the Greeks it is not customary for men to have monastic women, nor women, men; nevertheless we shall not overthrow that which is the custom in this region.
>
> Theodore, Penitential.[3]

Female enthusiasm for the conventual forms of the religious life is apparent in England almost from the beginning of the Christian era, and certainly by the middle years of the seventh century. Women's religious houses flourished particularly in the later seventh and first half of the eighth century during which time they acquired much landed wealth through the active patronage of royal and noble families. By the year 900, however, the profusion of minsters for women has vanished: at the end of King Alfred's reign there remained few monastic congregations with female members. Those sites that were to house religious women in the tenth and eleventh centuries were largely unrelated to the women's

---

[1] Aldhelm, prose *De uirginitate*, §lx (ed. R. Ehwald, *Aldhelmi Opera Omnia*, MGH, AA, XV [Berlin, 1919], 228–323, at p. 323; trans. M. Lapidge and M. Herren, *Aldhelm. The Prose Works* [1979], p. 132).

[2] Bede, *HE*, IV, 23 (ed. and trans. B. Colgrave and R. A. B. Mynors [1969], pp. 410–11).

[3] Theodore, Penitential, II, vi, 8 (ed. P. W. Finsterwalder, *Die Canones Theodori Cantuariensis und ihre Überlieferungsformen* [Weimar, 1929], pp. 285–334, at p. 320; trans. J. T. McNeill and H. M. Gamer, *Medieval Handbooks of Penance* [New York, 1990], pp. 179–215, at p. 204).

minsters of the pre-Viking Age. The reasons for the marked variation in the history of female religious experience in England before and after 900 are a central concern of this study. Here a sketch is given of the development of women's monasticism in early Anglo-Saxon society, with some discussion of the place of women's monastic lands in royal and noble family strategies, the institution of the double house and the status of religious women outside the cloister.

The earliest English minsters for women

The first religious houses for women in southern England were founded in Kent in the 630s and 640s, with the direct support and active participation of members of the ruling Kentish royal house; the earliest foundations were probably at Lyminge, which was established for Æthelburh, daughter of King Æthelberht, after her flight from Northumbria on the death of her husband Edwin in 633, and at Folkestone, founded for his daughter Eanswith by Eadberht of Kent, who died in 640.[4] The first identifiable Northumbrian woman to 'take the vows and habit of a nun', was by Bede's account a certain Heiu, who founded a community at Hartlepool, probably in the 640s.[5] Before that time, any English woman attracted by the appeal of this way of life was, according to Bede, forced to travel abroad to join one of the communities of northern Francia. Just as men, because there were not yet many minsters founded in England used to go to enter the religious houses of the Franks or Gauls to practise the monastic life, so Bede asserted, 'they also sent their daughters to be taught in them and to be wedded to the heavenly bridegroom'.[6] Englishwomen apparently joined the monasteries of Faremoutiers-en-Brie, Chelles, and Andelys-sur-Seine, among them the daughter, step-daughter and grand-daughter of the East Anglian king Anna — Æthelburh, Sæthryth and Eorcengota — all of whom went to Faremoutiers-en-Brie, taking the role of abbess in succession.[7] Just why the East Anglian royal house was so respected at Faremoutiers is unclear; Bede seems particularly well informed about that nunnery's history, apparently having access to a written source from the house itself.[8] Chelles was the community chosen in retirement by the Northumbrian Hereswith, wife of Anna's brother, Æthelhere, to which community Hereswith's

---

        [4]   N. Brooks, *The Early History of the Church of Canterbury* (1984), p. 183; S. E. Rigold, 'The "double minsters" of Kent and their analogies', *Journal of the British Archaeological Association*, 3rd ser. 31 (1961), 27–37, at p. 31.
        [5]   *HE*, IV, 23 (pp. 406–8).
        [6]   Ibid., III, 8 (pp. 236–9).
        [7]   Ibid.; P. Hunter Blair, *The World of Bede* (1970), pp. 144–6; P. Sims-Williams, *Religion and Literature in Western England, 600–800* (1990), p. 111.
        [8]   See S. Hollis, *Anglo-Saxon Women and the Church* (1992), pp. 258–61.

sister, Hild was also attracted.[9] Hild was, however, persuaded by the Irish missionary Aidan not to follow her sister but rather to remain in England; returning home from East Anglia, Hild 'lived the monastic life with a small band of companions' on one hide of land beside the River Wear before succeeding Heiu as abbess of Hartlepool.[10]

Frankish influences were particularly important to the development of early English monasticism, not just for the opportunities northern Gallic houses provided for men and women to satisfy their religious devotion in the communal life, but because of the direct stimulus provided by Frankish ecclesiastics in England.[11] The Life of Bertila, abbess of Chelles (c. 660–c. 710), reported that 'faithful kings from the parts of Saxondom across the seas would ask her through trusty messengers to send them some of her followers for teaching or sacred instruction ... or even those who might establish monasteries of men and women in that region'. In response to such requests Bertila sent 'chosen women and very devout men' to England, with saints' relics and many volumes of books, by this means multiplying the 'yield of souls to God'.[12] The first abbess of Wenlock in Shropshire, Liobsind, may have been Frankish.[13] Berta, the first abbess of the community at Bath founded in 675 can with more confidence be thought a Frank, and the congregation there continued its French connections under its second abbess (an Englishwoman called Beorngyth), in the person of Beorngyth's deputy, a certain Folcburg.[14] It may also have been at least in part through Frankish influence that the most common model for female monastic organisation was the double house, the mixed-gender congregation under a female head.[15]

The period of the greatest expansion in monasticism in England followed directly after the success of Irish and other missionaries among the English from the 630s onwards, when most of the Anglo-Saxon royal families were brought to the Christian faith; in the second half of the seventh century numerous minsters were founded throughout England, among which houses including women were

---

[9]   *HE*, IV, 23 (pp. 406–7).
[10] Ibid.
[11] J. Campbell, *Essays in Anglo-Saxon History* (1986), pp. 49–67; Rigold, 'The "double minsters"', pp. 32–3; Sims-Williams, *Religion*, pp. 119–20.
[12] *Vita Bertilae*, ch. 6 (ed. W. Levison, MGH, SS rerum Merovingicarum, VI [Hannover and Leipzig, 1913], 95–109, at pp. 106–7); trans. Sims-Williams, *Religion*, p. 110.
[13] This was suggested by H. P. R. Finberg, *The Early Charters of the West Midlands* (2nd edn, 1972), pp. 202 and 208–9, who has been followed by Campbell, *Essays*, p. 58. That *Liobsynda* was a Frankish name, and not rather the misrendering by a thirteenth-century scribe of the Old English name *Leofsith* or *Leofswith* has been questioned by Sims-Williams, *Religion*, p. 111.
[14] BCS 43 (S 51) and BCS 57 (S 1167); Sims-Williams, *Religion*, pp. 111–12.
[15] See further below, pp. 49–56.

Map 3   Female religious houses, *c.* 630–*c.* 900

prominent.[16] There seems no reason to doubt the genuineness of the statements of personal piety and spiritual aspiration that are found in charters donating land for the foundation of minsters or are ascribed to aspiring monastics by Bede or early hagiographers; the appeal of the monastic life was primarily a religious one, for all that monastic houses came to be woven into the dynastic structures of aristocratic society. A further significant spur to this growth in the religious life must have been the fulfilment of the need to provide for the spiritual care of the newly converted lay population, and particularly for those dwelling far from the royal court, where baptism and Christian teaching were more unfamiliar. Such indeed were the evangelising imperatives of the early Christian period that all religious houses, including those occupied by women, became in effect pastoral centres, even if it had not been for this purpose that their founders had sought to establish a minster.[17]

The reasons why women entered the cloister varied considerably and — where these can be determined — often reveal as much about the families to which they belonged as about the individual women themselves. Some women were dedicated to religion by their parents and placed in the cloister in infancy in order to satisfy their family's devotion vicariously; there these daughters could intercede on behalf of their kin, so ensuring the permanent preservation of its memory.[18] Oswiu of Northumbria gave his one-year-old daughter Ælfflæd to God in fulfilment of a vow; the young Mildrith was brought to Minster-in-Thanet and then sent to Chelles for a monastic education; and Leoba was placed in the minster at Wimborne while still a child.[19] Others of the adult women visible within female religious houses may have been educated from childhood within the Church without necessarily having from the outset been destined for life within a nunnery; their election to take vows could have been a conscious decision, made in

[16]   See Campbell, *Essays*, pp. 61–2 for discussion of the equivalent growth in monasticism in seventh-century Francia. The most recent analysis of the importance of royal patronage in the foundation of women's religious houses is that offered by M. A. Meyer, 'Queens, convents and conversion in early Anglo-Saxon England', *Revue bénédictine*, 109 (1999), 90–116.

[17]   J. Godfrey, 'The place of the double monastery in the Anglo-Saxon minster system', in *Famulus Christi*, ed. G. Bonner (1976), pp. 344–50, at pp. 344–5. I have made this case elsewhere, see my 'Parochial ministry in early Anglo-Saxon England: the role of monastic communities', *Studies in Church History*, 26 (1989), 43–54 and 'Anglo-Saxon minsters: a review of terminology', in *Pastoral Care Before the Parish*, ed. J. Blair and R. Sharpe (1992), pp. 212–25, at pp. 216–24.

[18]   For discussion of child oblation in general see J. Boswell, *The Kindness of Strangers* (1988), ch. 5; and M. de. Jong, *In Samuel's Image* (Leiden, 1996); and for a Frankish context, G. Muschiol, *Famula Dei. Zur Liturgie in merowingischen Frauenklöstern* (Münster, 1994), pp. 300–12. For examples of Anglo-Saxon child oblates see De Jong, *In Samuel's Image*, pp. 46–55, and for discussion of *puellae oblatae*, ibid., pp. 39–40 and 60–66.

[19]   Ælfflæd: *HE*, III, 24 (pp. 290–3); Mildrith: D. W. Rollason, *The Mildrith Legend* (1982), pp. 11–13 and 76; Leoba: Rudolf, *Vita Leobae*, ch. 6 (ed. G. Waitz, MGH, SS, XV.I [Hannover, 1887], 118–31, at p. 124).

preference to whatever marriage awaited them outside.[20] Equally women brought up in the world might turn to the cloister as a refuge from an unwanted betrothal or marriage; the collection of penitential canons ascribed to Archbishop Theodore permitted a girl to enter a religious house rather than marry the man to whom her parents had betrothed her.[21] The same canons directed that once a girl reached the age of sixteen or seventeen she was no longer in her parents' power, could not be forced into marriage against her will and might become a nun if she so wished.[22] There are various early Irish instances of women going to extreme lengths in order to enter the Church to avoid marriage, usually in direct contravention of their families' wishes.[23] Other examples of early medieval women (none of them English) who contrived to contract severe illness or hideous deformity sufficient to release them from the obligation to marry and permit them instead to enter nunneries have been collected by Jane Schulenburg, who has seen such behaviour as motivated by the heroic desire for the preservation of virginity.[24]

A vocation to the monastic life came to some women in maturity after experience of the world; Hild had lived thirty-three years in the secular habit before she chose to follow her sister's example and take the veil.[25] According to the Penitential ascribed to Archbishop Theodore, men and women were permitted to leave a marriage in order to enter the monastic life, provided that they had their partner's consent.[26] One indication of the number of formerly married women found within minsters is the identification made by Aldhelm in his prologue to his

---

[20]   Reference was made to the taking of vows by early medieval English nuns in Theodore, Penitential, I, xiv, 5 (*votum uirginitatis*) and I, xiv, 7 ('Mulier non licet uotum uouere sine consensu uiri') (ed. Finsterwalder, *Die Canones*, p. 307); for the consecration of a virgin with a veil, ibid., II, iii, 6–8 (p. 316). The Council of *Clofesho* of 747 directed that all wandering clergy, including *sanctimoniales*, should be sent back to the minster where they had first taken the habit of holy profession ('ubi primitus habitum sanctae professionis sumpserant'): ch. 29 (ed. A. W. Haddan and W. Stubbs, *Councils and Ecclesiastical Documents Relating to Great Britain and Ireland* [3 vols., 1869–78], III, 360–85, at p. 374).

[21]   Theodore, Penitential, II, xii, 34 (ed. Finsterwalder, p. 330; trans. McNeill and Gamer, p. 211); cited by Boswell, *The Kindness*, p. 254.

[22]   Theodore, Penitential, II, xii, 37 (ed. Finsterwalder, *Die Canones*, pp. 330–1).

[23]   L. M. Bitel, 'Women's monastic enclosures in early Ireland', *Journal of Medieval History*, 12 (1986), 15–36, at pp. 22 and 29.

[24]   J. T. Schulenburg, 'The heroics of virginity: Brides of Christ and sacrificial mutilation', in *Women in the Middle Ages and the Renaissance*, ed. M. B. Rose (Syracuse, New York, 1986), pp. 29–72, at pp. 51–4. As Schulenburg has pointed out (p. 53), one chapter of the law-code of the seventh-century Lombard king, Rothair, permitted men to retrieve their property and marry another woman if their betrothed became leprous, or mad or blind in both eyes, such illness being due not to the man's fault but to the woman's 'weighty sins': Rothair's Edict, ch. 180 (ed. F. Bluhme, *Leges Langobardorum*, MGH, Leges, IV [Hannover, 1869], 42; trans. K. F. Drew, *The Lombard Laws* [Philadelphia, Pennsylvania, 1973], pp. 84–5).

[25]   *HE*, IV, 23 (pp. 406–7).

[26]   Theodore, Penitential, II, xii, 8, 13 (ed. Finsterwalder, *Die Canones Theodori*, pp. 327–8).

work on virginity addressed to the nuns of Barking of an intermediate condition lying between true virginity and the married state which he called chastity. This was the state of one who 'having been assigned to marital contracts, has scorned the commerce of matrimony for the sake of the heavenly kingdom'.[27] Cuthburg separated from her husband Aldfrith of Northumbria during his lifetime and returned to her native Wessex where she established a minster at Wimborne.[28] When the East Anglian Æthelthryth finally obtained the permission of her husband, Ecgfrith of Northumbria, to enter the religious life (supposedly following twelve years of unconsummated marriage), she was placed by her husband in the minster at Coldingham, which was governed by his aunt, Æbbe. She also preferred to return to her native kingdom, getting herself appointed as an abbess and establishing a new house at Ely.[29] It seems that within female monastic communities the *virgines* were sometimes seen as a distinct group (not necessarily a very numerous one), separate from the other *ancillae Christi*; the latter were often called *feminae* perhaps indicating that these were women who had formerly been married.[30] A virgin, one who had vowed herself to God and assumed the garment of the blessed Mary, was truly the 'bride of Christ'.[31]

Entry to the religious life was a recognised route for widows, affording them greater personal safety and other advantages over life in a secular environment, notably freedom from an unwanted second marriage and greater control for themselves and their daughters over the fate of their own landed estates.[32] From the Church's perspective the cloister provided a suitable environment for the safe custody and appropriate occupation of active women

---

[27] Aldhelm, prose *De uirginitate*, §xix (ed. Ehwald, p. 249; trans. Lapidge and Herren, *Aldhelm*, p. 75). A general discussion of the categorisation of women by the early medieval Church may be found in R. Metz, 'Le statut de la femme en droit canonique médiéval', *Recueils de la Société Jean Bodin*, 12 (1962), 59–113.

[28] ASC 718. It is possible that Cuthburg went to Barking before returning to Wessex (as was asserted by P. Stafford, *Queens, Concubines and Dowagers* [Athens, Georgia, 1983], p. 179), since a woman of that name is included among the dedicatees of Aldhelm's *De uirginitate*, but this could equally have been another woman of the same name.

[29] *HE*, IV, 19 (pp. 392–3).

[30] D. Schneider, 'Anglo-Saxon women in the religious life: a study of the status and position of women in an early mediaeval society'(PhD thesis, University of Cambridge, 1985), pp. 49–50; see above, pp. 26–7.

[31] Legatine councils, A.D. 786, ch. 16 (ed. E. Dümmler, *Epistolae Karolini Aevi*, II, MGH Epistolae IV [Berlin, 1885], 19–29, at p. 25, no. 3): 'Virginem namque, quae se Deo uouerit et ad instar sanctae Mariae uestem induerit, sponsam Christi uicitare non dubitamus'.

[32] S. F. Wemple, *Women in Frankish Society* (Philadelphia, PA, 1981), pp. 104–5, 138–40, 156–7; D. Baltrusch-Schneider, 'Klosterleben als alternative Lebensform zur Ehe?', in *Weibliche Lebensgestaltung im frühen Mittelalter*, ed. H.-W. Goetz (Cologne and Vienna, 1991), pp. 45–64, at pp. 52–6; J. L. Nelson, 'The wary widow', in *Property and Power in the Early Middle Ages*, ed. W. Davies and P. Fouracre (1995), pp. 82–113, at pp. 84–5; J. T. Schulenburg, 'Female sanctity: Public and private roles, ca. 500–1100', in *Women and Power in the Middle Ages*, ed. M. Erler and M. Kowaleski (Athens, GA, 1988), pp. 102–25, at pp. 108–9. Compare also the comments made by K. J. Leyser, *Rule and Conflict in an Early Medieval Society* (1979), p. 68.

widowed in early and middle life; Henry Mayr-Harting has suggested that it may have been in part to provide for the large numbers of aristocratic and royal women thus affected that so many double houses were founded in the seventh century.[33] Widows were expected to assume the religious habit and veil and to take vows that were meant to be binding for life, although Theodore's Penitential addressed the problem presented by the remarriage of avowed widows.[34] Ambitious aristocratic dowagers and queen-mothers, deprived by widowhood of the political role they had played as wives, may well have been further attracted by the potential opportunity afforded them by the monastic life to continue to exercise power and influence as ecclesiastical landowners (bearing in mind the landed wealth and social prominence of many minsters). Widowed queens who had married into foreign ruling houses tended to return to their own country in order to take the veil rather than rely on the dubious protection of their husband's kin;[35] Æthelburg, wife of Edwin of Northumbria, went back to her native Kent on Edwin's death in 633, as did Eormenhild when her Mercian husband, Wulfhere, had died.[36] Interestingly, Eormenhild's mother Seaxburg (an East Anglian) had remained in Kent when her husband Eorconberht died, founding her own nunnery at Sheppey, but once her daughter returned home and joined her mother's house, Seaxburg went back to East Anglia and her sister's house at Ely.[37] Iurminburh, the second wife of Ecgfrith, did not enter any of the minsters associated with her husband's family (such as Whitby or Coldingham), preferring instead her sister's house at Carlisle.[38] In the early ninth century Eadburh, widow (according to Asser, murderess) of Beorhtric of Wessex, was unable to go home to Mercia where the dynasty of her father Offa had not survived, but was forced instead to flee to Francia to the protection of Charlemagne, who gave her a large convent of nuns.[39]

---

[33]   H. Mayr-Harting, *The Coming of Christianity to Anglo-Saxon England* (3rd edn, 1991) , p. 250. For examples of widows who entered monastic houses on their husbands' deaths (frequently taking over their management) see R. H. Bremmer, 'Widows in Anglo-Saxon England', in *Between Poverty and the Pyre*, ed. J. Bremmer and L. van den Bosch (1995), pp. 58–88, at pp. 80–1.

[34]   Theodore, Penitential, II, xii, 14–15 (ed. Finsterwalder, *Die Canones*, p. 328). See Wemple, *Women*, pp. 284–5. The importance to our understanding of female devotion in the later Anglo-Saxon period of widows who had assumed the religious life is such that the position of widows is considered separately as a distinct category in chapter 5.

[35]   As has been demonstrated by Schneider, 'Anglo-Saxon Women', pp. 247–9.

[36]   Æthelburg's flight to Kent was described by Bede, *HE*, II, 20 (pp. 204–5); for discussion of Eormenhild's career see the summaries of the texts of the Mildrith Legend given by Rollason, *The Mildrith Legend*, pp. 84–7 and Brooks, *The Early History*, p. 183.

[37]   *HE*, IV, 19 (pp. 392–3); see Stafford, *Queens*, p. 177.

[38]   Bede, *Vita sancti Cuthberti*, chs. 27–8 (ed. and trans. B. Colgrave, *Two Lives of Saint Cuthbert* [1940], pp. 142–307, at pp. 242–3 and 247–8).

[39]   Asser, Life of King Alfred, chs. 14–15 (ed. W. H. Stevenson, *Asser's Life of King Alfred* [1904], pp. 12–14; trans. S. Keynes and M. Lapidge, *Alfred the Great* [1983], pp. 71–2); see Keynes and Lapidge, *Alfred the Great*, p. 236, nn. 31–2. King Offa's widow, Cynethryth, inherited the minster at Cookham in Berkshire from her husband, a house over which the Mercian

Many other, non-royal women, also sought the cloister as widows, for example Æbbe, widow of the reeve Osfrith, whom St Wilfrid cured of paralysing illness during her husband's lifetime,[40] or Ceolburh, widow of Æthelmund, whose *obit* is recorded in the Anglo-Saxon Chronicle in 807.[41] The ninth-century will of the Kentish reeve Abba made different provisions for his wife, Heregyth, according to whether she remarried, went on a pilgrimage, or entered a minster.[42]

Less than strictly pious aspirations may have determined the entry of other groups of women to the religious life: Pauline Stafford has described nunneries as 'emphatically the favoured way of disposing of surplus daughters'.[43] Some of the women placed in minsters by their families may indeed have arrived reluctantly, forced into the cloister by relatives unwilling or unable to marry them in the world. The role of monastic houses in caring for the sick and disabled made them suitable places for the disposal of such deformed or sickly girls as had contrived to survive through infancy.[44] A well-endowed nunnery might accept a lower financial gift than a young man's family would require as dowry, and there was the added advantage that land alienated from a family's holdings in a minster's support would not pass to another kin group. Further, women devoted to God were, it might be presumed, extremely unlikely to become pregnant; not only would this substantially enhance their own life-expectancy, but it could bring benefits to their whole family by restricting the number of competing heirs in the next generation and may well have played a role in the dynastic policies of noble as well as royal families. Karl Leyser argued (in the immediate context of the rapid expansion of female monastic houses in tenth-century Saxony, but with direct comparison to England and Francia three centuries earlier) that the foundation of nunneries should be understood as providing at least in part a solution to the perennial noble anxiety about the fate of its daughters, transferring the burden of keeping such women safely outside the immediate kin group but within their own social

---

house and the archbishops of Canterbury had long disputed: BCS 291 (S 1258); Brooks, *The Early History*, pp. 103–4, 116, 131; Sims-Williams, *Religion*, p. 160.

[40]   *Vita sancti Wilfridi*, ch. 37 (ed. and trans. B. Colgrave, *The Life of Bishop Wilfrid by Eddius Stephanus* [1927], pp. 74–7).

[41]   ASC *s. a.* 805; Ceolburh was identified by John of Worcester as abbess of Berkeley: *Chronicon, s.a.* 807 (ed. and trans. R. R Darlington *et al.* (1995), II, 232–3); Bremmer, 'Widows', p. 80. See BCS 313 (S 1187), and the discussion of the history of the house at Berkeley in part II, *s.n.* Berkeley.

[42]   Harmer, *SEHD*, no. 2 (S 1482). These provisions are explored at greater length in chapter 5.

[43]   P. Stafford, 'Sons and mothers: Family politics in the early Middle Ages', in *Medieval Women*, ed. D. Baker (1978), pp. 79–100, at p. 97.

[44]   This issue was discussed by Boswell, *The Kindness*, pp. 240–1, who noted the disapproval of the practice even in the early Church, citing a letter of Jerome's complaining about parents who dedicated to virginity daughters who were deformed or defective in some way. See also J. Boswell, '*Expositio* and *oblatio*: the abandonment of children and the ancient and medieval family', *American Historical Review*, 89 (1984), 10–33, at p. 21.

milieu.[45] It should not be forgotten, however, that to group celibate women together thus in a physically isolated environment was an innovative social experiment marking a radical departure from the norms of Germanic custom, and the continued existence of such congregations must always have been precarious.[46] It is easy to see how demographic pressures could radically alter social attitudes towards nunneries: the maintenance of celibate women was a luxury affordable only in a society with an expanding (or at least static) population. A period of plague or prolonged and costly warfare might occasion the rethinking of marital (or rather reproductive) strategies.

The early Anglo-Saxon women's religious house was thus essentially an aristocratic institution; as we have seen, the inspiration as well as the economic means to found such places came from the royal courts and was followed by the rest of the nobility. In this sense all early Anglo-Saxon minsters must be considered to have been of the world, and not strictly withdrawn from it; consequently we need not be surprised at the prominence of so many Anglo-Saxon female congregations in the social and political landscape as well as within the Church.[47] The closeness of the link between royalty and nunneries, and especially double houses is particularly striking. For example, the Durham *Liber Vitae* listed the names of kings and abbots to be commemorated separately (and further divided the male heads of monastic houses according to their clerical rank), but placed queens and abbesses in the same category, almost as if the titles were synonymous.[48] Many of the earliest English female houses were occupied and governed by members of the royal families responsible for their foundation, abbesses frequently being succeeded by their sisters or daughters. The Kentish royal minsters of Lyminge and Folkestone have already been mentioned; Minster-in-Thanet and Minster-in-Sheppey were also royal foundations.[49] Similarly, the first minster at Ely had links with the East Anglian royal family.[50] Whitby was founded by Hild, who was related to the Deiran royal house and to whose care had been given Ælfflæd, the daughter of King Oswiu, who was devoted to God in

---

[45]   Leyser, *Rule and Conflict*, p. 64.

[46]   M. Clunies-Ross, 'Concubinage in Anglo-Saxon England', *Past and Present*, 108 (1985), 3–34, at pp. 32–3.

[47]   I have considered this matter at length elsewhere: 'The role of the minster in earlier Anglo-Saxon society', in *Monasteries and Society in Medieval England*, ed. B. Thompson (Stamford, 1999), pp. 35–58. The issue has also been addressed by P. Wormald, 'Bede, "Beowulf" and the conversion of the Anglo-Saxon aristocracy', in *Bede and Anglo-Saxon England*, ed. R. T. Farrell (1978), pp. 32–95, and J. Campbell, 'Elements in the background to the life of St Cuthbert and his early cult', in *St Cuthbert*, ed. G. Bonner *et al.* (1989), pp. 3–19.

[48]   *Liber Vitae ecclesiae Dunelmensis*, ed. J. Stevenson, *Liber Vitae ecclesiae Dunelmensis*, Surtees Society, 8 (1841), pp. 3–5; the implications of the equation of abbesses with queens in this text were noted by Dagmar Schneider, 'Anglo-Saxon women', p. 34.

[49]   Brooks, *The Early History*, p. 183.

[50]   Ely's first abbesses were the daughters of Anna, king of the East Angles: *HE*, IV, 19 (pp. 392–5).

infancy in fulfilment of her father's vow before the battle of Winwæd; the Whitby community (which Ælfflæd was later to govern) played an important role in the promotion of the cult of that royal family, particularly that of King Edwin.[51] Repton, similarly, had responsibility for the commemoration of Mercian kings, and St Peter's Gloucester had close links with the Hwiccean royal family;[52] a link between the early eighth-century minster at Wimborne (founded by Cuthburg, a sister of King Ine of Wessex) and the West Saxon royal house was maintained at least as far as the late ninth century.[53]

The keeping of the headship of a house within the same kin group was only one means by which a family's hold on a piece of ecclesiastical property might be maintained. Indeed that the founder's kin would tend to continue to see such a house as its own possession is clear, for example, from the expectations that Wihtred, king of Kent, had of the Kentish royal minsters, apparent both from his grant of ecclesiastical privileges and in his law code.[54] Whether successive generations of the same family would continue to share the original founder's view that dedication to religious purposes was the most appropriate use for the land could, of course, not be guaranteed. Patrick Wormald has commented on the paradox that charters (documents designed to free land from the claims of secular kindreds) came increasingly to relate to land in which the kindred retained a legitimate interest, something clearly visible from various charters preserved in Worcester's archive.[55] It was just this confusion over the blurring of the boundaries between sacred and secular against which Bede railed (in somewhat exaggerated fashion) in his letter to Bishop Ecgbert of York, complaining about thegns who set up false minsters and procured lands for their wives for constructing minsters allowing these laywomen to become mistresses of the

---

[51]   *HE*, III, 24, IV, 23 (pp. 290–3, 408–9); anon, *Liber beatae Gregorii papae*, chs. 18–19 (ed. and trans. B. Colgrave, *The Earliest Life of Gregory the Great* [1968], pp. 100–5).

[52]   M. Biddle and B. Kjølbye-Biddle, 'The Repton Stone', *ASE*, 14 (1985), 233–92, at pp. 233–6; Sims-Williams, *Religion*, pp. 122–5.

[53]   Anglo-Saxon Chronicle 718 and 900; see further part II, *s. n.* Wimborne. Pauline Stafford has commented on the possibility that royal women who found themselves not entirely willingly placed within the cloister may have been more than happy to use the legitimacy of their own blood to bolster the political ambitions of junior branches of their own family lines, citing the example of the Wimborne nun as a case in point: 'Sons and mothers', p. 97.

[54]   S. E. Kelly, *Charters of St Augustine's Abbey, Canterbury* (1995), no. 10 (S 20); Wihtred of Kent, laws, ch. 1.1 (ed. F. Liebermann, *Die Gesetze der Angelsachsen* [3 vols., Halle, 1903–16], I, 12); B. Yorke, '"Sisters under the skin?" Anglo-Saxon nuns and nunneries in southern England', in *Medieval Women in Southern England*, ed. K. Bate *et al.* (1989), pp. 95–117, at p. 99; Brooks, *The Early History*, pp. 192–3. Consider also the dispute between the Mercian kings and archbishops of Canterbury in the late eighth and early ninth centuries over the control of the Kentish religious houses: ibid., pp. 175–97.

[55]   P. Wormald, *How do we know so much about Anglo-Saxon Deerhurst?* Deerhurst Lecture 1991 (1993), at p. 5; P. Wormald *apud* J. Campbell, ed., *The Anglo-Saxons* (1982), pp. 87–8, and 123. Among the Worcester charters is a document recording the dispute between an abbess and her own mother over ownership of a minster at Withington in Gloucestershire; see further below, p. 57.

handmaids of Christ.[56] One of the questions in the mid-eighth-century *Dialogues* attributed to Archbishop Ecgbert raised the issue of the disputed inheritance of minsters, and another addressed problems occasioned by the lay headship of minsters and the means by which such heads might be brought under episcopal control.[57]

These instances are not unique to England in this period. Family policy may similarly have been a determining feature governing the creation (and dissolution) of nunneries in early medieval Ireland, many of which had only an ephemeral existence. Noting the wide discrepancy between the large number of pious women known from early medieval Ireland and the 'minute number' of women's houses that are attested there, Kathleen Hughes suggested that women's houses were designedly impermanent foundations, attributing this phenomenon to the fact that in Irish law a woman obtained only a life interest in any land that she inherited. The enclosures within which women religious lived often lay on their own family's land, their congregations being tolerated just for the duration of the founder's life, until the land reverted to the kin on her death.[58] Social and cultural attitudes to nuns in early medieval Ireland have been studied by Lisa Bitel, who has attributed the invisibility of early nuns and the disappearance of women's communities other than Kildare from the annals from the later eighth and ninth centuries to a variety of factors, notably ecclesiastical suspicion of female spirituality and the distrust of secular society of the potential power offered to women by communal celibacy. Women's houses, she has argued, seem not to have occupied the same place in the Irish kin-dominated economic system as male ones, where abbacies passed from father to son; nor was a nunnery easily secularised. A house whose members ceased to be celibate, or got married, was no longer a nunnery.[59]

In Francia, too, women's religious houses could only function within the constraints imposed by the social group from which most of their founders came and the changing strategies of individual families as much as external social, economic or military pressures would influence the long-term fate of a nunnery.

---

[56]   Bede, *Epistola ad Ecgberhtum*, §12 (ed. C. Plummer, *Venerabilis Baedae Opera* [1896], I, 405–23, at pp. 415–16). The highly rhetorical nature of this letter has long been recognised, but Patrick Sims-Williams has shown more significantly that Bede's letter lies in a long tradition of monastic polemic, comparing the specific complaints Bede made against smaller, informal monastic houses with similar ones articulated by Cassian and Fructuosus: *Religion*, pp. 126–30.

[57]   Ecgberht, Dialogue, questions 11 and 7 (ed. Haddan and Stubbs, *Councils*, III, 403–13, at pp. 408 and 406). The question posed here about the inheritance of minsters by heirs of both genders was quoted by C. S. Taylor in his discussion of the status of Berkeley minster in the early ninth century to which it is directly relevant: 'Berkeley minster', *Transactions of the Bristol and Gloucestershire Archaeological Society*, 19 (1894–5), 70–84, at pp. 73–5 and part II, *s.n.* Berkeley.

[58]   K. Hughes, *Early Christian Ireland. Introduction to the Sources* (1972), pp. 234–5.

[59]   Bitel, 'Women's monastic enclosures', p. 29.

The case of the nunnery established for the ninth-century Aquitanian nun, Immena, by her father discussed by Jane Martindale illustrates the broad point to particular effect. A nunnery was created at Sarrazac by Count Rudolf for his daughter Immena; he intended to be buried there and charged to Immena the responsibility for praying for his soul and preserving the memory of the family. After the Count's death, however, the nunnery was dissolved by Immena's brother Rudolf, archbishop of Bourges, and its lands used to endow a new male congregation at Beaulieu. The *commemoratio* of the family was to be maintained, but it could apparently more effectively be continued by the male monks of Beaulieu than by a convent of women unable to celebrate memorial masses.[60] A study made by Jean Verdon of the sources for women's monasteries in early medieval France has pointed to two periods — the seventh and eleventh centuries — for which the sources are relatively plentiful and when many new nunneries founded, separated by three centuries when fewer new institutions were established (or were recorded in the surviving literature). In the north Verdon identified a total of 126 nunneries, of which thirty-eight were seventh-century foundations and fifty dated from the eleventh century; of the total, six nunneries were created at places where there had earlier been a male congregation, and twenty-one pre-tenth-century foundations were replaced by male religious during the tenth and eleventh centuries. The overall numbers of female houses in southern France were much smaller and there Verdon counted only forty-six establishments, of which eight were founded in the seventh century, nine in the ninth and fifteen in the eleventh century; only one previously female house was reported to have been subsequently taken over by men. However, since Verdon made few attempts to assess the evidential quality or reliability of the evidence he employed, it is impossible to determine from his summaries of foundation-patterns how much institutional continuity there was across the First Viking Age.[61] A more recent study of religious women in the Midi (loosely interpreted as most of the region south of the Loire and west of the Rhône) has argued rather that in this area in the early medieval centuries 'feminine monasticism was virtually non-existent', although women did find other, non-cloistered outlets for the expression of their devotion.[62] Scholars are not wholly agreed as to precisely when in the central

---

[60]   J. Martindale, 'The nun Immena and the foundation of the abbey of Beaulieu: a woman's prospects in the Carolingian Church', in *Women in the Church*, ed. W. J. Sheils and D. Wood (1990), 27–42, at pp. 36–40. See also J. L. Nelson, 'Kommentar', in *Frauen in Spätantike und Frühmittelalter*, ed. W. Affeldt (Sigmarinen, 1990), pp. 325–32, at p. 329.

[61]   Jean Verdon published his findings for northern and southern France separately: 'Recherches sur les monastères féminins dans la France du Sud aux ix–xi siècles', *Annales du Midi*, 88 (1976), 118–38 and 'Recherches sur les monastères féminins dans la France du Nord aux ixe–xie siècles', *Revue Mabillon*, 59 (1976), 49–96.

[62]   E. Magnou-Nortier, 'Formes féminines de vie consacrée dans les pays du Midi jusqu'au début du XII siécle', in *La femme dans la vie religieuse du Languedoc (XIIIe–XIVe s.)*, Cahiers de Fanjeaux, 23 (1988), 193–216, at pp. 193–5. On religious women in Merovingian Gaul see now Muschiol, *Famula Dei*, ch. 2 ('Fromme Frauen in Gallien').

middle ages the expansion of women's monastic houses began in France, but the later ninth and tenth centuries are generally agreed to represent the nadir of communal female religious expression in that country.[63]

If women's religious houses were to succeed, to function for more than one generation providing continuously and effectively for the needs of their founders in this world and the next, they needed to obtain economic security through the acquisition of permanent landed endowments. While secular founding families could still lay claim to their estates, nunneries were always vulnerable (and their commemorative functions threatened) since dynastic strategies might change. But there was no less a need for nunneries to obtain protection from the physical dangers of the lay world beyond the kin-group. The founders of many early Anglo-Saxon female religious houses may have sought to isolate their inhabitants from their lay neighbours either by local topography in the case of a site like the isle of Ely and coastal locations such as Whitby, Wareham, or Sheppey, or by a man-made barrier.[64] Rudolf's Life of Leoba described the high walls that were supposedly built round Wimborne, and Bede wrote of the gate and door shutting off the separate parts of Æthelhild's minster near Partney, and implied that there was an enclosure surrounding Barking.[65] Largely, minsters for women seem originally to have been placed away from royal courts, bishop's sees and such urban centres as there were in the early period, although their economic as much as their spiritual activities were such that many must inevitably have accumulated population around them, as male minsters did.[66] Geographical segregation did not always bring the desired physical safety: Bede's Life of

---

[63] Mary Skinner has attempted to quantify the number of early houses in France supporting women that appear to have failed to survive into the eleventh century, ascribing a variety of reasons to their failure: 'Benedictine life for women in central France, 850–1100: a feminist revival', in *Medieval Religious Women I: Distant Echoes*, ed. J. A. Nichols and L. T. Shank (Kalamazoo, Michigan, 1984), pp. 87–113, at pp. 90–1. Bruce Venarde (*Women's Monasticism and Medieval Society: Nunneries in France and England, 890–1215* [Ithaca, New York and London, 1997], pp. 28–51) has catalogued and mapped the number of French nunneries active in the tenth and eleventh centuries, and argued for substantial expansion from about the year 1080.

[64] None of these places were, however, inaccessible; each of those named here lay on a major waterway.

[65] For Wimborne see Rudolf, *Vita Leobae*, ch. 2 (ed. Waitz, p. 123); Æthelhild's nunnery was described by Bede, *HE*, III, 11 (pp. 246–9), and Barking *HE*, IV, 10 (pp. 364–5). Secular dwellings were also normally formally separated from their surroundings by a physical barrier of some kind, but that the monastic cloister had different connotations from the noble enclosure is clear from the injunction made at the 747 council of *Clofesho*, that seculars were not to be permitted to wander freely within monastic enclosures, *intra claustra monasterii*: Council of *Clofesho* 747, ch. 20 (ed. Haddan and Stubbs, *Councils*, III, 369); quoted by Schneider, 'Anglo-Saxon women', p. 40, n. 23.

[66] Campbell, *Essays*, p. 141 (citing the example of Whitby, which 'with its numerous buildings, its crafts and its maritime contacts must have been considerably more like a town than were most places'). This is discussed further by me in 'The role of the minster'.

Cuthbert provides a story about a group of nuns who had been forced to flee from their own minster through fear of a Pictish army, and had to be given another place of refuge by the saint.[67] Certainly female religious houses appear to have been particularly vulnerable to external attack, notably to the Danish raids of the First Viking Age, but isolated male houses were attacked with equal frequency and other factors are likely to have been relevant here as well as the gender of the minsters' occupants. This does, however, raise the issue of the joint occupation of a number of early Anglo-Saxon religious houses by men and women, a practice which, it has been suggested, may have arisen in part to provide physical protection for nuns.[68]

Double minsters[69]

The double house — the community of male and female religious living in varying degrees of segregation under the overall authority of an abbess — is an institution peculiar to early medieval Francia and England (and translated from England into the newly converted German lands);[70] it differs both from the earlier mixed houses of the Eastern Church and from later medieval double houses such as those founded by Gilbert of Sempringham which were always governed by men.[71] Not enough is known about the internal organisation of religious houses for either gender in early Anglo-Saxon England for it to be possible to say with certainty what proportion of minsters occupied by women during the pre-Viking Age were double, rather than all-female establishments.[72] A pertinent factor here is that, just as there is no gender-specific term in Latin or Old English equivalent to the modern 'nunnery' by which to denote a monastic community occupied solely by

---

[67] Bede, *Vita sancti Cuthberti*, ch. 30 (pp. 254–5). Compare also the example of Vezelay given by Janet Nelson ('Kommentar', p. 329), where within a generation of the convent's foundation the nuns were replaced by monks 'on account of the frequent assaults of the secular world'.

[68] J. Nicholson, '*Feminae gloriosae*: Women in the age of Bede', in *Medieval Women*, ed. D. Baker (1978), pp. 15–29, at p. 20. For the fate of minsters during the First Viking Age see further below, chapter 3.

[69] Several commentators have recently drawn attention to the fact that the term 'double house' is a modern anachronism; for example S. Elkins, *Holy Women of Twelfth-Century England* (Chapel Hill, NC, 1988), pp. xvii–xviii; B. Golding, *Gilbert of Sempringham and the Gilbertine Order c. 1130–1300* (1995) pp. 74–5. It has, however, conventionally been the label used by historians to denote early English religious communities occupied by men and women together and will be retained in this discussion.

[70] S. Hilpisch, *Die Doppelklöster: Entstehung und Organisation* (Münster, 1928), pp. 44–5; for the development of double houses in early medieval Spain see ibid., pp. 52–5 and P. Hunter Blair, *Northumbria in the Days of Bede* (1976), pp. 135–6.

[71] Schneider, 'Anglo-Saxon women', pp. 31–2. Golding, *Gilbert*, ch. 2 ('The making of the Rule').

[72] Rigold, 'The "double minsters"', p. 27; Sims-Williams, *Religion*, p. 120.

women, nor does the language of the sources for the pre-Viking-Age Church distinguish houses with mixed congregations from single-sex establishments. A monastic house was called a *monasterium* (Old English *minster*) regardless of the number, sex or occupation of its occupants;[73] the most explicit description of a double house is found in Bede's Ecclesiastical History where on one occasion he referred to the house at Whitby as 'famulorum famularumque Dei monasterium'.[74] The sole exception to this general rule noted before the tenth-century monastic revolution is the case of the women's convent at Winchester, founded by King Alfred's widow, Ealhswith, probably with the assistance of Edward the Elder; that congregation was sometimes described in Old English charter-texts as the 'nuns' minster' in order to distinguish it from the Old and New Minsters in the same city, and is usually called the Nunnaminster by modern historians as a result.[75]

The purpose served by the men within a double community has been much debated. That they were present largely to defend the weaker sex has already been suggested, and the need for the physical protection of congregations of women must have been particularly pressing when so many were established at a distance from other population centres.[76] The presence of men in women's houses has also been attributed to the need for those capable of undertaking heavy manual labour.[77] Alternatively, some of the men in the congregation may have been priests, whose role was to say mass, hear confession and offer spiritual direction to the nuns (and celebrate commemorative masses for their benefactors) as well as to provide for the sacramental needs of the lay population.[78] Simple pragmatism could equally have lain behind the establishment of some mixed establishments, the pooling of resources into one economically viable estate producing a sufficient surplus to support a congregation of women and men dedicated

---

[73]   Foot, 'Anglo-Saxon minsters'. The modern word nunnery is probably adapted from the Anglo-French *nonnerie*, derived from the word for a nun, *nonne*; the *Oxford English Dictionary* (2nd edn) cites no use of the word in English earlier than 1275. Instead, pre-Conquest writers qualified *monasteria* by describing them as being 'of nuns' or 'of virgins'. There is one instance in the Old English Bede, where the original Latin *monasterium uirginum* has been rendered as *nunmynster* (*HE*, V, 3; *The Old English Version of Bede's Ecclesiastical History of the English People*, V, 3, ed. & trans. T. Miller, 2 vols., [1890], II, 390).

[74]   *HE*, IV, 26 (pp. 428–9); cited by Hilpisch, *Die Doppelklöster*, p. 47.

[75]   Robertson, *ASCharters*, no. 29 (S 1419): *on nunan ministre*; Robertson, *ASCharters*, no. 53 (S 1376): *on nunnan mynstre*; Robertson, *ASCharters*, no. 49 (S 1449) and Whitelock, *ASWills*, no. 20 (S 1503): *into nunnan mynstre*; Harmer, *SEHD*, no. 21 (S 1515): *to Nunnanmynstre*.

[76]   J. T. Schulenburg, 'Strict active enclosure and its effects on the female monastic experience (500–1100)', in *Medieval Religious Women I: Distant Echoes*, ed. J. A. Nichols and L. T. Shank (Kalamazoo, Michigan, 1984), pp. 51–86, at p. 76, drawing a parallel between the situation of double houses in England, France, Belgium and Germany.

[77]   Schneider, 'Anglo-Saxon women', p. 15; Nicholson, *'Feminae gloriosae'*, pp. 19–20.

[78]   Godfrey, 'The place of the double monastery', pp. 346–7; E. de Moreau, 'Les "monastères doubles": leur histoire surtout en Belgique', *Nouvelle Revue Théologique*, 66 (1939), 787–92, at p. 790.

to the service of God. That there were men able to leave the confines of the cloister in furtherance of the minster's economic interests has been seen by Schulenburg as further helping to preserve the autonomy of nuns' communities without imperilling the women's own enclosure.[79]

The most comprehensive list compiled to date of double houses mentioned in written sources is that made by Dagmar Schneider, who has identified with confidence eighteen such houses and more tentatively four others; she has found a further twenty female houses, known primarily from charters, where the presence (or absence) of religious men cannot be determined, nor can anything be said about the various houses (some surely identifiable with those named in other sources) of which we know no more than the names of the abbesses.[80] The nature of the evidence is also such that a substantial proportion of the minsters known to have had female occupants between 630 and 871 is attested only by chance reference in unique sources; equally some such houses, even if witnessed in more than one text, are only reported to have been active during a relatively confined chronological period. What can frequently not be determined is for how many generations beyond the point at which we have a glimpse of their activities, these places continued to support congregations either of women, or of men and women together.[81] Further, it is impossible to say with confidence whether or not there were any exclusively female religious houses in England in the pre-Viking Age.

---

[79]   Schulenburg, 'Strict active enclosure', p. 76.

[80]   Schneider, 'Anglo-Saxon women', pp. 19–20. Longer lists of double houses and possible double houses have been compiled by Roberta Gilchrist (*Gender and Material Culture. The Archaeology of Religious Women* [1994], at pp. 28–9); although she has usefully collected places not considered by Schneider where archaeological evidence might point to the presence of female religious, her use of documentary evidence is rather problematical and cannot be relied upon in the same way as can Schneider's meticulous research. To take just two examples, the supposition that there was an early nunnery, 'Helenstow', at Abingdon was first advanced by Marc Meyer and is based on a reading of Abingdon's post-Conquest cartulary-chronicle which close scrutiny cannot sustain (M. A. Meyer, 'Patronage of West Saxon royal nunneries in late Anglo-Saxon England', *Revue bénédictine*, 91 [1981], 332–58, at pp. 345–6). A more cautious reading of the written evidence has been advanced by John Blair, who has sought rather to defend the existence of such an early nunnery on archaeological grounds, namely the representation in Abingdon's thirteenth-century chronicle of an image of a cruciform disc-headed pin, resembling extant eighth-century examples excavated at Whitby and Flixborough: *Anglo-Saxon Oxfordshire* (1994), pp. 64–5. See further part II, *s.n.* Abingdon. More straightforwardly, I find it impossible to read any allusion to a double house at Malmesbury in Bede, *HE*, V, 18 (pp. 512–17). Other interpretations as well as that of monastic occupancy have also been advanced for some of the sites on whose archaeological evidence Gilchrist has depended, notably Brandon and Flixborough, where the simple use of cruciform-headed pins need not necessarily be taken as indicative of monastic use of a site. I am grateful to Dr Chris Loveluck (director of the Flixborough project) for advice on this matter.

[81]   Jane Schulenburg has also commented on the ephemeral aspect of so many women's monasteries, attributing this to a number of causes including the economic mismanagement of young inexperienced abbesses or the fraud of their lay representatives: 'Strict active enclosure', p. 71.

No house is specifically stated to have been a 'man-free zone', indeed the notion of strict gender segregation and male exclusion is never articulated in early English texts. Archbishop Theodore expressed some dismay at the English custom of mixed congregations but did not attempt to prohibit religious men and women from living together in mixed communities.[82] The 747 council of *Clofesho* tried to control behaviour within women's minsters, but sought only to exclude secular males from all monastic enclosures, not least because of the gossip to which their presence might lead.[83] The basis on which Schneider has differentiated between certainly double and other female houses is by means of an argument from silence: that no men are mentioned in any of the sources pertaining to these places. Since it is clear that there was no one right rule by which monastic houses were organised in the period before the monastic revolution of King Edgar's reign, it may be inappropriate to apply the criteria of exclusion and enclosure of the later age to the earlier period.[84]

Whatever the imperatives dictating a community's composition at one time, these did not necessarily remain constant. Bede's prose Life of St Cuthbert provides an example of a community at Tynemouth where there had during the saint's childhood been a noble company of men, although this was later, 'changed like all else by time', a congregation 'of virgins who serve Christ'.[85] There may have been instances, Dagmar Schneider has suggested, in which men governed communities with some female members; three minsters at Stonegrave, Coxwold and *Donaemuthe* were, for example, granted by their abbess to an abbot in the mid-eighth century.[86] The terms on which a minster was founded did not necessarily predetermine who was later to occupy the house. In the mid-eighth century Æthelberht, king of the South Saxons, granted 18 hides at Wittering in Sussex to a certain Diosza for the construction of a minster (*ad construendum monasterium*); after the list of witnesses to this grant there followed a statement by Diosza transferring responsibility for the new minster to his sister and

---

82   Theodore, Penitential, II, vi, 8, quoted at the head of this chapter. The Frankish 506 council of Agde had attempted to direct that monasteries for women should be set up far away from male houses lest the snares of the devil lead to the spreading of malicious rumours: Council of Agde, 506, ch. 28 (ed. C. Munier, *Concila Galliae A.314–A.506*, CCSL, 148 [Turnhout, 1963], p. 205): 'Monasteria puellarum longius a monasteriis monachorum, aut propter insidias diaboli aut propter oblocutiones hominum collocentur'. Quoted by de Moreau, 'Les "monastères doubles"', p. 791.

83   Council of *Clofesho*, 747, ch. 20 (ed. Haddan and Stubbs, *Councils*, III, 369).

84   See my 'Anglo-Saxon minsters'. I am grateful to Steve Bassett for helping to clarify my thinking on the question of all-female communities.

85   Bede, *Vita sancti Cuthberti*, ch. 3 (pp. 160–3). Cuthbert himself visited the female community and was entertained by the abbess Verca: ibid., ch. 35 (pp. 264–5).

86   Letter of Pope Paul I to Archbishop Ecgberht of York and Eadbert, king of Northumbria, 757x758 (ed. Haddan and Stubbs, *Councils*, III, 394–5; trans. Whitelock, *EHD*, no. 184). Schneider, 'Anglo-Saxon women', p. 24. Compare the situation of Bath, originally a minster for holy virgins, it was occupied only by men in the mid-eighth century; see below, n. 95.

determining that the land (and thus presumably its minster) was to pass to his sister on his death for her to hold as she wished, to which arrangement both King Æthelberht and Sigeferth, bishop of Selsey, were said to have agreed.[87] The gender of this minster's inhabitants was clearly a secondary issue behind the more pressing matter of the securing of the property, with its ecclesiastical privileges, in the possession of a single family. Among other congregations whose composition can be shown to have altered is Berkeley in Gloucestershire; in the mid-eighth and later ninth centuries there were men living at Berkeley, but the house may have had an abbess early in the ninth century, and there was certainly a female congregation there in the eleventh century.[88] The constitution of the minster at Winchcombe in Gloucestershire, also apparently a double house at the end of the ninth century, may similarly have fluctuated both before and after the First Viking Age.[89] Early Anglo-Saxon minsters thus seemingly had fluid populations whose composition fluctuated according to the particular desires and needs of the individual families with which they were most closely associated, local pastoral requirements, and the condition of any neighbouring religious institutions. This may afford an insight into contemporary attitudes of monastic organisation less precise and more accommodating of variety than those possible once the Church hierarchy had imposed a single system of communal religious organisation, deviance from which was considered an abuse.

The extent to which the men were segregated from the women in double houses appears to have varied considerably; the ninth-century Life of Leoba asserted that the two sexes at Wimborne were entirely separated behind high walls, but this as much else in that Life reveals more about Carolingian ideals of monastic organisation than about the true nature of a house in eighth-century Wessex.[90] There are, however, other reports of the separation of male and female dwellings in early English houses, for example at Æthelhild's minster near Partney there was a door shutting off the women's part of the house, which lay at some distance both from the men's quarters and the guest-house.[91] At Barking, men and women had separate sleeping quarters, but this does not necessarily indicate that men were excluded from the women's part of the minster and both groups may

---

[87]   *Charters of Selsey*, ed. S. E. Kelly (1998), no. 7 (S 46; A.D. 733x754); discussed by Kelly ibid., pp. 38–40. There Susan Kelly has drawn attention to a similar arrangement made for a minster at Bradfield in Berkshire, where a nobleman called Hæha founded a minster with his sister Ceolswith (or Cille) and made over his inherited property to his sister; Ceolswith became abbess of the double community, with her brother serving as a monk under her authority, although he later reclaimed his lands and had his monastic vows dissolved: BCS 29 (S 1179) and see also BCS 101 (S 241). The history of Bradfield will be explored fully in Susan Kelly's forthcoming edition of the Abingdon charters for the British Academy.

[88]   See part II, *s.n.* Berkeley.

[89]   For the evidence that there was a double community at Winchcombe in 897 see BCS 575 (S 1442); discussed further below in part II, *s.n.* Winchcombe.

[90]   Rudolf, *Vita Leobae*, ch. 2 (ed. Waitz, p. 123); see Schneider, 'Anglo-Saxon women', pp. 42–3, and n. 38; Hollis, *Anglo-Saxon Women*, pp. 271–82.

[91]   *HE*, III, 11 (pp. 248–9).

indeed have shared use of the church, as can be seen to have happened elsewhere.[92] There is no evidence that the sexes were separated at Whitby, nor most famously, at Coldingham, where the visiting Irishman Adomnan was so shocked to find the inmates 'sunk in slothful slumber'.[93] Boundaries may also have been blurred in circumstances where one founder created two supposedly autonomous houses one for women and the other for men. Nor can it necessarily be presumed that the female house of such a pair would have been a single-sex foundation. Barking, founded by Eorcenwold, bishop of London, for his sister Æthelburh seems always to have been a double house, although set up at the same time as a house for men at Chertsey;[94] similarly, as Patrick Sims-Williams has shown, although foundation-charter for Bath issued by Osric, sub-king of the Hwicce, referred to the king's intention to establish monasteries of men and of virgins serving God ('sparsim uirorum sparsimque uirginum deo famulantium'), the *monasterium sanctarum uirginum* at Bath may always have housed some men.[95] Aristocratic endowments caused the Church some problems in the early centuries; Ecgbert's Dialogues raised the difficulty occasioned by the inheritance of a minster by a man and a woman jointly and although the terms of the reply given suggest that this was thought to be an abuse, it nevertheless suggests that such instances arose.[96]

The lack of rigid isolation of the religious women from men in a number of double houses may have been one of the factors lying behind Theodore's stated disapproval — or at least only grudging acceptance — of the institution.[97] His reservations were not, seemingly, shared by native English churchmen and there is every reason to see the mixed congregation as the accepted norm. Few women in this early period seem to have had to resort to the length of seeking the physical and economic shelter of an otherwise all-male monastic house; men seem more frequently rather to have attached themselves to congregations of women. The inclusion of the names of five women among the monks listed in the *Liber Vitae* of Durham was noted by Dagmar Schneider, who wondered tentatively if these might have been female recluses associated with the male house. Since she has also observed that the same five names are found in the same sequence in the list

---

[92]   Ibid., IV, 7 (pp. 356–7). Aldhelm's poem on a church of St Mary built by Bugga (*Carmen ecclesiasticum* III, lines 50–58, ed. Ehwald, *Aldhelmi Opera*, pp. 16–17, trans. M. Lapidge and J. Rosier, *Aldhelm. The Poetic Works* [1985], p. 49), presents a picture of the joint psalmody of the *fratres* and of the *turba sororem* and readings from Holy Scripture by *lector lectrixue* at this double minster; quoted by Hilpisch, *Die Doppelklöster*, p. 48.

[93]   *HE*, IV, 25 (pp. 424–7).

[94]   Ibid., IV, 6 (pp. 354–7).

[95]   BCS 43 (S 51); Sims-Williams, *Religion*, pp. 120–1. The minster had become an all male establishment by 758: BCS 327 (S 265).

[96]   Ecgberht, Dialogue, ch. 11 (ed. Haddan and Stubbs, *Councils*, III, 408; transl. Taylor, 'Berkeley', pp. 73–4); see Schneider, 'Anglo-Saxon women', pp. 24–5; Sims-Williams, *Religion*, p. 118, n. 18.

[97]   Theodore, Penitential, II, vi, 8 (ed. Finsterwalder, *Die Canones*, p. 320).

of queens and abbesses, it is in fact more likely, as she herself suggested, that their inclusion with the monks is an error.[98] A forged Crowland charter purporting to date to before 833 states that a certain Æthelthryth lived as a recluse at Crowland in the time of Abbot Siward, but this story cannot inspire confidence.[99] Otherwise the first English examples of religious women living beside congregations of men date from the tenth century; these are, as Patricia Halpin's work has shown, more numerous in the last century before the Conquest than has widely been recognised.[100]

The ready availability of outlets for women to practise the religious life in each of the early Anglo-Saxon kingdoms, together with the fluidity of available organisational arrangements, may at least to some extent explain the absence of specific references in the sources to religious women who failed to conform to contemporary monastic standards: there was before the tenth century no one 'right rule' by which to live.[101] This is not to say that there were not agreed standards of religious behaviour, nor was there any apparent reluctance among eighth-century churchmen to criticise religious women who fell short of these ideals, particularly in respect of their obligation to maintain their vows of chastity; Bede criticised the inhabitants of Coldingham for their irregular behaviour, and Boniface warned in his letter to Æthelbald of Mercia, 746/7 of the prostitution and adultery of nuns (*meretrices monasteriales* and *adulterium nonnarum*).[102] The wearing of

---

[98] London, British Library, Cotton MS Domitian vii, fo 40r, col 1, lines 17–21; compare fo 14r, col 2, lines 1–5; a facsimile-edition of the manuscript was prepared by A. Hamilton Thompson: *Liber Vitae Ecclesiae Dunelmensis: a Collotype Facsimile of the Original Manuscript with Introductory Essays and Notes*, Surtees Society 136 (London, 1923); the text had previously been printed by Stevenson, *Liber Vitae ecclesiae Dunelmensis*, pp. 41 and 4. These entries have been discussed by Schneider, 'Anglo-Saxon women', p. 25.

[99] BCS 409 (S 189); Schneider, 'Anglo-Saxon women', p. 25, n. 86.

[100] The places where veiled women were found living beside male monastic or cathedral congregations are discussed as a group below (chapter 6, §e) enlarging the number of examples gathered by Halpin, 'Women', p. 104. Individual instances are explored in detail in the second part of this study, *s.n.* Abbotsbury, Abingdon, Bedwyn, Bury St Edmunds, Durham, Ely, Evesham, Glastonbury, Hereford, St Alban's, St Paul's, Westminster, Worcester. It would seem that Dagmar Schneider was mistaken when she argued that the only genuine example from Anglo-Saxon England of a woman attached to a male house to be the Æthelflæd who associated herself with Glastonbury in the time of St Dunstan: 'Anglo-Saxon women', p. 25; Æthelflæd's case is explored further in part II, *s.n.* Glastonbury.

[101] The phrase is Æthelwold's from his 'Account of King Edgar's establishment of monasteries' (ed. and trans. Whitelock *et al.*, *Councils and Synods*, I, 142–54, no. 33, at pp. 148–9): 'there were only a few monks in a few places in so large a kingdom who lived by the right rule (*þe be rihtum regule lifdon)*'.

[102] *HE*, IV, 25 (pp. 424–7); Boniface, *Epistola* 73 (ed. M. Tangl, *Die Briefe des Heiligen Bonifatius und Lullus*, MGH, Epistolae selectae I [Berlin, 1916], 151–2). Similar anxiety about sexual relations with nuns is reflected in the prohibition on *connubia* with *ancillae Dei* made at the legatine council of 786, ch. 15 (ed. Dümmler, p. 25, no. 3). The taking of a *nunne* out of a mynster was also forbidden in King Alfred's law-code, ch. 8 (ed. Liebermann, *Die Gesetze*, I, 54), perhaps influenced by the text of the 786 synod: Keynes and Lapidge, *Alfred the Great*, p. 307, n. 15.

inappropriately luxurious dress also occasioned unfavourable comment. In his prose treatise on virginity Aldelm discussed the 'shameless impudence of vanity and the sleek insolence of stupidity' which could be discerned among those living 'cloistered under the discipline of the minster'; women were criticised for allowing 'dark-grey veils for the head to give way to bright and coloured head-dresses, which are sewn with interlacings of ribbons and hang down as far as the ankles'.[103] Further, deviance from an accepted standard lay especially in the appropriation of supposedly monastic lands by those who were nominally still seculars; the sources may in fact here conceal more widespread violation of the highest standards set by the normative literature. This raises the issue as to whether religious vocations could only be expressed via the cloister, or whether religious women were also to be found living in or at the margins of the world during the pre-Viking Age.

Beyond the cloister

That women could, and did, devote themselves to the religious life without leaving their own homes (and — more significantly — without the lands by which they were supported being permanently removed from the control of their kindred) was not apparently considered to be an abuse during the early Anglo-Saxon period. The flexible contemporary conception of religious devotion encompassed wide variations of expression from the extremes of the ascetic anchorite to the understated piety of a group of religiously-minded nobles. Distinguishing a small congregation gathered round an aristocratic *deo devota* from an all-female or double minster established by means of charter on land intended permanently for religious use is far from easy, largely because of the nature of the sources on which we are dependent. Much of our information derives from normative literature, which was designed to define and enforce ideals to which few, if any, actual communities conformed absolutely. Most historical and hagiographical writing about religious women originated within monastic communities (frequently those anxious to promote the sanctity of their former members) and so tends inevitably to focus on the communal expressions of devotion, and the adherence of their subjects to existing models of saintly behaviour. Charter-evidence for female land-ownership before the tenth century is not plentiful (and, as was discussed earlier, is restricted to southern England) and, perhaps more significantly for our purposes, no women's wills survive from any period earlier than the tenth century.[104]

---

[103] Aldhelm, prose *De virginitate*, §lviii (ed. Ehwald, *Aldhelmi Opera*, pp. 317–18, trans. Lapidge and Herren, *Aldhelm*, pp. 127–8).

[104] The significance of widows' testamentary arrangements and the possibility that they may constitute written record of abnormal bequests has recently been explored by Julia Crick:

Some of the women recorded as direct recipients or indirect beneficiaries of charters alienating land for religious purposes may never actually have intended to take full vows of monastic profession and renounce all their personal property, let alone the material comforts of their aristocratic lifestyle. Possession of land granted by charter offered a number of advantages to the title-holder, as was recognised all too often by Bede's contemporaries.[105] Consider for example the dispute between a religious woman, Hrothwaru, who had been bequeathed a minster at Withington by her grandmother Dunne (described both as *sanctimonialis* and *famula Dei*), and Hrothwaru's mother, a married woman, who tried to maintain that the charters proving her daughter's ownership had been stolen rather than give up her hold on the minster.[106] Yet such women need not have been fraudulent hypocrites without reverent intentions. Alcuin wrote late in the eighth century to a *deo deuota femina* called Hundrud who, although possibly a professed nun,[107] was patently living not inside a minster but at the royal court: 'Let your thoughts be in soberness of life before God, your conversation governed by truth and your work ennobled by chastity, that by your example your juniors may be trained, your elders pleased and all edified, that in the king's palace (*in palatio regis*[108]) the devotion of the religious life may be observed in your conduct'. Alcuin further charged Hundrud (his *dulcissima soror*) with greetings for others at the court, particularly Offa's queen and her son, Ecgfrith.[109] It is unwise to make too much of this sole example, yet one might speculate as to whether Hundrud was a widow who had assumed the dress distinctive to her state and vowed to remain continent while continuing to live in the world. Merovingian Frankish Church councils permitted both virgins and widows to take vows of chastity and live pious lives in their own homes so long as nothing in their

---

'Men, women and widows: widowhood in pre-Conquest England', in *Widowhood in Medieval and Early Modern Europe*, ed. S. Cavallo and L. Warner (1999), pp. 24–36. I am grateful to Dr Crick not only for allowing me to see this paper before its publication but for a number of fruitful conversations about widows in Anglo-Saxon society.

[105]   See the comments made above about the complaints in Bede's letter to Ecgberht over lay ownership of ecclesiastical land.

[106]   BCS 156 (S 1429) and see also BCS 217 (S 1255). Schneider has argued ('Klosterleben', p. 57, n. 54), that Hrothwaru's mother was a nun, identifying her with the *sanctimonialis*, Bugce, who was the beneficiary of the original grant with her mother, Dunne, but Sims-Williams (*Religion*, p. 132) has discounted this possibility.

[107]   Dümmler took Alcuin's recommendation *ut ... regularis uitae deuotio in tua uideatur conuersatione* to be an indication that 'ergo Hundruda monacha fuit': *Epistolae*, II, 105, n. 4 (no. 62). I am not convinced that the phrase has to be thus understood: the religious life could, as I here suggest, be pursued equally outside the confines of the cloister as within.

[108]   Namely at the court of Offa of Mercia (757–796).

[109]   Alcuin, *Epistola* 62 (ed. Dümmler, pp. 105–6, transl. S. Allott, *Alcuin of York c. A.D. 732 to 804* [1974], p. 49). The letter is dateable no more closely than to between 789 and 796 (the death of both Offa and Ecgfrith). There appears to have been no direct association between Hundrud and the minster of *Inmercum* mentioned — in somewhat distant terms — towards the end of this letter.

behaviour compromised their continent state.[110] The prevalence in Frankish areas of the practice of widows taking vows and remaining within their own homes is suggested by the forcible terms in which it was condemned in ninth-century Church councils by bishops anxious to control such women and force them inside the cloister.[111]

In pre-Viking-Age England such *deo deuotae* are not easily distinguished from the inhabitants of more formally organised minsters for women, and would frequently have failed to find mention in the written record if their adoption of a new lifestyle had involved no formal transfer of landed wealth and hence produced no written record.[112] The brothers, sons, and nephews of unmarried women and widows may have countenanced the loss of income from a small part of a larger family estate by paying lip-service to a vocation with which they had little sympathy, knowing that the land could be re-appropriated by them or their male heirs on the death of the devout incumbent.[113] But the reservation of such land to religious purposes was always dependent on the *deo sacrata* avoiding the overt opposition of the rest of her kin group. There cannot have been many women, even the most affluent widows, who could afford to indulge in outward and economically independent displays of religious zeal in the face of the concerted disapproval of the rest of their kin; such a woman could of course join an already established monastic house, but only at the cost of accepting restrictions on her individual autonomy and personal wealth. The significance of the role played by widows within the wider argument I shall be elaborating about the nature of women's expression of religious devotion in England after the First Viking Age

---

[110] For a general discussion of this legislation see O. Pontal, *Histoire des conciles mérovingiens* (Paris, 1989), pp. 129–30 and 273–4 and Muschiol, *Famula Dei*, pp. 43–51. Reference was made to veiled women living in their own homes in legislation mostly concerned with prohibiting women who had taken the veil from marrying at, for example, the Council of Epaon, 517, ch. 20 (ed. C. de Clercq, *Concilia Galliae A.511–A.695*, CCSL, 148A [Turnhout, 1963], p. 29); Council of Orleans, 549, ch. 19 (ibid., p. 155): ' ... uel illae, qua in domibus propriis, tam puellae quam uiduae, conmutatis uestibus conuertuntur ...'; Council of Paris 614, ch. 15 (ibid., p. 279): 'De uiduabus et puellis quae sibi in habitu religionis in domos proprias tam a parentibus quam per se uestem mutauerint'; Council of St-Jean-de-Losne 673/5, ch. 13 (ed. de Clercq, *Concilia Galliae*, p. 316), quoted below, chapter 5, n. 13. See also De Jong, *In Samuel's Image*, pp. 39–40.

[111] W. Hartmann, *Die Synoden der Karolingerzeit im Frankenreich und in Italien* (Paderborn, 1989), pp. 424–6. This ninth-century literature is discussed in detail in chapter 5.

[112] Bremmer ('Widows', p. 81) has also struggled with the invisibility of these women, citing examples dating from the later period adjacent to his illustrations of cloistered widows, all of whom were active before the First Viking Age.

[113] John Blair has suggested (personal communication) that I may over-emphasise the transience of some early women's houses on the grounds that such a high proportion of early-recorded minsters (including, for example, Bibury and Withington) show clear signs of minster status later on. On the other hand, Blair has often tended to stress instances of stability and to argue for continuity of use where it may be more appropriate to envisage the re-use of a former religious site following a period of secularisation.

will become apparent later. The position of widows in the early medieval Church, the treatment of their behaviour in Church councils and the liturgical arrangements made for their blessing and consecration are considered at greater length in chapter 5.

Religious houses for women in early Anglo-Saxon England

The absence of a rigid framework defining limited circumstances in which religious women were permitted to express their vocations and a coincident flexibility in the interpretation of the roles available to women as ministers, at least in a missionary context, does much to explain the vitality of the female religious life in pre-Viking-Age England and also offers some pointers towards the changes in women's experience in the tenth and eleventh centuries. The success, and also ultimately the failure, of the institution of the double house lay in the capacity of Frankish and Anglo-Saxon society to harness to the missionary needs of their nascent churches the energies and talents of royal and noble women. The acceptance of the idea that women could fulfil spiritual functions — as teachers, preachers, and ministers of baptism, as well as the caritative functions of alms-giving, caring for the sick and raising and educating children — gave the Church a valuable impetus in its first few generations when the supply of competent clergy was very limited. That women could play a useful missionary role was still accepted in the eighth century when Boniface drew on female talents in founding new houses in Franconia, at least one of which was double, namely Heidenheim.[114] The prevalence of these attitudes must go a long way towards explaining the flowering of female religious devotion in an institutionalised, communal environment in the seventh and eighth centuries. The double house provided an outlet for the satisfaction of the religious devotion and administrative energy of Anglo-Saxon royal and aristocratic women as the heads and active members of communities which played a significant role in the political, economic and social landscape as well as in the ecclesiastical sphere, satisfying the spiritual needs of their lay neighbours by the example of their prayerful life of worship as well as through active pastoral ministry.

It is furthermore significant that, because there was no single model of how the religious life should be lived by women together, a wide variety of forms of devout expression could easily be assimilated within the system. In addition to the overwhelmingly royal institution of the double house — founded for members of ruling families and playing a significant role in the commemoration of their dead — houses were created on family lands by the secular aristocracy, who had no need to fear that these would permanently be lost from the kin. Bede

---

[114] *Ex Wolfhardi Haserensis Miraculis sanctae Walburgis Monheimensibus*, ch. 3 (ed. O. Holder-Egger, MGH, SS XV.I [Hannover, 1887], 535–55, at p. 540); Schulenburg ('Strict active enclosure', p. 66) has commented on Walburga's active role.

disapproved of the ease with which such communities could be established (for men or women) and expressed anxiety as to the extent to which irregular, pseudo-minsters were condoned by eighth-century kings, willing to grant charters for the permanent alienation of land for ecclesiastical purposes. His voice was not heard until the reformers of King Edgar's reign (particularly Bishop Æthelwold) sought to limit the interference of seculars on monastic lands.[115]

---

[115] Bede, *Epistola ad Ecgbertum*, chs. 10–13 (ed. Plummer, I, 413–7); for use of Bede's letter by the tenth-century reformers see A. Gransden, 'Traditionalism and continuity during the last century of Anglo-Saxon monasticism', *Journal of Ecclesiastical History*, 40 (1989), 159–207, at pp. 165–70. Late-eighth and ninth-century kings tempted to take lands back from the church may, however, have heeded Bede's caution all too willingly. An attempt was made to legislate against the secular overlordship of minsters at the council of *Clofesho* in 803 (ed. Haddan and Stubbs, *Councils*, III, 545–7; trans. Brooks, *The Early History*, p. 179). Compare also Council of Chelsea, 816, chs. 7–8 (ed. Haddan and Stubbs, *Councils*, III, 579–85, at p. 582).

Chapter 3

The disappearance of the early
Anglo-Saxon nun

The relative profusion of sources relating to Anglo-Saxon religious women in the seventh and eighth centuries (commensurate with those available for men's monastic communities in the same period) and their consequent prominence within the early medieval English Church contrasts starkly with the meagreness of the written record for female religious — but not for male — in the last two centuries before the Conquest.[1] Observing the diminution in the extant evidence for nuns and nunneries across the Anglo-Saxon period we have noted that there is a clear relationship between a minster's possession of landed wealth and its representation in the historical record. The paucity of surviving charters in favour of tenth- and eleventh-century English nunneries could thus be taken to reflect their relative poverty in comparison both with contemporary monastic houses for men and with women's communities of the pre-Viking Age. If economic causes were the key to understanding the reduction in the evidence across the First Viking Age, how could we explain the sharp economic decline of double houses and minsters for women from their relative prosperity in the late seventh and early eighth centuries? Must we suppose something radical to have happened to Anglo-Saxon attitudes towards female religious (or indeed to women in general) during the ninth century in order to explain the near silence of tenth- and eleventh-century writers over the activities of individual religious women or congregations of nuns? Sweeping statements were made about nuns collectively, at least by Bishop Æthelwold in his various rhetorical writings justifying the need for reform in the Church of King Edgar's day,[2] but particular communities are more difficult to find. Accounting for the later invisibility of women religious is much more difficult than is its demonstration.

Possible contexts for the limitations of the later literature for the purpose of the study of religious women will be discussed in the next chapter when the tenth-century monastic revolution is considered in greater detail, although it is impossible to arrive at any satisfactory answers from silence.[3] One question

---

[1]   The more abundant evidence for male religious does, however, relate predominantly to reformed, Benedictine houses; the late Anglo-Saxon record for non-monastic male clergy is also fairly meagre.

[2]   See below, chapter 4, pp. 88–9.

[3]   There is also considered, and rejected, the notion that the authors of the surviving sources deliberately concealed female religious activity from view.

should, however, be addressed first: did the early Anglo-Saxon nun simply disappear during the First Viking Age? Driven, as is the entirety of this project, by the evidence, this chapter explores the most difficult period of pre-Conquest monastic history when the sources are the least plentiful, the ninth century. Investigating the possibility that the silence of the sources does reflect the disappearance of the early English nun, it identifies three contexts in which any argument explaining this phenomenon would have to be set. Her demise might be attributable to the apparent decline of the double house as an institution beyond the mid-eighth century; to the impact on the English Church of Carolingian ecclesiastical reforms which sought to limit women's influence and restrict their spheres of activity within the Church; or to the effects of viking raiding on English monastic life. While not pretending to arrive at any conclusive answers, this necessarily brief discussion does aspire to identify the problems to which any speculative solutions must respond.

The demise of the Anglo-Saxon double house

The last double house (a mixed community under the authority of an abbess) for which there is certain evidence is the community of Abbess Æthelthryth, widow of Æthelwold Moll, to whom Alcuin wrote in 796.[4] There are instances from the late ninth century of apparently mixed houses ruled by abbots at Wenlock and Winchcombe,[5] and there may have been a community of men and women at Cheddar in the same period, the gender of whose ruler is not known.[6] From the first half of the tenth century instances of a few single religious women who lived in the neighbourhood of male communities (for example the *nunne* Æthelthryth at Bedwyn, or the widow Æthelflæd, whose house was in the enclosure of Glastonbury abbey[7]), but no new genuinely double houses seem to have been established beyond the middle years of the eighth century. Unless the reformers' references to *canonici* in the 960s who 'married wives illicitly, divorced them and took others'[8] should be read as veiled allusions to the continuance of the practice of male and female religious cohabiting within the same monastic enclosure (and this seems unlikely, for had these women had been vowed to God the reformers

---

4   Alcuin, *Epistola* 106 (ed. E. Dümmler, *Epistolae Karolini Aevi*, II, MGH, Epistolae IV [Berlin, 1895], 152–3); D. B. Schneider, 'Anglo-Saxon women in the religious life: a study of the status and position of women in an early mediaeval society' (PhD thesis, University of Cambridge, 1985), p. 26.

5   Wenlock BCS 587 (S 221); Winchcombe: BCS 575 (S 1442).

6   BCS 1219 (Latin version of S 806); see further below, part II, *s.n.* Cheddar.

7   'B', *Vita S. Dunstani*, chs. 10–11 (ed. W. Stubbs, *Memorials of St Dunstan*, Rolls Series 63 [1874], 3–52, at pp. 17–19); see part II, *s.n.* Glastonbury.

8   Wulfstan of Winchester, *Vita sancti Æthelwoldi*, ch. 16 (ed. and trans. M. Lapidge and M. Winterbottom, *Wulfstan of Winchester, The Life of St Æthelwold* [1991], pp. 30–1).

would surely have had much to say about their failure to preserve their vows of chastity), there is no evidence for any mixed congregation in England beyond the early years of the tenth century. That the model of mixed-sex communities had gone out of fashion seems probable, but explaining why that should have been so is much harder. If the decline of the double house is in some way linked with a new reluctance among the Anglo-Saxon nobility and aristocracy to patronise female houses with landed wealth (observable from the decline in the number of charters issued in favour of female houses from the mid-eighth century onwards) then answers need to be sought in contemporary aristocratic attitudes to women in religion or to women as landholders. The final demise of the double house as an institution may have coincided with changes in social (or perhaps more significantly, ecclesiastical) attitudes to women, and particularly the enforcement of a Pauline view of their incapacity for ministry in the aftermath of the Carolingian reforms.[9] While it is relatively easy to explain how it was that the mixed community could not have flourished in the climate of the tenth-century Benedictine monastic revolution (when strict gender segregation, monastic enclosure and regularity of observance were imposed on all congregations), it is difficult to see this process in terms of its effect on double houses as other than the regularisation of a shift in the pattern of religious observance that had in fact occurred much earlier.

Asking the same question about the decline of the double house, Dagmar Schneider has dwelt on the royal associations of double houses during the early Anglo-Saxon period, the predominance of royal women among their abbesses, and the significant role played by these communities in preserving their natal families' memorial cults.[10] Later in the pre-Conquest period the roles open to queens were more limited, their relationship with religious houses was restricted to nominal headship rather than active management, the one exception being Ælfthryth's apparent direct involvement with the organisation of the nunnery at Barking after the exile of its abbess, Wulfhild.[11] The political power formerly exercised by seventh-century abbesses was not shared by their tenth- and eleventh-century counterparts; the close association between the West Saxon royal house and the nunneries it sponsored in the tenth century did not extend to the engagement of their inmates in contemporary political affairs.[12] Thus Dagmar Schneider has attributed the decline of the double house to changes in the concept of kingship, to wider social movements that tended to restrict the independent action of women and to the integration of monastic houses within more rigidly defined ecclesiastical hierarchies, made explicit in the literature of the tenth-century

---

[9]   See below, pp. 66–70.

[10]   Schneider, 'Anglo-Saxon women', pp. 33–4.

[11]   Goscelin, *Vita sanctae Wulfhildae*, ch. 9 (ed. M. Esposito, 'La vie de Sainte Vulfhilde par Goscelin de Cantorbéry', *Analecta Bollandiana*, 32 (1913), 10–26, at pp. 21–2); see part II, *s.n.* Barking.

[12]   Schneider, 'Anglo-Saxon women', p. 35.

reform.[13] Relevant also to the comparative positions of royally patronised houses
in later Anglo-Saxon England with those of the pre-Viking Age are the changes
effected in the political landscape in the eighth and ninth centuries as the smaller,
independent royal houses of England were either subsumed within those of their
larger and more powerful neighbours or brought down during the Danish wars. By
the time that there are significant signs of a revival of interest in monasticism, in
the reign of King Æthelstan, there is only one royal house left in England, with
landed interests firmly focussed in the south.

The ecclesiastical context of the redefinition of the religious role of
women is certainly an important one, to which we will return shortly, but there are
other relevant factors here. Although Schneider is right to concentrate on the link
between royalty and double houses this was not the sole outlet for female religious
expression in the pre-Viking Age; the rest of the aristocracy also patronised
women's houses. The commemoration of the dead of one particular kin group
could as well have been performed for non-royal families by women living in the
family minsters established by their own kin and can be seen as reflecting an
attitude in earlier Anglo-Saxon society towards the importance of women within
the kin group that extended beyond royal circles.[14] Explanation for the apparent
reduction in the foundation of new women's religious houses must therefore also
be sought at least in part within the context of aristocratic patterns of landholding
and endowment. Did the double house decline as a consequence of changes in the
way in which women could hold land (either by means of gift or through
inheritance) which meant that female religious and the minsters that housed them
found it more difficult, or even impossible, to acquire sufficient landed wealth to
remain economically viable? On this reading, the demise of the double house
would become a secondary consequence of a wider decline in female monasticism
generally, the mixed community being imperilled because of its female
membership. Its only hope of salvation would then be to follow the path that
certainly was taken by some double houses and change its membership in order
to become a purely male institution.

The period when double houses proliferated may have coincided with a
time when land devoted to ecclesiastical use was freed from many, if not all,

---

[13]   Ibid., pp. 36–7, and D. Baltrusch-Schneider, 'Klosterleben als alternative
Lebensform zur Ehe?', in *Weibliche Lebensgestaltung im frühen Mittelalter*, ed. H.-W. Goetz
(Cologne and Vienna, 1991), pp. 45–64, at pp. 77–8.

[14]   Nor was this peculiar to England. Janet Nelson has drawn attention to the small
number of Frankish nunneries that functioned over long periods as centres of lay piety, specifically
in their prayerful commemoration of the dead, noting the significance of the nunnery at
Remiremont in catering for the spiritual needs of peasant as well as noble patrons: J. L. Nelson,
'Women and the word in the earlier middle ages', in *Women in the Church*, ed. W. J. Sheils and
D. Wood (1990), 53–78, at pp. 66–7.

secular liabilities;[15] the point at which charters in favour of female communities start to become more infrequent corresponds to the period when charters first began to state explicitly that military obligations were required of all booked land. Once the booking of a portion of a family's estate for the creation of a minster no longer secured exemption for that land from the military services owed to the king — and indeed once straightforward grants of bookland started to be made to the laity — ecclesiastical landholding would have appeared less tax-efficient to the nobility than it had done to previous generations.[16] Some families may have preferred henceforth to satisfy the spiritual aspirations of their male as much as their female members in ways that did not lead to the permanent alienation of land outside the kin group. Instead of endowing a minster for a particularly devout relative, a family might have chosen to allow her (or him) a life interest in a portion of their estates that would revert to the kin on the recipient's death. Any sort of family minster may thus have looked less than attractive in this altered fiscal climate, yet we have already seen in the last chapter that there were earlier instances of devout women living 'in their own homes' not away from their kin in enclosed minsters. We might speculate as to whether this form of female religious expression became more common after the middle years of the eighth century.

It is difficult to disentangle these possible factors (which can only adequately be explored in the context of a much fuller analysis of female landholding and inheritance in the early middle ages than is appropriate here) from the alternative explanation that it was the double house *per se* to which the later eighth-century aristocracy took exception. Was there a growing noble reluctance to patronise mixed-sex congregations because of contemporary anxieties about, or frank disapproval of, the cohabitation of supposedly celibate men and women? How significant was the issue raised by Karl Leyser in relation to Ottonian Saxony of the necessity to prevent too many women from breeding further heirs to dilute a noble family's line?[17] We confront once more the issue of the silence of the sources and our ignorance of the fate of so many early Anglo-Saxon women's monastic houses. There might have been sexual scandals far worse than that of Coldingham of which prudish monastic chroniclers forbore to write. Those who

---

[15] Whether land granted by means of charter was always freed from all obligations including that of the provision of military service remains a contested issue; E. John, *Land Tenure in Early England* (2nd edn, 1964), pp. 67–73; N. P. Brooks, 'The development of military obligations in eighth- and ninth-century England', in *England Before the Conquest*, ed. P. Clemoes and K. Hughes (1971), pp. 69–84; R. P. Abels, *Lordship and Military Obligation in Anglo-Saxon England* (Berkeley and Los Angeles, California, 1988), pp. 43–57; and most recently, E. John, *Reassessing Anglo-Saxon England* (1996), pp. 51–3.

[16] For a recent discussion of the rights and obligations attached to bookland see T. Charles-Edwards, 'Anglo-Saxon kinship revisited', in *The Anglo-Saxons from the Migration Period to the Eighth Century*, ed. J. Hines (1997), pp. 171–210, at pp. 192–8.

[17] K. J. Leyser, *Rule and Conflict in an Early Medieval Society* (1979), p. 64.

subsequently acquired the endowments of former religious houses might actively
have sought to obscure details of the events surrounding a minster's dissolution.
If male communities in the ninth century had been gradually becoming less strictly
monastic and more similar to congregations of secular priests that shift would also
have served to occlude the women.[18] Of equal importance are the desires of the
female monastics themselves. While there were clearly features of the religious
life that appealed to substantial numbers of Englishwomen during the seventh and
early eighth centuries and made it an attractive alternative to marriage, life in the
cloister may have seemed less enticing if claustration began more forcibly to be
imposed at the same time as married women acquired a greater social status.[19]
Here we must turn to the articulation of just these notions in the legislation of the
Frankish emperors Charles the Great and Louis the Pious, reflecting changes in the
Church's attitude to women which may arguably have also been felt in England.[20]

Ecclesiastical reform

The second oecumenical council at Nicea in 787 decreed that double houses
should never be set up, because these always occasioned scandal and offence,
although those communities that were already in existence were to be permitted
to continue provided that they followed the recommendations of St Basil.[21] No
such definitive statement against the double house was articulated at an English
or Frankish council in the eighth or ninth century (although the recommendations
of Nicea were of course known, in a flawed Latin translation, at the court of
Charlemagne) but various measures were promulgated at Frankish Church
councils in order to bring women's religious houses under closer episcopal
control, and particularly to enforce the claustration of nuns.[22] Bishops were given
authority to intervene in the affairs of nuns' houses if they failed to observe their
rules, abbesses were only permitted to leave their monasteries if summoned by the

---

[18]   I owe this insight to John Blair (personal communication).
[19]   S. F. Wemple, *Women in Frankish Society. Marriage and the Cloister 500–900*
(Philadelphia, PA, 1981), pp. 154 and 171; C. Fell, *Women in Anglo-Saxon England and the
Impact of 1066* (1984), ch. 3.
[20]   For a broad-ranging survey of ecclesiastical attitudes to women in the early middle
ages see Nelson, 'Women and the word'.
[21]   Council of Nicea, 787, ch. 20 (ed. J. D. Mansi *et al. Sacrorum conciliorum nova et
amplissima collectio*, [Florence, 1759–98], XIII, col. 437). See S. Hilpisch, *Die Doppelklöster:
Entstehung und Organisation* (Münster, 1928) p. 22. Quoted E. De Moreau, 'Les "monastères
doubles": leur histoire surtout en Belgique', *Nouvelle Revue Théologique*, 66 (1939), 787–92, at
p. 791.
[22]   J. T. Schulenburg, 'Strict active enclosure and its effects on the female monastic
experience (500–1100)', in *Medieval Religious Women I: Distant Echoes*, ed. J. A. Nichols and
L. T. Shank (1984), pp. 51–86, at pp. 56–8; Wemple, *Women*, pp. 166–71.

king or with their bishop's permission,[23] and abbesses and nuns were not even to leave their houses in order to go on pilgrimage to Rome or to other venerable places, because of the dangers inherent in the inevitable relationships they would strike up with men on such trips.[24] Those female houses that had not previously been regulated were to be brought under tighter control: 'Concerning very small monasteries where nuns live without a rule: it is our will that a community based on the rule be formed in a single place; and let the bishop look to where it can be formed. And that no abbess is to presume to go outside the monastery without our command or to allow those subject to her to do so; and their monasteries are to be well fenced off; and in no circumstances are they to presume to write or sing vulgar songs there'.[25] Contact with men was to be kept to the absolute minimum; nunneries were no longer to have responsibility for educating boys, poor people and pilgrims in search of charity were to be kept outside the nunnery gate and even the visits of bishops and monks were to be restricted.[26]

One significant issue for those reformers trying to restrict female monastic freedoms was that of the essential incapacity of their sex to govern their own lives, or their estates, effectively. The *Institutio sanctimonialium* (the rule for women religious compiled by Amalarius of Metz and enforced at the Council of Aachen of 816/7) stated specifically that it was because of the greater fragility of their sex that women needed to be strictly cloistered.[27] By removing the men from their houses and forcibly shutting the women off from the outside world the women

---

[23] Council of Verneuil, 755, ch. 6 (ed. A. Boretius, *Capitularia regum Francorum*, MGH, Leges II [Hannover, 1883], I, 34, no. 14); Council of Riesbach, Freising and Salzburg, 800, ch. 27 (ed. A. Werminghoff, *Concilia Aevi Karolini*, I, MGH, Leges III, Concilia II, 1 [Hannover and Leipzig, 1906], p. 210, no. 24); Council of Mainz, 813, ch. 13 (ibid., p. 264, no. 36); Council of Tours, 813, ch. 30 (ibid., p. 290, no. 38). Compare the earlier Council of Herstal 779, ch. 3 (ed. Boretius, *Capitularia*, I, 47, no. 20; trans. P. D. King, *Charlemagne. Translated Sources* [1987], p. 203): 'Monasteries of holy women are to observe a holy rule; and every abbess is to maintain unbroken residence in her monastery'.

[24] Council of Cividale del Friuli, 796–7, ch. 12 (ed. Werminghoff, *Concilia*, II, 1, pp. 193–4, no. 21); Wemple, *Women*, p. 168; Schulenburg, 'Strict active enclosure', pp. 56–7. Compare Boniface's recommendation to Archbishop Cuthbert that English *mulieres* and *uelatae feminae* should be prevented from going on pilgrimage to Rome: *Epistola*, 78 (ed. M. Tangl, *Die Briefe des Heiligen Bonifatius und Lullus*, MGH, Epistolae selectae I [Berlin, 1916], p. 169).

[25] *Duplex legationis edictum*, 789, ch. 19 (ed. Boretius, *Capitularia*, I, 63, no. 23; trans. King, *Charlemagne*, p. 221): 'De monasteriis minutis ubi nonnanes sine regula sedent ...'.

[26] *Capitula ecclesiastica ad Salz data*, 803–4, ch 7 (ed. Boretius, *Capitularia*, I, 119, no. 42); *Institutio sanctimonialium*, ch. 18 (ed. Werminghoff, *Concilia*, II, 2, p. 455, no. 39B); Council of Cividale del Friuli, 796/7, ch. 12 (ed. Werminghoff, *Concilia*, II, 1, pp. 193–4, no. 21); Council of Paris, 829, ch. 46 (ed. Werminghoff, *Concilia* II, 2, p. 640, no. 50). Wemple, *Women*, pp. 168–9.

[27] *Institutio sanctimonialium*, ch. 18 (ed. Werminghoff, *Concilia* II, 1, p. 449, no. 39B): 'Quanto enim idem sexus fragilior esse dinoscitur tanto necesse est mairorem erga eum custodiam adhiberi'. See Schulenburg, 'Strict active enclosure', p. 58. For further discussion of this rule see below, chapter 4, pp. 107–10.

were perforce rendered economically dependent.[28] In a climate in which the predominant form of female religious expression — the double house — had gone out of favour, new approaches and models of communal living had to be adopted for the next generations of aspiring nuns to find the means to satisfy their devotion. In the Carolingian world the all-female community was not only actively advocated in the reforming literature, but was patronised and promoted by Charlemagne and Louis the Pious and their nobility.[29] But the case of the Aquitainian nun, Immena, to which Jane Martindale has drawn attention, should sound a note of caution here. Immena was dedicated to the religious life by her parents, being established on family lands at a place called Sarrazac with a congregation of nuns living according to a *regula puellarum* with the specific intention that she and her successors would preserve the family's memory in prayerful commemoration. Yet, the parents' confidence in the efficacy of their daughter's prayers was not shared by Immena's brother, Rudolf archbishop of Bourges, who redistributed the nunnery's lands in favour of a new monastery — for monks — at Beaulieu.[30] There were disadvantages in all-women houses, particularly where the absence of men meant that no memorial masses could be celebrated.

Carolingian ecclesiastical reforms brought with them more than the strict segregation of the sexes, being much concerned with the unique characteristics and powers of the priesthood, they led also to the articulation of strongly-worded prohibitions against the exercise by women of any quasi-sacerdotal powers.[31] In part this was a question of authority: women were not to exercise any kind of dominion over men, but were always to be viewed as their spiritual inferiors. Of equal relevance was the issue of ritual purity. Women's public roles were to be limited to the lighting of candles and ringing of Church bells; within the cloister their functions were restricted to psalmody, singing and prayer together with the care of sick and impoverished women and the education of young girls.[32] Veiled

---

28   Schulenburg, 'Strict active enclosure', p. 77.

29   Wemple (*Women*, pp. 171–3) has drawn attention to the prominence of many of the abbesses and other inmates of these houses and the political role taken by all monasteries in the ninth century.

30   J. Martindale, 'The nun Immena and the foundation of the Abbey of Beaulieu: a woman's prospects in the Carolingian Church', in *Women in the Church*, Studies in Church History, 27, ed. W. J. Sheils and D. Wood (1990), 27–42; above, chapter 2, p. 47. E. Magnou-Nortier, 'Formes féminines de vie consacrée dans les pays du Midi jusqu'au début du XIIᵉ siécle', in *La femme dans la vie religieuse du Languedoc (XIIIᵉ–XIVᵉ s.)*, Cahiers de Fanjeaux, 23 (1988), 193–216, at pp. 204–5.

31   See R. McKitterick, *The Frankish Church and the Carolingian Reforms, 789–895* (1977), pp. 1–18 and 52–65.

32   Council of Riesbach, Freising and Salzburg, 800, ch. 22 (ed. Werminghoff, *Concilia*, II, 1, p. 210, no. 24); Council of Mainz, 847, ch. 16 (ed. W. Hartmann, *Die Konzilien der karolingischen Teilreiche, 843–859*, MGH Leges III, *Concilia*, III [Hannover, 1984], 169–70,

women were to be denied access to sacred space: they might not enter the sanctuary of a church, approach the altar, touch the consecrated vessels, administer sacerdotal vestments for priests, or distribute the consecrated elements to communicants at the mass.[33] Even within their own cloisters the role of abbesses was more tightly circumscribed; in Charlemagne's 789 *Admonitio generalis* abbesses were forbidden any longer to give blessings by placing their hands and making the sign of the holy cross upon men's heads, or to veil virgins.[34] The most explicit statements against freedom of female action were made at the 829 Council of Paris, where amazement was expressed that 'women, whose sex by no means makes them competent, despite the laws, were able to gain licence to do things that are prohibited even to secular men'.[35] It is scarcely surprising that in such a climate Archbishop Rudolf should have thought his family's cult better commemorated by a community of monks than by his sister Immena's all-female convent at Sarrazac.

The zeal for reform was not felt in England in the early ninth century in quite the same way as in Francia; its main advocate, archbishop Wulfred was more interested in the organisation of cathedral and male monastic communities than he was in female forms of the monastic life.[36] There had been some efforts at ecclesiastical reform in the previous century. Inspired by Boniface's recommendations and his reports of his own attempts to regulate the Frankish church, the 747 council of *Clofesho* had dealt with a number of matters relating to monastic organisation making general recommendations about the behaviour of nuns and abbesses and on the advisability of limiting contact between avowed women and all men, including priests and monks.[37] Episcopal control over minsters was enforced via the canons of the council held at Chelsea in 816, bishops being encouraged to exert more influence over the appointment of abbots

---

no. 14; *Institutio sanctimonialium*, chs. 28 and 22 (ed. Werminghoff, *Concilia* II, 1, pp. 455 and 452, no. 39B); Wemple, *Women*, p. 169; Schulenburg, 'Public and private', p. 115.

[33] *Admonitio generalis*, ch. 17 (ed. Boretius, *Capitularia*, I, p. 55, no. 22); Council of Paris 829, ch. 45 (ed. Werminghoff, MGH, *Concilia* II, 2, p. 639, no. 50).

[34] *Admonitio generalis*, ch. 76 (ed. Boretius, *Capitularia*, I, p. 55, no. 22; transl. King, *Charlemagne*, p. 218).

[35] Council of Paris, 829, ch. 45 (ed. Werminghoff, *Concilia*, II, 2, pp. 639–40, no. 50); quoted Wemple, *Women*, p. 167.

[36] Brooks, *The Early History*, pp. 155–64; B. Langefeld, '*Regula canonicorum* or *Regula monasterialis uitae*? The Rule of Chrodegang and Archbishop Wulfred's reforms at Canterbury', *ASE*, 25 (1996), 21–36. Not that Wulfred ignored women's houses: his policies brought him into bitter conflict with Abbess Selethryth of Lyminge and Minster-in-Thanet (Brooks, *The Early* History, pp. 183–5) and later with Cwenthryth, abbess of Winchcombe and of Minster: ibid., pp. 190–7.

[37] Council of *Clofesho*, 747, ch. 20 (ed. A. W. Haddan and W. Stubbs, *Councils and Ecclesiastical Documents Relating to Great Britain and Ireland* [3 vols., 1869–78], III, 360–85, at p. 369).

and abbesses,[38] but in general this council was more preoccupied with the dangers presented to the monastic life by the misappropriation of Church lands by seculars and with the control of priestly ministry than with the minutiae of internal monastic organisation.

That Frankish ecclesiastical reforms eventually had some impact on the organisation of the English church, notably on the regulation of the monastic life, cannot be doubted on the basis of what we know of the stimuli behind the tenth-century monastic revolution. But that the redefinition of the role of women within the Church was already articulated within an Anglo-Saxon context as early as the mid-eighth century, when the first diminution in the fervour for the female religious life becomes apparent, is far from clear. Since English texts do not pronounce the same prohibitions against the quasi-ministerial functions of women at this date, it is hard to specify a chronology of liturgical reform or sacramental restriction in which to set the waning of aristocratic interest in the patronage of houses of women monastics. Or indeed to be certain that to attempt such a model is not to reconstruct the sequence of events in the wrong order. Might it not equally be that once men and women religious had stopped living together, or were at least no longer doing so in such numbers, that new donations made *pro remedio animae* and as acts of commemoration for the souls of the departed would inevitably be directed towards those, now mostly male, congregations whose members comprised priests able to celebrate masses for the dead? The iteration of Pauline notions of the fragility and unworthiness of the female sex could be secondary to that shift, a confirmation of the rightness of the new order. Various factors confound our inquiry here, centrally as has already been stressed, the general lack of ninth-century sources. It is possible to overstate the case for a decline in women's monasticism. We have already noted the probable survival of women within religious congregations at Wenlock, Winchcombe and (less plausibly) Cheddar in the 890s.[39] Asser bore witness to the fact that the female desire for the monastic life was not entirely lacking among the English in the 880s, when King Alfred was apparently able to find plenty of women keen to join the nunnery he had established for his daughter, Æthelgifu, at Shaftesbury, in contrast to the difficulties he experienced in peopling his all-male foundation at Athelney.[40] Unless this is to be attributed to nothing more than the desire of these nobles to benefit from the social cachet (and indisputable material prosperity) surrounding an institution occupied by royalty, it suggests that there was in

---

[38]   Council of Chelsea, 816, chs. 4 and 7 (ibid., pp. 579–85, at pp. 580–2).

[39]   Above, p. 62.

[40]   Asser, Life of Alfred, ch. 98 (ed. W. H. Stevenson, *Asser's Life of King Alfred* [1904], p. 85; trans. S. Keynes and M. Lapidge, *Alfred the Great* [1983], p. 105). For the account of the reluctance of noble or freeborn men of the king's race willing to undertake the monastic life, which obliged Alfred to appoint John of the Old Saxons to rule as abbot over a number of people of Gallic origin (and at least one 'member of the pagan race', namely a viking) at Athelney see ibid., chs. 93–4 (pp. 80–1).

Wessex, at least, an untapped source of female devotion at the end of the ninth century.[41]

There were, however, other, external factors that started to play a part in threatening the survival of the whole of the Christian Church as an institution during the course of the ninth century. In that extreme need, the peculiar requirements of women religious (now denied the missionary role that could have made them valuable) must have seemed somewhat less pressing.

The Danish raids

The impact of Danish military activity in the ninth century on the communal religious life generally and on its female expression in particular was, by whatever standard it is measured, devastating.[42] In the coastal areas of Kent and Northumbria where Danish attack was most frequent not one of the communities of women known to have existed in the late seventh century was still active at the Norman Conquest; most had disappeared from the historical record as female minsters by the early tenth century. We have already seen that there were other factors in ninth-century England that militated against the continuance of independent monastic houses for women, or mixed congregations under female governance, and that also had a part to play in the demise of these institutions: a marked discontinuity in the sites of female religious observance is apparent even in those areas of England far from Danish raiding and settlement. Some attention needs, however, also to be paid to the damage potentially done to women in religion by the viking wars, even if these are ultimately to be dismissed as the principal cause of this apparent decline in women's monasticism.

It has become fashionable recently to question the extent of the damage done by the Danes to the non-fighting populations of western Europe and to doubt that the vikings were directly responsible for perpetrating acts of violence or rape

---

[41]   The same factors — lack of local competing institutions to satisfy female spiritual desires, and the attractive aura of royal blood — may have been equally influential in ensuring the success of the new nunneries sponsored by the West Saxon royal house in the tenth century: the Nunnaminster at Winchester, Romsey, Wilton, Amesbury and Wherwell.

[42]   I have looked elsewhere at the extent of the danger presented to the Church by the Danish wars of the ninth century: 'Violence against Christians? The Vikings and the Church in ninth-century England', *Medieval History*, 1 (1991), 3–16. Guy Halsall has challenged my views in his 'Playing by whose rules? A further look at Viking atrocity in the ninth century', *Medieval History*, 2.2 (1992), 2–12. However, in focussing on what might have constituted 'normal' warfare in the eighth and ninth centuries, he has not actually dissented from my conclusion that the vikings 'had serious detrimental effects upon the Church' during the ninth century. For a Frankish perspective see also S. Coupland, 'The rod of God's wrath or the people of God's wrath? The Carolingians' theology of the Viking invasions', *Journal of Ecclesiastical History*, 42 (1991), 535–54.

against innocent communities of defenceless nuns.[43] Certainly most of the accounts of viking atrocity date from beyond the ninth century, many from after the Conquest.[44] For example, it is only in the twelfth-century house-history of Ely the *Liber Eliensis*, that we find a detailed account of the attacks of a Danish army led by Inguar and Hubba between 866 and 871, extending to the burning of Æthelthryth's minster and the slaughter of its inmates.[45] Similarly, an account of how nuns from other places including Whitby took refuge from 'Hinguar' and Hubba in the (fortified) double house at Tynemouth but were later massacred there by the vikings 'and translated by martyrdom to heaven' is given in the early thirteenth-century *Flores Historiarum* of the St Albans monk, Roger of Wendover and repeated and amplified by Matthew Paris in his *Chronica Majora*.[46] Equally, there are many instances from English, Frankish and Irish chronicles of Christian

---

[43]   The revisionist position was first advanced by Peter Sawyer in his *The Age of the Vikings* (1963, 2nd edn, 1971), but has been sophisticated by a number of writers over the last thirty years. For an extreme view consider the remarks made by Janet Nelson in a BBC 'Timewatch' programme about the Vikings broadcast in 1995, quoted by D. N. Dumville, *The Churches of North Britain in the First Viking Age* (1997), p. 9.

[44]   The only contemporary witness to the bloody destruction of an Anglo-Saxon minster is Alcuin, who wrote from the Continent after the first Danish raid on Lindisfarne in June 793 to express his dismay at the shedding of blood on the altar of St Cuthbert (Alcuin, *Epistolae*, nos. 16–22, ed. Dümmler, pp. 42–59). Alcuin was not an eye-witness and deliberately used a heightened tone and appropriate biblical imagery to support his argument that only a great sin could have merited such a terrible punishment; it is clear from others of his letters that despite the violence of the 793 raid, within a year the community was functioning again: Alcuin, *Epistolae*, no. 24 (ed. Dümmler, p. 65).

[45]   *Liber Eliensis*, I, chs. 38–41 (ed. E. O. Blake [1962], pp. 52–5); for the possibility that the author had access to an account of the Danish invasions including a roll of their leaders see Blake, ibid., p. xxix. See below part II, *s.n.* Barking for details of the late eleventh-century account of the slaughter of the nuns of Barking given by Goscelin in his *Lecciones de sancta Hildelitha*, ch. 2 (ed. M. L. Colker, 'Texts of Jocelyn of Canterbury which relate to the history of Barking Abbey', *Studia Monastica*, 7 [1965], pp. 455–8, at p. 455).

[46]   Roger of Wendover, *Flores Historiarum*, *s.a.* 1065 (ed. H. O. Coxe, 5 vols. [1841–4], I, 504–5); Matthew Paris, *Chronica Majora*, *s.a.* 1065 (ed. H. R. Luard, Rolls Series 57 (7 vols. 1872–80), I, 531. It is possible that Roger of Wendover's source for this story was a Life of St Oswine written by a monk of St Albans who had gone to the abbey's cell at Tynemouth in 1111, but the printed version of that life does not make any mention of the presence of nuns at Tynemouth during the Viking Age: *Vita Oswini regis Deirorum*, ed. Surtees Society, *Miscellanea Biographia* (1838), pp. 11–14. John Leland provided another account of the burning of Tynemouth by *Hynguar* and Hubba and may have had access to a now lost version of the Life of Oswine, but he also made no reference to nuns at the abbey: *De Rebus Britannicis Collectanea*, ed. T. Hearne (2nd edn, 6 vols., 1774), IV, 114. The story of the martyrdom of nuns at Tynemouth is generally reported at second-hand via W. S. Gibson, *The History of the Monastery Founded at Tynemouth* (2 vols., 1846–7), I, 15–18, as for example by D. Knowles and R. N. Hadcock, *Medieval Religious Houses. England and Wales* (2nd edn, 1971), pp. 78–9. Further discussion, including an exploration of Leland's probable sources was provided by H. H. E. Craster, *Tynemouth Priory* (1907), at pp. 40–1. I am extremely grateful to Stephen Thompson for verifying these references for me.

armies perpetrating acts of violence against Christian places of worship: the opportunities for the acquisition of plunder presented by undefended sites of movable wealth were recognised by all parties in the ninth century. The provisions made in a number of early medieval European secular law-codes for the physical protection of religious women indicate that the violation of the chastity of nuns and consecrated widows was threatened at least as much by their compatriots (and co-religionists) as by the members of foreign armies.[47] But while accepting that the Danes were not motivated by anti-Christian fervour and that Christians also attacked churches and raped consecrated women, it is not necessary — nor is it, as David Dumville has recently argued, at all plausible — to imagine that the ninth-century laws of war were so much more sophisticated than those of our own century that the sea-borne warbands that attacked, and over-wintered on islands that had been home to communities of religious women did so without availing themselves of the physical pleasures denied them on their journey. We need pay little attention to Roger of Wendover's highly coloured account of the self-mutilation of the nuns of Coldingham, who supposedly chose to make themselves too horrible to view by cutting off their own noses in order that the Danes would kill them without compromising their virtue.[48] Yet we may still accept that virgin nuns would have felt particularly vulnerable in the face of sea-borne raiders of any nationality, and that contemporary rumours of the danger presented by the vikings could have inflamed those fears. It is not entirely implausible to imagine that the Israelite heroine Judith (who used her beauty to lure the Assyrian leader Holofernes into his tent alone with her and then cut off his head while he slept) might have been presented as an inspirational example to Anglo-Saxon nuns of a slightly later generation, especially since in the fragmentary Old English poem in which her deeds were celebrated she has been transformed from a young,

---

[47] Compare the penalties imposed in King Alfred's laws on those who made sexual advances to a *nunne* (Alfred, ch. 8, ed. F. Liebermann, *Die Gesetze der Angelsachsen*, [3 vols., Halle, 1903–16], I, 54) with the provisions made for the physical protection of nuns and women dedicated to God in Lombard and Bavarian codes: Laws of Liutprand (A.D. 723), ch. 30.I and A.D. 724, ch. 76.VII (ed. F. Bluhme, *Leges Langobardorum*, MGH, Leges, IV [Hannover, 1869], pp. 122–3 and 138; trans. K. F. Drew, *The Lombard Laws* [Philadelphia, PA, 1973], pp. 159–60 and 176); *Lex Baiwariorum*, I, xi (ed. E. von Schwind, MGH, Leges, V, 2 [Hannover, 1926], pp. 283–4, trans. T. J. Rivers, *Laws of the Alemans and Bavarians* [Philadelphia, PA, 1977], p. 122). Discussed by J. T. Schulenburg, 'The heroics of virginity: Brides of Christ and sacrificial mutilation', in *Women in the Middle Ages and the Renaissance*, ed. M. B. Rose (Syracuse, New York, 1986), pp. 29–72, at pp. 43–4.

[48] Roger of Wendover, *Flores historiarum*, s.a. 870 (ed. Coxe, I, 300–2); quoted Schulenburg, 'The heroics', pp. 47–8. Schulenburg has provided two other examples of virgin nuns who mutilated their faces and cut off their noses to protect their chastity from infidels, one from eighth-century Frankia (St Eusebia of St Cyr near Marseille) and the other from early medieval Spanish monastery of St Florentine near Ecija, although that story is again reported in a later Chronicle: ibid., pp. 46–8.

continent widow into a 'holy virgin'.[49] If the consecrated women of Minster-in-Sheppey and Minster-in-Thanet escaped with their lives and virginity intact from the ninth-century viking raids, it was because they had fled their homes for better defended sites (whether secular or ecclesiastical) before the Danes arrived.[50]

When considering the possibility that the First Viking Age marked a low-point in women's monasticism in England there is more to be discussed than the fact of individual houses being attacked by Danish raiding parties in search of movable wealth, or the damage to their buildings or lands from the effects of warfare or deliberately started fires, or the jeopardising of the chastity of the nuns at the hands of seamen bent on sexual pleasure. Even more harmful to the continuance of female religion was the conflict felt by the worldly families of women religious, the secular aristocracy, over the need for the lands for the defence of the kingdom against this external threat. In the face of frequent military incursions the maintenance of strategically vulnerable women's religious houses and their protection from destruction must have looked like a luxury no sane king or nobleman could afford to sustain. It is here that the preservation of monastic lands within the control of founding families becomes once more a pertinent issue. If a charter served not to alienate land permanently from the kin into the ecclesiastical orbit but rather to satisfy the piety of female relatives while preventing them from disposing of their estates outside the kin group, then it is scarcely surprising that in time of need such lands were taken back within the men's control. While scholars can argue about the actual physical damage done to named monastic houses and a case can be made for seeing the late-eighth-century English Church in general as already in need of reform before the Danish coastal raids became frequent and seriously troublesome, the fact remains that viking attacks acted as a spark in an already volatile situation.

By the end of the First Viking Age a substantial number of houses, male and female, had vanished into oblivion. As Asser suggested, the decline in the desire for the monastic life perceptible among the English may have been because of 'the depredations of foreign enemies whose attacks by land and sea are very frequent and savage, or else because of the people's enormous abundance of riches of every kind'.[51] The ecclesiastical order might, alternatively as Fulk, archbishop of Rheims, surmised, have fallen into ruin 'whether by the frequent invasion and

---

[49]   *Judith*, line 56 (ed. and trans. A. S. Cook, *Judith. An Old English Epic Fragment* [Boston, MA, 1888], pp. 6–7): 'seo halge meowle'. See Schulenburg, 'The heroics', pp. 38–9; and M. Clayton, 'Ælfric's *Judith*: manipulative or manipulated?', *ASE*, 23 (1994), 215–27, at pp. 225–7.

[50]   The community of St Mildrith's seems to have been joined with that of Lyminge early in the ninth century, and the latter community acquired for itself a place of refuge in the city of Canterbury: BCS 317 (S 160). Viking armies wintering on the island of Thanet were reported in the Anglo-Saxon Chronicle *s.a.* 851, 853 and 865, and on the island of Sheppey in the year 855.

[51]   Asser, Life of Alfred, ch. 93 (ed. Stevenson, *Asser*, p. 81; transl. Keynes and Lapidge, *Alfred the Great*, p. 103).

onslaught of Vikings, or through decrepitude, or through the carelessness of its bishops or the ignorance of those subject to them'.[52] But, to quote Asser again, there seems no question that 'this kind of monastic life came all the more into disrespect', a general trend in which women need not have been especially disadvantaged, but from which female religious houses may have proved less able to recover than their male counterparts.

Yet, although it is clear that the ecclesiastical life in England in the First Viking Age was damaged, the extinction of any single monastic community as a direct consequence of Danish activity is, as David Dumville has shown, hard to demonstrate. Many religious institutions, male and female, certainly found it difficult to sustain a communal devotional life during the ninth century and some did pass permanently out of the historical record from this time;[53] much land that had previously belonged to the Church appears from later records to have fallen into lay hands. In the case of minsters whose pre-Viking Age charters have survived to be incorporated in the archives of later houses such as Barking or Glastonbury, one might surmise that the community had not wholly collapsed.[54] Determining the fate of individual congregations in the ninth and early tenth centuries is made more difficult by the recorded attitude of the monastic reformers of King Edgar's reign, notably Æthelwold, who had such a highly developed sense of what constituted a *monasterium* that he denied the existence of more than one such community in England before Abingdon's revival.[55] It seems wiser to reserve judgement as to the arrangements made by these early minsters across the First Viking Age, following Dumville in expressing caution before postulating their total demise, particularly in the case of those whose early charters survived to be incorporated into later monastic archives at the same site. On the other hand, the occupation of the same site by religious before and after the Danish wars is, on its own, insufficient evidence to argue that the later congregation was descended from the earlier, let alone that it might have traced an unbroken history.[56]

It may be advisable here to clarify the distinction between continuity in the use of a given site and the continuous maintenance of a specific congregation of

---

[52]   Fulk, letter to Alfred, trans. Keynes and Lapidge, *Alfred the Great*, pp. 182–3.

[53]   This is the case notably for the pre-Viking Age minsters of Northumbria whose early archives have not survived; whether their collapse was a consequence of Danish raiding or of later Danish settlement cannot be determined. Many of these places were again to support a church, frequently one of more-than-average importance in the late eleventh and twelfth centuries, but this in itself is not evidence of the continued ecclesiastical use of these sites across the period for which the sources are silent.

[54]   D. N. Dumville, *Wessex and England from Alfred to Edgar* (1992), pp. 29–36.

[55]   Æthelwold, 'An account of King Edgar's establishment of monasteries' (ed. and trans. Whitelock *et al.*, *Councils and Synods*, I, 142–54, at pp. 148–9, no. 33).

[56]   Those historians such as John Blair who have tended to place more confidence in the evidence for continuity before and after the First Viking Age would argue that although my reservations about site occupancy are valid for any one case in isolation, the overall pattern does point to widespread continuity.

religious women. Several places can be shown to have been occupied by religious of either gender (or both) at various times during the pre-Conquest period, perhaps with short interruptions about which contemporary sources are frequently silent. Few congregations can, however, match the genuinely continuous maintenance of the community of St Cuthbert, whose members abandoned their island home on Lindisfarne to travel with their precious relics around Northumbria before settling first at Chester-le-Street and finally at Durham, having retained a corporate identity intact across two centuries of insecurity of place.[57] The key to the successful preservation of this congregation lay surely in the saintly embodiment of its communal ideal; just as in the parallel case of the monks of St Philibert who moved through fear of the vikings from Noirmoutier to Tournus, the community was identified through its possession of relics of a notable saint and their collective promotion of his cult.[58] The only female congregation of our period which appears to have retained its communal identity after relocation to a new site is that of St Mildrith, and once again this community was united by its possession of relics of historical significance to the nuns.[59] Early in the eleventh century the women of Shaftesbury appear temporarily to have resorted to the refuge which Æthelred gave them at Bradford (which grant was motivated to a large degree by the need to provide a safe environment for the relics of Edward the Martyr of which the cloistered women had charge), but this was not a permanent relocation since the majority of the congregation returned subsequently to Shaftesbury (leaving a small cell behind to continue in religious devotion at Bradford).[60] In view of the obvious impracticability of religious women leaving such security as their own convents could provide and wandering unprotected through the countryside, it is unsurprising that there are no other recorded examples of migrant religious women, nor that the community of St Mildrith moved such a short

---

[57]   The Lindisfarne community was described as the 'church of St Cuthbert' as early as the 790s: Alcuin, *Epistola*, 16 (ed. Dümmler, p. 42). The first vernacular reference to the community of St Cuthbert is found in the record of the manumissions made by Ælfred *lareow*, priest of the Church of Durham in the second quarter of the eleventh century, and entered on the last leaf of the (now burnt) gospel book which King Æthelstan had given the community in 934 (British Library, Cotton MS Otho B. ix); see H. H. E. Craster, 'Some Anglo-Saxon Records of the See of Durham', *Archaeologia Aeliana*, 4 ser 1 (1925), 189–98, at p. 190. The peregrinations of this community during the Viking Age have been explored by Eric Cambridge, 'Why did the community of St Cuthbert settle at Chester-le-Street?', in *St Cuthbert, His Cult and His Community*, ed. G. Bonner *et al.* (1989), pp. 367–86.

[58]   Ermentarius, *Miracula S Filiberti* (ed. O. Holder-Egger, *MGH, Scriptores* XV.I, pp. 298–303). On the role of the cults of the dead in forging and sustaining communal religious identity see C. Cubitt, 'Universal and Local Saints in Anglo-Saxon England', in *Local Saints and Local Churches*, ed. R. Sharpe and A. Thacker (forthcoming).

[59]   One might remember that a number of male communities newly established in the tenth century at locations formerly occupied by nuns chose to venerate the female saints of early Anglo-Saxon England associated with their sites, for example Æthelwold's foundation at Ely.

[60]   *Charters of Shaftesbury Abbey*, ed. S. E. Kelly (1996), no. 29 (S 899).

distance. The question of the fate of congregations whose early documents survived the viking period must remain open, although theoretically these might also represent instances where a community's identity was sustained via the person or persons who preserved these documents, even though the site of the minster was abandoned.

Even bearing this distinction in mind there was indubitably, as far as the female religious experience was concerned, little institutional continuity across the First Viking Age. The only one of the sites where female congregations of religious were located in the seventh and eighth centuries that was still housing nuns at the Conquest was Barking, but it is not clear that that community had a continuous existence or whether the tenth-century nunnery was refounded on the site of the earlier minster.[61] It is just possible that descendants of the community of St Mildrith on Thanet were still active in the city of Canterbury in 1086; at the time of the Domesday survey the lands of Minster-in-Thanet had come into the possession of St Augustine's, Canterbury and there was only a church with one priest left on the island, but a congregation of St Mildrith's is attested in the eleventh century and four nuns who held land in alms of the abbot of St Augustine's in 1086 might, conceivably, have been the remnant of the former Thanet community.[62] Some additional tenth- and eleventh-century female houses could trace their origins back into the early period (namely Berkeley, Boxwell, Castor, Cheddar, Leominster, Wareham, Warwick, Wenlock, Wimborne, and Winchcombe), although none of these proved able to support a congregation to the end of the Anglo-Saxon period. Other communities of female religious newly founded in the tenth century had a similarly ephemeral existence, disappearing from the historical record before the Conquest: Abingdon, Ramsey, Reading and Southampton (*Hamtunia*).[63] The places at which religious women were found living in groups during the tenth and the eleventh centuries were not, by and large, the sites of early Anglo-Saxon nunneries or double houses and might indeed be taken to mark innovations in religious expression as much as in geographical location.[64] The Benedictine house created at Ely by St Æthelwold was for monks, not nuns. However many female communities it is possible to find during this period (and much more generous estimates than have been advanced by other historians are made in chapter 6 and in the survey of the places where congregations of women religious may have lived during this period which constitutes part II of this study[65]), the inequality of the representation of religious

---

[61] See part II, *s.n.* Barking.

[62] art II, *s.n.* Minster-in-Thanet.

[63] Those places that seem to have supported female religious for a part, but not the whole, of the period covered by this survey are discussed as a group below, chapter 6, §d.

[64] See below, chapter 6.

[65] The estimates made by other historians as to the numbers of religious houses for women active in the later pre-Conquest period have been reported above in the historiographical survey provided in chapter 1.

women as opposed to men in the contemporary literature remains marked and requires some explanation.

If an argument is to be advanced about why female religious houses vanish from the sources during and after the ninth century, it is necessary to attempt to quantify as far as possible just which early houses did cease to function, and when the most substantial decline in female monasticism occurred. It should be remembered that the decline in the number of charters issued for women's communities began in the second half of the eighth century, before the start of the Viking Age and may reflect a disenchantment with this form of religious observance which the Danish wars only served to accelerate.[66] Bearing in mind how difficult it can be to establish precisely when a religious congregation of either gender was founded, determining at which point a minster ceased to function (or no longer included any women) is even harder. A permanently dissolved community was obviously unable to record a narrative of the circumstances surrounding its demise, a task that was seldom likely to have been taken up by those who acquired its lands and title-deeds thereafter. The preservation, albeit often in the archives of male religious houses, of the pre-Viking Age royal diplomas of some early English minsters for women does at least suggest that their communal past had not entirely been forgotten, but the circumstances in which the later holders acquired such estates are seldom fully elaborated (and would frequently not make edifying reading). Various female religious houses that have been identified as active in the period before the ninth century are known only from chance references that illustrate just one instance in the community's history, as has already been mentioned; how long such places continued to house women beyond that one moment of visibility cannot be discovered. Many of the royal double houses which are better witnessed in their early years can only be assumed to have ceased to function as female communities on the grounds that they are later absent from the written record, not because any early medieval source provides a definitive statement about their dissolution. A significant contributory factor here is obviously the general decline in the production of Latin literature of all kinds in England in the first three quarters of the ninth century which has served to obscure historical understanding of this period,[67] but it is exacerbated in the case of female religious houses by the lack of

---

[66]   P. Wormald, 'St Hilda, saint and scholar (614–80)', in *The St Hilda's College Centenary Symposium*, ed. J. Mellanby (1993), pp. 93–103, at p. 95.

[67]   Much attention has been devoted by scholars to the state of Latin learning in the ninth century, for example N. Brooks, 'England in the ninth century: the crucible of defeat', *TRHS* 5 ser 29 (1979), 1–20, at pp. 14–16 and J. Morrish, 'King Alfred's letter as a source on learning in England', in *Studies in Earlier Old English Prose*, ed. P. E. Szarmach (Kalamazoo, MI, 1986), pp. 87–107. It has recently been exhaustively explored by Michael Lapidge, who has made a compelling case for accepting King Alfred's assertion that there were at the time of his accession few men south of the Humber with any knowledge of Latin: *Anglo-Latin Literature, 600–899* (1996), pp. 409–54, no. 16.

interest evinced in their activities by ecclesiastical writers in the tenth and eleventh centuries. An argument about the fate of these houses made from the pre-Conquest literature tends, therefore, to become an argument advanced from silence, while later medieval historians and particularly antiquaries such as Leland and Tanner have tended to extrapolate from that silence and turn the presumption that a house failed during the period into a definitive statement about its destruction at the hands of the Danes. The task of tracing back into the medieval period the origins of these stories about the demise of these early nunneries would certainly merit further investigation.

In exploring the fate of early Anglo-Saxon minsters, modern scholars have tended to turn to the handlist of pre-Conquest religious houses which constitutes the first appendix to David Knowles's and R. N. Hadcock's *Medieval Religious Houses, England and Wales*. Despite its obvious limitations and the frequently tentative conclusions it voices, this text has acquired an evidential status among historians such that its authority is often cited without caution. Robin Fleming and Jane Tibbetts Schulenburg, for example, have used this handlist as evidence for the effects of Danish raiding on England in the ninth century.[68] Schulenburg's statement (made in the context of a comparative study of the decline of female monastic houses in western Europe between the fifth and the eleventh centuries) that 'at least forty-one houses for women (including double houses) were destroyed by the Danes' formed the basis of Shari Horner's attempt to provide an historical context for the Old English poem *Juliana* and her argument about the particular relevance of the experience of early Christian martyrs to Anglo-Saxon nuns facing rape and martyrdom at the hands of the pagan vikings.[69] Equally, the section relating to tenth- and eleventh-century Anglo-Saxon circumstances in Bruce Venarde's ambitious book about women's monasticism in England and France between 850 and 1215 is heavily dependent on Knowles and Hadcock.[70]

A careful reading of Knowles's and Hadcock's appendix of pre-Conquest foundations reveals — as the authors were in fact themselves quite ready to admit — that the list was compiled largely from the *Collectanea* and Itinerary of the sixteenth-century antiquary, John Leland, Thomas Tanner's *Notitia Monastica* (first published in 1695), Dugdale's *Monasticon Anglicanum* (an early nineteenth-

---

[68] R. Fleming, 'Monastic lands and England's defence in the Viking Age', *English Historical Review*, 100 (1985), 247–65, and for a critical reading of this paper see Dumville, *Wessex*, ch. 2. See also J. T. Schulenburg, 'Women's monastic communities, 500–1100: Patterns of expansion and decline', *Signs. Journal of Women in Culture and Society*, 14 (1989), 261–92, at pp. 268–9 and 275–7; and idem., 'The heroics', pp. 45–6.

[69] S. Horner, 'Spiritual truth and sexual violence: the Old English *Juliana*, Anglo-Saxon nuns and the discourse of female monastic enclosure', *Signs. Journal of Women in Culture and Society*, 19 (1994), 658–75, at p. 659 (quoting Schulenburg, 'Women's monastic communities', p. 275).

[70] B. Venarde, *Women's Monasticism and Medieval Society* (Ithaca and London, 1997), pp. 24–8.

century edition of an originally seventeenth-century text). Use has further been made of the relevant volumes of the *Victoria County History*, many of which were published in the early years of this century, drawing overwhelmingly on antiquarian histories at least for those periods when the contemporary sources are least plentiful. On the basis of this research, Knowles and Hadcock identified approximately fourteen English religious houses occupied by women in the seventh and eighth centuries that failed to survive as far as *c.* 800;[71] a further twenty-nine houses previously occupied by women they asserted to have been destroyed, or to have ceased to function at some point during the ninth century. For the vast majority of this group Knowles and Hadcock ascribed dates of destruction in the 860s and 870s (coinciding with the period when the Danes caused the most political upheaval in Britain). These houses are listed in the table. Of the total number of houses listed, ten find place in the analytical survey of women's communities that makes up the second part of this study as the putative sites of female congregations between the late ninth and mid-eleventh centuries (these are marked with a dagger). For the rest, although the manner and circumstances of their destruction, dissolution, or desertion cannot necessarily readily be established, that they have disappeared from the historical record as female religious houses by the start of the tenth century seems clear.[72]

I have dwelt at such length on this minor point and presented the information in this form in order to sound a note of caution. As a starting point for further research Knowles' and Hadcock's list is invaluable and has no parallel. As the evidence on which to base any conclusions about male or female religious houses before the Conquest it must, however, be accepted as being seriously deficient.[73] Further study might reveal other institutions to add to their list, and increase the total number of institutions attested in the pre-Viking-Age that appear no longer to have supported women after *c.* 880, but such efforts would not alter the essential point at issue here: a substantial number of minsters for women vanished from the historical record during the course of the later eighth and ninth centuries and failed to reappear as the home of a community of women religious in the tenth century. Various of the houses listed in the table appear from the dates

[71]   These supposed female congregations were at Abingdon, Aldingbourne, Aylesbury, Bath (converted to a male house), Coventry, Gloucester (SS Peter and Paul), Eastry, Ebbsfleet, Hartlepool, Malling, *Penitanham*, Tadcaster, Withington and Wytham.

[72]   John Blair points out that of the places listed in table 1 only six (Boxwell, East Dereham, Ebchester, Eltisley, Hoo and South Shields) were not to his knowledge churches of status in the eleventh century. This will support his impression of the substantial continuity of place in religious observance across the pre-Conquest period, but does not affect my argument that their *female* communities were no longer demonstrably resident.

[73]   It is striking for how many of the houses said by Knowles and Hadcock to have ceased to support women during the First Viking Age the date of *c.* 870 is attached to the institution's demise, and it is far from clear why this should be so. I hope to return to the historiography of the monastic experience of the Danish wars on a future occasion.

assigned to their dissolution by Knowles and Hadcock to have still supported women religious into the start of our period, for example the Mercian double house at Repton which is usually presumed no longer to have been home to a religious community beyond the winter of 873–4 when a viking army overwintered there.[74] However, since my concern in this study is with the female experience of the religious life beyond the start of King Alfred's reign, and not primarily with the fate of pre-Viking-Age minsters for women, only those communities of religious women that can be shown from written evidence of any date to have been active within our period (rather than hesitating on the point of dissolution) are surveyed below. Others might quarrel with my application of this criterion and question whether, for example, Boxwell and St Osyth's at Chich have genuine claim to inclusion, or if Burton-on-Trent has been rightly omitted.[75] Such quibbles do not alter the question at the heart of this study: how can the

---

[74] Anglo-Saxon Chronicle, *s.a.* 874. There is no evidence that religious life continued here after the Danes' departure in 874, although Repton was once more a church of significance, with a large cemetery, in the twelfth century. A mass burial found west of the Anglo-Saxon church and outside the defences built by the Danes containing approximately 250 disarticulated bodies can be dated to 873–4 from the silver pennies found with the deposit; these are probably members of the Danish army, either a group that had died together of some epidemic disease, or others brought from further afield for burial at Repton. See M. Biddle and B. Kjølbye-Biddle, 'Repton and the Vikings', *Antiquity*, 66 (1992), 36–51. It is no longer thought, as was once suggested, that the grave is filled with the slaughtered members of the monastic community.

[75] Boxwell was said by Leland to have been destroyed by the Danes (*The Itinerary of John Leland in or about the Years 1535–1543*, ed. L. Toulmin Smith, 5 vols. [1964], IV, 133); St Osyth's housed a religious community in the eleventh century, maintaining the cult of its patron saint, but there is no evidence that congregation included women. The identification of a pre-Viking-Age minster for women at Burton on Trent depends on the authority of the eleventh-century Life of the Irish saint, Modwenna (Monenna), supposedly active across a period from the time of St Patrick to that of Aldfrith, king of Northumbria 686–705. According to her hagiographer, Conchubranus, she established a minster for women in England, which was believed in the twelfth-century by the monks of Burton to have been on an island in the Trent called Andresey: *Vita sanctae Monenne*, I, 15, III, 3 (ed. and transl. Ulster Society for Medieval Latin Studies, *Seanchas Ard Mhacha* 9 [1979], 270–3 and 10 [1982], 432–5). It is difficult to extract much that is historically useful from this narrative, which offers no evidence for the presence of an active female community at Burton during the period covered by this study; the same source has also been taken to provide evidence for the presence of a tenth-century female community at Polesworth. Had an early women's house ever existed in the vicinity of Burton it is impossible to say when it might have ceased to support the activities of religious women. The historical abbey of Burton was founded in the early eleventh century by Wulfric Spott: *Charters of Burton Abbey*, ed. P. H. Sawyer (1979), no. 28 (S 906: King Æthelred's confirmation of the abbey's privileges and the lands granted by Wulfric, dated 1004); *Charters of Burton Abbey*, ed. Sawyer, no. 29 (S 1536: the will of Wulfric, describing the abbey's foundation and endowment, dateable 1002x1004). For a summary of received opinion about this putative minster see Knowles and Hadcock, *Medieval Religious Houses*, p. 469.

Table 1

The supposed 'destruction' of women's religious houses in the ninth century
(after Knowles and Hadcock, *Medieval Religious Houses*, Appendix 1)

	House	*Date of supposed destruction*
‡	Barking	870
	Beverley	*c.* 867
‡	Boxwell	?
	Burton on Trent	874
	Carlisle	*c.* 875
‡	Castor	*c.* 870
‡	Chester SS Peter and Paul	after 875?
	East Dereham	*c.* 870
	Ebchester	*c.* 875?
‡	Eltisley	*c.* 870?
	Ely	870
‡	Folkestone	before 927
	Hackness	*c.* 870
	Hanbury, Threekingham and Weedon	875
	Hoo	ninth century
‡	Leominster	ninth century
‡	Minster-in-Sheppey	before 900
	Oxford, St Frideswide	*c.* 874?
	Peakirk	*c.* 870
	Repton	874
‡	St Osyth at Chich	870?
‡	Shaftesbury	before 888?
	South Shields	*c.* 865–75?
	Thorney	*c.* 870
	Tynemouth	865–75
	Watton	ninth century?
	Westbury-on-Trym [cf Berkeley ‡]	ninth century?
	Whitby	*c.* 867

‡   Signifies a house surveyed among the communities of women religious in part II.

apparent demise of female monasticism across the First Viking Age be reconciled with the fact that there were many more women's religious congregations active in England in the last two centuries before the Conquest than the eight nunneries recorded as landholders in Domesday Book, those patronised by the West Saxon royal house to which historians have conventionally paid attention?

A second note of caution must be introduced here. We observed earlier that the decline in the evidence for the foundation of new female religious houses and the endowment of existing ones long preceded the onset of the Danish wars, being visible from about the middle of the eighth century.[76] While it may well be imagined that the disruptions during and after the viking wars did women's (and indeed men's) religious houses no good, it cannot be denied that the fervour for endowing women's monastic houses found among the early Christian Anglo-Saxon aristocracy had already begun to diminish before the onset of Danish raids, and before the effects of the Carolingian reforms and the restrictions they placed on women's freedom of movement, association and action could have been felt in England. (Which is not to say that the spiritual devotion of Englishwomen had in any way decreased, merely that their capacity to acquire and retain land for exclusively religious use was in some manner diminished.) Explanations for the decline of the endowed women's minster must be sought in the same sphere as must the causes of that institution's considerable early success, namely in the dynastic and landed strategies of the Anglo-Saxon nobility and, perhaps even more significantly, royalty. In which case, it needs to be accounted for primarily within an English, and indeed an English aristocratic, milieu rather than by recourse to explanations arising from external pressures or influences.

The First Viking Age has been used as a convenient chronological division across which the diminution in female religious houses can be measured, not least because of the difficulties addressed here of establishing precisely when before or during the ninth century individual early communities ceased to function. Yet, whatever were the factors that led particular families to choose to accommodate the vocations of their female members within their larger estate-strategies rather than to make separate provision potentially removing the land from the kin's control, these were felt before the Danish wars began. Once Carolingian ecclesiastical notions of the behaviour appropriate to women in religion and the restrictions consequent on the imposition of tighter external control on their communities began to be articulated in an English context (together with ideas of uniform regularity of observance), the contrast with the situation in the late seventh and early eighth centuries became much more sharply marked. However, we see in the tenth century the consequences of a longer period of change in English attitudes to the endowment and support of religious houses for women, changes that as we have shown can be attributed to no single cause but need to be

---

76   Wormald, 'St Hilda', p. 95; above, p. 26.

placed within several overlapping contexts, all masked by the greater obscurity produced by the viking wars and the general dearth of written evidence from the ninth century.

Chapter 4

Women and the tenth-century monastic revolution

> In some places also [Edgar] established cloistered women [*mynecœna*] and entrusted them to his consort Ælfthryth, that she might help them in every necessity.
>
> Æthelwold, 'An account'.[1]

> It is right that priests, and equally vowesses [*nunnan*] as well, live according to rule and maintain their chastity if they wish to dwell in a minster or command respect in the sight of the world.
>
> Wulfstan, Institutes of Polity.[2]

Bishop Æthelwold was to assert that before the reform of the male community at Abingdon in the 960s the 'right rule of life' was maintained in England at no more places than one, namely Dunstan's house at Glastonbury.[3] Nevertheless, even ignoring the bishop's insistence on Benedictine regularity as the defining feature of monasticism (an anachronism in England before the revolution of religious observance in Edgar's reign), it is hard to identify many places where women religious might have lived in the early years of the tenth century. From the large numbers of female houses witnessed before the First Viking Age only Barking could lay certain claim to a community of female religious in the 950s, and its history may well have been interrupted during the viking wars.[4] Otherwise, there are fewer than ten establishments that might be thought for any reason to have sustained a communal existence into the reign of King Alfred and beyond, none of which Æthelwold would have categorised with places exemplary of 'right living'. It can with varying degrees of confidence be asserted that there were around the turn of the ninth century religious women at Bedwyn, Cheddar,

---

[1]   Æthelwold, 'An account of King Edgar's establishment of monasteries' (ed. and trans. Whitelock *et al.*, *Councils and Synods*, I, 142–54, at p. 150, no. 33).

[2]   Wulfstan, *I Polity*, 85 (ed. K. Jost, *Die "Institutes of Polity, Civil and Ecclesiastical"* [Bern, 1959], p. 129, trans. following M. Swanton, *Anglo-Saxon Prose* [2nd edn, 1993], pp 187–201, at p. 199).

[3]   Æthelwold, 'An account' (ed. and trans. Whitelock *et al.*, *Councils*, I, 148–9, no. 33).

[4]   Whitelock, *ASWills*, no. 2 (S 1483); *Charters of Barking Abbey*, ed. C. R. Hart (forthcoming), no. 9 (S 552a). Full details of the sources for each of the places mentioned in this paragraph are given in the analytical survey in part II; brief attention was paid to the fate of women's minsters in the Viking wars above in chapter 3, and will be again in chapter 6, §a.

Wareham, Wenlock, Wimborne, and Winchcombe, but whether any of these places housed women beyond that single moment for which evidence of their presence has survived is less clear.[5] Similar uncertainty surrounds the histories at the end of the First Viking Age of the congregations of Berkeley, Castor, Leominster, and the fate of the women of St Mildrith, formerly of Minster-in-Thanet; each of these early minsters was said again to have housed religious women in the eleventh century. Just two new female religious houses were founded during the reigns of Alfred and Edward the Elder: King Alfred's own establishment at Shaftesbury and the house begun by his wife at Winchester. A cursory glance at map 1 will, however, reveal that more than sixty places can be identified from written sources as the sites of congregations of women religious during the last two centuries before the Conquest. In the light of the evident discontinuity in female monastic observance across the First Viking Age, this apparent profusion of late Anglo-Saxon female houses might be thought to point to a notable flowering of women's monasticism after the middle years of the tenth century, to which the rhetoric surrounding the monastic revolution of Edgar's reign seems, indeed, to bear witness.

The tendency of much of the recent scholarly literature has been to enlarge our understanding of the vitality of female monasticism before the Conquest through the collection of as many examples as possible of places where women can be shown to have been living a religious life during the tenth and eleventh centuries. A wider recognition of the flexibility and diversity of female modes of religious expression in the later Anglo-Saxon period will permit the identification of many more women's houses than a rigid Benedictine interpretation of what constitutes a nunnery would allow.[6] Various writers have remarked on the incongruity of historians' persistent preoccupation with only a handful of these late Anglo-Saxon women's houses, and have challenged the negative presumptions made in earlier generations about the significance of nuns in this period. But to address the issue as Patricia Halpin and Marc Meyer have recently sought to do is to pose a rather different question from that asked, for example, by David Knowles, who did recognise that there were religious women outside the Benedictine nunneries of southern England.[7] In identifying so many

---

5   Bedwyn: H. Merritt, 'Old English entries in a manuscript at Bern', *Journal of English and Germanic Philology*, 33 (1934), 343–51, at pp. 346–7; Cheddar: Robertson, *ASCharters*, no. 45 (S 806); Wareham: Asser, Life of Alfred, ch. 49 (ed. W. H. Stevenson, *Asser's Life of King Alfred* [1904], p. 36); Wenlock: BCS 587 (S 221); Wimborne: Anglo-Saxon Chronicle, *s.a.* 900; Winchcombe: BCS 575 (S 1442). Of these only Wareham can be shown to have housed women later in the tenth century: Anglo-Saxon Chronicle 982.

6   This has been argued effectively by Patricia Halpin, 'Women religious in late Anglo-Saxon England', *Haskins Society Journal*, 6 (1994), 97–110. Her work follows on from that of Marc Anthony Meyer, especially his 'Patronage of West Saxon royal nunneries in late Anglo-Saxon England', *Revue bénédictine*, 91 (1981), 332–58.

7   D. Knowles, *The Monastic Order in England* (2nd edn., 1963), pp. 136–7 and notes.

religious women located away from the royally patronised communities that have dominated the contemporary sources, Meyer and Halpin have raised an important question about how female congregations of this period ought to be categorised, but Meyer in particular has failed directly to address that problem. Has this work on the places where women religious lived in the later tenth and eleventh centuries provided evidence for the siting of additional nunneries, like the royal West Saxon houses? If so, we must reconsider why it is that these institutions have been so ill-served in the historical record.[8]

Alternatively, have examples rather been accumulated of devout women living communally (or as avowed individuals) outside the cloister in which case, how should these properly be fitted into the framework of late Anglo-Saxon ecclesiastical organisation? By concentrating on evidence for groups or single women 'affiliated in uncertain terms with nearby men's foundations', Patricia Halpin has taken the instances she has collected to exemplify 'women practising alternative religious lifestyles', arrangements that were not officially recognised and ran counter to the ideals of the tenth-century reformers.[9] The problem of official recognition is one to which we shall return (for her analysis might here be challenged), but even were this explanation sufficient to explain the position of women living under the shadow of male congregations, it cannot encompass all the non-Benedictine types of female religious observance surveyed in this study. If it is indeed the case that more persistent investigation of the sources leads to the identification of religious women, not of institutions, it is necessary to address the terminological issue that finding poses, namely how such *religiosae feminae* should — singly and collectively — be described. This is not a trivial question; indeed it will be shown that the issue of how to label and categorise differences in religious lifestyle was one that exercised later Anglo-Saxon ecclesiastical legislators. Before the language of the post-reform female religious life can be investigated it is, however, necessary to look more closely at the impact on women of the wider revolution in monastic organisation in the tenth century.

Women and the tenth-century monastic revolution

The rhetoric surrounding the revolution in monastic organisation in mid-tenth-century England extended as much to female as to male congregations of

---

[8]   This was precisely the question that Sally Thompson asked about the sources for nunneries in England after the Norman Conquest: 'Why English nunneries had no history: a study of the problems of the English nunneries founded after the Conquest', in *Distant Echoes*, ed. J. A. Nichols and L. T. Shank (Kalamazoo, Michigan, 1984), pp. 131–49. As I have suggested above, pp. 20–21, although Thompson was addressing many of the same issues that concern us here, there are fundamental differences between the types of congregations with which she and I are concerned, as will become apparent during the course of this chapter.

[9]   Halpin, 'Women', p. 107.

religious.[10] The *Regularis concordia*, agreed at a council at Winchester in the 970s at which abbesses were represented, directed that Edgar's queen Ælfthryth 'should be the protectress and fearless guardian of the communities of nuns; so that he himself helping the men and his consort the women there should be no cause for any breath of scandal'.[11] Attention was paid at the council to the particular need to protect religious women. Archbishop Dunstan was quoted as adding an injunction that monks and other men, regardless of their rank, should be kept out of nunneries, and that those with spiritual authority over *sanctimoniales* should use their powers in the women's best interests, so that their entry into a nunnery would not hinder the sisters' regular observance.[12] In the vernacular account of Edgar's establishment of monasteries written as a prologue to his translation of the Rule of St Benedict and quoted at the head of this chapter, Bishop Æthelwold placed equal emphasis on the creation of nunneries and on the role of Ælfthryth as their protectress; the king was said ever to be inquiring about the welfare of the monks, and he kindly exhorted her to take thought for the nuns in the same way, following his example.[13] Æthelwold further warned abbesses in particular against the dangers of the world outside the cloister:[14]

---

[10]   The most recent contribution to the fate of women in the tenth-century monastic revolution is Pauline Stafford, 'Queens, nunneries and reforming churchmen: Gender, religious status and reform in tenth- and eleventh-century England', *Past and Present*, 163 (1999), 3–35.

[11]   *Regularis concordia*, proem, ch. 3 (ed. and trans. T. Symons [1953], p. 2). That abbesses were present at this council is clear from ibid., proem, ch. 4 (pp. 2–3): Edgar 'synodale concilium Wintoniae fieri decreuit. .... non tantum episcopi uerum etiam abbates ac abbatissae ... uoti compotes referri non distulerunt'. Dagmar Schneider has drawn attention to the fact that abbesses were specifically listed among the participants at Church councils in the later Anglo-Saxon period, although their presence was rarely recorded before the Viking Age: 'Anglo-Saxon women in the religious life: a study of the status and position of women in an early mediaeval society' (PhD thesis, University of Cambridge, 1985), pp. 295–9.

[12]   *Regularis concordia*, ch. 7 (ed. and trans. Symons, pp. 4–5). Bruce Venarde has taken the explicit discussion of religious women in the *Regularis concordia* to be 'a reflection of the importance of religious women in the earlier tenth century' and has argued that 'there was considerably more continuity of practice between the early and late tenth century in nunneries than in the communities of monks': *Women's Monasticism and Medieval Society* (Ithaca, New York and London, 1997), pp. 25–6. One could quarrel with both statements.

[13]   Æthelwold, 'An account' (ed. and trans. Whitelock *et al.*, *Councils*, I, 150, no. 33). This text may have been written after Edgar's death during the period of the anti-monastic reaction (D. Whitelock, 'The authorship of the account of King Edgar's establishment of monasteries', in *Philological Essays*, ed. J. L. Rosier [The Hague, 1970], pp. 125–36, at p. 136, reprinted in Whitelock, *History, Law and Literature in 10th-11th Century England* [1981], no. VII) but, if so, it may be seen that Ælfthryth did not relinquish her role as guardian of nunneries on her husband's death.

[14]   Æthelwold, 'An account' (ed. and trans. Whitelock *et al.*, *Councils*, I, 153, no. 33).

> We also instruct abbesses to be deeply loyal and to serve the precepts
> of the holy rule with all their hearts, and we enjoin by the command
> of God Almighty, that none of them presume senselessly to give
> God's estates either to their kinsfolk, or to secular great persons,
> neither for money nor flattery.

Secular legislation of the later tenth and eleventh centuries similarly encompassed religious women as well as monks in its directives concerning appropriate monastic behaviour or the protection of ecclesiastical property. All the servants of God, among whom women were specifically mentioned, were instructed in two of King Æthelred's codes issued early in the eleventh century to 'submit to their duty and live according to their rule and zealously intercede for all Christian people'.[15] Women religious, together with widows, were accorded particular protection in law; penalties were imposed on those who injured a woman who had taken vows of religion and on those who did violence to a widow,[16] while retribution awaited any who attempted to marry veiled women. In his letter to the English of 1019/1020, Cnut ordered that if anyone tried to marry a consecrated vowess or a cloistered woman 'he is to be an outlaw before God and excommunicated from all Christendom and to forfeit to the king all that he owns unless he desists quickly and atones very deeply to God'.[17] It is thus apparent that female religious vocations were recognised and provided for within the structures of the later Anglo-Saxon Church. However, once one looks beyond the general admonitions in the prescriptive literature in search of contemporaneous references to individual religious women or their congregations, it is striking how poor is the evidence and the extent to which it focuses on that one geographical cluster of houses already identified as occupying a privileged place in the historical record.

Scholars of female involvement in the reform movement have, perhaps inevitably, tended to devote their energies to those nine or so female monastic institutions for which the fullest sources have survived, as was discussed in the first chapter.[18] Generally it has been presumed that the royal connections of most of these houses would have caused them to play a significant part in the royally-

---

[15] V Æthelred, ch. 4; VI Æthelred, ch. 2; and compare also I Cnut, ch. 6a (ed. F. Liebermann, *Die Gesetze der Angelsachsen* [3 vols., Halle, 1903–16], I, 238, 246, 288). The provisions of VI Æthelred, ch. 3 (ibid., I, 249) concerning disputes within reformed houses relate both to houses of *canonici* and of *sanctimoniales*, see Stafford, 'Queens, nunneries and reforming churchmen', pp. 22–3 and n. 47, where the chapter is quoted and translated in full

[16] VI Æthelred, ch. 39 (ed. Liebermann, *Die Gesetze*, I, 256). The legal protection of widows is discussed below in chapter 5.

[17] Cnut, letter to the English 1019/1020, ch. 16 (ed. Liebermann, *Die Gesetze*, I, 274). For the language of this clause and the distinction made in legal texts between *nunne* (vowess) and *mynecænu* (cloistered woman), see further below, pp. 96–103.

[18] These are Amesbury, Barking, Horton, Romsey, Shaftesbury (and its cell at Bradford-on-Avon), Wherwell, Wilton and the Nunnaminster at Winchester. This group of houses has most recently been discussed by J. Crick, 'The wealth, patronage, and connections of women's houses in late Anglo-Saxon England', *Revue bénédictine*, 109 (1999), 154–85.

Map 4   Nunneries in England, 940–1066

sponsored movement for the revival of monasticism in the reign of Edgar,[19] yet this is something it is hard to demonstrate. The Nunnaminster at Winchester is the sole house in this group explicitly to be mentioned in any contemporaneous account of the process by which the precepts of the Rule of St Benedict were introduced to the monasteries of Edgar's reign. Wulfstan of Winchester in his Life of Æthelwold recorded in considerable detail the ejection of the community of clerks from the Old Minster at Winchester and their replacement with Benedictines, trained at Æthelwold's house at Abingdon, dwelling at some length on the reasons why such drastic measures were necessary.[20] The reorganisation of the Nunnaminster he dealt with much more succinctly and without justificatory explanation: '[Æthelwold] had plans too for the third monastery at Winchester, known in English as the Nunnaminster ... Here he established flocks of nuns, placing over them Æthelthryth'.[21] Otherwise the reform of women's houses was described by Wulfstan only in his blanket summary of the outcome of Æthelwold's efforts: 'And so it came about, with the king's agreement, that thanks both to Dunstan's counsel and activity and to Æthelwold's unremitting aid, monasteries were established everywhere in England, some for monks, some for nuns (*quaedam sanctimonialibus*), governed by abbots and abbesses who lived according to the Rule'.[22] Later medieval historians followed Wulfstan in reporting the institution of cloistered women at Winchester,[23] but the only other house for

---

[19]   See for example Knowles, *The Monastic Order*, pp. 48–52, or T. Symons, '*Regularis concordia*: History and derivation', in *Tenth-Century Studies*, ed. D. Parsons (1975), pp. 37–59, at pp. 40–1: 'To [a list of male communities reformed by the mid-970s] we may be fairly safe in adding at least three houses of nuns: the Nunnaminster (Winchester), Shaftesbury and Wilton'. Symons' authority was given here as F. M. Stenton, *Anglo-Saxon England* (3rd edn, 1971), p. 445. But Stenton's point was not that these three nunneries had been formally reformed, rather that they were active during the first half of the tenth century when the organised male religious life was in abeyance. The particular significance of the association between women's houses and the West Saxon queen has now been explored by Stafford, 'Queens, nunneries and reforming churchmen', especially pp. 16–22.

[20]   Wulfstan, *Vita S Æthelwoldi*, chs. 16–18 (ed. and trans. M. Lapidge and M. Winterbottom, *Wulfstan of Winchester, The Life of St Æthelwold* [1991], pp. 30–3). The influences inspiring Æthelwold's actions have been discussed by P. Wormald, 'Æthelwold and his continental counterparts: Contact, comparison, contrast', in *Bishop Æthelwold*, ed. B. Yorke (1988), pp. 13–42.

[21]   Wulfstan, *Vita S Æthelwoldi*, ch. 22 (ed. and trans. Lapidge and Winterbottom, pp. 36–9): 'In tercio quoque Wintoniensi coenobio, quod Anglice Nunnamenster appellatur ...'. See also Ælfric, *Vita S Æthelwoldi*, ch. 17 (ibid., p. 76): 'In Monasterio namque Nonnarum ordinauit sanctimoniales, quibus matrem praefecit Ætheldritham'.

[22]   Wulfstan, *Vita S Æthelwoldi*, ch. 27 (ibid., pp. 42–3); compare Ælfric, *Vita S Æthelwold*, ch. 18 (pp. 76–7).

[23]   The Nunnaminster's reform by Æthelwold was described by William of Malmesbury, *De gestis pontificum Anglorum* §78 (ed. N. E. S. A. Hamilton, Rolls Series, 52 [1870], p.174). John of Worcester's account (*Chronicon, s.a.* 963, ed. and trans. R. R. Darlington *et al.*, *The Chronicle of John of Worcester, II The Annals from 450 to 1066* [1995], 416–17), however,

which there is a later medieval reform narrative — if it can so grandiloquently be described — is Romsey. John of Worcester reported that King Edgar had placed cloistered women at the monastery of Romsey which his grandfather, Edward the Elder had built.[24]

The monastic revolution for men involved the endowment of new institutions adhering to the regular life as well as the reorganisation of existing ones, but none of this group of well-sourced women's houses found their origins while Edgar was king.[25] Early in Æthelred's reign Edgar's widow supposedly established two houses for women (at Amesbury and Wherwell) neither of which can easily be shown to have fitted directly into the Benedictine movement.[26] Chatteris was the most recent foundation to find mention among the female religious landholders in Domesday Book;[27] unlike the rest of the nunneries privileged in the historical record, this was a noble foundation, established by Eadnoth, bishop of Dorchester, for his sister. As a former member of Oswald's community at Worcester and later abbot of Ramsey, Eadnoth had unimpeachable reform-connections, but the account of his establishment of Chatteris survives only in a twelfth-century account of the benefactors of Ely and makes no allusion to the mode of observance practised by the first women.[28] The one remaining nunnery from this group that should be mentioned in the context of the tenth-century monastic revolution is Barking, whose history in this respect presents particular interpretative problems. As already mentioned, uncertainty surrounds the circumstances in which the religious life was revived at Barking after its presumed interruption during the viking wars, the archaeological evidence

---

referred to the institution of nuns only in general terms: 'St Æthelwold ... established monks at the Old Minster after the expulsion of the secular clergy. For he, who was the king's special counsellor, urged him most vigorously to expel the secular clergy from the monasteries, and to command that monks and nuns should be installed in them'.

[24]   John of Worcester, *Chronicon, s. a.* 967 (ed. and trans. Darlington *et al.*, II, 416–19).

[25]   Unless Horton is to be understood as newly founded by Edgar; according to Goscelin's Life of St Wulfhild, ch. 4 (ed. M. Esposito, 'La vie de Sainte Vulfhilde par Goscelin de Cantorbéry', *Analecta Bollandiana*, 32 [1913], 10–26, at p. 17), the king gave Barking and five other nunneries (*domus familiarum*) to Wulfhild, one of which was at Horton. There is no evidence for a female religious house at Horton before this period, although an abbess of Horton was mentioned in the *Liber Vitae* of Hyde Abbey: *Liber Vitae: Register and Martyrology of New Minster and Hyde Abbey, Winchester*, ed. W. de G. Birch (1892), p. 57. See further part II, *s.n.* Horton.

[26]   Both were reputedly founded by Edgar's widow Ælfthryth, allegedly as an act of penance for her involvement in the murder of Edward the Martyr, and were apparently closely connected. See further part II, *s.n.* Amesbury, Wherwell. Barbara Yorke ('"Sisters under the skin?" Anglo-Saxon nuns and nunneries in southern England', in *Medieval Women in Southern England*, ed. K. Bate *et al.* [1989], pp. 95–117, at pp. 97–8) has spoken of a 'wave' of new female monastic foundations in the later period, of which the first was Shaftesbury, but so sporadic is their endowment during the tenth century it can really be characterised as little more than a ripple.

[27]   Crick, 'The wealth', p. 170.

[28]   *Liber Eliensis*, II, 71 (ed. E. O. Blake [1962], pp. 140–1).

apparently pointing to considerable activity on the site in the first half of the tenth century; it is unclear whether hagiographical accounts of Queen Ælfthryth's assumption of direct control over the nunnery following her ejection of its abbess, Wulfhild, could be thought to have brought the house within the orbit of the reform.[29]

If it is difficult to demonstrate the direct involvement of these nine most celebrated nunneries in the Benedictine revival,[30] it is even harder to show how any other tenth-century female community played a part in that movement. In contradistinction to male houses, for which several reform narratives have survived, there are no surviving accounts of the process by which any nunnery was reformed beyond those already mentioned relating to the Nunnaminster at Winchester and Romsey. The silence of the extant sources on this subject raises various questions. It might indicate that no such narratives were composed in the tenth century. If they were not, does this reflect a contemporary opinion that female houses were not in need of reform, that there was nothing to report, or is it rather indicative of a reluctance on the part of the tenth-century reformers to record such information, a deliberate suppression of events that did occur?[31]

It is remarkable that none of the literature of the period mentioned specifically the abuses supposedly perpetrated by female religious, although the indolence, gluttony, material greed and immorality of the unreformed male clerks was frequently commented upon.[32] Is it possible that English nunneries were not

---

[29]   Goscelin, *Vita S Wulfhildae*, ch. 9 (ed. Esposito, p. 21); see further part II, *s.n.* Barking.

[30]   The sources can be approached differently, as recently by Pauline Stafford, who has argued ('Queens, nunneries and reforming churchmen', pp. 22–30) that although the sources are reticent as to how precisely reform was effected, the changed climate following the promulgation of reforming ideals presented nunneries with opportunities further to distance themselves from lay control.

[31]   For a recent and rather different approach to this problem of 'houses without history' see Stafford, 'Queens, nunneries and reforming churchmen'.

[32]   Æthelwold criticised the behaviour of unreformed clergy in the proem to the *Regularis concordia* (§2, ed. and trans. Symons, pp. 1–2); and in 'An account' (ed. and trans. Whitelock *et al.*, *Councils*, I, 150, no. 33). Æthelwold's biographer, Wulfstan of Winchester, explained the saint's intolerance of the 'detestable blasphemers against God': *Vita S Æthelwoldi*, ch. 16 (ed. and trans. Lapidge and Winterbottom, pp. 30–1). The terms of King Edgar's privilege for the New Minster, Winchester (ed. Whitelock *et al.*, *Councils*, I, 121–33, no. 31 [S 745]), were also highly critical of the unreformed clergy, particularly §vii. Similar charges were put into the mouth of Pope John XII in a papal privilege supposedly dated 963 and granting permission for the ejection from Winchester of the 'canons hateful to God and to all the worshippers of the catholic faith' (ed. Whitelock *et al.*, *Councils*, I, 109–13, no. 29), but Julia Barrow has recently shown this to be a twelfth-century forgery: 'English cathedral communities and reform in the late tenth and the eleventh centuries', in *Anglo-Norman Durham*, ed. D. Rollason *et al.* (1994), pp. 25–39, at pp. 37–8. Byrhtferth of Ramsey also commented on the evils of unreformed monks: *Vita S Oswaldi* (ed. J. Raine, *The Historians of the Church of York*, Rolls Series 71 [3 vols., 1879–94], I, 399–475, at p. 411).

in fact forcibly reformed as were male houses such as Milton, Chertsey and the Old and New Minsters at Winchester,[33] or at least that reform of women's houses was not undertaken on the same scale as that for men? Unreformed female communities may have been organised around looser systems which proved more amenable to restructuring in accordance with the imposed norms of the Rule of St Benedict, without the necessity to resort to the confrontational methods adopted by Æthelwold elsewhere. The silence of the sources might here indicate the peaceful adoption of the Rule of St Benedict by congregations of placid and compliant women. It may indeed have been that there was no systematic 'reform' of female institutions: they were expected rather to institute the precepts of the *Regularis concordia* on their own initiative, perhaps with the local bishop making a later visitation to verify that the finer details were being properly observed.[34]

Alternatively it is possible that there was some larger ideological rationale behind the apparent silence of contemporary witnesses on this score, perhaps an anxiety that overt allusion to the failings of women dedicated to God might bring the institution of monasticism into disrepute. If the West Saxon and Mercian aristocracy was to be persuaded to go on committing its daughters to the religious life, noble families would need some assurances about the physical and moral security of the institutions to which their women would be consigned. Any vilification of the lives of those already within nunneries might have much more serious repercussions for future recruitment than would the dissemination of similar criticisms of male houses, so leading reforming authors to ignore the vices and immorality of unreformed religious women. (Since no such scruples had prevented Boniface, Alcuin or the compilers of the canons of the eighth-century reforming church councils from castigating the luxury, sexual immorality and spiritual indolence of the nuns in their day, this must reflect an alteration in attitudes in the post-Viking Age towards the consigning of daughters to the religious life.[35]) The issue of recruitment is of particular relevance if Leyser's argument about the flourishing of tenth-century Saxon nunneries is thought pertinent to English circumstances also: noblemen seeking to prevent their daughters from producing further heirs who would dilute their familial lines would have needed substantial reassurances about the continuing chastity of noble nuns.[36] One may reasonably assume that some reforming measures were undertaken (certainly Edith was visited at Wilton by Æthelwold and the criticisms

---

[33]   Anglo-Saxon Chronicle, 964. Bishop Æthelwold does appear to have taken a particularly tough line over clerical behaviour, for secular clerks were not so energetically expelled from other religious houses by either St Oswald or St Dunstan.

[34]   Goscelin's Life of Edith appears to imply that this was much the way in which the 'reform' of Wilton was effected: S. Ridyard, *The Royal Saints of Anglo-Saxon England* (1988), p. 141, n. 5.

[35]   Examples of the sorts of criticisms levelled against eighth-century religious women by their contemporaries have been collected above, chapter 2, n. 102.

[36]   K. J. Leyser, *Rule and Conflict in an Early Medieval Society* (1979), p. 64.

he then made of her over-luxurious dress might be indicative of his taking a general interest in the way the house was conducted[37]), however it is impossible to determine when the new forms of life were instituted at any given nunnery, whereas some relative, if not highly accurate, chronology for the progress of the male reform can be invented.[38]

Could it be simply that female communities of any type were so few in the third quarter of the tenth century that their reorganisation excited little comment? It is, admittedly, unclear just how many communities for women there were in England at the time of the Winchester council, one might hazard a guess at six or eight monastic or semi-monastic houses plus the various establishments gathered more informally round individual *religiosae feminae*.[39] There were not, however, very many communities for men active in this period either, yet their reform was described contemporaneously. Religious women of aristocratic background would have had as many vested interests in the lands and material wealth of the communities to which they belonged as their male counterparts, as well as being firmly committed to a monastic lifestyle which many had practised since childhood. It is hard to conjecture that they — or their families — would have acquiesced silently to the major social and economic upheaval their forcible ejection from the minsters would have created. But this is to argue from silence. We hear the defeated clerks at second-hand, through the rhetoric of the reformers: from this battle, the victors' despatches only have been preserved. Female non-combatants were — seemingly — mute.

It should further be noted that distinctions cannot readily be drawn in the later tenth century and beyond between women's houses which agreed to adopt the new modes of regulation and those — if such there were — that chose to continue in their former way of life. Investigation into this matter is hampered not only by the lack of explicit references to the reorganisation of individual women's communities, but also by an imprecision in the vocabulary employed for communal religious houses in this period. Are we to assume that at least after the

---

[37] William of Malmesbury, *Gesta regum Anglorum*, II, 218 (ed. and trans. R. A. B. Mynors *et al.* [1998] I, 402–3).

[38] Narratives of the progress of the reform have been constructed by Knowles (*The Monastic Order*, ch. 3) and D. H. Farmer, 'The progress of the monastic revival', in *Tenth-Century Studies*, ed. D. Parsons (1975), pp. 10–19; neither accounts satisfactorily for the fate of women's houses in the movement.

[39] Venarde has calculated that there might have been four or five communities for women at this time: *Women's Monasticism*, p. 25. Approximately one dozen religious houses that had been occupied by women at some point during the pre-Viking Age may still (or once more) have numbered women among their communities at the turn of the ninth century. Of these, however, only four appear to have housed women in the late tenth or early eleventh centuries: Barking, Berkeley, Wareham, and Leominster; see below chapter 6, §a. The number of women's houses potentially needing reform can be increased if we add the new establishments founded from Alfred's reign onwards, namely Shaftesbury, possibly Romsey, Wilton, and the Nunnaminster at Winchester; see below, chapter 6, §b.

reforming council at Winchester that issued the *Regularis concordia*, all these *monasteria* housing women were, or were meant to be, essentially Benedictine? This presumption has certainly underlain much historical writing on the period. If correct, this would mark a substantial departure from the modes of religious expression adopted by women in the pre-Viking Age when no single rule of life predominated, and calls into question once more the silence of the sources in not reporting such a revolution in monastic practice. In fact, the view that only one organisational system prevailed beyond Edgar's reign can be challenged, since it takes no account of the distinctions drawn in the secular laws between the adherents of different lifestyles within the Church.

Beginning with these legal texts, study of the language used in contemporary sources to describe religious women may offer a way forward from the impasse we have reached in our attempt to explore the issue of women's involvement in the monastic revolution of Edgar's reign from the perspective of the institutions housing cloistered women. The limitations of this approach (which has generally been adopted by such historians of the reform as have taken an interest in women) have been starkly illustrated by the preceding discussion: few of the questions raised can be answered in any but the most general of terms, and numerous problems remain unsolved. More profitable is the pursuit of these issues via the veiled women themselves.

The language of the religious life in later Anglo-Saxon England

It has already been seen that there were in the pre-Viking Age no gender-specific nouns for men's and women's religious houses; collectively communities of women, of women living with men, and all-male congregations were all called *monasteria*. More contemporaneous information has survived relating to the reform of monasteries for men in Edgar's reign, but male religious houses still continued to be called 'minsters' (or *monasteria*) beyond this time, regardless of whether their inmates were following the precepts of the Rule of St Benedict or were rather secular clergy, engaged in pastoral ministry.[40] Only in the second of King Edgar's law-codes in chapters concerning the payment of tithe and other church-dues are types of secular church further differentiated, the 'old minster to which the territory belongs' being distinguished from later churches built within their sphere of pastoral authority.[41]

---

[40]   Consider, for example, V Æthelred, chs. 6 and 7 (ed. Liebermann, *Die Gesetze*, I, 238), where both monk and canon were said to live in a minster. Compare also the eleventh-century Latin paraphrase of VI Æthelred, chs. 3.1, 4 (ibid., p. 249) where *monasterium* is used for the habitations of both *monachi* and *canonici*.

[41]   II Edgar, ch. 1.1 (ed. Liebermann, *Die Gesetze*, I, 196): 'to þam ealdan mynstre, þe seo hernes tohyrð'. In the translation of Edgar's code in the *Quadripartitus* (a collection and Latin translation of pre-Conquest law-codes made *c.* 1114), tithe was said to be payable 'ad matrem

There was no equivalent female model to the secular mother church, since women were forbidden any active pastoral role. All female religious houses (just as in the earlier period) were described as *monasteria*, although sometimes a women's *monasterium* might explicitly be said to have been 'of nuns' (*sanctimoniales*) or of the female servants (*famulae*), or handmaidens (*ancillae*) of God. It was suggested earlier that the lack of a specific noun to denote nunneries in this period was one among a number of signs that strict gender segregation played no part in English monasticism before the tenth century.[42] Although the female convent founded at Winchester early in the tenth century by King Alfred's wife, Ealhswith, and her son Edward the Elder was generally described as the nuns' minster (the Nunnaminster) to differentiate it from the two male communities in the city, this term does not seem to have acquired a wider usage.[43] Otherwise the vocabulary of female monastic institutions remained as imprecise in the tenth and eleventh centuries as in the earlier period, but the same does not hold true of the language used to describe the inmates of *monasteria*.

The revolution in religious observance effected under Bishop Æthelwold's direction during the reign of Edgar introduced into England for the first time a separation between the lifestyles of monastics who lived *regulariter*, according to the precepts of the Rule of St Benedict, and seculars, who followed a different rule of life and — in the case of males — were more obviously engaged in active pastoral ministry outside the cloister. This tight distinction between the two groups of religious could not have pertained in the pre-reform period when no single rule of life predominated; nor could such a separation between the adherents of different systems of communal organisation have constituted, as Æthelwold implied it did, a restoration of a past order.[44]

The shift apparent in the vocabulary used of religious women in the normative sources of the later tenth and eleventh centuries marks a more significant departure from the terminological practice of the pre-Viking Age than it does for male religious; the distinct status that separated monks from other *clerici* not in priestly orders was already reflected in the literature of the earlier age.[45] The division created by the Æthelwoldian revolution between the lifestyles of regular, enclosed religious and seculars living in the world was mirrored in the refining of the language by which the two groups were described, and the adoption

---

ecclesiam, cui parochia adiacet'; the early twelfth-century so-called *Instituta Cnuti* translated the 'old minsters' of the original as the 'antiquae ecclesiae ad quas iuste parrochiani pertinent' (ibid., p. 197).

[42] Above, chapter 2.

[43] See above, chapter 2, n. 75; compare also BCS 824 (S 526): '*monasterio monialium quod in Wyntonia urbe situm sit ...*'.

[44] Æthelwold 'An account' (ed. and trans. Whitelock, *et al.*, *Councils*, I, 144–5, 152–3, no. 33). See also A. Gransden, 'Traditionalism and continuity during the last century of Anglo-Saxon monasticism', *Journal of Ecclesiastical History*, 40 (1989), 159–207, at pp. 165–70.

[45] See above, chapter 1, p. 28.

of precise terms marking a departure from the practice of the pre-Viking period.[46] This is seen most obviously in some of the law-codes of Æthelred and Cnut whose provisions were drafted by Wulfstan (archbishop of York 1002–1023).[47] Here, in chapters relating to the obligations of the servants of God collectively, the responsibilities of cloistered religious, *munecas* and *mynecenas* (monks and cloistered women), were distinguished from those of the secular clergy, *preostas* or *canonicas*, paired with their female equivalents, termed *nunnan*, secular vowesses.[48] In translating these nouns thus I am seeking to preserve the shades of meaning inherent in the Old English where *mynecenu* denotes the female equivalent of a monk, namely a woman living within an enclosed, all female monastic house, as opposed a veiled woman living under vows in the world.[49] In a code issued by Æthelred in 1008 following a council held at Enham it was decreed 'that men of every order are each to submit willingly to that duty which befits them both in religious and secular concerns. And especially God's servants — bishops and abbots, monks and cloistered women, priests and vowesses — are to submit to their duty and to live according to their rule and to intercede zealously for all Christian people'.[50] The same pairing of *munuc* and *mynecenu* in contrast with *preost* and *nunne* is found in a compilation of Wulfstan's writings, possibly draft material for a sermon that was never in the end written.[51] The monk and the

---

[46]   These linguistic shifts are discussed in detail in my 'Language and method: the Dictionary of Old English and the historian', in *The Dictionary of Old English*, ed. M. J. Toswell, Old English Newsletter, Subsidia 26 (1998), 73–87. A brief summary may also be found in M. Clayton, 'Ælfric's *Judith*: manipulative or manipulated?', *ASE*, 23 (1994), 215–27, at pp. 225–7. The changes have also been noted by Stafford, 'Queens, nunneries and reforming churchmen', p. 10.

[47]   For Wulfstan's role in the drafting of eleventh-century secular legislation see D. Whitelock, 'Archbishop Wulfstan: homilist and statesman', *TRHS*, 4 ser. 24 (1942), 25–45, at pp. 35–8, 41; P. Stafford, 'The laws of Cnut and the history of Anglo-Saxon royal promises', *Anglo-Saxon England,* 10 (1982), 173–90, at pp. 173–7.

[48]   The significance of the distinction being made in this legislative material between cloistered female religious and women living under religious vows outside enclosed monasteries was discussed by Dorothy Whitelock, *The Will of Æthelgifu* (1968), p. 34; see also Schneider, 'Anglo-Saxon women', pp. 82–4; Yorke, '"Sisters"', pp. 108 and 117, n. 91; and R. Gilchrist, *Gender and Material Culture* (1994), p. 34.

[49]   The reasons why these terms have been chosen in preference to any of the available alternatives are given in full below.

[50]   V Æthelred, chs. 4–4.1 (ed. Liebermann, *Die Gesetze*, I, 238): '7 huruþinga Godes þeowas — biscopas 7 abbudas, munecas 7 mynecena, preostas 7 nunnan — to rihte gebugan 7 regollice libban 7 for eall Cristen folc þingian georne'. The same sentence was repeated almost unaltered in VI Æthelred, ch. 2.2; I Cnut, ch. 6a (pp. 246 and 288), except that for *preostas* the noun *canonicas* was used.

[51]   This text is included as number 50 in A. Napier's edition of Wulfstan's homilies: *Wulfstan. Sammlung der ihm zugeschriebenen Homilien nebst Untersuchungen über ihre Echtheit* (Berlin, 1883), pp. 266–74, at p. 271; see D. Bethurum, *The Homilies of Wulfstan* (1957), pp. 39–41.

cloistered woman were thus seen as a group distinct from the secular priest and his
female counterpart the *nunne*. In this intepretation I differ from Marc Meyer, who
has taken this clause to signify a distinction 'between nuns and women who have
retired from the active life to the monastery: the latter are classed with canons (i.e.
priests serving collegiate minsters) and the nuns are grouped with monks';[52] I
cannot agree that secular vowesses lived among the Benedictine nuns of the
reformed nunneries.[53] Similarly, in the letter he wrote to the people of England in
1019/1020, Cnut directed that no one was to be so presumptuous as to take to wife
a consecrated vowess or a cloistered woman: 'on gehadodre nunnan oððe on
mynecenan'.[54] The equivalence of *nunnan* with the secular clergy is seen most
clearly in Wulfstan's Institutes of Polity, where the archbishop made
recommendations about the obligation pertaining to religious collectively (*be
gehadedum mannum*) to live rightly and set an example to the rest of the laity,
before going on to define more precisely the roles first of abbots, then of monks
(*be munecum*), then of cloistered women (*be mynecenan*), and finally of priests
together with vowesses (*be preostan* and *be nunnan*).[55] Of cloistered women
Wulfstan wrote, 'It is right that, just as we said before about monks, *mynecena*
behave monastically, and not associate with secular men nor have all too much
intimacy with them, but ever live according to rule and always separate themselves
from worldly concerns as diligently as they can'.[56] His recommendations for the

[52]   M. Meyer, 'Land charters and the legal position of Anglo-Saxon women', in *The
Women of England from Anglo-Saxon Times to the Present*, ed. B. Kanner (1980), pp. 57–82, at
p. 60.
[53]   Dagmar Schneider has taken a similar line to mine: 'Anglo-Saxon women', p. 85,
n. 18.
[54]   Cnut, letter to the people of England 1019/1020, ch. 16 (ed. Liebermann, *Die
Gesetze*, I, 274). The verb *gehadian* means to ordain, or consecrate; the participle derived from it
— *gehadod* — is equivalent to the Latin, *ordinatus*, and is generally used of men in holy orders.
The nominative singular feminine form would in early West Saxon be *gehadodu nunne*; whether
this would have been used as late as the time of Cnut is unclear. See A. Campbell, *Old English
Grammar* (1959), §643.5.e; K. Brunner, *Altenglische Grammatik* (3rd edn, Tübingen, 1965),
§414.2. This particular coupling of participle and noun occurs primarily in the later Anglo-Saxon
laws in chapters similar to this one prohibiting marriage with consecrated women, also in the same
context in Wulfstan's homilies. One homily of Ælfric's praised female continence: 'there are
however, widows who live in continence, consecrated as vowesses for the love of the Saviour (*to
nunnan gehadode for ðæs hælendes lufon*); 'Homily for the nativity of Mary, the blessed virgin',
lines 367–8 (ed. B. Assmann, *Angelsächsische Homilien und Heiligenleben* [Darmstadt, 1964],
p. 39, no. 3). Each recorded instance puts the vowess in the dative form, often as the victim of a
potential action done 'to' her. I have to thank Katherine O'Brien O'Keeffe for assistance on this
matter.
[55]   Religious in general: I *Polity*, 68–77, II *Polity*, xxii.145–169; monks: I *Polity*, 81–3,
II *Polity*, xii.173–84; cloistered women: I *Polity*, 84, II *Polity*, xiii.185; priests and avowed women:
I *Polity*, 85, II *Polity*, xiv.186 (ed. Jost, *Die "Institutes"*, pp. 109–29).
[56]   Wulfstan, I *Polity*, 84, II *Polity*, xiii.185 (ed. Jost, *Die "Institutes"*, p. 128; trans.
Swanton, *Anglo-Saxon Prose*, pp. 198–9).

secular *nunnan* imply that such women might be found either in their own houses or living in communities: 'It is right that priests, and equally vowesses as well, live according to rule and maintain their chastity if they wish to dwell in a minster or command respect in the sight of the world'.[57]

The writings of Ælfric generally sustained the same terminological distinction between cloistered *mynecena* and women under vows who lived in the world; for example, in his first Old English letter for Wulfstan Ælfric used *mynecenu* as the female equivalent of the *munuc*.[58] But in one of his pastoral letters to Wulfsige, bishop of Sherborne, having described the seven orders of the Church, Ælfric excluded from these the orders of monks and abbots (*munuchad* and *abbudhad*), 'which are of another nature and are not reckoned in this number, nor also is the nuns' order (*nunnanhad*) named with them'.[59] Whether Ælfric meant here to signify only the female equivalent of *munuchad*, or rather deliberately intended to encompass less formally constituted *nunnan* as well as the woman who lived in a cloister is not entirely clear. Dagmar Schneider has presumed *nunnanhad* to signify religious women in general (as I should also prefer to do), but Roberta Gilchrist has taken the noun to denote 'the nuns' order comparable to the monks' and abbots' orders'.[60] In this context one might also mention the early eleventh-century so-called Northumbrian Priests' Law, where penalties were imposed on those who lay with *nunnan* ('Gif hwa wið nunnan forlicge ....); although it is again unclear whether the referent of that noun encompassed all religious women, or signified only those outside the cloister, we know of no Benedictine congregations (male or female) in the north during this period.[61] In his Glossary, Ælfric explained the Latin *monacha* (or *monialis*) to mean *mynecenu*, and *nonna* to signify *arwurþe wydewe oððe nunne*, 'an honourable widow or vowess'.[62] This passage reinforces the impression we have

---

[57]   I *Polity*, 85, II *Polity*, xiv.186 (ed. Jost, *Die "Institutes"*, p. 129; trans. Swanton, p. 199). Schneider, 'Anglo-Saxon women', p. 84.

[58]   'First Old English Pastoral Letter for Wulfstan, Archbishop of York', ch. 117 (ed. Whitelock *et al.*, *Councils*, I,184, no. 45): 'Munuchad 7 mynecena, abbodas 7 abbedessan ne synd na getealde to þyssum seofon hadum'.

[59]   Ælfric, 'Pastoral letter for Wulfsige III, bishop of Sherborne', ch. 45 (ibid., p. 205, no. 40).

[60]   Schneider, 'Anglo-Saxon women', p. 83, and n. 11; Gilchrist, *Gender*, p. 34.

[61]   Northumbrian Priests' Law, ch. 63 (ed. and trans. Whitelock *et al.*, *Councils*, I, 466, no. 63). Gilchrist has stressed (*Gender*, p. 34) that this legislation must suggest that that there were female religious communities of some sort in the north of England. For possible examples of such — clearly non-cloistered — congregations, see part II, *s.n.* Corbridge and Durham.

[62]   *Ælfrics Grammatik und Glossar*, ed. J. Zupitza (Berlin, 1880), p. 299, lines 12–14 (based on the text found in Oxford, St John's College, MS 154). The full series reads: '*monacha uel monialis* mynecynu. *anachorita* ancra. *eremita* westensetla. *nonna* arwyrþe wydewe oððe nunne'. Compare the text (from London, British Library, MS. Cotton Julius A.ii) printed by T. Wright, *Anglo-Saxon and Old English Vocabularies*, 2nd edn. ed. R. T. Wülcker (2 vols, 1884),

derived from the secular law-codes that two discrete types of religious woman existed within the later Anglo-Saxon Church, and supplies the additional information that the second category — of those who vowed to be continent but did not live in regular, enclosed monastic communities — might often include widows.[63] In his homily for the nativity of the Blessed Virgin Mary (dated by Peter Clemoes to 1005x1006) Ælfric singled out among examples of devout female behaviour widows, 'who live in continence, consecrated as vowesses for the love of the Saviour'.[64] Wulfstan, however, treated widows separately from both *mynecena* and *nunnan* in his Institutes of Polity, advising them to follow the example of the prophetess Anna and live in continent prayer, engaged in fasting and alms-giving.[65] Questions relating to the particular status of widows require separate investigation, to which we will turn in the next chapter.

In vernacular texts written after the monastic revolution of Edgar's reign it is thus apparent that a clear distinction was drawn between cloistered religious and those living in the world. Men and women who lived an enclosed, regular life (*munecas* and *mynecena*) were distinguished from secular priests (*preostas* or *canonicas*) and their female counterparts living outside the cloister, who were called — confusingly to the modern reader — *nunnan*.[66] The same clarity is not, however, visible in contemporary Latin sources. The Old English noun *nunne* is obviously a loan-word from the late Latin *nonna*, which signified firstly a venerable, aged woman, or grandmother, and only secondarily 'a nun';[67] we saw in the discussion of language before the Viking Age that both the Latin and Old English words were used before the tenth-century reform to denote any sort of religious woman, and were not reserved to those women who had adopted a secular, or canonical rather than regular life.[68] I have been unable to parallel in

---

I, 308. The example was quoted by Whitelock, *The Will*, p. 34, and following her by G. R. Owen, 'Wynflæd's wardrobe', *Anglo-Saxon England*, 8 (1979), 195–222, at p. 219.

[63]   The taking of religious vows by widows had a long history in the early medieval Church; see below, chapter 5.

[64]   Ælfric, homily for the nativity of the Virgin Mary (ed. Assmann, *Angelsächsische Homilien*, p. 39, lines 367–8, no 3): 'Synd swa þeah þa wudewan, ðe wuniað on clænnysse to nunnan gehadode for ðæs hælendes lufon'.

[65]   I *Polity*, 93–7, II *Polity*, xv.198–202 (ed. Jost, *Die "Institutes"*, pp. 136–7). The behaviour of Anna was described in Luke, 2: 36–8.

[66]   *A Microfiche Concordance to Old English*, ed. A. diPaolo Healey, and R. L. Venezky (Toronto, 1982, produced under the auspices of the Dictionary of Old English project) provides one apparent exception to this rule, the entry for 963 in the E text of the Anglo-Saxon Chronicle, where in relation to Æthelwold's reform of Winchester it is said that the bishop established two monasteries, one of monks (*muneca*) and the other of *nunna*. This is, however, a twelfth-century addition to the Chronicle-text, made at Peterborough, and does not reflect tenth-century usage.

[67]   C. Du Cange, *Glossarium mediae et infimae Latinitatis*, revised edn. D. P. Carpenter and G. A. L. Henschel (10 vols. Niort, 1883–7), *s v. nonnus*; J. F. Niermeyer, *Mediae Latinitatis Lexicon Minus* (Leiden, 1976), *s.v. nonna*.

[68]   Above, chapter 1, pp. 26–8.

Latin texts from the last century before the Norman Conquest an equivalent shift in semantic meaning to that shown in Old English, so that it cannot be demonstrated that *monacha* and *sanctimonialis* came to signify followers of the regular life while *nonna* was reserved for secular women under vows. For example, in a Latin letter to Wulfstan, Ælfric condemned the offspring of adulterers and those born of *nonnae*, apparently using the noun of all religious women, not specifically either those within or without the cloister.[69] In part the imprecision of the Latin texts in contrast to the tightness of the vernacular vocabulary might reflect the increase in importance of the vernacular to the reformed Church and hence the predominance of Old English in the normative literature from the period after the agreement of the *Regularis concordia*. The latter text was directed only at cloistered religious and did not consider an alternative style of religious living. It may also be relevant that, whereas the ninth-century Carolingian normative literature drew a distinction between the *canonicus* who was to live the secular life as set out by Chrodegang and the *monachus* who was to live according to the precepts of the Rule of St Benedict, only one mode of life was envisaged for all *sanctimoniales*, who were regrouped under uniform principles drawing on both canonical practice and monastic custom.[70]

It is only in the early twelfth century in the Latin versions of the laws of Cnut that there is made direct translation of the legal clause given first in V Æthelred and repeated in the vernacular version of VI Æthelred and I Cnut where *munecas 7 mynecena*, were contrasted with *preostas* or *canonicas* and *nunnan*. In those Latin translations *monachae* and *sanctimoniales* are the nouns used to translate *mynecena*, and *nonnae* is used for *nunnan*.[71] Archbishop Wulfstan had been responsible for the original drafting of the laws agreed at Enham in 1008 (the code known as V Æthelred) and for the production of two somewhat modified versions of this code for circulation in his northern province, a Latin one intended for the higher clergy and a vernacular version for general circulation (both described as VI Æthelred).[72] However, the archbishop's Latin paraphrase did not

---

[69]   Ælfric, letter to Wulfstan A.D. 1002x1005, ch. 5 (ed. Whitelock *et al.*, *Councils*, I, 248, no. 45): 'De adulteriis nati et de nonnis generati'.

[70]   M. Parisse, 'Les chanoinesses dans l'empire germanique (ixe–xie siècles)', *Francia*, 6 (1978), 107–26, at p. 112.

[71]   In the translation of I Cnut, ch. 6a made in the *Quadripartitus* (*c.* 1114) the pairing is of *monachi, monachae, canonici, nunnae* (ed. Liebermann, *Die Gesetze*, I, 288); in the so-called *Instituta Cnuti* (which date from 1103x1120) the whole clause reads: 'et precipue hoc precipimus seruis et ancillis Dei, uidelicet episcopis, abbatibus, abbatissis, monachis, sanctimonialibus, canonicis, presbyteris, nonnis, ut regulariter uiuant ...' (p. 289). The version of Cnut's laws known as the *Consiliatio Cnuti* (which date from 1110x1130), omitted the phrase about secular clergy and vowed women entirely, referring only to *episcopi, abbates, monachi et monache* (ibid., p. 289).

[72]   The relationship between Æthelred's fifth and sixth law-codes and the role of Wulfstan in their drafting was considered by K. Sisam, *Studies in the History of Old English Literature* (1953), pp. 278–287; see also Whitelock *et al.*, *Councils*, I, 338–43. The same clause was repeated in I Cnut, where Wulfstan's influence is again apparent.

translate the vernacular provisions sentence by sentence and omitted some passages, including this particular clause which defined the servants of God; in its place in VI Æthelred was given a strongly worded statement to abbots and abbesses about the strict imposition of the Rule of St Benedict.[73] Wulfstan's Latin version of VI Æthelred did translate the prohibition made in the vernacular version against marriage to a consecrated women (*gehadode nunne*), directing that no one was to join himself with a *deo sacrata* or any other illicit person.[74]

While collecting examples of current Latin terminology for women religious, the language employed in Domesday Book should also be considered. The noun most commonly used for religious women in all the county surveys was *monialis* (that indeed is the noun indexed in the new Phillimore edition of Domesday Book, *s. v.* nun).[75] The inhabitants of the nunneries at Amesbury, Chatteris, St Mary's Elstow, Winchester, and at Holy Trinity in Caen were all collectively thus described, as were the four *moniales* who held land near the city of Canterbury in alms of the abbot of St Augustine's, the 'nuns of Hereford' (*moniales de Hereford*), and the residue of the female community from the disbanded house at Leominster.[76] Most of the individual religious women mentioned in Domesday Book as the holders of small pieces of land were also described by the title *monialis*.[77] The only exceptions are single instances from the Lincolnshire, Suffolk and Somerset surveys. A solitary religious woman, Cwenthryth who held land at Canwick in Lincolnshire was termed a *monacha*.[78] The description of the burh of Bury St Edmunds in Little Domesday mentioned the presence at the abbey of twenty-eight *nonnae*, who lived with the poor.[79] In the survey of Somerset successive entries relate to lands held in alms of the king: twelve acres in the lands of Curry (together with woodland and pasture of 80 acres

---

[73] VI Æthelred (Latin), ch. 2 (ed. Liebermann, *Die Gesetze*, I, 247).

[74] VI Æthelred, ch. 12.1: 'Ne on gehalgodre ænigre nunnan, ne on his gefæderan, ne on ælætan ænig Cristen man ne gewifige æfre'; VI Æthelred Latin, ch. 12: 'Nemo igitur inlicitis coniunctionibus se inquinet, id est cum cognatis uel cum coniugatis uel cum Deo sacratis seu cum aliis inlictis personis' (ed. Liebermann, *Die Gesetze*, I, 250–1). This clause was not found in V Æthelred, but it was repeated in I Cnut (ch. 7.1, ibid., p. 290); compare the twelfth-century translations of Cnut's first code: the *Quadripartitus* translates *gehalgode nunne* as *sanctimonialis*, where the *Instituta Cnuti* reads *consecrata sanctimonialis aut nonna* (ibid., pp. 290–1).

[75] This analysis is based on the indices to the Phillimore Domesday: J. McN. Dodgson and J. J. N. Palmer, *Domesday Book 37: Index of Persons* (1992) and and J. D. Foy, *Domesday Book 38: Index of Subjects* (1992).

[76] Domesday Book, I, fo 68va (Wiltshire, 16.5): Amesbury; fo 193ra (Cambridgeshire, 11.2): Chatteris; fos 217ra–b (Bedfordshire, 53.1, 3–4): St Mary's Elstow; fos 43vb, 48rb (Hampshire, 14.6, 44.1): the Nunnaminster at Winchester; fo 166va (Gloucestershire, 23): 'aecclesia monialium de Cadomo'; fo 12rb (Kent, 7.11); fo 181vb (Hereford, 2.17); fo 180ra (Hereford, 1.10b): Leominster.

[77] These instances are discussed together in the introduction to part II, §a.

[78] Domesday Book, I, fo 337vb (Lincolnshire, 67.27).

[79] Ibid., II, fo 372r (Suffolk, 14.167).

valued at 5s) held by Editha, a *monialis*; and two-and-a-half virgates at *Honecote* held by *duae nonnae*.[80] Roberta Gilchrist has argued that *monialis* (or *monacha*) and *nonna* were used in the Domesday survey throughout England in the same way that *mynecenu* and *nunne* were taken in the laws to denote distinct classes of religious woman both of whom might live in groups (as the example of the *duae nonnae* from Somerset indicates); the *monialis* (*monacha* or *mynecenu*) she has seen as the inhabitant of a formal monastic community, the *nonna* living in a less formal environment.[81] It is not, however, obvious that the language of Domesday Book can be read so precisely, nor that any great significance can be attached to the two instances in which *nonna* is used in preference to the otherwise apparently standard *monialis*. Markedly different economic circumstances characterised the positions of the Somerset *monialis* Edith (supported by the income from twelve hides of land) and the two *nonnae* at Honecote who had recourse to only a couple of virgates,[82] but to argue that the religious nature of their lives also differed significantly is impossible from this evidence. The language of Domesday Book is not likely to enhance our understanding of the variations of female religious expression found in the eleventh century; the commissioners appear, throughout England, to have used a single noun, *monialis* as a generic term for a religious as opposed to a lay woman. That we might in fact prefer to categorise most if not all of these women (other than those clearly belonging to large, formally constituted nunneries) together with vowesses living outside the cloister and not with enclosed Benedictines will be argued below:[83] such an issue was, however, of no relevance to a survey concerned primarily with land tenure.

A language for historians

The revolution in monastic organisation promoted by Bishop Æthelwold with the support of King Edgar, although ostensibly imposing on all religious congregations a single mode of life (the Rule of St Benedict with the revisions set out in the *Regularis concordia*), in fact created a dual system whereby communities of seculars, following a different rule, lived side-by-side with enclosed Benedictine houses. This duality is made explicit, as we have seen, in the different labels applied in the normative texts (at least those written in Old English) to the adherents of the separate regimes. Yet recognition of this distinction and its significance is of only limited use in historical explanation unless it is reflected in the adoption by the modern English writer of an equivalently differentiated vocabulary to denote devout woman of the two sorts.

---

[80]   Ibid., I, fo 91va (Somerset, 16.12–13).
[81]   Gilchrist, *Gender*, pp. 33–4.
[82]   A virgate is a quarter of a hide.
[83]   See the introduction to part II, §a.

Here the problem of translating the vernacular terms becomes acute, since the Old English word used of a woman who dwells in a cloister, *mynecenu*, has no direct modern equivalent. The modern English noun 'nun' (a woman devoted to the religious life under certain vows; usually one ... who lives in a convent under a certain rule) is derived from the Old English *nunne*, and perhaps the Old French *nonne*, both of which stem ultimately from the late Latin *nonna*, feminine of *nonnus*, a title usually given to elderly persons.[84] In the eleventh century the noun *nunne* signified not the cloistered woman meant by the modern term but rather the female counterpart to the secular priest or canon. There is an obvious potential confusion here, exacerbated by the lack of consistency among translators of the normative texts of the later Anglo-Saxon period, who have employed a diversity of words and phrases that introduces an ambiguity totally at odds with the precision of the original texts.[85] It is possible, as Dorothy Whitelock demonstrated, to sustain the contrasts drawn in the original texts by translating *mynecenu* as 'nun' and *nunne* as 'woman dedicated to God'.[86] The merit of this usage is that the terms adopted in translation have the same referents as the original Old English words. However, 'professed nun' has also been used by other scholars to translate *on gehadodre nunnan* and the phrase 'a woman who has taken religious vows' has been used for *mynecenu*.[87] Michael Swanton, who has translated Wulfstan's Institutes of Polity, chose to render *mynecenu* as 'woman in orders', and *nunne* as 'nun'.[88] The disadvantage of this last example is that the word 'nun' conjures up the wrong referent; it implies notions of claustration and regularity that were explicitly not intended by Wulfstan to apply to secular religious women.

For these reasons, I have preferred to avoid the word 'nun' altogether when translating these passages, and to make a contrast instead between cloistered woman and vowess. There is a noun cloistress, described by the *Oxford English Dictionary* as obsolete or rare, which signifies 'a female tenant of a cloister, a nun', the feminine of *cloisterer*. Just one instance of its use is given, from

---

[84]   *Oxford English Dictionary*, 2nd edn., *s.v.* nun.

[85]   Translation into German is much easier, for the masculine *der Mönch* has a feminine equivalent, *die Mönchin*, and the Old High German noun, *Nunne*, survives as the modern German *die Nonne*; these nouns were used consistently by Liebermann to preserve the distinctions made in the Old English. See also his discussion of *Nonne* in his glossary to the laws, *Die Gesetze*, II, 596–7.

[86]   As, for example, in Whitelock's translation of V Æthelred, ch. 4.1 (*EHD*, I, 443, no. 44). Translating the same clause, Agnes Robertson chose to render the terms as 'nun' and 'women under religious vows': *The Laws of the Kings of England from Edmund to Henry I* (1925), pp. 80–1. Compare Yorke, '"Sisters"', pp. 108 and 117, n. 91.

[87]   Robertson, *The Laws*, pp. 144–5 (translating Cnut's letter to the English, 1019/20, ch. 16); and compare her translation of VI Æthelred, ch. 12.1 where *on gehalgodre ænigre nunnan* has also been translated as 'a professed nun' (ibid., p. 95). In a code which dates to before the monastic revolution — I Edmund — Robertson used 'nun' to translate *nunne*: I Edmund, 4, pp. 6–7.

[88]   Swanton, *Anglo-Saxon Prose*, pp. 198–9.

Shakespeare's *Twelfth Night* (I.i.27), where the metaphor of a claustration is used to evoke Olivia's grief at the death of her brother: 'Like a cloistress she will veilèd walk'. If it were chosen to translate the Old English *mynecenu* it would have the advantage of being unambiguous, for it signifies precisely the same religious state as is conveyed by the Old English noun and, being rare, it does not carry with it implications of any specific sort of cloistered existence or life under any particular rule. I have hesitated, however, before reviving an obsolete word (and one which is singularly inelegant in its plural form) and have elected instead to use the equally precise term 'cloistered woman'. The two labels, cloistered woman and vowess,[89] signify distinct life-styles and hence point to the existence of discrete sorts of women's *monasteria*: the better documented, regular monastic congregation (the Benedictine 'nunnery') where women lived within the cloister, and the less formally constituted community in which a vowess might dwell, were she not living alone.[90]

One alternative response has been made to the linguistic distinctions of religious person introduced in the aftermath of the monastic revolution which merits separate consideration. The importance of the contrast between *mynecenu* and *nunne* was noted by Dagmar Schneider; to her mind the difference between the two sorts of religious (male and female) lay in the rule of life each was to follow. Monks and nuns were to live, as the *Regularis concordia* made clear, according to the Rule of St Benedict, whereas the lives of 'canons and canonesses', she has argued, were to be regulated according to the provisions imposed on non-monastic Frankish religious at the 816 synod of Aachen.[91] This understanding has enabled her to reflect the distinctions visible in the contemporary vernacular literature by translating *mynecenu* as 'nun' and *nunne* as

---

[89]   Vowess may seem equally archaic to some readers; my reasons for its use are defended below, p. 110.

[90]   Here I depart from Barbara Yorke ('"Sisters"', p. 108) for whom the difference between the two sorts of women lay in the fact that while both were able to retain private estates, nuns lived in a community whereas vowesses were allowed to live on their own estates; Wulfstan's Institutes of Polity, however, as we saw, makes it clear that *nunnan* could also be found in minsters. Roberta Gilchrist (*Gender*, p. 34) has also pointed out that *nunnan* could live communally, supporting her view by reference to the evidence of Domesday Book discussed above. Sustaining in historical analysis the distinctions between the houses occupied by the two religious types would be easier had the contrasts drawn in the language relating to religious people been translated into the coining of separate nouns to signify distinct sorts of community. The parallel between the semi-monastic life followed by English vowesses of the tenth and eleventh centuries and the informal *via media* of the later continental Beguines is striking, and presents the possibility of using the noun 'beguinage' to describe their communities; compare Gilchrist, *Gender*, pp. 170–2. This does not, however, seem appropriate to Anglo-Saxon circumstances.

[91]   Schneider, 'Anglo-Saxon women', pp. 85–7; idem., 'Klosterleben', p. 59. The *Institutio canonicorum* has been edited by A. Werminghoff, *Concilia Aevi Karolini*, I, MGH, Leges III, Concilia II, 1 [Hannover and Leipzig, 1906], pp. 308–421, no. 39A; the *Institutio sanctimonialium*, ibid., pp. 421–56, no. 39B.

'canoness', a system that has obvious advantages of clarity, consistency, and conformity to current linguistic practice. Its disadvantage is that it may, as Schneider herself has recognised, impose a more rigid model of a bipartite religious life than the sources will actually allow. Moreover, that the rules imposed at Aachen were widely followed even in a Frankish context is difficult to demonstrate.[92] Although plausible, the notion that the *Institutio sanctimonialium* regulated tenth-century English communities of 'canonesses' needs to be investigated further and may not entirely be provable.

In view of the demonstrable influence of the early ninth-century reforms of Louis the Pious on the shaping of the English tenth-century reform, the obvious available rules to govern the lives of seculars outside the monastic, Benedictine cloister are those composed by Chrodegang and Amalarius of Metz.[93] Chrodegang's rule for canons, *Regula canonicorum*, was known in tenth-century England, indeed a translation of the 'enlarged' version was made apparently at the Old Minster in Winchester at the school of which Æthelwold was master; fragments of the *Institutio canonicorum* compiled by Amararius of Metz which were codified at Aachen in 816 have also survived in English manuscripts.[94] It is more difficult to demonstrate satisfactorily that the *Institutio sanctimonialium* of 816 was used as a guide for secular vowesses in England, since it is not witnessed in any extant manuscript of Anglo-Saxon provenance; it can be shown in the generation after the reform that Archbishop Wulfstan knew the text.[95] It may also be objected that the *Institutio sanctimonialium* as promoted at the 816 Aachen council was not intended to treat canonesses separately from cloistered nuns. Although different modes of life were recommended to *canonici* and *monachi*, all religious women, *sanctimoniales*, were grouped together and directed to follow one rule of life. The intention of that council it has been argued was to bring all women together within a single, unified mode of life that owed something to

---

[92]   Only four ninth-century manuscript copies of the *Institutio sanctimonialium* have survived: S. F. Wemple, *Women in Frankish Society* (Philadelphia, PA, 1981), p. 170.

[93]   Wormald, 'Æthelwold', pp. 16–19; D. Bullough, 'The continental background of the reform', in *Tenth-Century Studies*, ed. D. Parsons (1975), pp. 20–36, at pp. 23–7.

[94]   *The Old English Version of the Enlarged Rule of Chrodegang*, ed. A. S. Napier, EETS, os 150 (London, 1916); M. Lapidge, 'Æthelwold as scholar and teacher', in *Bishop Æthelwold*, ed. B. Yorke (1988), pp. 89–117, at p. 109. See also M. Bateson, 'Rules for monks and secular canons after the revival under King Edgar', *EHR*, 9 (1894), 690–708, at pp. 699–700; Schneider, 'Anglo-Saxon women', pp. 85–6; A. Cabaniss, *Amalarius of Metz* (Amsterdam, 1954), pp. 49–50; J. Barrow, 'English cathedral communities and reform in the late tenth and the eleventh centuries', in *Anglo-Norman Durham*, ed. D. Rollason *et al.* (1994), pp. 25–39.

[95]   As Jost showed, in I *Polity* 85, II *Polity* XIV 186 (ed. Jost, *Die "Institutes"*, p. 129), Wulfstan was quoting Amalarius, *Regula sanctimonialium*, viii (ed. Migne, *PL* 105, col 96) = *Institutio sanctimonialium*, ch. 8, ed. Werminghoff, *MGH, Concilia* II, I, p. 444, lines 11–14, no. 39B.

canonical as well as to monastic practice.[96] The *Institutio* recommended
claustration of nuns by restricting their contact with the outside world and with
men, communal eating and sleeping, while at the same time permitting them to
retain their own possessions, to have servants, and to live in their own houses.[97]

Since so much of the English normative literature is vague in its
injunctions to non-cloistered religious women it is difficult to establish whether
any one rule was recommended for the regulation of their life, let alone to
determine which specific rule that were. That secular priests and canons had their
own rule was made explicit in the various versions of the 1008 code of King
Æthelred.[98] In his Institutes of Polity, having instructed the residents of the cloister
to behave monastically, Wulfstan directed secular priests were to live regularly
(*regollice libban*) and included vowesses, *nunnan*, in the same injunction;[99]
it might be presumed that he envisaged that the same rule of life would be followed
by both sexes,[100] but it is difficult to establish what rule that might have been. As
archbishop, Wulfstan took considerable interest in the activities and demeanour
of the male clergy in his province, an interest reflected by the sorts of texts that he
copied into his so-called 'commonplace book': passages from penitentials,
liturgical texts, excerpts from canon law, Carolingian capitularies, writings of
Theodulf of Orleans, Amalarius of Metz and Alcuin.[101] Wulfstan compiled the so-
called Canons of Edgar (almost all of which deal with the behaviour and
obligations of priests) and he was probably also responsible at least for overseeing
the Northumbrian Priests' law.[102] He certainly knew the *Institutio canonicorum*
and *Institutio sanctimonialium* of 816, for he made use of both in his Institutes of
Polity and quoted the former in one of his homilies. Moreover, passages from the

---

96   Parisse, 'Chanoinesses', p. 112. Suzanne Wemple has also pointed out (*Women*,
p. 168) that once regulation was made in 816 (through the *Institutio sanctimonialium*) of the
general advice given at 813 Council of Châlons recommending that canonesses should be a
separate order, there was in fact little to distinguish the obligations of Benedictine nuns and
canonesses. This would further increase the difficulty of determining in an English context which
system of organisation might have been in use.

97   *Institutio sanctimonialium*, chs. 20–1 (ed. Werminghoff, *MGH*, *Concilia*, II, 1,
pp. 451–2, no. 39B).

98   V Æthelred, ch. 7 (ed. Liebermann, *Die Gesetze*, I, 238); VI Æthelred, ch. 4 (p. 248,
Latin p. 249): 'And canons where there is property such that they can have a refectory and
dormitory, are to hold their minster with right observance, and with chastity, as their rule directs'.
But compare I Cnut, 5.2 (ed. Liebermann, I, 286, trans. Robertson, *The Laws*, p. 160): 'If an
accusation is brought against a secular priest (*mæssepreost*) who does not live acording to a rule,
he shall clear himself in the same way as a deacon who lives according to a rule (*regollife*)'.

99   Wulfstan, I *Polity*, 85, II *Polity*, xiv.186 (ed. Jost, *Die "Institutes"*, p. 129).

100   That was the assumption made by Schneider, 'Anglo-Saxon women', p. 87.

101   D. Bethurum, 'Archbishop Wulfstan's commonplace book', *Proceedings of the
Modern Language Association*, 57 (1942), 916–29.

102   Whitelock, 'Archbishop Wulfstan', pp. 40–1. The 'Canons of Edgar' have been ed.
and trans. Whitelock *et al.*, *Councils*, I, 313–38, no. 48; the Northumbrian Priests' Law, ibid.,
pp. 447–68, no. 63.

Institutio canonicorum are copied in two of the manuscripts containing Wulfstan's 'commonplace book'; in a third there is a short piece in Old English entitled *De regula canonicorum* that has been shown to be a translation made by Wulfstan himself of a chapter from Amalarius' rule.[103] Wulfstan did not, however, extend this concern with the conduct of priests under his charge to an equivalent preoccupation with the regulation of non-cloistered women beyond the very general injunctions that have already been quoted. The remarks made by Ælfric in his summary of the book of Judith about *nunnan* who live disgracefully without repenting sufficiently of their sins suggest once more that there was a recognised standard to which the devout secular vowess was expected to conform (at least one of chastity, since the particular sin these vowesses wore so lightly was that of fornication),[104] but tells us nothing more about how the lives of such women might have been regulated.[105]

That such evidence as there is about the way of life pursued within late Anglo-Saxon female communities appears to echo as much the *Institutio sanctimonialium* as the *Regularis concordia* (which itself provided more of a general framework for the monastic life, rather than a set of rules to be rigidly followed) is a direct consequence of the fact that almost all our information is derived from normative sources, which themselves reflect the normative literature of the Carolingian reform.[106] This undermines Schneider's case that the *Institutio*

---

[103] Bethurum, 'Archbishop Wulfstan's commonplace book', p. 919; Whitelock, 'Archbishop Wulfstan', pp. 40–1; for discussion of this manuscript (Oxford, Bodleian Library, MS. Junius 121) see N. R. Ker, *Catalogue of Manuscripts Containing Anglo-Saxon* (Oxford, 1957, reissued 1990), no. 338 (the passage translating Amalarius is art. 12).

[104] Ælfric, 'On the book of Judith' (ed. Assmann, *Angelsächsische Homilien*, p. 115, lines 429–42, no. 9). Sister Mary Byrne has commented on the ideal model that Ælfric constructed here of the union of humility and chastity personified in Judith: *The Tradition of the Nun in Medieval England* (Washington, D.C., 1932), pp. 48–9.

[105] The status of the woman to whom Ælfric addressed the epilogue to his account of the biblical widow Judith has been debated. Clemoes argued that the text as a whole was written for a 'nun', noting that the opening words of the text 'Leofan men' found in only one manuscript, did not originate with Ælfric, and that he did not consider this to be a homily: introduction to *Angelsächsische Homilien*, ed. Assmann, p. xxxviii. Kenneth Sisam suggested that the recipient might have been an abbess: *Studies in the History of Old English Literature* (1953), p. 67, n. 2. Mary Clayton has, however, explored the language of the female religious life in the later tenth century to argue much more plausibly that this text was directed at women who had taken vows of chastity without entering nunneries, suggesting that in this instance the dedicatee was probably a virgin rather than a widow: 'Ælfric's *Judith*', pp. 225–7. For the presence of widows in such communities see further below, chapter 5.

[106] Schneider herself has made this point ('Anglo-Saxon women', p. 87), which weakens substantially her case that 'the *Institutio sanctimonialium* was used to a far greater extent than the survival of manuscripts of Anglo-Saxon provenance would suggest', ibid., p. 86. Nevertheless she has proceeded to analyse the provisions of the former text for the organisation of the female religious life, demonstrating on a number of occasions similarities between its provisions and those of the *Regularis concordia*.

was used as a practical guide for canonesses in later Anglo-Saxon England; the logic of her argument is flawed by her necessary dependence on prescriptive texts and by an inherent circularity arising from the similarities to which she has drawn attention between the *Institutio sanctimonialium* and the *Regularis concordia*. Attractive though the suggestion is — particularly in the light of the insistence of the tenth-century reform movement on uniformity of observance — it cannot be demonstrated conclusively that the *Institutio* was imposed as a system for the regulation of secular female religious communities in later Anglo-Saxon England separate from that prescribed for cloistered women.

Four distinguishing traits that mark out canonical from the cloistered life for women have been identified by Michel Parisse (in the context of a thirteenth-century dispute between the canonesses of Epinal and the bishop of Toul over the women's mode of life). These are: the absence of a formal monastic profession; residence in individual houses; the retention of personal possessions (land as well as moveable wealth); and the maintenance of the possibility of leaving the religious life in order to get married.[107] Parisse has inquired whether such characteristics of what are in later centuries called secular canonesses may be found in earlier periods and he has indeed discovered notable parallels in the organisation of some noble female houses particularly in Lotharingia and Germany in the tenth and eleventh centuries. The same features can also be found in a number of tenth- and eleventh-century English women's religious communities and might be thought distinctive not so much of conformity to a canonical notion of appropriate female religious behaviour as of a way of life characterised by diversity and difference from the cloistered norm. The case for using the modern noun canoness in respect of non-cloistered English religious women is thus unpersuasive; it calls to mind a referent inappropriate for the variety of forms of religious expression found among women in the later Anglo-Saxon period. I return once more to the noun 'vowess' as a translation for *nunne*. This has the merit of expressing the idea of dedication to a life of religion, possibly made via a formal liturgical ceremony, but does not prejudge the means by which the *nunne* chose to express her devotion (whether individually or in a community).[108] The word vowess can also embrace both the unmarried virgin, who for whatever reason has preferred not to enter a Benedictine house, and the widow, dual referents that were taken by Ælfric to be signified by the Latin *nonna*.[109] It is time to look more closely at the position of widows in the Anglo-Saxon Church.

---

[107] Parisse, 'Chanoinesses', p. 109.

[108] Tenth-century pontificals and sacramentaries provided prayers and rituals for the blessing or consecration of virgins and of widows dedicated to God, both involving the blessing of the clothes symbolic of their altered state; see further the section on liturgy in chapter 5.

[109] *Ælfrics Grammatik und Glossar*, ed. Zupitza, p. 299, lines 13–14.

Chapter 5

Widows and vowesses

A woman who vows not to take another husband after her husband's death and when he is dead, false to her word, takes another and is married a second time, when she is moved by penitence and wishes to fulfil her vow, it is in the power of her husband to determine whether she shall fulfil it or not.

Theodore, Penitential, II, xii, 14.[1]

And each widow is to remain unmarried for twelve months; she is afterwards to choose what she herself will. .... A widow is never to be consecrated [to religion] too hastily.

II Cnut, chs. 73 and 73.3.[2]

A certain widow who was called Oswynn dwelt near the saint's burial-place in prayers and fastings for many years after. She would every year cut the hair of the saint and cut his nails soberly and lovingly, and keep them in a shrine as relics on the altar.

Ælfric, *Passio S Eadmundi.*[3]

In our exploration of the participation of women in the tenth-century monastic revolution we have got closer to being able to answer the question raised at the beginning of the first chapter: how should we characterise women, particularly widows who had obviously made some commitment to the religious life but were equally clearly not living in enclosed Benedictine communities? Such women might be thought of as *nunnan*, vowesses, as described in the laws and Wulfstan's Institutes of Polity,[4] but for widows the issue of their former marital status may be pertinent here, particularly in the light of the equation made by Ælfric between the *nunne* and the 'worthy widow' (that is, presumably, one who had listened to the Church's teachings and chosen devout continence not remarriage).[5] It may be helpful to make one further digression and explore the evidence for the position

---

[1] Theodore, Penitential, II, xii, 14 (ed. P. W. Finsterwalder, *Die Canones Theodori Cantuariensis und ihre Überlieferungsformen* [Weimar, 1929], pp. 285–334, at p. 328; trans. J. T. McNeill and H. M. Gamer, *Medieval Handbooks of Penance* [New York, 1990], pp. 179–215, at p. 209).

[2] II Cnut, chs. 73 and 73.3 (ed. F. Liebermann, *Die Gesetze der Angelsachsen*, ed. F. Liebermann (3 vols., Halle, 1903–16), I, 360; trans. following Whitelock, *EHD*, I, 465–6, no. 49).

[3] Ælfric, *Passio Sancti Eadmundi regis et martyris*, lines 189–94 (ed. and trans. W. W. Skeat, *Ælfric's Lives of Saints* [EETS, reprinted 1966], II, 328–9, no. 32).

[4] See above, pp. 98–100.

[5] *Ælfrics Grammatik und Glossar*, ed. J. Zupitza (Berlin, 1880), p. 299, lines 13–14.

and treatment of widows in the early Church and in western Europe in general before the First Viking Age, before we turn to look more specifically at the position of widows in the later Anglo-Saxon Church. New prayers were introduced in the late tenth century to the liturgical rites for the consecration and blessing of widows, probably reflecting the increasing frequency with which widows were choosing at this time to enter a life of religion rather than remain, potentially available to remarry, in the world. The central part of this chapter will explore these rites in some detail, raising thereby some important questions about the development of the liturgy in England at the close of the tenth century as shown through the transmission of pontifical texts. Only then can we return to the problem of the categorisation of the particular situations of Wynflæd, Æthelgifu and the various unmarried daughters of Edward the Elder, and readdress the wider argument about the nature of the evidence to which their cases point.

Devout widows in the early Church

The widow, as a person possessed both of sexual experience and potentially of some independent means, presented a number of problems to ecclesiastical hierarchies in the early medieval West; the Church's efforts at controlling such women were directed primarily at restricting widows' freedom by forcing them into a life of chastity. To their noble kin, however, widows' temporal possessions offered tempting prizes to be administered carefully (within the family or via a new marriage if the woman were still young enough) to the mutual advantage of all concerned. It was in the interests of neither group that previously married women should enjoy too much freedom; the dangers of young, idle widows were obvious to all and demanded both secular and spiritual control.[6]

In societies where aristocratic mortality was high the fate of those of both genders whose spouses predeceased them, particularly those widowed young, acquired a particular significance.[7] A variety of choices was open to a woman in this situation, all potentially driven by her need to obtain some replacement for the male guardian she had lost.[8] The terms of the various arrangements made in his

---

[6]   I Timothy, 5: 13; J. Bremmer, 'Pauper or patroness: the widow in the early Christian Church', in *Between Poverty and the Pyre*, ed. J. Bremmer and L. van den Bosch (1995), pp. 31–57, at pp. 35–8 and 40.

[7]   K. J. Leyser, *Rule and Conflict in an Early Medieval Society* (1979), pp. 51–62; M. Parisse, 'Des veuves au monastère', in *Veuves et veuvage dans le haut Moyen Age*, ed. M. Parisse (1993), pp. 255–74, at pp. 255–7 and 262–7; R. H. Bremmer, 'Widows in Anglo-Saxon England', in *Between Poverty and the Pyre*, ed. J. Bremmer and L. van den Bosch (1995), pp. 58–88, at pp. 81–2; J. L. Nelson, 'The wary widow', in *Property and Power in the Early Middle Ages*, ed. W. Davies and P. Fouracre (1995), pp. 82–113, at pp. 84–5.

[8]   References to widows in earlier Anglo-Saxon law-codes are concerned largely with their physical protection and material support; see T. J. Rivers, 'Widows' rights in Anglo-Saxon

will by the ninth-century Kentish reeve Abba for the disposal of his property after his death illustrate clearly the options facing his wife should she survive him. If he had had a son, his son was to inherit his landed property and enjoy it with his mother. If Abba were to die childless his wife could only retain his lands as long as she were willing to hold them *mid clennisse*, continently. Abba's brother was instructed to assist the widow in the management of the estate, ensuring that it raise sufficient profit for her support. Should Abba's widow remarry she would lose her husband's land, but were she to enter a minster or go on a pilgrimage she would receive a substantial monetary gift and alms were to be given on her behalf to the minster at Lyminge.[9]

As this will has shown, a wife whose husband predeceased her could remarry, in which case much of any inheritance she had from her late husband would be lost to her, and such wealth as she did retain would pass from her own control into that of her new husband.[10] Alternatively she could remain as a lay woman in the world without remarrying, looking either to her surviving relatives or to the Church for physical and material protection. Although in England a formal duty to protect widows was laid on the king and the Church only in the late pre-Conquest period,[11] there were references to the need to provide physical protection for widows in earlier Anglo-Saxon law-codes. The laws of Æthelberht of Kent demanded compensation for the violation of a widow's *mund* and other codes considered the need for the material support of such women and their children.[12] The provisions made in early Frankish councils point to a third option open to widows. Widows could take vows to remain continent for the rest of their lives and, having assumed the dress distinctive to their state, live either within a monastic community, or stay in their own homes (albeit under threat of being consigned to the cloister should they fail to remain chaste).[13] English Church

---

law', *American Journal of Legal History*, 19 (1975), 208–15, at pp. 210–12; Bremmer, 'Widows', pp. 59–60, and for examples from the early English law-codes, below n. 12. Julia Crick's forthcoming paper 'Men, women and widows: widowhood in pre-Conquest England', in *Widowhood in Medieval and Early Modern Europe*, ed. S. Cavallo and L. Warner (1999), pp. 24–36 does much to enhance our understanding of the behaviour of widows in Anglo-Saxon society.

9   Harmer, *SEHD*, no. 2 (S 1482). For a general discussion of this will see T. Charles-Edwards, 'Anglo-Saxon kinship revisited', in *The Anglo-Saxons from the Migration Period to the Eighth Century*, ed. J. Hines (1997), pp. 171–210, at pp. 197–8.

10   Crick, 'Men'; Nelson, 'The wary widow', p. 87–9.

11   Rivers, 'Widows' rights', pp. 211 and 213; see below, nn. 54–8.

12   Æthelberht, chs. 75–6 and 78 (ed. Liebermann, *Die Gesetze*, I, 7–8); Hlothhere and Eadric, ch. 6 (*ibid.*, p. 10); Ine, ch. 38 (p. 94). Rivers, 'Widows' rights', pp. 210–12.

13   Synod of St-Jean de Losne, 673/5, ch. 13 (ed. C. de Clercq, *Concilia Galliae A.511–A.695*, CCSL, 148A [Turnhout, 1963], p. 316): 'Illas uero, quas Domini sacerdotes religioso ordine uiuere cognouerint, liceat eis *in domibus earum caste pieque conuersare*; ut uero, si neglegentes de castitate earum extiterint, ad eas reuertentes in monasterio trudantur'; quoted by B. Jussen, 'On Church organisation and the definition of an estate: the idea of widowhood in late

councils did not codify the same explicit recommendations about the appropriate behaviour of widows, but we have already seen that there is reason to think that Anglo-Saxon widows also chose the continent life, in which case these comparisons are relevant.[14]

The Church had since patristic times preferred women not to remarry on their husband's death; for Tertullian all those who entered into second marriages were certain to be damned, while Jerome saw those who remarried as equivalent to prostitutes.[15] Widows were thus encouraged to remain single and devote their continence to God. Bede's homily on the wedding at Cana (John, 2: 1–11) offered some consolation to the chastely married: if there were 'fault in an immaculate marriage bed', he argued, Christ would not have consecrated that state with the first of his miracles:[16]

> But since conjugal chastity is good, the continence of a widow is better, and the perfection of a virgin is best, to demonstrate his approval of the choice of all these ranks while yet determining the merit of each, he deigned to be born from the inviolate womb of the virgin Mary; soon after being born he was blessed by the prophetic voice of the widow Anna; then as a young man he was invited by those celebrating a marriage, and he honoured them by the presence of his power.

The collection of penitential canons attributed to Archbishop Theodore permitted a man to remarry one month after the death of his wife (as long as he did not marry a relative of his first wife), but specified that a woman must wait a year before taking a second husband.[17] Alternatively, a woman could take vows and live as a religious, but such a decision was meant to be lifelong.[18] When Alcuin wrote to Æthelburh, abbess of Fladbury, on the murder of her brother-in-law, Æthelred of

---

antique and early medieval Christianity', *Tel Aviver Jahrbuch für deutsche Geschichte*, 22 (1993), 25–42, at p. 31, n. 18. See also W. Hartmann, *Die Synoden der Karolingerzeit im Frankenreich und in Italien* (Paderborn, 1989), p. 425; G. Muschiol, *Famula Dei. Zur Liturgie in merowingischen Frauenklöstern* (Münster, 1994), pp. 45–6. Compare also the canons referring to widows issued at the Councils of Orleans and Paris quoted above, chapter 2, n. 110.

[14]   Above, pp. 41–3 and 56–9.

[15]   Bremmer, 'Pauper', pp. 34–41; Jussen, 'On Church organisation', p. 27; Nelson, 'The wary widow', p. 84; Crick, 'Men' .

[16]   Bede, *Homelia*, I.14, lines 9–16 (ed. D. Hurst, *Baedae Homiliae evangelii*, CCSL 122 [Turnhout, 1955], p. 95; trans. L. T. Martin and D. Hurst, *Bede the Venerable. Homilies on the Gospels* (2 vols., Kalamazoo, Michigan, 1991), I, 134.

[17]   Theodore, Penitential, II, xii, 10 (ed. Finsterwalder, *Die Canones*, p. 327); compare II, xii, 27 (p. 329). Julia Crick has drawn attention to the significant distinction made in these canons between a woman whose husband has died, who is described either as *uxor* or *mulier* and a widow who has taken religious vows, for whom the noun *uidua* is reserved (and often paired with her religious counterpart, the *uirgo*): 'Men'.

[18]   The problem of how to treat those who had taken vows of chastity but nevertheless married a second time were addressed in Theodore, Penitential, II, xii, 14–15 (ed. Finsterwalder, *Die Canones*, p. 328), quoted at the head of this chapter.

Northumbria, he was quite clear about the advice that should be given to the king's widow: 'Some of this ruin has brought you hot tears, I know, for your beloved sister. Now she is widowed she must be urged to soldier for Christ in a convent ('in cenobio militet Christo') that her temporal grief may lead to eternal joy'.[19]

The behaviour appropriate to widows specified in the New Testament served as a model for later commentators. The example of the prophetess Anna, daughter of Phanuel who, widowed after seven years of marriage, had reached the age of eighty-four years living in the Temple serving God with fasting and prayer night and day, was often invoked as a model to be emulated, as in Bede's homily quoted above.[20] In his sermons, Caesarius of Arles advised the widows in his congregation to refrain from remarrying: 'The good widows who do not love pleasure and do not gossip are neither nosy nor envious nor arrogant, those widows who serve God through fasting, prayer and charity, just as the holy Anna did, these widows unite with the holy Anna herself into many thousands of widows'.[21] Equally significant was the definition of the true widow found in Pauline epistles; she was of mature years, the relict of only one husband, dressed 'in holy attire' (*in habitu sancto*), was known for her good works, sensible and edifying conversation 'and continued in supplications and prayers, night and day'.[22] The fourth-century commentary on Paul's first epistle to Timothy by Ambrosiaster dealt at length with widows, laying particular emphasis on the ascetic features of their lifestyle, and thereby drawing the widow characterised by continence, prayer and mortification closer to the perfect condition of virgins and monks.[23] It is clear that there was in late fourth-century Rome a number of widows of the Church (*uiduae Ecclesiae*) who having made a formal promise not to remarry, devoted themselves entirely to God, adopted a distinctively modest dress and were honoured by the Church; the faithful were urged to provide for their

---

19   Alcuin, *Epistola* 102 (ed. E. Dümmler, *Epistolae Karolini Aevi*, II, MGH, Epistolae IV [Berlin, 1895], 1–493, at p. 149; trans. S. Allott, *Alcuin of York c. A.D. 732 to 804* [1974], p. 55, no. 42). Compare also *Epistola* 103 (pp. 149–50), where Alcuin urged Æthelburh to encourage her widowed sister to serve God faithfully and continue making progress towards the salvation of her soul.

20   Luke 2: 36–8. Compare also the *Collectio canonum hibernensis*, bk 45, caps 6 and 12 (ed. F. W. H. Wasserschleben, *Die irische Kanonensammlung* [Giessen, 1874], pp. 181 and 183, translated M. Ní Dhonnchadha, '*Caillech* and other terms for veiled women in medieval Irish texts', *Éigse*, 27 [1994–5], 71–96, at pp. 90–1): 'Now in the New Testament, Anna, who recognised the Lord as an infant, was the first widow. .... Augustine says: there are two kinds of veiled women: firstly virgins who imitate Mary in body and nature; secondly, penitents who imitate Anna and who ought to remain under the hand of the pastor until death'.

21   Caesarius of Arles, sermon 6, §7 (ed. G. Morin, *Sancti Caesarii episcopi Arelatensis Opera, I: Sermones* [Maredsous, 1937], p. 35); trans. Jussen, 'On Church organisation', p. 36.

22   I Timothy 5: 3–16; Titus 2: 3–5.

23   R. Gryson, *The Ministry of Women in the Early Church* (Collegeville, Minnesota, 1976), pp. 97 and 103.

material support.[24] Many of Jerome's letters extolled the ideal of the Christian widow and reinforce our notion that these were a distinct and significant body within the Church in his day.[25] Whether their distinctive dress marked them out as a specific sub-category of women whose husbands had predeceased them can be disputed.

Late antique custom marked a wife's bereavement in two ways: by defining a period after her husband's death when she was to remain chaste (and punishing her if she became pregnant during that time); and by insisting on her adoption of black clothes as a sign of mourning. At the council of St-Jean-de-Losne of 673/5 it was decreed that 'women who have lost their husband and according to old custom change their dress and desire to live as widows should be under the protection of the ruler'.[26] Similarly, at Cividale del Friuli in 796–7, *puellae scilicet uel uiduae* making vows of virginity or continence were said to put on as a sign of chastity the black quasi-religious (*quasi religiosa*) garment in accordance with old custom.[27] Jussen has argued that these directives indicate not that such bereaved women all assumed a life of religion, but merely that the assumption of a distinctive dress signifying mourning was an outward sign expected of *all* widows, *relictae*. In Jussen's opinion, *vestem mutare* should therefore be taken to mean 'loss of the husband', a view which has important implications for his understanding of the early Frankish synodal texts concerning the behaviour of widows.[28] Bringing a sociological approach to the synodal literature, Jussen has seen widows as a defined social category, a particular sub-group of which, called *uiduae* in these texts, was being defined as a social estate with a unique morality, able to earn honour from their visible performance of acts of charity, prayer and fasting.[29] There are some difficulties in this approach. While it is the case that these synodal records have little to say about non-religious widows (except in the provisions concerning incest), their absence from this

---

[24]   Gryson, *The Ministry*, p. 97.

[25]   For example, Jerome's letters to Eustochium and to Marcella, nos. 22 and 38 (ed. I. Hilberg, *Sancti Eusebii Hieronymi Epistulae* [2 vols., Vienna, 1910], I, 143–211, 289–93). See also Bremmer, 'Pauper', pp. 46–9.

[26]   Synod of St-Jean de Losne, 673/5, ch. 12 (ed. de Clercq, *Concilia Galliae*, p. 316): 'Feminae sane, quae earum uiros amiserint et ad uiduitatem studio priscam consuetudinem atque ueste mutata permanere uoluerint, sub tuitionem principis habeantur'. Quoted by Jussen, 'On Church organisation', p. 32; Nelson, 'The wary widow', p. 85. See Muschiol, *Famula Dei*, pp. 46–7.

[27]   Council of Cividale del Friuli, 796–7, ch. 11 (ed. A. Werminghoff, *Concilia Aevi Karolini*, I, MGH, Leges III, Concilia II.1 [Hannover and Leipzig, 1906], p. 193, no. 21).

[28]   Jussen, 'On Church organisation', pp. 33 and 35. This view does not take account of the fact that the chapter of the 796/7 Cividale council just quoted relates as much to virgins as to widows; for virgins the *nigra uestis* cannot have signified mourning, even if it might so have done for the widows.

[29]   Jussen, 'On Church organisation', p. 42, and quoting Caesarius, Sermo 6, §7 (as above, n. 21).

literature should not surprise us.[30] Little was said in these texts about women who were virgins other than those who had entered the cloister, nor did lay married women attract much attention. That these decrees reveal most about the religious organisation of women (virgins and deaconesses as well as widows) is to be expected from texts concerned primarily with ecclesiastical organisation and the boundaries between the Church and the world.

Much of the secondary literature concerning the status of widows within the late antique and early medieval Churches in the West has been concerned with issues surrounding the functions allowed to religious women during the first Christian centuries and particularly the increasing restrictions placed from the late fourth century onwards on their exercise of levitical (viz. sacramental) functions.[31] It is far from clear that in the western Church women ever assumed any of the duties of the diaconate: the dignity of the *diaconissa* seems not to have denoted a true function in the West, as it did in the eastern Church where deaconesses were particularly involved with the preparation of adult females for baptism and in their receipt of that sacrament.[32] In the early Christian West this was rather an honorary title, associated with the particular liturgical blessing bestowed on widows who dedicated themselves to religion.[33] Anxiety that women might have been admitted to the levitical ministry was, however, voiced at the council of Nîmes of 394/396, and injunctions against this supposed abuse were repeated in the fifth and sixth centuries.[34] The prohibition on the ordination of women was stated most explicitly at the First Council of Orange in 411: 'Deaconesses are absolutely not to be ordained; and if there are still any of them, let them bow their head under the benediction which is given to the congregation'.[35] As Roger Gryson has argued, these *diaconissae* are probably best understood as widows who received a blessing

---

30   *Contra* Jussen, 'On Church organisation', p. 31.

31   The clearest exposition of the subject is found in Gryson, *The Ministry*, a study written explicitly as a contribution to the debate over the ordination of women in the late-twentieth century in order to clarify the arguments provided by historical precedent. More wide-ranging analysis has been provided by Bremmer, 'Pauper'.

32   E. Palazzo, 'Les formules de bénédiction et de consécration des veuves au cours du haut Moyen Age', in *Veuves et veuvage dans le haut Moyen Age*, ed. M. Parisse (Paris, 1993), pp. 31–6, at p. 32. Attention is drawn here to the fifth-century *Statuta ecclesiae antiqua* of Gennadius of Marseille, who directed that the care of preparing women for baptism was to be entrusted to widows or *moniales*: *Statuta*, ch. 100 ('recapitulatio', ch. 12) (ed. C. Munier, *Concila Galliae A.314–A.506*, CCSL, 148 [Turnhout, 1963], p. 184).

33   Gryson, *The Ministry*, pp. 100–2; Muschiol, *Famula Dei*, pp. 295–300.

34   Gryson, *The Ministry*, p. 108; Council of Orange, 441, ch. 29 (ed. Munier, *Concilia Galliae*, p. 85); Council of Epaon, 517, ch. 21 (ed. de Clercq, *Concilia Galliae*, p. 29); and Council of Orleans, 533, ch. 17 (ibid., p. 101); second council of Tours, 567, ch. 20 (ibid., pp. 184–8). H. Le Bourdellès, 'Les ministères féminins dans le haut moyen âge en Occident', in *La Femme au Moyen-Age*, ed. M. Rouche and J. Heuclin (Maubeuge, 1990, pp. 11–23, at p. 15.

35   Council of Orange, 441, ch. 25 (ed. Munier, *Concilia Galliae*, p. 84): 'Diaconae omnimodis non ordinandae: si quae iam sunt, benedictioni quae populo impenditur capita submittant'; Gryson, *The Ministry*, p. 102.

on their *professio*, or formal entry into the religious life, an occasion marked by
their taking of a vow of continence, assumption of distinctive clothing, and receipt
of a blessing: 'The *professio* to persevere in widowhood, made before the bishop
in the *secretarium*, will be marked by the clothing of the widow imposed by the
bishop. Anyone who abducts one of these women, or she who violates such an
agreement, must be punished'.[36] These two canons make explicit both the lay
status of such women and the fact that the profession they made distinguished
them from other lay women (and, I would argue, from other *relictae*, other women
who had survived the decease of their husbands). The synodal texts were trying
to standardise widows' lifestyles, to push them closer to other social types (veiled
women and virgin nuns) who also changed their dress as part of their initiation
into the Church, and by constantly reinforcing the Pauline picture of the ideal
widow they defined a state characterised by specific behaviour.

That widows remained laywomen and were never to be ranked with the
clergy is clear from these early Church councils, yet the liturgical evidence
demonstrates quite clearly that entry to the *ordo uiduarum* was formally marked
by a ceremony involving blessings and prayers, and formal reclothing.[37] There are
many respects in which the blessings found for widows in early sacramentaries
differ little from those prescribed in the same texts for the consecration of virgins;
in the blessing of the clothes that would mark out their new state, virgins and
widows alike were instructed to preserve their chastity in accepting clothes that
would dignify them before God and help to keep them from temptation.[38]
Consolation was sought for a widow for the tribulations of her widowed state, just
as the prophet Elijah had consoled the widow of Zarephath (better known as the
widow with the cruse of oil);[39] heavenly glory was the ultimate reward for
reverently preserved chastity. The lack of extant English liturgical books from
before the tenth century means that we are dependent on continental
sacramentaries for evidence about the liturgical provisions for widows made in the
pre-Viking Age; the prayers found in those manuscripts for the consecration of

---

[36]   Council of Orange, 441, ch. 26 (ed. Munier, *Concilia Galliae*, p. 85); translated by
Gryson, *The Ministry*, p. 103; quoted by Jussen, 'On Church organisation', p. 34.
[37]   Palazzo, 'Les formules', pp. 32–3; R. Metz, 'Le statut de la femme en droit
canonique médiéval', *Recueils de la Société Jean Bodin*, 12 (1962), 59–113, at p. 93; S. F.
Wemple, *Women in Frankish Society* (Philadelphia, Pennsylvania, 1981), pp. 284–5, n. 58. I
cannot follow Jussen's interpretation of this literature where he has reached the conclusion that
'among widows there were no official initiation rites': 'On Church organisation', p. 41.
[38]   Palazzo, 'Les formules', p. 33.
[39]   'Consolare domine hanc famulam tuam uiduitatis laboribus constrictam sicut
consolare dignatus es sareptenam uiduam per heliam prophetam.' Cited here from the *Liber
sacramentorum Gellonensis*, ed. A. Dumas, CCSL 159 [Turnhout, 1981], p. 409, §2615. The story
of Elijah's visit to the widow from Zarephath is found in I Kings 17:10–16; allusion is made to it
also in Luke 4:26. See Bremmer, 'Pauper', p. 32.

widows were first attested in an English context in tenth-century pontificals and sacramentaries.[40]

Widows who opted for continence and did not remarry can thus be seen to have had a defined status and gradually demarcated role within the early Church; accorded considerable respect, they had an honoured place in the — non-clerical — ecclesiastical hierarchy. [41] In the East their role was absorbed by the order of deaconesses, but in the West widows were largely, but not wholly, assimilated within the monastic Church. The status of widows who, with the Church's explicit approval, chose continence rather than remarriage came to be solemnified by a series of blessings and prayers preserved in early sacramentaries which celebrated the widow's formal adoption of the clothes distinctive to a life in religion. In many cases these prayers echoed those employed for the consecration of virgins and both groups were classed among the minor orders of the Church, neither being ordained, nor having any clearly defined liturgical or ministerial role.[42] A widow was not, necessarily, consigned to the cloister on her consecration; the Frankish canons allowed for her to live chastely and piously as a religious in her own home: *liceat eis in domibus earum caste pieque conuersare*.[43] Similarly in England it has already been seen that many of the inmates of pre-Viking Age religious communities had formerly been married, some, like Cuthburg the founder of the minster at Wimborne,[44] left their spouses by mutual agreement, others, however, came to the cloister in widowhood. The diversity of experience and religious expression encompassed within the Anglo-Saxon understanding of the monastic life is more likely to provide an explanation for the lack of criticism of women who lived a religious life outside the cloister in English sources than is the presumption that all widows were cloistered.[45] The attention paid by Aldhelm in

---

[40]   See further below, pp. 127–34.

[41]   The picture of the *ordo uiduarum* presented by Tertullian was one of an elderly and dignified group of some social standing, permitted to sit at the front of the church with the bishop, elders and deacons: Bremmer, 'Pauper', pp. 40–1.

[42]   Palazzo, 'Les formules', pp. 32–4.

[43]   Council of St.-Jean-de-Losne, ch. 13 (ed. de Clercq, *Concilia Galliae*, p. 316), quoted by Jussen, 'On Church organisation', p. 31, n. 18. Wemple, *Women*, p. 105; E. Magnou-Nortier, 'Formes féminines de vie consacrée dans les pays du Midi jusqu'au début du XIIe siécle', in *La femme dans la vie religieuse du Languedoc (XIIIᵉ–XIVᵉ s.)*, Cahiers de Fanjeaux, 23 (1988), 193–216, at pp. 207–9. And see the other texts quoted above in chapter 2, n. 110.

[44]   Anglo-Saxon Chronicle 718; compare also the account given by Bede of Æthelthryth, who preserved her virginity through twelve years of marriage to Ecgfrith of Northumbria before persuading him to allow her to take the veil: *HE*, IV, 19–20 (ed. and trans. Colgrave and Mynors, pp. 390–3); Bremmer, 'Widows', p. 80–1.

[45]   Attempts were made at some Church councils to return female as well as male monastics to the cloisters from which they had departed (for example at *Clofesho*, A.D. 747, ch. 29, ed. A. W. Haddan and W. Stubbs, *Councils and Ecclesiastical Documents Relating to Great Britain and Ireland* [3 vols., 1869–78], III, 374, quoted above, chapter 2, n. 20) but generally greater concern was voiced over wandering clergy and the validity of their ordinations than over any putative irregularities committed by devout widows living quietly and harmlessly outside

his treatise on virginity to the virtue accruing to chaste widows is one indication
of the significance of this body of religious women within the early Anglo-Saxon
Church:[46]

> For if the uncontaminated virginity of Mary bore for us the incarnate
> Word of God in celestial childbirth, yet when the circle of one forty-
> day span had been measured out, the prophetess Anna, the daughter
> of Phanuel, prophesied the same redeemer through the presentiment
> of the Holy Spirit, and accordingly both grades, consecrated to both
> virgins and widows, are honoured in the very beginning of the divine
> nativity.

Widows and vowesses in the later Anglo-Saxon Church

Already denied the status of deaconess and a place among the ordained clergy
since the fifth century, religious widows were further constrained by Carolingian
reformers in the ninth century who tried to bring them under episcopal control and,
as far as possible, impose claustration on them, preventing them from living in
their own homes.[47] At the council of Paris in 829 widows were instructed not to
veil themselves indiscreetly, but to wait for thirty days before making a choice
about their future with the bishop's advice; at the end of the period of mourning
they might remarry, or 'if they decide instead to devote themselves to God, they
are to be admonished and instructed that they should not do so in their own homes,
but should submit themselves as maidservants to God under the direction of a
spiritual mother in a convent'.[48] They were not to continue living in their own
houses, nor 'living indiscreetly and using a noxious liberty of their own' were they

---

minster communities. Note again the Frankish parallel of *deo sacratae* living in the world:
Muschiol, *Famula Dei*, pp. 43–63.

[46]   Aldhelm, *De uirginitate*, ch. xiii (ed. R. Ehwald, *Aldhelmi Opera Omnia*, MGH,
AA, XV [Berlin, 1919], pp. 242–3; trans. M. Lapidge and M. Herren, *Aldhelm. The Prose Works*
[1979], p. 70).

[47]   Wemple, *Women*, pp. 259–60, n. 45; Nelson, 'The wary widow', p. 90. J. T.
Schulenburg, 'Strict active enclosure and its effects on the female monastic experience
(500–1100)', in *Medieval Religious Women I: Distant Echoes*, ed. J. A. Nichols and L. T. Shank
(1984), pp. 51–86, at pp. 77–9; idem, 'Female sanctity: Public and private roles, ca. 500–1100',
in *Women and Power in the Middle Ages*, ed. M. Erler and M. Kowaleski (Athens, Georgia, 1988),
pp. 102–25, at pp. 115–19.

[48]   Council of Paris, 829, ch 44 (ed. Werminghoff, *MGH, Concilia*, II, 2, pp. 638–9, no.
50; trans. Nelson, 'The wary widow', p. 90): 'ut non in domibus propriis sed in monasteriis sub
spiritalis matris regimine Deo se seruituras subdant'. See also *Episcoporum relatio*, 829, ch. 15
(ed. A. Boretius and V. Krause, *Capitularia regum Francorum*, MGH, Leges II, [Hannover, 1897],
II, 42, no. 196): 'Deprehendimus etiam et aliam neglegentiam, quod quaedam feminae sine
consensu sacerdotum uelum sibi incaute inponant'. Quoted by Nelson, 'The wary widow', p. 90.

to wander about in different places to the peril of their souls.[49] The objections of the senior clergy were clear: widows released to some extent from the control of their male relatives (and from the possibility of remarriage) by becoming *deo sacratae* needed to be reined in by their spiritual guardians lest either they used the veil as an excuse for licentiousness, or, subverting the natural order, they assumed the liberty of taking control over property as the female guardians and administrators (*excubatrices et administratrices*) of churches.[50]

These provisions can be interpreted, as they have been by Suzanne Wemple, as part of the Church's attempts to impose monogamy by preventing widows from using vows taken insincerely as a licence for sexual freedom, but they also reflect the increasing desire of the episcopacy to control female action, both their spiritual observance and the 'noxious liberty' that gave them control over property.[51] In its intention of preventing widows from establishing house-convents this conciliar legislation clearly failed. The council of Mainz of 888, while reiterating the instruction that widows should not be veiled too quickly, allowed those who had made a profession of chastity either to be cloistered regularly in a monastery or to guard the chastity of their profession intact while remaining at home.[52]

The fate of a widow's inheritance was also of obvious concern to her children, her husband's kin and even her original family and, as Janet Nelson has stressed, the ecclesiastical legislation must be considered in its secular context of the royal and aristocratic interests vested in the protection of widows' property, especially their landholdings. Peculiarly vulnerable to exploitation of their wealth, widows needed protection from the assaults of the secular world; the same Frankish councils that attempted to restrict widows' own freedom of action also imposed heavy penalties on their abduction by seculars avaricious for their wealth.[53] The earliest surviving account from Anglo-Saxon England of an instance

---

[49]   *Episcoporum relatio*, 829, ch. 17 (ed. Boretius and Krause, *MGH Capitularia*, II, 42, no. 196; trans. Nelson, 'The wary widow', p. 91). Compare the Council of Tribur 895, ch. 25 (ibid., pp. 227–8, no. 252).

[50]   Council of Paris, 829, ch. 42 (ed. Wermingohoff, *Concilia*, II, 2, pp. 638–9, no. 50); discussed by Nelson, 'The wary widow', p. 92.

[51]   Wemple, *Women*, pp. 105 and 259–60, n. 45 and Nelson, 'The wary widow', p. 92. Compare Schulenburg ('Strict active enclosure', p. 79): 'In large part, the basic rationale for narrow enclosure seems to have been the desire of *controlling* woman's sexuality through enforced isolation, not guarding her autonomy'.

[52]   Council of Mainz, 888, ch. 26 (ed. J. D. Mansi, *Sacrorum conciliorum nova et amplissima collectio* [Florence, 1759–98], XVIII, cols. 71–2): 'De uiduis praecipimus, ut nequaquam cito uelentur ... Si autem propositum castitatis assumpserint, aut monasterii claustris regulariter constringantur, aut domi manentes castitatem suae professionis integerrime custodiant'. Discussed by Wemple, *Women*, p. 173, and Nelson, 'The wary widow', pp. 91–3.

[53]   *Capitulare ecclesiasticum* 818/9 ch. 22 (ed. A. Boretius, *Capitularia regum Francorum*, MGH, Leges II [Hannover, 1883], I, 278, no. 138). The example of the widow Erkanfrida, examined in detail by Nelson ('The wary widow', pp. 95–113), demonstrates forcibly

in which the Church (in the person of the archbishop of Canterbury) acted as guardian for a widow is found in a charter dating from Edgar's reign.[54] However, a formal duty to protect widows was only laid on the king and the Church early in the eleventh century; it finds articulation first in the later law-codes of Æthelred, which are attributed to the authorship of Wulfstan, archbishop of York.[55] In Æthelred's fifth law-code it was decreed that every widow who conducted herself rightly was to be under the protection of God and the king; each was to remain without a husband for a year, 'she is afterwards to choose what she herself will'.[56] Further recommendations were made in Æthelred's sixth code: anyone who injured a vowess (*nunne*) or did violence to a widow was obliged to make amends to the utmost of his ability both to the Church and the state;[57] it was also ordered on the same occasion 'that they should not be constantly oppressing the widow and the orphan, but that they should diligently cheer them'.[58] Cnut's laws, too, sought to protect widows from the violence of the secular world.[59] Wulfstan's homiletic writings reiterated some of these legal injunctions; Liebermann made direct comparison between the recommendation that widows were to have special royal protection and a passage in a collection of Old English prose apparently in Wulfstan's style which was probably compiled by the archbishop himself, although never worked up fully into a sermon.[60] The oppression and abuse of widows (who were being wrongly forced to marry, impoverished and greatly humiliated) was one of the aspects of English society criticised by the archbishop

---

the vulnerability and dependence of the widow and her need to seek assistance in carrying out her wishes from a secular lord and the protection of the saints in her choice to become a *deo sacrata*.

[54]   Robertson, *ASCharters*, no. 44 (S 1447).

[55]   Rivers, 'Widows' rights', pp. 211 and 213. On Wulfstan's role as a lawmaker see D. Whitelock, 'Archbishop Wulfstan: homilist and statesman', *TRHS*, 4 ser. 24 (1942), 25–45, at pp. 35–8, and 41; P. Stafford, 'The laws of Cnut and the history of Anglo-Saxon royal promises', *Anglo-Saxon England*, 10 (1982), 173–90, pp. 173–77.

[56]   V Æthelred, ch. 21 (ed. Liebermann, *Die Gesetze*, I, 242; trans. Whitelock, *EHD*, I, 445, no. 44). This clause was repeated as VI Æthelred, ch. 26; compare also II Cnut, ch. 73 (ed. Liebermann, *Die Gesetze*, I, 254, 360).

[57]   VI Æthelred, ch. 39 (ed. Liebermann, *Die Gesetze*, I, 256). Compare II Cnut, ch. 52: 'If anyone takes a widow by force he is to compensate for it with the wergild' (ibid., p. 346).

[58]   VI Æthelred, ch. 47 (ibid., p. 258). Liebermann saw a possible influence of Exodus 22: 22 in this clause: *Die Gesetze*, III, 177.

[59]   II Cnut, ch. 52 (ed. Liebermann, *Die Gesetze*, I, 346). For a general discussion of this legal material enforcing widows' protection see M. P. Richards and B. J. Stanfield, 'Concepts of Anglo-Saxon women in the laws', in *New Readings on Women in Old English Literature*, ed. H. Damico and A. H. Olsen (Bloomington and Indianapolis, Indiana, 1990), pp. 89–99, at pp. 94–5; Bremmer, 'Widows', p. 68.

[60]   Liebermann, *Die Gesetze*, III, 173 (notes to V Æthelred, ch. 21); this text was printed as one of Wulfstan's homilies by A. Napier, *Wulfstan. Sammlung der ihm zugeschriebenen Homilien* (Berlin, 1883), no. 50 (the passage in question lies at p. 271), but for consideration of the place of this compilation in the Wulfstan corpus see the discussion by D. Bethurum, *The Homilies of Wulfstan* (1957), pp. 39–41.

in the most famous of his homilies, delivered in 1014 as a warning that to these and other sins could be attributed the rising tide of viking attack.[61]

Widows' own behaviour also attracted a good deal of attention in the prescriptive literature of the later Anglo-Saxon period. Secular law did not forbid remarriage, which was potentially a significant element of family strategy, both in situations where women were left with young children and where there was a substantial inheritance. The Church, however, placed more pressure on widows not to remarry than in earlier centuries. A one-year period when a widow should remain without a husband in mourning was imposed in secular law, after which she might 'choose what she herself desires'.[62] Any widow who took a husband within the space of that year would lose her morning gift and all her inheritance from her first husband; even if remarried by force she would lose her possessions unless she left her new spouse for good.[63] While St Paul had not only allowed for but actively encouraged the remarriage of women widowed young (whom he considered unsuitable to a life in religion),[64] later Anglo-Saxon ecclesiastics discouraged second marriages and were utterly opposed to the taking of more than two marital partners. In the recommendations he made to laymen in his Institutes of Polity, Wulfstan argued that a second marriage should not be accompanied by the priestly blessings given to a first, and that those who did remarry were to do penance for their actions.[65] The same restrictions were placed on remarriage in the Old English version of Halitgar's Penitential where Christians were told not to marry more than twice, widows advised to remarry young, and all subsequent marriages were denied ecclesiastical blessing: 'so as to make clear to them that it had been better for them to have remained chaste'.[66]

---

[61]   Wulfstan, 'Sermo Lupi ad Anglos' (ed. D. Whitelock, *Sermo Lupi ad Anglos* [3rd edn., 1963], p. 51, trans. Whitelock, *EHD*, I, 930, no. 240): '⁊ wydewan syndan fornydde on unriht to ceorle ⁊ to mænege foryrmde ⁊ gehynede swyþe'. Bremmer, 'Widows', pp. 74–5.

[62]   V Æthelred, ch. 21.1, VI Æthelred, ch. 26.1, II Cnut, ch. 73 (ed. Liebermann, *Die Gesetze*, I, 242, 254, 360).

[63]   II Cnut, chs. 73a, 73.2 (ed. Liebermann, *Die Gesetze*, I, 360). All these provisions are designed in large part to allow widows the space to make their own decisions about their future without being forced into uncongenial (or disadvantageous) decisions by the pressure from the rest of their kin.

[64]   I Timothy, 5: 14 (and see also I Corinthians 7: 8–9); St Paul's teachings on remarriage have been discussed in a late-antique historical context by Bremmer, 'Pauper', pp. 36–8.

[65]   I *Polity*, 90, II *Polity*, xxi.190–5 (ed. K. Jost, *Die "Institutes of Polity, Civil and Ecclesiastical"* [Bern, 1959], pp. 132–4; trans. M. J. Swanton, *Anglo-Saxon Prose* [2nd edn, 1993], p. 199); Bremmer, 'Widows', p. 77. Compare Ælfric's pastoral letter for Wulfsige III, chs. 26–8 (ed. and trans. Whitelock *et al.*, *Councils and Synods*, I, 201, no. 40): 'And no priest may be at the marriage anywhere where a man takes another wife or a woman takes another husband, nor bless them together; as if one thus indicated to them, that it were better for them if they remained in chastity. Yet the layman may with the apostle's permission marry a second time if he loses his wife, but the canons forbid the blessings to it and have appointed penance for such men to do'.

[66]   *Die altenglische Version des Halitgar'schen Bussbuches*, II, 20 (ed. J. Raith [Darmstadt, 1964], p. 27); discussed by Bremmer, 'Widows', pp. 76–7.

The ideal widow would opt for chastity after the example of biblical widows such as Anna or Judith.[67] Ælfric's summary of the book of Judith commended the example of this widow to its reader (possibly a *nunne*[68]), stressing 'how chastely she lived before Christ's nativity'.[69] In many ways Judith presented the closest biblical model for late Anglo-Saxon widows, notably because she continued to live in her husband's house after his death. Ælfric summarised the story of Manasses' *laf*, describing how after her husband's death (from sunstroke while harvesting) she had lived shut away on the upper floor of the house, fasting except for on the Sabbath and plainly dressed;[70] once she had saved the city of Bethulia from the siege of the Assyrian leader Holofernes (by allowing him to attempt to seduce her but killing him while he slept), she had then returned to her home and lived continently there for the remainder of the 100 years of her life, freeing her maidservant on her death.[71] Before suggesting too confidently, however, that Ælfric had in mind a widowed vowess when he wrote this piece, it should be noted that in warning against the example set by the scandalous behaviour followed by *sume nunnan*, he reminded his reader of the punishments waiting in hell for those who violated vows of chastity: 'she is not again a virgin if she lies with anyone, and she will not have the reward of hundredfold fruit'.[72] The maintenance of chastity required great struggle but brought the rewards of martyrdom.[73] The example of Judith is not the most obvious model for a never-married virgin (although the Old English poem *Judith* made its heroine a virgin rather than a widow).[74] One might nevertheless reflect once more on the fact that the biblical Judith was a widow who lived on family lands and not in a separately endowed establishment; in that sense she sets a good precedent for all *nunnan* whatever their marital history.

---

[67]   Bremmer, 'Widows', pp. 78–9, where reference is made also to the fragmentary Old English poem *Judith*. That poem, it has been suggested (J. T. Schulenburg, 'The heroics of virginity: Brides of Christ and sacrificial mutilation', in *Women in the Middle Ages and the Renaissance*, ed. M. B. Rose [Syracuse, New York, 1986], pp. 29–72, at pp. 38–9), was written (perhaps in the tenth century) to inspire religious women who faced sexual assault at the hands of Danish invaders with the heroic example of Judith, whose chastity remained uncompromised. Interestingly in the poem Judith appears as a never-married virgin, not as a widow.

[68]   M. Clayton, 'Ælfric's *Judith*: manipulative or manipulated?', *ASE*, 23 (1994), 215–27, at pp. 225–7.

[69]   Ælfric, 'On the Book of Judith', lines 434–5 (ed. Assmann, *Angelsächsische Homilien*, p. 115, no. 9). On the form of this text see above, chapter 4, n. 95.

[70]   Ælfric, 'On the Book of Judith', lines 196–208 (ed. B. Assmann, *Angelsächsische Homilien und Heiligenleben* [Darmstadt, 1964], p. 108).

[71]   Ibid., lines 399–401, p. 114.

[72]   Ibid., lines 432–3, p. 115. See Sister Mary Byrne, *The Tradition of the Nun in Medieval England* (Washington, D.C., 1932), p. 60.

[73]   Ælfric, 'On the nativity of Mary, the blessed virgin' (ed. Assmann, *Angelsächsische Homilien*, lines 294–7, 378–82, pp. 36 and 39, no. 3); Byrne, *The Tradition*, p. 52.

[74]   Mary Clayton has thus suggested that Ælfric's intended reader was a virgin vowess, living in a community of other *nunnan*: 'Ælfric's *Judith*', p. 227.

Although continence was the choice the Church would recommend for widows, among the injunctions concerning widows in Cnut's second law-code it was stated that 'a widow is never to be consecrated [to religion] too hastily'.[75] The enforcement of a one-year period of mourning in late Anglo-Saxon texts can interestingly be paralleled, as Julia Crick has recently shown, in the laws of the eighth-century Lombard king, Liutprand (those issued in his sixteenth year, A.D. 728): 'No man who holds the *mundium* of a woman may permit her to take the veil or assume the habit of a nun (*monachico habito induere*) within a year of the death of her husband'. The reason for the delay is explained; in the first throes of grief a woman may readily be persuadable into the cloister 'but when she has returned to herself and the desires of the flesh return, she may fall into adultery and behave as neither nun nor laywoman should'.[76] In eleventh-century England, too, the election of continence was, as much as a second marriage, only to be entered into after the woman had had time for due reflection, not at speed for the convenience of her relatives. The most comprehensive advice to widows as to their correct behaviour was given by Wulfstan in his Institutes of Polity; there he directed that they should follow the example of the prophetess Anna, who was with Simeon a witness to the infant Christ's circumcision according to the account given in Luke's Gospel:[77]

---

[75]   II Cnut, ch. 73.3 (ed. Liebermann, *Die Gesetze*, I, 360): '₇ ne hadige man æfre wudewan to hrædlice'. Discussed by Liebermann, ibid., III, s. v. 'Witwe', §9. Joel Rosenthal ('Anglo-Saxon attitudes: Men's sources, women's history', in *Medieval Women and the Sources of Medieval History*, ed. J. T. Rosenthal [Athens, Georgia and London, 1990], pp. 259–84, at p. 261) has interpreted this clause as reflecting a low opinion of women's constancy, but its context (with other clauses relating to the protection of widows from their avaricious male relatives) suggests that this was a measure designed for the protection rather than the restriction of widows. Compare the recommendation made at the Council of Paris 829 that widows should pause for reflection before rushing into the cloister (ch. 39, ed. Werminghoff, *MGH, Concilia*, II, 2, p. 637, no. 50); noted by D. Baltrusch-Schneider, 'Klosterleben als alternative Lebensform zur Ehe?', in *Weibliche Lebensgestaltung im frühen Mittelalter*, ed. H.-W. Goetz (Cologne and Vienna, 1991), pp. 45–64, at p. 55.

[76]   Crick, 'Men', n. 18. Laws of Liutprand, ch. 100.V (ed. F. Bluhme, *Leges Langobardorum*, MGH Leges, IV [Hannover, 1869], 148–9, trans. K. F. Drew, *The Lombard Laws* [Philadelphia, Pennsylvania, 1973], pp. 187–8). These provisions have recently been discussed more fully by Patricia Skinner: 'Maintaining the widow in medieval southern Italy' in *Widowhood in Medieval and Early Modern Europe*, ed. S. Cavallo and L. Warner (forthcoming, 1999). I am grateful to both Drs Crick and Skinner for allowing me to see these papers in advance of their publication.

[77]   Wulfstan, I *Polity*, 93–7, II *Polity*, xv.198–202 (ed. Jost, *Die "Institutes"*, pp. 136–7, trans. Swanton, *Anglo-Saxon Prose*, p. 199). For the prophetess Anna see Luke 2: 36–8.

VEILED WOMEN I

> It is right that widows should earnestly follow the example of Anna. She was in the temple day and night diligently serving. She fasted greatly and attended to prayers and called on Christ with mourning spirit, and distributed alms over and again and ever propitiated God as far as she could by word and deed, and now has heavenly bliss for a reward. So shall a good widow obey her lord.

Ælfric had equated the 'worthy widow' (namely one who had chosen continence over remarriage) with the *nunne*, the secular vowess,[78] and it has already been shown that Wulfstan considered *nunnan* could live in minsters as well as singly.[79] This royal and ecclesiastical legislation from the later Anglo-Saxon period can, Barbara Yorke has argued, be interpreted as an indication that 'widows who took a vow of chastity (so that they would not be forced by kinsmen to remarry)' were permitted 'to live independently on their own lands rather than having to band together in nunneries as seems generally to have happened in the seventh and eighth centuries'.[80] However, it seems more than probable that widows who had taken vows on their husband's death did sometimes also live, like *nunnan*, with small communities around them at the margins of the secular world, although this cannot be demonstrated with certainty.[81]

If it was common for secular women, and particularly widows, to imitate the state of professed women in the cloister by taking vows and wearing some of their distinctive clothing including the veil while remaining in the world, this would argue against the attempts made by some recent historians to shoehorn widows like Wynflæd and Æthelgifu into known congregations of cloistered religious.[82] Instead they should be seen as women who, adhering to contemporary ecclesiastical prohibitions on remarriage, occupied a recognised social position as avowed religious outside the cloister. Support for the notion that the Church was taking an increased interest in widows who took religious vows (in other parts of Europe as well as in England) can be found if we turn to the liturgical evidence.

---

[78]   *Ælfrics Grammatik und Glossar*, ed. Zupitza, p. 299, lines 13–14: 'nonna: arwyrþe wydewe oððe nunne'.

[79]   Wulfstan, I *Polity*, 85, II *Polity*, xiv.186 (ed. Jost, *Die "Institutes"*, p. 129). See above, chapter 4.

[80]   B. Yorke, '"Sisters under the skin?" Anglo-Saxon nuns and nunneries in southern England', in *Medieval Women in Southern England*, ed. K. Bate *et al.* (1989), pp. 95–117, p. 108.

[81]   D. Schneider, 'Anglo-Saxon women in the religious life: a study of the status and position of women in an early mediaeval society' (PhD thesis, University of Cambridge, 1985), pp. 84–5. It may be that the widow Æthelgifu had formed just such a community round her on her estate at Standon in Hertfordshire: D. Whitelock, *The Will of Æthelgifu* (1968) (S 1497); see further below, pp. 139–40.

[82]   See, for example, P. Halpin, 'Women religious in late Anglo-Saxon England', *Haskins Society Journal*, 6 (1994), 97–110; B. L. Venarde, *Women's Monasticism and Medieval Society: Nunneries in France and England, 890–1215* (Ithaca, New York and London, 1997), pp. 22–24.

Liturgical forms for the consecration of widows in the tenth and eleventh centuries

The more prominent status of widows in the later tenth-century Church is reflected by the development in the same period of new liturgical forms to mark their consecration into the religious life. The paucity of surviving English liturgical manuscripts dating from before the tenth century can make it difficult to demonstrate which features in the later manuscripts represent innovations in Anglo-Saxon practice. There is, however, some evidence that the refining of the liturgical status of widows (reported by Eric Palazzo first to have appeared in a German context in the mid-tenth century) is paralleled in England a little later. In a study of the forms for the blessing and consecration of widows in the high Middle Ages, Eric Palazzo has drawn attention to the fact that in the Romano-German Pontifical there is a much fuller *ordo* for the consecration of widows than that found in earlier texts; this pontifical (that is a collection of pontifical *ordines*, the procedures and prayers pronounced by a bishop at the ceremonies at which he officiated) was compiled in the diocese of Mainz, probably at the church of St Alban around the year 950.[83] Although the Romano-German Pontifical did not reach England until the middle years of the eleventh century, some of the prayers new to that collection concerning the blessing of religious women appear to have been copied into English manuscripts around the turn of the tenth century.[84]

Early sacramentaries contained prayers for the blessing of widows, invoking the parallel of the widow of Zarephath who was comforted by the visit of the Prophet Elijah; they pray for the widow's consolation, for the sanctification and benediction of her clothes (especially the veil) and ask for divine aid in keeping the consecrated woman in continence and modesty. The widow herself is enjoined to show humility, chastity, obedience, charity and to be noted for her performance of good works.[85] Although many of the prayers given for the blessing of widows in the Romano-German Pontifical are modelled on those of earlier sacramentaries, in one of the pieces — described by Palazzo as representing a unique witness in the liturgy — direct allusion is made to the figure who should serve as a model for the widow, the prophetess Anna.[86] This prayer is the last of the *ordo*, following the blessing and institution of her clothes and veil, and asks that the newly consecrated *famula* should serve God in his church with devout

---

[83]   M. Lapidge, 'The origin of CCCC 163', *Transactions of the Cambridge Bibliographical Society*, 8 (1981), 18–28, at p. 18; C. Vogel and R. Elze, *Le Pontifical romano-germanique du dixième siecle* (3 vols., Vatican City, 1963–72), III, 3–28.

[84]   Particular gratitude is owed to Sarah Larratt-Keefer for her patient assistance in helping me to make sense of this liturgical material and for drawing my attention to J. Brückmann's bibliographical survey of English pontificals: 'Latin manuscript pontificals and benedictionals in England and Wales', *Traditio*, 29 (1973), 391–458.

[85]   See above, chapter 2, and Palazzo, 'Les formules', pp. 32–3.

[86]   Palazzo, 'Les formules', pp. 34–5.

mind just as the prophetess Anna, having assumed the clothes of widowhood, for a long time served devotedly in the temple in fasting and prayer. [87] Invocation of the example provided by Anna is also employed in the preceding *ordo*, that for the making of a deaconess.[88] At the moment of the woman's consecration, before her endowment with the symbols of her new state (stole, veil, ring and wreath), is pronounced a prayer beginning 'Deus, qui Annam filiam Phanuelis'.[89] Here is sought for the deaconess the same spiritual qualities and heavenly rewards as were given to Anna, who was widowed after only seven years of marriage and spent the rest of her eighty-four years in chastity serving God in the temple, engaged night and day in prayer and fasting until she was, with Simeon, a witness to Christ's circumcision.[90]

I have been unable to find a version of this prayer in any earlier liturgical collection than the Romano-German Pontifical, nor indeed does the example of Anna seem specifically to have been recommended to widows in the prayers for their blessing and consecration included in earlier sacramentaries. Pointing out that the Romano-German Pontifical marks a ritualisation (typical of the spirit of this liturgical compilation as a whole) of the consecration of the widow unknown hitherto, Palazzo has inquired whether this should be put into the context of a new significance for widows within the bosom of religious communities in the same period.[91] Certainly the large number of female convents established in Saxony in the tenth century (Karl Leyser calculated that at least thirty-six houses for women were founded between 919 and 1024) could have given rise to new liturgical needs; few of these establishments followed the Rule of St Benedict, and in the context of the rather looser provisions of the canonical way of life a number of houses was founded for and dwelt in by widows, several with substantial personal

---

[87]   *Le Pontifical*, XXV, 14 (ed. Vogel and Elze, I, 61): 'ut sicut Anna prophetissa multis temporibus uestibus uiduitatis induta, in templo gloriae tuae ieiuniis et orationibus fideliter deseruiuit, sic et haec famula tua tibi soli Deo in ecclesia tua deuota mente deseruiat'.

[88]   It does not seem appropriate to investigate here in any detail the resurrection of the title *diaconissa* for senior religious women of the ninth- and tenth-century Church. Susanne Wemple has noted its reappearance at the council of Worms of 868, where (reiterating canon 15 of the council of Chalcedon of 451) it was stated that women over the age of forty might be ordained to the diaconate: Council of Worms 868, ch. 73, ed. Mansi, *Concilia*, XV, col. 882; see Wemple, *Women*, p. 146, and W. Hartmann, *Das Konzil von Worms, 868* (Göttingen, 1977), p. 40 and table 2, p. 126. The title *diaconissa* may have been associated with the office of the abbess at this time. Wemple has suggested that it might have been thought suitable for royal women who retired to nunneries that already had ruling abbesses, or for lay abbesses who held monastic houses as benefices from the king; there is, however, no evidence that these women sought to perform quasi-clerical roles: *Women*, pp. 46–7 and 173. See also Le Bourdellès, 'Les ministères', p. 22 on the use of the title deaconess by tenth- and eleventh-century abbesses in recognition of their religious power over nuns, which he has seen as the sole genuine instance from the medieval west of a female 'ministry'.

[89]   *Le Pontifical*, XXIV, 8 (ed. Vogel and Elze, I, 55–6).

[90]   Luke 2: 36–8.

[91]   Palazzo, 'Les formules', p. 35.

estates.[92] There is, however, also as the preceding discussion of the status of religious women in England has suggested, a putative Anglo-Saxon context for the development and use of new rituals for the benediction of widows, albeit most probably outside the cloister rather than within.

There are no surviving English manuscripts of the Romano-German Pontifical dating from before the third quarter of the eleventh century, the earliest copies being associated with Ealdred, archbishop of York (1060–69).[93] The most complete extant English manuscript is Cambridge, Corpus Christi College MS. 163, copied in a mid-eleventh-century Anglo-Caroline minuscule apparently from a version of the Pontifical brought back from Cologne by Ealdred.[94] Michael Lapidge has suggested that this manuscript, which provides all the *ordines* for the consecration of women (*consecratio sacre uirginis*; *ad ancillas Dei uirgines uelendas*; *ad diaconissam faciendam*; *consecratio uidue*) found in other copies of the Romano-German Pontifical, but not those for the ordination of abbots and monks, might have been copied at or for use in a nunnery.[95] Such a presumption raises difficult questions about the ownership of pontificals, and indeed the purpose for which episcopal books were made.[96] Although it might be imagined that a nunnery would — albeit rarely — have had a need for an *ordo* for the dedication of a new church or altar, it is harder to see what use a female community would make of a mass for the dedication of a baptistery, still less the *ordines* and subsequent masses for the ordination of bishops or deacons, or for the benediction of a king or emperor.[97] Must we seek to place this volume in a nunnery of such size that the diocesan bishop would frequently have been needed for the veiling of new inmates? It might rather be located either at one of the male religious houses to which women seem loosely to have been attached,[98] or perhaps at the house of a bishop, whose diocese encompassed a large number of female minsters (groups organised around widows and vowesses as well as regular nunneries) and whose existing liturgical books, while adequate for the ordination of abbots and monks, did not supply him with *ordines* for the consecration of these

---

[92]   Leyser, *Rule*, pp. 62–4 and n. 12, p. 164.

[93]   Lapidge, 'The origin', pp. 18–20; and idem., 'Ealdred of York and MS. Cotton Vitellius E. XII', *Yorkshire Archaeological Journal*, 55 (1983), 11–25, at pp. 20–4.

[94]   Lapidge, 'The origin', p. 22. This manuscript is very closely related to a, now damaged, manuscript London, British Library, MS. Cotton Vitellius E.xii: ibid., and Lapidge, 'Ealdred', pp. 21–2; see also D. N. Dumville, *Liturgy and the Ecclesiastical History of Late Anglo-Saxon England* (1992), p. 73.

[95]   Lapidge, 'The origin', pp. 23–6.

[96]   The same point was made by Dumville, *Liturgy*, p. 73. Compare also the pertinent remarks concerning female book-ownership made by Julia Crick, 'An eleventh-century prayerbook for women: the origins and history of the Galba prayerbook' (forthcoming).

[97]   A list of the contents of Cambridge, Corpus Christi College, MS. 163 has been printed by Lapidge, 'The origin', pp. 24–6.

[98]   For examples of such arrangements see Halpin, 'Women', p. 104, and below, chapter 6, §e

various sorts of religious women. On this supposition it might well be appropriate
to assign the manuscript to the Old Minster, Winchester where on other grounds
it might be thought to have originated.[99] The copying of at least this part of the
manuscript would then be seen to reflect a liturgical need occasioned by the
emergence of more diverse forms of female religious expression in southern
England.

The growth in the number of Anglo-Saxon religious women outside
regular convents has, however, been demonstrated from at least the middle years
of the tenth century, and one might have looked to find liturgical responses to this
development earlier than the episcopate of Ealdred of York. In fact at least two
English manuscripts (the Ecgberht and Claudius Pontificals), both datable on
palaeographical grounds to around the year 1000,[100] witness to the introduction of
a new prayer into the form for the consecration of widows, which may bear some
relationship to the prayers found in the Romano-German Pontifical. The origin of
the combined benedictional and pontifical usually referred as the Ecgberht
Pontifical (Paris, Bibliothèque nationale, MS. latin 10575) is unknown; it has no
connection with York or the eighth-century archbishop Ecgberht but is written in
a square-minuscule hand datable to *c.* 1000.[101] The pontifical contains two orders
of *Benedictio uirginum et uiduarum*, with the form for the blessing of a cross
(normally given in other pontificals as part of the consecration of a church and its
contents) inserted between them.[102] The second *ordo* begins with the blessing of
the clothes for a widow or virgin ('Deus qui uestimentum salutare'; 'Deus
bonarum uirtutum dator'; 'Visibilium et inuisibilium rerum creator deus';
'Inlumina quesumus domine oculos maiestatis tuae'); the pall is placed on the
widow who is told to receive the veil of widowhood that she will wear unstained
at the last Judgement ('Accipe uidua pallium'). Under the rubric *benedictio
uiduarum*, this second *ordo* then inserts a prayer beginning 'Deus, qui annam

---

99   Lapidge, 'The origin', pp. 22–3.
100 For discussion of the date of these manuscripts see Dumville, *Liturgy*, pp. 78–9 and
85–6 and the bibliographical references cited there.
101 The Ecgberht Pontifical has been edited by H. M. J. Banting, *Two Anglo-Saxon
Pontificals* (1989), pp. 3–153.
102 Banting, *Two Anglo-Saxon Pontificals*, p. 122, n. 17. The first *ordo* (pp. 116–19)
follows prayers for the blessing of virgin nuns, of virgins and blessings for a nun, virgin or widow.
It provides two prayers for the blessing of the clothes of a virgin or widow, 'Deus aeternorum
bonorum fidelissime promissor' and 'Deus bonarum uirtutum dator', at the moment when the virgin
or widow receives the *sacrum uelamen* is uttered the instruction, 'Accipe puella (*uel* uidua)
pallium' and the prayer 'Omnipotens sempiterne deus adiuua quas uirginitatis (*uel* uiduitatis)
honore dignatus es decorare'. The rite continues with the prayers of consecration of a virgin said
by a bishop, and then under the rubric *Consecratio uidue* offers the two prayers 'Consolare domine
hanc famulam tuam uiduitatis languoribus constrictam' and 'Deus castitatis amator et continentiae
conseruator'. All of these prayers can be paralleled in earlier sacramentaries. Following a prayer
for the veiling of *ancillae Dei*, are prayers for inclusion in a mass at the consecration of a virgin
or widow.

filiam phanuelis'.[103] The rite concludes with prayers for the *consecratio uiduae*: 'Consolare domine hanc famulam tuam uiduitatis laboribus' and 'Da quesumus omnipotens deus'.

All of these prayers can be found in earlier sacramentaries with the exception of that concerning the prophetess Anna, which occurs in only one other English manuscript of this period, the combined pontifical and benedictional in British Library MS., Cotton Claudius A. iii, folios 84r–v, written in an Anglo-Caroline minuscule hand of *c.* 1000 (Claudius Pontifical I).[104] In this pontifical the rites for blessing virgins and widows are separated, but there is still much duplication between the rites. The *ordo* for the blessing of a widow follows immediately from that for a virgin, and supplies with the same four prayers for the blessing of her clothes as in the Ecgberht Pontifical ('Deus qui uestimentum salutare'; 'Deus bonorum uirtutum dator', 'Visibilium et inuisibilium rerum creator deus', 'Illumina quesumus domine oculos maiestatis tuae'). Under the rubric *Benedictionem uiduarum* occurs next the new prayer, 'Deus qui Annam'; this is followed by the standard consolatory prayer ('Consolare domine hanc famulam tuam') before the rite concludes with the imposition of the veil on the widow's head and the instruction, 'Accipe uidua pallium'.

Claudius A. iii is a composite manuscript, portions of which have a close association with Archbishop Wulfstan: the earliest of the Pontificals was almost certainly Wulfstan's own. The addition to what is now folio 31v of a verse inscription in Old English recording that the *halgungboc* had been bound by a certain Thureth (a Northumbrian earl of Æthelred's reign[105]) suggests a northern connection rather than one with the see of Worcester.[106] The manuscript contains also Latin and Old English texts of the law-code of King Æthelred known as VI Æthelred written in an early eleventh-century hand; the Latin version of the *synodalia decreta* states that these were promulgated at a council at Enham (held in 1008) and that Wulfstan had taken part in their drafting; further the vernacular version (headed 'Concerning the ordinance of the councillors', *Be witena gerædnessan*), has corrections in Wulfstan's own hand.[107] King Æthelred's fifth and sixth codes are the first dateable law-codes drafted in Wulfstan's prose style and might be thought to reflect something at least of Wulfstan's particular interests. They happen, furthermore, to be the first English codes issued since the

---

[103]   Ibid., p. 122.

[104]   The manuscript has been edited by D. H. Turner, *The Claudius Pontificals* (1971). See also N. R. Ker, *Catalogue of Manuscripts Containing Anglo-Saxon* (Oxford, 1957, reissued 1990), pp. 177–8, no. 14; Dumville, *Liturgy*, p. 78.

[105]   D. Whitelock, 'Wulfstan at York', in *Franciplegius*, ed. J. B. Bessinger and R. P. Creed (New York, 1965), pp. 214–31, at pp. 217–18.

[106]   Dumville, *Liturgy*, pp. 78–9.

[107]   We have already had occasion to discuss Wulfstan's role in the drafting of this legislation and in the making of two versions for circulation in his northern province, see above, p. 98.

sixth century to deal with the protection of widows, placing them specifically under the protection of God and the king, as well as making recommendations as to the proper conduct of bereaved women.[108] Wulfstan's interest in widows and his inclusion of a chapter on their behaviour in his Institutes of Polity in which he made direct reference to the example provided by the prophetess Anna have already been discussed.[109] That Wulfstan should also have owned a manuscript introducing novel liturgical forms for the blessing of widows which draw similarly on Anna as a model raises the question as to how much responsibility should be attributed to the archbishop personally for the liturgical reflection of the increased significance of widows within the late Anglo-Saxon Church.

Although not identical to the prayer with the same incipit given in the order for the consecration of a deaconess in the Romano-German Pontifical, the form of the prayer 'Deus, qui Annam filiam Phanuelis' found in the Claudius and Ecgberht Pontificals beginning with so full a statement of the qualities of the prophetess Anna is closer to the Romano-German Pontifical than to any other source I have been able to identify. The prayer draws attention to the career of Anna and invokes for the woman being blessed the qualities of the ideal widow of the sort praised in Pauline epistles: the proper instruction of young women, chastity, discrimination tempered with compassion, generosity with humility, sobriety with humanity and perpetual meditation on the work of God.[110] This prayer is not found in any of the other tenth- and eleventh-century pontificals whose contents I have been able to identify.[111] Rites for the blessing or consecration of widows are found in the Dunstan (or Sherborne) Pontifical,[112] the

---

[108] VI Æthelred, chs. 26–26.1 (=V Æthelred, chs. 21–21.1); II Cnut, ch. 73 (ed. Liebermann, *Die Gesetze*, I, 254, 242, 360). Other pertinent chapters in VI Æthelred are ch. 12 (pp. 250–1), which may be compared with I Cnut, ch. 7 (p. 290), also drafted by Wulfstan; and with the collection of homiletic and legal material by Wulfstan printed by Napier, *Wulfstan*, no 50, at p. 271). Also VI Æthelred, chs. 39 and 47 (ed. Liebermann, *Die Gesetze*, I, 256–9), neither of which occurs in V Æthelred.

[109] Wulfstan, I *Polity*, 93–7, II *Polity*, xv, 198–202 (ed. Jost, *Die "Institutes"*, pp. 136–7); see above, p. 101.

[110] Compare I Timothy, 5: 3–16; Titus 2: 3–5.

[111] There is no order for the blessing of widows in the part-pontifical preserved in Sidney Sussex MS. 100 (Δ.5.15), part 2 (ed. Banting, *Two Anglo-Saxon Pontificals*, pp. 157–70), nor are prayers for blessing widows included in Durham, Cathedral Library, MS A. IV. 19: *The Durham Collectar*, ed. A. Corrêa (1992).

[112] Paris, Bibliothèque nationale, MS. latin 943, fos. 85v–86v. I am most grateful to Patrick Conner for checking a microfilm of this manuscript on my behalf. The manuscript's contents have been described in the greatest detail by V. Leroquais, *Les Pontificaux manuscrits des bibliothèques publiques de France* (4 vols., Paris, 1937), II, 6–10. The first intended owner of this manuscript was almost certainly Dunstan, archbishop of Canterbury 959/60–988; for discussion of the manuscript's date see Dumville, *Liturgy*, pp. 82–4.

Lanalet Pontifical,[113] the Anderson (or Brodie) Pontifical,[114] the combined benedictional and pontifical of Archbishop Robert.[115] Prayers for the blessing of a widow (and her clothes) are also among the *ordines* from the Romano-German pontifical copied into the Leofric Missal.[116] All of these versions of the rite supply the prayers familiar from eighth-century sources and duplicate those given in the Ecgberht and Claudius Pontificals; none includes either of the prayers from the Romano-German Pontifical that invokes the example of the prophetess Anna.[117] Eric Palazzo has argued that the use of the model of Anna as an inspiration for widows in the prayer for their consecration in the Romano-German Pontifical represented a liturgical innovation.[118] The evidence accumulated for this study can offer an historical explanation in tenth- and eleventh-century England for the question that Palazzo raised about the significance of widows in the contemporary Church. However, I must refer back to the liturgists the problem of the sources of this prayer, and the relationship between the Romano-German Pontifical *ordo* for deaconesses and the blessings for widows in the Ecgberht and especially the Claudius Pontificals. Liturgical scholars may similarly be best placed to explore the possible routes by which ideas about the role and duties of widows might have been exchanged between the diocese of Mainz and England (especially the circle of Archbishop Wulfstan) around the year 1000.

That it had in the tenth century become more common for widows formally to dedicate their continent state to God and to seek ecclesiastical blessing and the solemn imposition of the outward symbols of their devoted condition may account for the introduction of new prayers into the rite for widows' initiation in at least two Anglo-Saxon pontificals. In the aftermath of Æthelwold's monastic revolution and the imposition of a more rigidly defined form of conventual monasticism, increasing formalism may also have marked the arrangements made by those electing consciously to fulfil their vocations outside the cloister. Spiritual aspirations such as these were certainly not innovative (consider for example the arrangements made in his will by the ninth-century reeve Abba should his wife

---

[113]   Rouen, Bibliothèque municipale, MS. A. 27 (368) (ed. G. H. Doble, *Pontificale Lanaletense* [1937], pp. 43–4); see Dumville, *Liturgy*, pp. 86–7, where the manuscript is dated to the early eleventh century.

[114]   London, British Library, MS. Add. 57337; a late-tenth or early-eleventh-century Anglo-Caroline manuscript from Christ Church, Canterbury: Dumville, *Liturgy*, p. 77. I am most grateful to Dr Justin Clegg of the British Library for checking the text for the benediction of a widow on fo. 72r of this manuscript on my behalf.

[115]   Rouen, Bibliothèque municipale, MS. Y.7 (369) (ed. H. Wilson, *The Benedictional of Archbishop Robert* [1903], pp. 138–40); the Anglo-Caroline hand of this manuscript has been dated by David Dumville to the second quarter of the eleventh century: *Liturgy*, p. 87.

[116]   Oxford, Bodleian Library, MS. Bodley 579 (2675) (ed. F. E. Warren, *The Leofric Missal* [1883], pp. 226–7).

[117]   *Le Pontifical*, XXIV, 8 ['Deus qui Annam'] and XXV, 14 ['Domine Deus, uirtutum caelestium dominator'] (ed. Vogel and Elze, I, 55–6, 61).

[118]   Palazzo, 'Les formules', p. 35.

elect to remain chaste on his death[119]), but they appear to have been marked in the
new climate by more precise arrangements than in previous centuries, when
diversity and flexibility of expression characterised the religious life as much
inside the cloister as without. It does seem reasonable to surmise that it was
Wulfstan's familiarity with the prayer recommending the example of Anna in the
ordo for blessing a widow in his own Pontifical that inspired him to choose as an
inspiration that prophetess 'who now has heavenly bliss for a reward', when he
urged the good widows of his own day to obey their Lord.[120]

Veiled women in later Anglo-Saxon England

This, finally, brings us back to the issue with which we began this study: the
precise identification of the status of individual religious women mentioned in
sources of the tenth and eleventh centuries. Following the monastic revolution of
Edgar's reign there were, as we have seen, two parallel modes of religious living,
the monastic and cloistered and the non-cloistered and secular. The normative
literature coined distinctive labels to differentiate between the adherents of the two
systems: the men and women who inhabited regular monasteries were termed
munecas and mynecenas, while the female equivalent of the secular priest (*preost*
or *canonicus*) was described as a *nunne*. Dorothy Whitelock explained these terms
succinctly: 'a *nunne* is distinguished from a *mynece*, a "cloistered nun". It means
a woman who has taken vows of chastity without entering a community. Widows
often did this'.[121] The one question that has still been left open is the precise
relationship between the *nunne* and the chaste widow. Both took vows, wore
distinctive clothes and occupied a liminal position in the world that was neither
wholly secular nor fully religious. The widow's consecration we have just
discussed; rites for the blessing of virgins were similar and could have been
celebrated for women who were to remain outside the cloister as well as for
intending Benedictines.[122] Whether virgin or widow a woman could take vows,
put on the habit and veil, and live either on her own estates or in a small
community. A number of such women can be identified in tenth- and eleventh-

---

[119]   *SEHD*, no. 2 (S 1482); cited in full above, p. 113.

[120]   Wulfstan, Wulfstan, I *Polity*, 93–7, II *Polity*, xv, 198–202 (ed. Jost, *Die "Institutes"*,
pp. 136–7, trans. Swanton, *Anglo-Saxon Prose*, p. 199). Other possible biblical models for the
behaviour of chaste widows were examined by Bremmer, 'Widows', p. 78.

[121]   Whitelock *et al.*, *Councils*, I, 347, n. 4 (in explanation of V Æthelred, 4.1). Quoted
by R. Gilchrist, *Gender and Material Culture. The Archaeology of Religious Women* (1994),
p. 34.

[122]   The consecration of virgins and the status of women within early medieval canon
law have been extensively studied by René Metz; see particularly, *La consécration des vièrges
dans l'église romaine* (Paris, 1954) and 'Le statut de la femme'. Pertinent to this discussion is also
Magnou-Nortier, 'Formes féminines', pp. 195–203.

century Anglo-Saxon England, for example the *nunne* Æthelthryth who witnessed
a woman's manumission performed in the minster at Bedwyn, the divorced
woman Ecgfrith who took the veil at the church of Durham, or the devotee of the
martyred king, Edmund, whose habits were quoted at the head of this chapter.[123]

Should we assume that all those described in the sources as *nunnan* had
previously been married? A woman who had never been married need not
necessarily have been wholly without property and dependent on her father and
brothers for support, although that might often have been her situation. Daughters
could inherit from both their parents (alongside or in default of sons), and their
inheritance could include land as well as moveable wealth.[124] The women named
as legatees in extant Anglo-Saxon wills were frequently recipients of reversionary
grants, they were bequeathed the use of an estate which was ultimately to pass into
other hands, either that of male kin, or more likely an ecclesiastical beneficiary;
Julia Crick has recently drawn attention to the frequency with which women's
inheritance took this form.[125] Any woman — virgin daughter or bereaved wife —
who possessed land in this fashion (either in her own right to dispose of as she
wished, or for her use during her lifetime only) could have chosen to continue to
live on her land, enjoying the profits of the estate after having taken a vow of
chastity and adopted the dress distinctive to that state. If such a short-lived
arrangement failed to find mention in any surviving documentary source we need
scarcely be surprised; as long as the land ultimately reverted to the intended
beneficiary, its use in the interim would not necessarily be worthy of comment.[126]
A widow who elected to live as a *nunne* in the world on the lands she had
inherited might have inspired an unmarried daughter to adopt the same lifestyle
with her, the two of them forming the basis of a tiny community. Such a virgin
daughter, inheriting that estate from her dead mother would, herself properly
described as a *nunne*, preserve the quasi-religious character of the household for
another generation. But on her own death she would have no child to whom to
leave the land which, reverting to other parts of the kin group, might thereafter
return to wholly secular use. It is easy to see how such ephemeral religious houses
were disadvantaged in the historical record, private arrangements of this nature

[123] Single vowesses are considered as a group below, chapter 6, §f.
[124] Nelson, 'The wary widow', p. 85.
[125] In a paper entitled 'Beyond the nunnery: Uncloistered religious women before the
Conquest', read to the fourth International Medieval Congress at the University of Leeds, July
1997.
[126] The same phenomenon, of women described as *Deo sacratae* or *deuotae feminae*,
some widows but many who have certainly never been married, has been explored by Elisabeth
Magnou-Nortier in south-western France, where she has shown that this form of religious
expression was more common than cenobitic monasticism, which for women was almost non-
existent in the area: 'Formes féminines'. She has also confronted the difficulties of the paucity of
the documentary evidence and its restriction to women of high aristocratic birth, wondering how
many other women there were who lived in the world but fulfilling a vow dedicating their lives to
God: ibid., pp. 203–9.

requiring no documentary confirmation unless this was secured by arrangements for the reversion of the land to a religious house;[127] instead of speculating as to the factors that obscured the arrangements made by these vowesses from our view, we might rather express surprise that so many have left any written documents at all.[128]

At the beginning of the first chapter attention was drawn to the wills of two tenth-century women of whom it is difficult to say with confidence whether they were members of monastic communities, or secular women with pious aspirations who continued to live in the world. Should they properly be linked with Æthelhild, the virgin daughter of Edward the Elder who was said by William of Malmesbury to have scorned marriage and taken the lay habit? It seems that we can now answer this question and identify both the unmarried Æthelhild and the two widows as *nunnan*. The case histories of the latter are worth exploring in greater detail for the wider issues that they raise.

Wynflæd is identifiable as the mother of Ælfgifu, the first wife of King Edmund and mother of King Edgar, who was buried at Shaftesbury where she was commemorated as a benefactor.[129] This is also probably the same Wynflæd, described as *quaedam religiosa sanctae conuersacionis monialis femina*, who was the beneficiary of a charter of King Eadmund's dated 942, which granted her land at Cheselbourne and Winterbourne in Dorset;[130] the charter was preserved in the archive of the nunnery at Shaftesbury, but it is questionable whether Wynflæd should be included among the professed inmates of that community. Eadmund's diploma for Wynflæd is one of a group of charters dating from the mid-tenth century which granted land to individual religious women (*religiosae feminae*), few of whom can confidently be assigned to any known monastic congregation. Some historians have attempted to locate a number of these women within the

---

[127] Alternatively, as David Dumville has suggested (*Wessex and England from Alfred to Edgar* [1992], p. 177), charters may have been issued granting lands for this purpose to particular women, but because the estates in question thereafter descended into private, not ecclesiastical, hands, this documentation may have been lost. Pauline Stafford has also recently commented on the difficulties of tracing such women within the historical record: 'Queens, nunneries and reforming churchmen: Gender, religious status and reform in tenth- and eleventh-century England', *Past and Present*, 163 (1999), 3–35, at pp. 30–35.

[128] Examples of women practising religious lifestyles outside the cenobitic framework have also been explored by B. Venarde, *Women's Monasticism and Medieval Society* (1997), pp. 24 and 46–7. *Deovotae* and *deodicatae* women in the Catalan regions of Spain between the ninth and the eleventh centuries have been studied by Monserrat Cabré y Pairet, who has drawn attention to the gender-specific nature of this form of religious expression, and the lack of equivalent masculine nouns: '"Deodicatae" y "deovotae": La regulación de la religiosidad femenina en los condados catalanes, siglos IX–XI', in *Las mujeres en el cristianismo medieval. Imágenes teóricas y cauces de actuación religiosa*, ed. A. Muñoz Fernández (Madrid, 1989), pp. 169–82, at pp. 171–4.

[129] S. E. Kelly, *Charters of Shaftesbury Abbey* (1996), pp. xiii–xiv, 56.

[130] Kelly, *Charters of Shaftesbury*, no. 13 (S 485).

communities in whose archives the charters were preserved, on which presumption Wynflæd has been taken as a member of the Shaftesbury community, or at least a close associate of that abbey.[131] But to do so is to make unwarrantable assumptions about the structures within which female religious operated in this period. The existence of such grants might on the contrary be seen as further instances of devout women making their own flexible arrangements outside the boundaries of organised, communal religion;[132] the *religiosae feminae* of the charters could in vernacular texts of the early eleventh century have been termed *nunnan*.[133] Perhaps these women were forced to turn to the king in order to acquire land on which to live as vowesses because they had not inherited landed property of their own, and had male relatives unwilling to allow them any part of the family estate on which to satisfy their devotion. Alternatively they might have been reverting to the older strategy of asking the king to turn family land into bookland, thus circumventing family claims.

Wynflæd was clearly a widow at the time when she drew up her will, but those who have discussed this document have found it hard to determine whether Wynflæd was then living a secular life, was a member of a nunnery, or whether she might more appropriately be placed at the margin of both worlds. Her will begins with bequests to an unnamed church, including a gift of two silver cups to 'the refectory' for the benefit of the community, and a monetary gift to each servant of God; this establishment was apparently distinct from Wilton, which is identified as the recipient of a separate gift, but is probably Shaftesbury, which house Wynflæd named later in her will.[134] Wynflæd was obviously close to this congregation and her bequests included her *nunscrude*, her 'nun's clothing', but she was not necessarily a cloistered *mynecenu*. She had clearly in widowhood retained control of her landed estates and their stock as well as a number of valuable personal possessions; since she made mention of her untamed and tame horses, she would further appear to have been breeding and training horses.[135]

---

[131]   G. R. Owen, 'Wynflæd's wardrobe', *Anglo-Saxon England*, 8 (1979), 195–222, at pp. 197–9; Halpin, 'Women religious', p. 103.

[132]   Susan Kelly in considering the status of the *religiosa femina*, Ælfthryth, recipient of a grant from King Eadred of land in Dorset in 948 (Kelly, *Charters of Shaftesbury*, no. 16; S 534) wondered if the women who received these grants were expected to live independent religious lives on their estates, or gather new communities around them: Kelly, *Charters of Shaftesbury*, p. 68.

[133]   This group of charters has been discussed by Schneider, 'Anglo-Saxon women', pp. 221–2; Dumville, *Wessex*, pp. 177–8; N. P. Brooks, 'The career of Saint Dunstan', in *St Dunstan*, ed. N. Ramsay *et al.* (1992), pp. 1–23, at p. 7; M. A. Meyer, 'Land charters and the legal position of Anglo-Saxon women', in *The Women of England*, ed. B. Kanner (1980), pp. 57–82, at pp. 60–1; Venarde, *Women's Monasticism*, p. 24. See further below, chapter 6, §f.

[134]   Whitelock, *ASWills*, no. 3, p. 109; Kelly, *Charters of Shaftesbury*, p. 56.

[135]   Whitelock, *AS Wills*, no. 3, pp. 14–15. The individual items bequeathed include a cross and two silver cups, an engraved ring (or bracelet) and two brooches, two buffalo-horns and a number of drinking cups, nine chests (for holding linen and bedding) and a little spinning box,

Strict Benedictine observance would forbid such retention of individual property to any who had taken a full monastic profession,[136] but is hard to determine what sort of rule Shaftesbury might have been following in the middle years of the tenth century. Even had the congregation been reformed during Edgar's reign, it is unlikely that the precepts of the Rule of St Benedict would have governed its life as early as the time at which Wynflæd drew up her will.

The clothing which Wynflæd bequeathed does little to clarify the issue as to her status. She left one of her black tunics and her best holy veil and headband to Ceolthryth, and a gown, cap and headband to Æthelflæd the White. Afterwards Æthelflæd was told to supply from Wynflæd's *nunscrud* the best she could for Wulfflæd (freed earlier in the will on condition that she would serve Wynflæd's daughter) and for Æthelgifu (a seamstress who was not freed, but given to the testatrix's grand-daughter) and to supplement the gift with gold so that each of them should have sixty pennyworth.[137] While the assumption of the veil was generally taken as a mark of entry to the communal religious life, widows taking vows were distinguished by their clothing as having taken vows of continence, their distinctive dress being conferred at the time of their consecration to religion.[138] In discussion of Wynflæd's wardrobe Gale Owen has drawn attention to a group of eleventh-century glossed Aldhelm manuscripts where the holy veil, *haligrift*, is taken as the typical garment of a widow.[139] Whitelock suggested that Wynflæd might either have been lay-abbess of the monastery with which she had connections, or that she might have taken vows of chastity as a widow; Susan Kelly has argued that she might have been a lay associate of Shaftesbury.[140] In terms of the categories defined in the early eleventh-century secular law codes and in the writings of Wulfstan and Ælfric such women would be termed *nunnan*, secular vowesses. To define Wynflæd as a *nunne* appears to offer the best resolution of the apparent ambiguities presented by her will. It further raises the

---

a number of garments (some of high quality) as well as a considerable quantity of bed-clothing, linen, tapestries, household utensils, and other small things including books.

[136]   As pointed out by Whitelock, *AS Wills*, p. 109.

[137]   Whitelock, *The Will of Æthelgifu*, pp. 14–15.

[138]   The rites for the consecration of widows, as was shown above, contain both prayers for the blessing of their clothes and at the moment of their vesting. Gale Owen drew attention ('Wynflæd's wardrobe', pp. 198 and 219) to the fact that Wynflæd also bequeathed to her daughter a ring which could, at least in later period be a mark of a professed widow, although I have not found mention of the bestowing of rings on widows in liturgical texts of this period. The rite for the consecration of a deaconess in the Romano-German Pontifical bestowed on her a veil, *uelamen* and ring ('Accipe anulum fide signaculum spiritus sancti, ut sponsa Christ uoceris, si fideliter ei seruieris', XXIV, 12, ed. Vogel and Elze, *Le Pontifical*, I, 57); but in the same text virgins and widows were only reclothed in new *uestimenta*, having the veil placed on their heads. For the suggestion that the ring was a symbol of professed widowhood see J. L. André, 'Widows and Vowesses', *Archaeological Journal*, 49 (1892), 69–82, at pp. 78–9.

[139]   Owen, 'Wynflæd's wardrobe', p. 219.

[140]   Whitelock, *ASWills*, p. 109; Kelly, *Charters of Shaftesbury*, p. 56.

possibility that the later prescriptive literature, in defining a distinction between *mynecenu* and *nunne* was at least to some extent normalising pre-existing conditions.

The testatrix Æthelgifu is at first sight more difficult to identify and her status even less clear, but she also fits better into the model we have defined of the lay vowess than into any other category. Æthelgifu may have been the widow of a thegn called Æthelric, and it is possible that this testator is the same woman Æthelgifu recorded among the witnesses to the lawsuit agreed early in the 990s between a certain Wynflæd (not the testator of that name) and Leofwine.[141] She left, however, no certain trace outside her will, which can be dated no more closely than to 990x1001. Æthelgifu made a number of testamentary bequests to the Church, indeed she devoted an enormous proportion of her property to religious purposes. Via this will Æthelgifu made grants to the Benedictine abbey of St Albans, to the minsters of Hitchin, Braughing and Welwyn, and to 'her priests'. Whitelock suggested that these were probably not Æthelgifu's personal chaplains but rather independent priests with holdings to cultivate and pastoral obligations to their neighbours.[142] Æthelgifu may have had a closer relationship with the priest Edwin, whom she intended to free on her death, although he does not appear to have been connected with her principal estate at Standon; she bequeathed to Edwin the church plus half a hide of land for his lifetime with a man, and Byrhstan's sister in return for Edwin's saying of masses and prayers for Æthelgifu's soul (and on condition that he continue to keep the church in repair). Æthelgifu also made arrangements for the manumission of three women, Ælfwaru (daughter of the huntsman Wulfric), Leofrun, and Æthelflæd, on condition that each was to chant four psalters a week for a month and one psalter a week for a whole year after her death.[143] Although slaves, these women must have had some kind of education if they were to be able to fulfil the terms on which they were freed; either they must have been sufficiently literate to be able to read the psalter, or to have been so familiar with its recitation that all three of them had the entire text by heart. Such familiarity could surely only have come from the regular and frequent chanting of the psalter as part of a liturgical (perhaps monastic) round.

Should we take this, as Whitelock did, as an indication that Æthelgifu had established a little religious community among the members of her household, while continuing to live on her own estates (perhaps that at Standon, with which the huntsman Wulfric was associated, which is the only one of Æthelgifu's estates to produce wine)?[144] The clothing that Æthelgifu bequeathed is less ambiguously secular than that left by Wynflæd; she bequeathed her brightest kirtle, a blue kirtle

---

[141]   Robertson, *ASCharters*, no. 66 (S 1454); the identification was made by Whitelock, *The Will of Æthelgifu*, p. 27.

[142]   Whitelock, *The Will of Æthelgifu*, pp. 32, 34.

[143]   Ibid., pp. 12–13, lines 50–2.

[144]   Ibid., p. 34.

which was untrimmed, three purple, or silk, kirtles, and other dun-coloured kirtles. She also left a headband worth at least twenty-five mancuses, naming five women as the intended recipients of five-mancus pieces cut from this band,[145] and referred furthermore to her 'best head-dresses'. The noun used here, *heafodgewædo*, might mean head-dress but is also found, as Whitelock pointed out, in the Old English Genesis to translate the Latin *velamen*, veil.[146] Æthelgifu, like Wynflæd, may thus have worn the veil. She too, as Whitelock argued, should be seen as a vowess, a *nunne*.

Such disproportionate attention has been paid to these two women in order to exemplify and particularise the theoretical argument advanced in this chapter and the last that there were two distinct categories of religious woman in the English Church following the monastic revolution of Edgar's reign. Their example serves furthermore to supply a link between this lengthy and discursive argument and the evidence which is set out in part two of this study. When Dorothy Whitelock concluded that Æthelgifu should be seen as a lay vowess she supported her argument with reference to the legal material, Wulfstan's Institutes of Polity, and the equation of widow and vowess made in Ælfric's Glossary. She also drew attention to two widows and a woman who had taken a vow of chastity who were mentioned in the twelfth-century *Liber Eliensis* as beneficiaries of the male community at Ely. One of these widows, Æthelflæd, was said to have devoted herself to religion in widowhood after the example of the blessed Anna.[147] Further examples can also be invoked in support of the proposition advanced in Wynflæd's case that this way of life was not newly instituted in the aftermath of the Benedictine revolution but was available earlier in the tenth century as a means by which devout women (especially widows) could fulfil a religious vocation while retaining control of their own estates. It has already been suggested that the various single religious women recorded as the recipients of mid-tenth-century charters might be best understood in this light. The woman, Æthelthryth, described as a *nunne* who is named together with the congregation of the church of Bedwyn in Wiltshire among the witnesses to a manumission dating from the early tenth century recorded on a blank leaf of a gospel book from that church (now in Bern) could similarly be seen as a secular vowess.[148] She may well have had her dwelling near the church and availed herself of the priestly services offered by that community, but she is more likely to have lived independently as a vowess than

---

[145]   Whitelock drew attention (ibid., p. 12, n. 7) to other instances of the division of a *bend*: the will of Brihtric and Ælfswith, his wife: Whitelock, *ASWills*, no. 11 (S 1511) and the will of Wulfwaru: Whitelock, *ASWills*, no. 21 (S 1538).

[146]   Whitelock, *The Will of Æthelgifu*, p. 12, n. 10.

[147]   *Liber Eliensis* II, 64 (ed. E. O. Blake [1962]); Whitelock, *The Will of Æthelgifu*, p. 34; see further part II, *s n.* Ely.

[148]   Bern, Burgerbibliothek, MS 671, fo 76v; printed by H. Merritt, 'Old English entries in a manuscript at Bern', *Journal of English and Germanic Philology*, 33 (1934), 343–51, pp. 346–7.

to have been in any formal sense attached to this male congregation.[149] A choice between the cloistered and non-cloistered religious life was also open to the female relatives of Edward the Elder, according to the testimony of William of Malmesbury. Three of the king's daughters were said to have avoided marriage, Eadflæd living chastely in a religious habit and her sister, Æthelhild, in a lay habit while their half-sister Eadburh, a virgin dedicated to Christ, joined the Nunnaminster at Winchester.[150] The king's second wife, Ælfflæd, apparently adopted some sort of religious life on the dissolution of her marriage c. 917, apparently outside a regular monastic house, since she retained possession of her own landed estates.[151] A similar life may have been followed by Edward the Elder's third wife Eadgifu, called *famula Dei* in a diploma by which her son Eadred granted her an estate in Sussex.[152] It seems reasonable to conclude that only two of Edward's female relatives chose the cloistered life (his daughters Eadflæd and Eadburh), the others preferring the greater flexibility of life as secular vowesses.

Conclusion

If it were to be accepted that there were throughout the tenth century religious women who took vows but who were not fully professed members of any regular, cloistered community, this would go a long way towards explaining the problem that has been identified with the sources for women's religious communities in England after the First Viking Age.[153] As we have already seen it is primarily the

---

[149] *Contra* B. Yorke, 'The Bonifacian mission and female religious in Wessex', *Early Medieval Europe*, 7 (1998), 145–72, at p. 167. For exploration of a different possible interpretation of this woman's identity see Dumville, *Wessex*, pp. 81–2, n. 120.

[150] William of Malmesbury, *GR*, I, 126 (ed. and trans. R. A. B. Mynors *et al.* [1998], I, 199–201); quoted at the head of chapter 1.

[151] Ælfflæd's career has been discussed by Meyer, 'Women', pp. 46–7 (where it was argued that she joined the Nunnaminster at Winchester) and 'The queen's "demesne"', pp. 91–2 (where she was described as a nun of Wilton). Ælfflæd was buried at Wilton, with her daughters Eadflæd and Æthelhild. The issue of her religious status and her possible relationship with Glastonbury is analysed in greater detail below, chapter 6, §e.

[152] Kelly, *Charters of Shaftesbury*, no. 17 (S 562). See M. A. Meyer, 'The queen's "demesne" in later Anglo-Saxon England', in *The Culture of Christendom*, ed. M. A. Meyer (1993), pp. 75–113, at pp. 93–4.

[153] This explanation also answers one of the questions raised by Catherine Cubitt in her recent review article of writing on the monastic revolution ('The tenth-century Benedictine reform in England', *Early Medieval Europe*, 6 [1997], 77–94, at p. 87): 'what was the impact of the Reform movement upon earlier traditions of female piety, such as the practice of aristocratic women living in pious retirement in association with monastic foundations?' Such women can be seen to have continued to occupy the liminal position between the Church and the world where *deo deuotae* were found in the pre-Viking Age, but had acquired more formal recognition in both

few institutions with permanent landed endowments that have found place in the historical record; the larger group of sites where women religious can be seen to have lived is less visible in the contemporary sources and hence, inevitably, in the later historiography. The latter might be seen as communities formed round a vowess living either on a single estate granted to her for that purpose or on inherited land. In many instances the disparity in the survival of sources may reflect a real difference between contrasting sorts of congregation, monastic, cloistered communities (that could only function if adequately endowed) being better recorded than the houses of secular religious women. If so, the sources could be taken as representative of a real situation: that there were at most nine or ten monasteries of cloistered women in later Anglo-Saxon England. A difficulty here is that the distinction that we have been able to demonstrate between the protagonists of the two lifestyles cannot be drawn in institutional terms; there is no contemporary language to define religious houses of different sorts.[154] Scholars who have in recent years attempted to expand the number of known female religious congregations in the later Anglo-Saxon period have advisedly chosen to look at the women themselves but, as was discussed earlier, such studies have left unanswered the question of how to categorise the institutions in which these women lived, other than by reference to their diversity.[155]

The distinction drawn in normative ecclesiastical texts between *mynecenu* and *nunne* first became necessary in the aftermath of the Benedictine revolution when a single standard had been imposed for the observance of all monastic communities and a meaningful contrast between the regular and secular lives newly devised. Only once the implications of the existence of two discrete categories of religious woman are properly understood, can the nature of the extant evidence be explained. But the choice as to life within an endowed minster or life outside as a vowess had already existed before Æthelwold introduced the precepts of St Benedict to the former category of institution. As well as the early tenth-century examples just discussed, instances were found of religious women who lived outside the cloister in the pre-Viking Age, some of whom are likely to have been widows.[156] The linguistic innovation of the later prescriptive material thus

---

secular and ecclesiastical spheres through the various prescriptive statements made about their behaviour.

[154]   Compare Gilchrist, *Gender*, p. 34, who has also sought to identify a two-tiered institutional structure. Bruce Venarde's recent book (*Women's Monasticism*) has drawn on Gilchrist's work and made much of the evidence for non-cloistered women in the later pre-Conquest period, but without entirely recognising that such women were often the focus of small communities. More female religious houses can be identified in England between 900 and 1066 than the fourteen Venarde has catalogued.

[155]   Above, pp. 86–7. Patricia Halpin saw the closest parallel to these late Anglo-Saxon houses as being the anchoritic female establishments common in the twelfth century: 'Women', p. 109.

[156]   See chapter 2, above pp. 56–59.

reflects and normalises pre-existing conditions, rather than inventing a new distinction. Might we argue, nevertheless, that the need for the coining of new linguistic terms indicates that the female pursuit of the religious life outside the cloister had become more common in the tenth century?

The disparity in source survival for women's houses between the early eighth and the later tenth centuries could at least in part be accounted for by an increase in the number of women who chose to live the religious life without seeking a landed estate on which future generations of female religious could be supported. Because they were designedly impermanent and ephemeral, houses of this type were less well evidenced than the, predominantly royal, houses that had permanent landed endowments: they existed in order to satisfy the spiritual (and to an extent material) needs of particular religious women in their own lifetime. From the sources we glimpse only a series of disjointed vignettes, capturing particular instants in the religious life of single women, or small groups of female companions. In comparison with those male and female monastic houses that succeeded in obtaining their own permanent lands to devote to religious purposes, these short-lived communities may seem unfortunate, but it is inappropriate to judge such foundations by the norms of regular monasticism, for which a landed endowment was an essential prerequisite. As vehicles for the satisfaction of the spiritual aspirations of individual women within a framework both acceptable to their kin and conforming to contemporary ecclesiastical standards (particularly over the question of remarriage of widows) such arrangements were highly successful.

On this reading, the apparent under-representation of women's religious houses in the sources from the later period need not be sought by reference to their peculiar poverty in comparison with men's houses, a gendered bias in the survival of evidence, nor in the deliberate obscuring of women in texts composed by male writers. Rather it reflects a shift in the pattern of landed endowment of female religious houses in England after the First Viking Age. Royal patronage was in the later period to prove virtually essential to the creation of a female religious establishment which could entertain any hopes of sustaining a long-lived existence. While the centrality of royal interest in and material support for nunneries was demonstrated also in the early period, the patronage of the one remaining English royal family, the house of Cerdic, was restricted in the tenth century to that family's heartlands in central and southern Wessex. The Mercian, East Anglian and West Saxon aristocracies evinced sufficient interest in the monastic ideal during the tenth century to assist Bishops Æthelwold and Oswald with the material endowment of new male congregations (at least during King Edgar's lifetime), but did not demonstrate much obvious interest in the permanent alienation of land to female religious use.[157] Historians have not previously

---

[157] The notable exceptions to this rule are Bishop Eadnoth, who used his family's lands to endow a women's house at Chatteris, and Ealdorman Ælfhere who was, with his daughters, a

accounted adequately for the seeming invisibility of veiled women, since they have only recently started to acknowledge the significance of the existence of a parallel track for religious women beside that of the cloistered life and to attend to its official recognition in the contemporary normative literature.[158] In part they have been too much influenced by the efforts of the tenth-century reformers to standardise monastic practice, but they have further been hampered by the confusion to modern English speakers of the restriction of the label *nunne* not to the Benedictine nun, but to her counterpart in the lay world. With these perceptions in mind, I turn now to the evidence itself and ask whether there are any other ways in which the extant data might be handled in order enhance our understanding of women's religious observance in the later Anglo-Saxon period.

significant patron of Barking Abbey. See further J. Crick, 'The wealth, patronage, and connections of women's houses in late Anglo-Saxon England', *Revue bénédictine*, 109 (1999), 154–85, at pp. 168–70.

[158] It is here that I depart from the otherwise convincing conclusions reached by Patricia Halpin, who argued ('Women', p. 107) that 'small groups of women or individual women religious affiliated in uncertain terms with nearby men's foundations' were accepted but not officially recognized.

Chapter 6

A typology of female religious communities in later Anglo-Saxon England

The quest for nunneries in the last two centuries before the Conquest needs to be placed on a new footing. That different labels were coined to characterise the women of the two groups is clear from the normative literature: *mynecena* were cloistered women and *nunnan* secular vowesses. Vowesses might live alone on their own estates or could, as Wulfstan indicated in his Institutes of Polity, also be found in minsters, that is living communally.[1] If vowesses and widows did sometimes gather small congregations of like-minded women around them, this model should be considered, as well as that of the regular cloister, in exploration of the evidence for female religious houses in the last centuries before the Norman Conquest. It may, as was suggested in the previous chapter, serve to explain the puzzle with which this study began of the somewhat contradictory terms of the wills of Wynflæd and Æthelgifu and the differences seen by William of Malmesbury between the lifestyles of the devout daughters of Edward the Elder. The situations of other *religiosae feminae* who appear, for example, as the recipients of modest land grants in the tenth century and cannot convincingly be shown to have been attached to any of the better known 'nunneries' may similarly have been closer to the model of the vowess than that of the cloistered woman.[2]

In previous attempts to make some sense of the extant sources for women's religious houses during and after the tenth-century monastic revolution, little use has been made of this duality of women's religious expression as a potential organisational motif.[3] Nor has the explanatory potential of the existence

---

[1]   Wulfstan, I Polity, 85, II Polity, xiv.186 (ed. K. Jost, Die "Institutes of Polity, Civil and Ecclesiastical" [Bern, 1959], p. 129).

[2]   Such a view challenges the efforts made particularly by Patricia Halpin to assign the recipients of such grants to known monastic congregations, or to see evidence for otherwise unattested nunneries on the lands granted to individual *religiosae feminae*: P. Halpin, 'Women religious in late Anglo-Saxon England', *Haskins Society Journal*, 6 (1994), 97–110, pp. 103–5; and compare also M. A. Meyer, 'Women and the tenth century English monastic reform', *Revue bénédictine*, 87 (1977), 34–61, pp. 46–51.

[3]   Roberta Gilchrist, recognising the existence of two classes of religious woman, has suggested (*Gender and Material Culture* [1994], p. 34) that historians might search for equivalent levels of ecclesiastical site, but the argument can be pushed much further than it is in her study. Most recently Pauline Stafford has also touched on the representation of female religious in the

of two parallel frameworks for women in religion profitably been explored in order to account for the paucity of sources describing their activities, or the institutions that housed them in this period. In the rest of this study, this better informed understanding of the variety of female religious experience in the later Anglo-Saxon period will be applied to the evidence that has survived for the specific places at which women fulfilled their vows. Here I devise an organisational framework within which to analyse the substantial quantity of data (of highly variable quality) relating to the congregations of women religious.

Since distinct types of evidence are available for different groups of houses it is clear that it is possible to do more than simply differentiate between those (largely West Saxon and royally patronised) communities of female religious that have dominated the literature, and the impoverished, transitory, and generally ill-attested residue (lamenting the general inadequacy of the surviving record the while). The evidence that the sources supply for communities of religious women (cloistered or not) in the later Anglo-Saxon period is examined in the second part of this study, which arranges in alphabetical sequence the sites where groups of such women can be shown to have lived. The criteria for inclusion there are that the survey should encompass every place at which an Anglo-Saxon, later medieval, antiquarian, or modern writer has witnessed to the presence of cloistered women or of more than one vowess living at any point between the accession of Alfred of Wessex and the Norman Conquest. To take 871 as the starting date for my survey is not an entirely arbitrary decision. This was designedly a study of women religious active beyond the First Viking Age and was therefore not intended to encompass those early minsters for women that faded from view before or during the viking wars. This policy thus excludes a number of houses which were allegedly destroyed, often it is said by the Danes, in the 870s as well as those that were abandoned or turned into secular households long before that time.[4] The historiography of this group of congregations (listed as table 1 in chapter 3) presents interesting problems quite different from the difficulties presented by the evidence for later female communities and although these would benefit from further exploration, they cannot distract us here. Space has been found here for that small number of religious communities which housed women during Alfred's reign but ceased to function or apparently changed in composition around the end of the ninth century. The demise of these minsters is less plausibly attributable to Danish military activity or to its wider social or economic consequences, but might reflect attitudes to the expression of female vocations that were to become more prevalent during the next two centuries. I have already

---

language of the laws: 'Queens, nunneries and reforming churchmen: Gender, religious status and reform in tenth- and eleventh-century England', *Past and Present*, 163 (1999), 3–35, at pp. 10–11

[4]   Further discussion of the criteria on which houses have been included, particularly in relation to those that apparently ceased to function during the First Viking Age, may be found above in chapter 3.

suggested that the shift whose effects we have witnessed in the patterns of the landed endowment of religious houses for women had begun rather earlier; nevertheless it appears that the alteration in the evidential picture becomes much more marked once the tenth-century reform had formalised the distinctions between cloistered and non-cloistered women.

Rather than just present the mass of data for individual communities of the later Anglo-Saxon period undigested, this chapter attempts to link houses together under a variety of different heads in order to determine whether the sharing of features such as a common pattern of historical development, or the fact of being recorded in only one particular kind of evidence reveals anything useful about the female experience of the religious life at this time. By drawing attention to the similarities between houses, the divisions invented here are also designed to help scholars interested in particular places or specific religious establishments to see which features the institutions with which they are concerned may have shared with others. The categories devised fall into two groups. The first concerns the nature and history of the women's congregations being studied: separate sections will explore those houses located on the sites of pre-Viking-Age minsters for women; new foundations from Alfred's reign onwards; communities in which the West Saxon royal family seems to have taken a particular interest; congregations which for one reason or another ceased to include women during the period covered by this survey; and the few groups of women who were apparently loosely attached to particular male religious foundations. Although strictly speaking this is a study of communal not individual religious expression, information relating to instances of single vowesses who cannot easily be attached to any known religious congregation has been gathered together. Arguments have already been advanced for thinking that these women may have formed the foci of small, informal congregations which justifies the inclusion of such women at this point. There is a second group of categories dictated by the nature of the evidence, that gathers congregations together according to the nature of the earliest extant text to witness to their existence. Since the range of sources reflecting female religious expression in the tenth and eleventh centuries was exhaustively analysed in chapter 1, these categories are only explored in detail in the introduction to part II. They are, however, briefly mentioned here — and mapped — since this evidential typology is as revealing as is the historical one for understanding the historiography of the nunneries of later Anglo-Saxon England.[5]

---

[5] The categories created are of women's communities recorded in contemporary pre-Conquest texts; female religious houses first reported in Domesday Book; congregations known from the report of post-Conquest, medieval writers; and those to which only antiquaries have borne witness. A final category groups those places at which modern authorities have sought to locate groups of nuns, for which the medieval or antiquarian evidence provides no support.

(a) Pre-Viking-Age minsters for women active beyond 871

In the period beyond the accession of King Alfred there were female religious communities at various sites where Anglo-Saxon minsters for women or double houses had been active in the pre-Viking Age; it can, however, rarely be determined whether these congregations had sustained an unbroken existence across the lacuna which characterises most of their archives during the first period of viking wars. Post-Conquest monastic hagiographers, cartularists, and historians frequently supplied accounts of the violent destruction of minsters at the hands of the Danes, the murder of their inmates and devastation of their lands, but such narratives are not based on contemporary accounts and appear to derive largely from their authors' imaginations and preconceived assumptions about the nature of viking warfare. All the primary evidence supporting the statements made about individual congregations of religious women is analysed fully in the separate entries for each place given in the analytical survey in the second part of this study, where explanation will be found for the various interpretative judgements made in order to reach the conclusions sketched here. For the benefit of the reader interested in the broader argument and not the specific details, brief citation of the most essential evidence is given for each place when it is first mentioned in this chapter, but that information is not repeated in cases where the same congregation is included under a number of heads; in general, secondary literature is not cited here.[6]

Despite the lack of contemporary accounts it nevertheless appears, as was argued above, that the viking wars did indeed imperil the existence of endowed female houses, although they need not have dampened female religious ardour.[7] In uncertain times a devout woman and her male kin may each have thought it preferable to satisfy her aspirations on land which still lay within the family's orbit rather than, either alienating land permanently from their control by endowing a new minster, or allowing the woman to leave her kindred and join a vulnerable congregation of other female religious. If, as is now customary, we were to reject later medieval chroniclers' accounts of the murder of defenceless nuns by marauding vikings, there would seem little alternative but to presume that the inmates of supposedly abandoned nunneries were taken back into their blood families (often, of course, the same families that had been responsible for the foundation or endowment of these houses). However, David Dumville has recently argued that the sanitisation of the vikings may have gone rather too far; it is hard to imagine that religious women did not suffer from being caught up in these conflicts.[8] A form of communal continuity could have been sustained at least in

---

6   Readers are thus directed to the individual entries in part II.
7   Above, chapter 3.
8   D. N. Dumville, *The Churches of North Britain in the First Viking Age*, Fifth Whithorn Lecture (1997), pp. 12–14; see above, chapter 3, pp. 71–3.

the memory of these laicised nuns and their families until such time as their congregations could be revived, or founded anew, armed with a documentary record stretching back beyond personal recollection. Where pre-Viking Age southern minsters for women are distinguished from their Northumbrian sisters is that the early charters of some of the former have been preserved, whereas all those relating to northern houses are lost.[9]

The best example of the revival of the religious ideal at the site of a pre-Viking Age minster for women is afforded by Barking, a seventh-century foundation where a female community was certainly functioning from the later 940s. Its fate between the time of Bede and 946x951 when it was mentioned in the will of ealdorman Ælfgar is unknown.[10] The preservation of its pre-Viking Age archive points, however, to some degree of continuity if not an unbroken history of correct monastic observance at the same site, and the archaeological record similarly suggests that the site was used for some purpose in the early tenth century.[11] A tale that the whole community of women had been burnt in their church at Barking by the Danes in 870 was first reported in a late eleventh-century hagiographical text by Goscelin of St Bertin, but is often reported as if it had the evidential authority of contemporary witness.[12]

Members of the former community of Minster-in-Thanet, founded in the seventh century, may similarly have preserved some vestiges of the religious life during the First Viking Age, although it seems likely that they were forced under pressure of sea-borne Danish raids to abandon the minster's exposed coastal site in favour of a more defended location, perhaps at Lyminge (with which Minster was associated early in the ninth century) or within the walls of Canterbury. A charter of King Eadred of 948 granting land in Kent alluded to the existence of a community of St Mildrith, but this need not necessarily have lain on the island of

---

9   This is to presume, as the literary sources appear to suggest, that Northumbrian kings as well as their southern counterparts issued charters to record grants conveying land to ecclesiastical use.

10   Whitelock, *ASWills*, no. 2 (S 1483).

11   K. MacGowan, 'Barking Abbey', *Current Archaeology*, 149 (1996), 172–8.

12   *Lecciones de sancta Hildelitha*, ch. 2 (ed. M. L. Colker, 'Texts of Jocelyn of Canterbury which relate to the history of Barking Abbey', *Studia Monastica*, 7 [1965], 383–460, at p. 455); compare William of Malmesbury, *GP*, §73 (ed. N. E. S. A. Hamilton, Rolls Series 52 [1870], p. 144). The burning of the community was cautiously reported by D. Knowles and R. N. Hadcock, *Medieval Religious Houses. England and Wales* (2nd edn, 1971), p. 256, but with much greater certainty by, for example, J. T. Schulenburg, 'The heroics of virginity: Brides of Christ and sacrificial mutilation', in *Women in the Middle Ages and the Renaissance*, ed. M. B. Rose (Syracuse, New York, 1986), pp. 29–72, at pp. 45–6, R. Fleming, 'Monastic lands and England's defence in the Viking Age', *EHR*, 100 (1985), 247–65, at pp. 255–6; and B. Venarde, *Women's Monasticism and Medieval Society* (Ithaca, New York and London, 1997), p. 23.

Map 5   Pre-Viking Age women's houses active *c*. 890–1066

Map 5   Pre-Viking Age women's houses active *c.* 890–1066

Barking
Berkeley [abandoned before 1066]
Boxwell [abandoned before 1066; reported only by antiquaries]
Castor [abandoned before 1066; reported only by antiquaries]
?Cheddar [abandoned before 1066]
Folkestone [abandoned before 1066]
Leominster [abandoned before 1066]
Minster-in-Sheppey [abandoned before 1066]
Minster-in-Thanet [relocated to Canterbury or vicinity; still active in
          1011 and ?mentioned in Domesday Book]
?Wareham [abandoned before 1066]
Warwick [abandoned before 1066; reported only by antiquaries]
Wenlock [abandoned before 1066]
Wimborne [abandoned before 1066]
Winchcombe [abandoned before 1066]

Thanet.[13] It seems that in the early eleventh century there was a congregation dedicated to Thanet's saint at Canterbury: in 1011 an Abbess Leofrun, whom John of Worcester identified as abbess of the monastery of St Mildrith, was among those captured by the Danes at the siege of Canterbury.[14] Leofrun's congregation might have had some connection with the former Thanet community, whose early charters survived to be incorporated into the archive of St Augustine's Abbey, which acquired the relics of St Mildrith and much of Minster's former endowment in the mid-eleventh century. Whether any connection should be drawn between these religious women and the four *moniales* reported in Domesday Book to be holding land near the city of Canterbury is not clear.[15] The pre-Viking Age minsters on Sheppey and at Folkestone are less likely to have sustained any sort of continued existence through the ninth to eleventh centuries. The nunnery that was founded at Sheppey in the twelfth century had no demonstrable connection with the early minster, all record of whose early land-holdings has been lost, although the late-seventh-century church building remained standing at least to roof level to be incorporated into the later medieval church.[16] There was still a community of women religious at Folkestone in the 830s, and some members of the male community are recorded in a document dating from 844, but the congregation may not have continued for long thereafter;[17] the difficulties of disentangling the history of this community are hampered by the fact that the charter that describes the sack of the minster, although purporting to date from 927, was forged at Christ Church Canterbury in the late eleventh century.[18] It seems unlikely that there were religious women at Folkestone for any significant part of our period; although the survival of the relics of Eanswith at the abbey might point to the maintenance of her cult, this was not necessarily performed by women. Similarly, although there was probably a church of secular priests at

---

[13]   BCS 869 (S 535). As I argue in part II, I do not accept Meyer's argument ('Patronage of West Saxon royal nunneries in late Anglo-Saxon England', *Revue bénédictine*, 91 [1981], 332–58, p. 345) that the religious life was revived on Thanet during the tenth century. Susan Kelly has helpfully observed (*The Charters of St Augustine's Abbey* [1995], pp. xxix), that that the cult of St Mildrith was remembered in the mid-tenth century and beyond is not in itself evidence that there was still a community to sustain it, let alone that this congregation lived on Thanet at that time. See further part II, *s.n.* Minster-in-Thanet.

[14]   Anglo-Saxon Chronicle 1011 CD; John of Worcester, *Chronicon, s.a.* 1011 (ed. and trans. R. R. Darlington *et al.* [1995], II, 468–9).

[15]   Domesday Book, I, fo 12rb (Kent, 7, 11).

[16]   N. Brooks, *The Early History of the Church of Canterbury* (1984), pp. 201–5; S. Thompson, *Women Religious* (1991), pp. 201–2. H. M. Taylor and J. Taylor, *Anglo-Saxon Architecture* (3 vols., 1965–78), I, 429–30.

[17]   Harmer, *SEHD*, no. 2 (S 1482); BCS 445 (S 1439).

[18]   BCS 660 (S 398); see Brooks, *The Early History*, pp. 202 and 367, n. 82.

Lyminge in Kent in the eleventh century, there is no trace of religious women there after the early ninth century.[19]

All of the houses just discussed were for at least a part of their early history double minsters, supporting congregations of both men and women, but none of them appears to have sustained a mixed congregation in the tenth or eleventh centuries. As was discussed in chapter three, the institution of the double house had a relatively short history in Anglo-Saxon England, flourishing only between the mid-seventh and the later eighth century. Although there are a few instances of religious women and men living together (or in close proximity) in the late ninth and early tenth centuries, this group of women's houses was not among them. There were no genuine double houses (mixed congregations under the overall headship of a woman) found in England after the end of the eighth century.[20]

Women religious are, however, recorded in the later Anglo-Saxon period living at some sites which had housed male congregations before the First Viking Age; whether any connection need be postulated between these early minsters and later female communities beyond the coincidence of site is in each case highly doubtful. A minster at Berkeley in Gloucestershire was apparently governed by abbots in the mid-eighth century and again in the later ninth century; although John of Worcester — possibly erroneously — located an abbess Ceolburh at this house early in the ninth century, there is no certain reference to the presence of women at Berkeley until the mention of an Abbess Ælfthryth in the early eleventh-century *Liber Vitae* of New Minster, Winchester.[21] An abbess of Leominster was mentioned in the Anglo-Saxon Chronicle for 1046,[22] but there is no evidence that the seventh-century minster founded there by Merewalh had ever held a community of nuns except for the surmise of Leland.[23]

Charter witness-lists indicate that mixed female and male communities existed at the turn of the ninth century at Wenlock and Winchcombe, both the sites of earlier double houses and perhaps also at Cheddar. Wenlock had been founded in the later seventh century, probably as a double house headed by an abbess; in

---

[19]   Goscelin, *Libellus contra inanes s. uirginis Mildrethae usurpatores*, ch. 11 (ed. M. L. Colker, 'A hagiographic polemic', *Mediaeval Studies*, 39 (1977), 60–108, at pp. 78–9); N. Brooks, *The Early History of the Church of Canterbury* (1984), pp. 201–5.

[20]   Above, chapter 3; D. Schneider, 'Anglo-Saxon women in the religious life: a study of the status and position of women in an early mediaeval society' (PhD thesis, University of Cambridge, 1985), p. 26.

[21]   BCS 187 and 218 (S 56 and 63), both witnessed by an abbot of Berkeley; Harmer, *SEHD*, no. 12 (S 218), a grant to a minster at Berkeley. Anglo-Saxon Chronicle, *s.a.* 805; John of Worcester: *Chronicon, s.a.* 805 (ed. and trans. Darlington *et al.*, II, 232–3); *Liber Vitae: Register and Martyrology of New Minster and Hyde Abbey, Winchester*, ed. W. de G. Birch (1892), p. 58

[22]   Anglo-Saxon Chronicle 1046 C.

[23]   *The Itinerary of John Leland in or about the Years 1535–1543*, ed. L. Toulmin Smith, 5 vols. (1964), II, 73.

901 a community at Wenlock, then apparently headed by a male superior, exchanged some land with Ealdorman Æthelred and Æthelflæd, which transaction was witnessed by five women, apparently members of the minster congregation.[24] The double house at Winchcombe, founded probably in the later eighth century, apparently supported a mixed congregation in 897, in which year it reached an agreement with the church of Worcester over land in Gloucestershire, which was witnessed by three women, who have been taken to have been members of Winchcombe's congregation.[25] It seems reasonable to assume a direct connection between both these early double houses and the congregations recorded c. 900, without necessarily postulating for each an unbroken history. Neither minster appears to have housed women beyond this time, although both seem to have supported male congregations in the tenth and eleventh centuries. One version of a (spurious) charter attributed to King Edgar referred to the presence of both female and male servants of God at Cheddar in the reign of King Edward the Elder; this document purported to confirm to the Old Minster at Winchester the liberty of Taunton and alluded to a previous exchange made between Edward the Elder and the community at Cheddar of land in Somerset.[26] There is no other evidence that Cheddar was ever occupied by women religious and it is far from clear that this evidence alone is sufficient to argue for a mixed congregation of religious in the early years of the tenth century.[27] More plausible is the notion that there was a congregation of women at the site of the pre-Viking Age double house of Wimborne in 900, when a *nunne* from there was seized unlawfully by the ætheling Æthelwold in his rebellion against his cousin Edward the Elder.[28] There is, however, no further allusion to the presence of religious women at Wimborne beyond this time. There may have been a religious community at that place during the tenth century, but the congregation recorded in Domesday Book is one of male seculars; it seems more likely that like Winchcombe and Wenlock, Wimborne ceased to support women at some time after c. 900.[29] It is not clear whether the *monasterium sanctimonialium* mentioned by Asser as lying within the *castellum* at Wareham was a new foundation of the later ninth century, or whether it had been established before the start of the First Viking Age.[30] Leland was probably

---

[24]   BCS 587 (S 221).

[25]   BCS 575 (S 1442).

[26]   Robertson, *ASCharters*, no. 45 (S 806): 'famulis famulabusque Domini on Ceodre degentibus'.

[27]   J. Blair, 'Palaces or minsters? Northampton and Cheddar reconsidered', *ASE*, 25 (1996), 97–122; B. Yorke, 'The Bonifacian mission and female religious in Wessex', *Early Medieval Europe*, 7 (1998), 145–72, at p. 167.

[28]   Anglo-Saxon Chronicle 900; John of Worcester, *Chronicon, s.a.* 901 (ed. and trans. Darlington *et al.*, II, 354–7).

[29]   Anglo-Saxon Chronicle 962; Domesday Book, I, fo 78va (Dorset, 14, 1).

[30]   Asser, Life of Alfred, ch. 49 (ed. W. H. Stevenson, *Asser's Life of King Alfred* [1904], p. 36). The Wareham inscriptions and the surviving church fabric both suggest that there

mistaken in believing this house to have been destroyed in the Danish raid on the Wareham in 876.[31]

Antiquaries have witnessed to the presence in the later ninth century of congregations of women religious at three additional places: Boxwell in Gloucestershire, Castor in Northamptonshire, and Warwick, Warwickshire. Of these, only Castor is attested in medieval sources as the site of a pre-Viking-Age minster for women, being associated with Cyneburga, the daughter of Penda of Mercia; Tanner reported the continued existence of this congregation until it was destroyed by the Danes in 1010, but the authority on which he based his opinion is unknown.[32] Leland reported that there were *nunnes* at Boxwell, and that they were 'destroyed as sum say by the Danes'; that we should take this as a reference to an early community of religious women which survived into but not beyond the pre-Viking age is far from clear, since it is impossible to verify Leland's account with reference to any medieval source relating to this church.[33] In his history of Warwickshire Dugdale recorded the burning down of a 'nunnery near to the church of St Nicholas' in the town of Warwick during raiding in the shire by Cnut's army, but it cannot be determined whether or not this supposed women's community was a recent foundation or could trace any sort of existence into the period before the start of King Alfred's reign.[34] These three instances illustrate well the difficulty of basing any sort of argument on antiquarian accounts; these putative communities find most appropriate place within the category of female religious houses first witnessed in texts dating from beyond the medieval period.

Few of the houses which supported congregations of women between the accession of Alfred and the Norman Conquest had long histories, and of those attested in this period which may have had connections with earlier foundations three (Wenlock, Wimborne, and Winchcombe) apparently ceased to support women during the early years of the tenth century. Other than Barking and possibly the community of St Mildrith's from Thanet, the other tenth- and eleventh-century female religious houses in England appear either to have been new foundations, or to have been less formally constituted establishments, groups of women more or less loosely attached to better endowed male houses, or congregations gathered around vowesses living on family lands. Various reasons might be postulated for this: female religious houses may have found it

---

was a minster of some sorts at Wareham, not necessarily one including women, long before the late ninth century; see further part II, *s. n.* Wareham.

31   Leland, *De Rebus Britannicis Collectanea*, ed. T. Hearne (2nd edn, 6 vols., 1774), III, 388. Wareham's tenth-century monastic history is addressed in the next section.

32   T. Tanner, *Notitia Monastica*, ed. J. Nasmith (Cambridge, 1787) [without pagination], Northamptonshire xiv. On Tanner's authority, Castor was included among destroyed monasteries in the appendix to the sixth volume of W. Dugdale, *Monasticon Anglicanum*, new edn J. Caley *et al.*, 6 vols. in 8 (1817–30), VI, 3, p. 1621.

33   Leland, *Itinerary*, IV, 133.

34   W. Dugdale, *The Antiquities of Warwickshire* (1656, 2nd edn. 1730), p. 376.

particularly difficult to survive the vicissitudes of ninth-century warfare (as much because their land was needed for defence, or the male relations of their inmates no longer felt able to support them in economically and militarily useless endeavour, because they had been the particular focus of Danish attack). Other pre-Viking Age female communities may have sustained a sufficient existence during the ninth century to be revived or refounded in Alfred's reign or beyond, but without having found place in the surviving historical record. It is also not impossible that women's houses now known only from sources which place them in the tenth or eleventh centuries had in fact had an earlier existence not recorded in any surviving documents, perhaps because the poverty or inadequacy of their original endowment was such that they never had charters recording their landholdings, and none of their inmates attracted the attention of contemporary chroniclers.

(b) New foundations for women religious made between 871 and 1066

It is striking how few of the sixty-odd institutions which some authority, however dubious, attests to have housed religious women during this period are said explicitly in sources of any date to have been newly created between the accession of King Alfred and the Conquest. In many instances this is clearly a consequence of the inadequacy of the surviving record, notably where that relates to the endowment of new religious houses for women.[35] A number of the institutions discussed within the evidential categories explored in part two (particularly those that were first attested in Domesday Book, or female communities that found mention only in post-Conquest histories) must in fact have been founded at some point in the later pre-Conquest period. The reported evidence for the presence of women is, in a handful of these cases, so slender as to prove unverifiable, the period of occupation of the site being essentially unknown. A few houses, such as those at Chester and St Albans, were reported to lie in towns that had previously housed male congregations,[36] and it is unclear whether the supposed female community at some time replaced the men or whether, as is demonstrable in other instances such as Bury St Edmunds, the women were in some informal fashion attached to a continuing male monastery.

Three houses, Polesworth, Wareham, and Woodchester, merit inclusion under this heading more by accident of the evidence concerning their origins than because a more compelling case can be made on their behalf. Polesworth in Warwickshire was said by chroniclers of the thirteenth-century abbey of St Albans

---

[35]   The infrequency with which religious houses for women are provided with extant foundation charters, even forged ones, was noted in chapter 1, p. 17.

[36]   If these communities were explicitly urban ones, they are unlikely to pre-date the tenth century.

to have been established for an Edith, sister of King Æthelstan, following the death of her husband, Sihtric of York.[37] Were this story true, it would clearly date Polesworth's foundation to the later 920s; however, Æthelstan's sister Edith is more conventionally held to have married the Saxon king Otto, and the tale may have arisen in an attempt to account for the placing of the relics of a saint Edith at Polesworth in the earliest of the surviving lists of saints' resting-places, a legend which may similarly have lain behind the dedication of the twelfth-century nunnery at Polesworth.[38] Wareham in Dorset has been included within this category since it is first mentioned as the site of a nunnery in the late ninth century;[39] how long before that time it had been founded cannot be determined, however, and it might in fact more properly, as we have already seen, find place with the pre-Viking Age institutions. Wareham's activities in the first half of the tenth century are unknown; it is not mentioned again until the obit of its abbess was reported in the Anglo-Saxon Chronicle for 982.[40] The inclusion of a supposed nunnery at Woodchester in Gloucester at any point in this survey arises from a misunderstanding of the account of that manor given in Domesday Book that was perpetrated by Camden and given wider currency by being repeated by Tanner in his *Notitia Monastica*.[41] It is not in fact likely that Earl Godwine's wife, Gytha, ever built a religious house at this place, although it is apparent from Domesday Book that she lived off the profits of the manor of Woodchester while she was staying at Berkeley (which nunnery her husband had dissolved).[42]

It is impossible to attach any date to the arrival at Cheddar of the *famulae Dei* who were thought (at least by a later medieval scribe copying a charter in favour of the Old Minster at Winchester) to have occupied that minster during the reign of Edward the Elder.[43] Nor is it known when the nunnery at Reading was created, whose abbess Leofrun was named among the *feminae illustres* commemorated in the *Liber Vitae* of Hyde Abbey.[44] We are on more secure ground over the origins of the nunnery at Shaftesbury, which may be taken — if

---

[37] Roger of Wendover, *Flores historiarum, s.a.* 925 (ed. H. O. Coxe [5 vols., 1841–4], I, 385–6); Matthew Paris, *Chronica Majora, s.a.* 925 (ed. H. R. Luard, Rolls Series 57 [7 vols. 1872–80], I, 446–7).
[38] *Die Heiligen Englands*, II, 18 (ed. F. Liebermann [Hannover, 1889], p. 13); Thompson, *Women*, p. 227.
[39] Asser, Life of Alfred, ch. 49 (ed. Stevenson, *Asser*, p. 36, trans. S. Keynes and M. Lapidge, *Alfred the Great* [1983], p. 82).
[40] Goscelin also alluded to the presence of a house of female religious in the town early in the reign of King Edgar: *Vita sanctae Wulfhildae*, ch. 4 (ed. M. Esposito, 'La vie de Sainte Vulfhilde par Goscelin de Cantorbéry', *Analecta Bollandiana*, 32 [1913], 10–26, at p. 17); M. A. O'Donovan, *Charters of Sherborne* (1988), p. lix.
[41] *Camden's Britannia*, ed. and trans. E. Gibson (1695), col. 247; Tanner, *Notitia Monastica*, Gloucestershire, xxxiv.
[42] Domesday Book, I, fo 164rb (Gloucestershire, 1, 63).
[43] Robertson, *ASCharters*, no. 45 (S 806).
[44] *Liber Vitae* of Hyde Abbey (ed. Birch, p. 58).

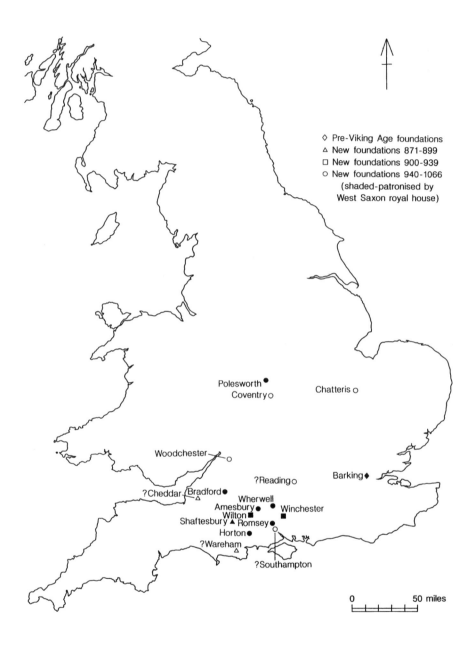

◇ Pre-Viking Age foundations
△ New foundations 871-899
□ New foundations 900-939
○ New foundations 940-1066
  (shaded-patronised by
  West Saxon royal house)

Polesworth ●
Coventry ○

Chatteris ○

Woodchester ○

?Reading ○

Barking ◆

?Cheddar Bradford ●
          △
              Wherwell
Amesbury ●   ●
Wilton   ■ Winchester
Shaftesbury ▲ Romsey ●   ■
Horton ●   ○
?Wareham
    △
      ?Southampton

0   50 miles

Map 6   The foundation and royal patronage of women's religious houses,
              871x1066

Map 6   The foundation and royal patronage of women's religious houses,
871x1066

New foundations
   i) of Alfred's reign
      ?Cheddar
      Shaftesbury
      ?Wareham

   ii) 900 x 939
      Wilton
      Winchester, the Nunnaminster

   iii) 940 x 1066
      Amesbury
      Bradford-on-Avon
      Chatteris
      Coventry
      Horton
      Polesworth
      ?Reading
      Romsey
      Southampton
      Wherwell
      Woodchester

Nunneries patronised by members of the West Saxon royal family
      Amesbury
      Barking
      (Bradford-on-Avon)
      Romsey
      Shaftesbury
      Wherwell
      Wilton
      Winchester, the Nunnaminster

we accept the biography of King Alfred attributed to the authorship of Asser as genuine — to have been newly founded in that king's reign. Asser described in some detail how the king established a community for his daughter, Æthelgifu, gathering round her a group of pious women.[45] The only other monastic community created by Alfred was that for men which he founded at Athelney.[46] Alfred's widow, Ealhswith, may have been responsible for initiating the foundation of a minster for women in Winchester, but this was probably only completed by her son, Edward the Elder.[47] A women's monastic community at Wilton was first mentioned in charters from the mid-tenth century but it cannot be determined how long before the date of the earliest of those documents the house may have been established.[48] The later medieval nunnery preserved a variety of different accounts of its origins. A dubiously authentic charter for Wilton attributed to King Edgar included a statement to the effect that the nunnery had been founded by Edgar's grandfather, Edward the Elder,[49] and William of Malmesbury reported that two of the latter king's daughters had been buried at Wilton, with which house they might conceivably have been connected.[50] A fifteenth-century poem from Wilton connected King Alfred with the refoundation in 890 of a women's minster that had first been created in the later eighth century.[51]

Few of the communities of women religious surveyed here can be shown to have been endowed specifically to advance the spiritual ideals promoted through the monastic revolution of Edgar's reign, even though the contemporary rhetorical writing concerning that movement made the involvement of women's houses in the revival explicit, and historians have tended to presume that most of the nunneries newly founded in the tenth century did play a part in the revival of monasticism, as we have already seen.[52] Romsey and Horton are the sole houses which might conceivably be thought to have been established at the height of the reform. There are, however, three conflicting versions of Romsey's origins: John of Worcester stated that King Edgar placed nuns in the house at Romsey which his

[45]   Asser, Life of King Alfred, ch. 98 (ed. Stevenson, *Asser*, p. 85).
[46]   Ibid., chs. 93–4 (pp. 80–1).
[47]   *Liber Vitae* of Hyde Abbey (ed. Birch, p. 5); Æthelweard, *Chronicon*, IV.4 (ed. A. Campbell [1962], p. 52); Leland attributed the Nunnaminster's foundation to King Alfred: *Collectanea*, I, 413.
[48]   BCS 699 (S 424), BCS 714 (S 438) and BCS 917 (S 582).
[49]   BCS 1304 (S 799); as it survives this is not an authentic document. It cannot have been invented later than the early fourteenth century (when it was copied into Wilton's cartulary) but it may preserve earlier legends about the abbey's origins.
[50]   William of Malmesbury, *GR*, II, 126 (ed. and trans. R. A. B. Mynors *et al.* [1998], I, 200–1). See above, chapter 5, p. 140 for discussion of the religious lifestyles adopted by Edward the Elder's former wives and daughters.
[51]   *S. Editha*, lines 598–609 (ed. C. Horstmann, *S Editha sive Chronicon Vilodunense* [Heilbronn, 1883], p. 14).
[52]   See above, chapter 4, pp. 87–91.

grandfather, Edward the Elder had founded, but William of Malmesbury thought Edgar himself responsible for the nunnery's creation.[53] The fourteenth-century *Vita S Elfleda* attributed the foundation both to an ealdorman Æthelwold, father of the saint, and to King Edgar.[54] The earliest extant texts to make mention of a religious community at Romsey date only from Edgar's reign: a charter by which Edgar gave land at Edington to the abbey in 968, and the report in the A and G versions of the Anglo-Saxon Chronicle for the year 971 of the burial at Romsey of the ætheling Edmund, infant son of King Edgar.[55] Little is known of the circumstances in which Horton was founded. Its existence as a nunnery during the reign of Edgar depends on the unsupported statement of Goscelin in the Life of St Wulfhild that this *domus familiarum* was given to the saint with four others when Wulfhild was established at Barking.[56] If any reliance were to be placed on this account, it could be taken as evidence also for the existence *c.* 960 of an otherwise unattested nunnery at *Hamtunia*, which I identify below as Southampton, one of the four nunneries given to Wulfhild. Whether this also should be seen as a new tenth-century creation is equally unclear. Neither Horton nor Romsey (nor, for that matter, Southampton) can thus convincingly be held to have been endowed specifically as a reformed (Benedictine) house. Shaftesbury, the Nunnaminster at Winchester, and Wilton were all certainly founded before the start of the revival, during the reigns of Alfred and Edward the Elder (and are therefore unlikely to have been Benedictine in origin, although each has been thought to have played a part in the monastic reform). Amesbury and Wherwell were founded beyond the peak of the reform in King Æthelred's reign,[57] as was the cell established by the women of Shaftesbury at Bradford on Avon, a site given them by that king as a refuge from the Danes.[58] In some ways Chatteris had the closest connections with the Benedictine movement; although not a royal foundation, it was established early in the eleventh century by a former disciple of Oswald's, translated by him from Worcester to Ramsey.[59] Later sources credited King Cnut with the attempted foundation of a religious house for women at Coventry, whose members were

---

[53]   John of Worcester, *Chronicon, s.a.* 967 (ed. and trans. Darlington *et al.*, II, 416–19). William of Malmesbury, *GP*, §178 (ed. Hamilton, pp. 174–5).

[54]   *Vita sanctae Elfledae* (ed. C. Horstmann, *Nova Legenda Angliae* [2 vols., 1901], I, 379–81, at p. 381).

[55]   BCS 1215 (S 765); Anglo-Saxon Chronicle *s.a.* 971 AG.

[56]   Goscelin, *Vita sanctae Wulfhildae*, ch. 4 (ed. Esposito, p. 17).

[57]   For the foundation of Amesbury see William of Malmesbury, *GP*, §87 (ed. Hamilton, p. 188); for Wherwell: ibid., §§78 and 87 (pp. 175 and 188).

[58]   *Charters of Shaftesbury*, ed. S. E. Kelly (1996), no. 29 (S 899).

[59]   Chatteris was said by Ely's house-history to have been founded by Eadnoth, bishop of Dorchester 1007x1009–1016, and formerly abbot of Ramsey: *Liber Eliensis*, II, 71 (ed. E. O. Blake [1962], pp. 140–1).

expelled in 1043; a second one planned by the same king for Ramsey was aborted at its inception.[60]

Despite the hesitations just voiced about the extent of these institutions' full adherence to the precepts expounded in the *Regularis concordia* (and over the issue as to whether their former residents may have been expelled as part of the reform), it seems reasonable to surmise that most if not all of the houses discussed under this heading conformed to some of the principles of reformed monasticism. All were, as far as we can tell, houses exclusively for women. Each (apart perhaps from Wareham and Reading for whom no such evidence has survived) had its own landed endowment, freed permanently from external interference by royal charter, sufficient that its economic viability would not be compromised by future claims to any personal lands the residents may have retained on entering the cloister. In intention (if not always in practice) we could describe the majority of these as institutions in which women had chosen to live corporately, under a rule, shut off in some measure from the lay world, in order to satisfy personal and collective spiritual aspirations. In other words, we could see these as 'nunneries', their inhabitants as 'cloistered women'. These are the places where the *mynecena* dwelt, the female equivalents of regular monks, for whom appropriate behaviour was specified in the prescriptive literature of the early eleventh century.[61]

All but three of the Anglo-Saxon women's religious houses which can be shown to have been newly founded after the accession of King Alfred had some association with the royal house. Chatteris is the only one said to have been established as a result of noble patronage, although that munificence found no record in extant pre-Conquest documentation, being reported only in the twelfth-century *Liber Eliensis*. Reading and Wareham were, however, despite their lack of royal patronage, mentioned in tenth- or eleventh-century sources, unlike the other institutions which may well have been founded in the same period, but about whose existence pre-Conquest authors were largely silent.[62] The significance of the question of royal involvement with these houses warrants further consideration, for it is that single factor above all others which can be shown to have privileged these cloistered female communities within the historical record.

(c) Nunneries patronised by members of the West Saxon royal family

The patronage of women's religious houses in the tenth century has previously attracted a good deal of attention, and the issue has recently been considered

---

[60]   Coventry: Leland, *Collectanea*, I, 50; *Itinerary*, II, 107. Ramsey: *Chronicon Abbatiae Rameseiensis* (ed. W. D. Macray [1889], p. 126).

[61]   V Æthelred, 4–4.1; VI Æthelred, ch. 2.2; I Cnut, ch. 6a (ed. Liebermann, *Die Gesetze*, I, 238, 246 and 288); Wulfstan, I *Polity*, 84, II *Polity*, xiii.185 (ed. Jost, *Die "Institutes"*, p. 128). See above, chapter 4, pp. 98–100.

[62]   Notably the houses discussed in the introduction to part II, §§b and c.

afresh by Julia Crick.[63] A separate category has here been devoted to the subject in order to demonstrate once again how restricted both in number and in geographical distribution were those nunneries which received material support from the West Saxon royal house during the tenth century. Although this was a period in which this particular family espoused a public position of considerable interest and financial involvement in the process of the revitalisation of monasticism (as evidenced for example by the preface to the *Regularis concordia*, and King Edgar's request that the Rule of St Benedict be translated into Old English in order that he might know more about the teachings and precepts of that rule[64]), the female recipients of the family's direct patronage comprise a select group. Only seven religious houses for women appear to have benefited directly from the munificence of members of the West Saxon royal family in the tenth and eleventh centuries: Amesbury, Barking, Romsey, Shaftesbury, Wherwell, Wilton and the Nunnaminster at Winchester. To these might have been added the community Polesworth (where thirteenth-century historians reported King Æthelstan's sister Edith to have lived after the death of her husband, Sihtric of York), but the evidence for its association with the royal house is so tenuous that it has been omitted from this category.[65] Barking is the only one of these houses to lie outside Wessex; the rest are concentrated in a cluster in western Hampshire, southern Wiltshire and eastern Dorset.[66] What — beyond geography — distinguishes this particular group of nunneries most strikingly is that these are all houses with which a recent member of the West Saxon royal family had a direct association. All were either founded by a king or queen, or lived in by a princess, queen, or royal concubine. It can be no coincidence that these were not only the

---

[63]   Meyer, 'Patronage'; J. Crick, 'The wealth, patronage, and connections of women's houses in late Anglo-Saxon England', *Revue bénédictine*, 109 (1999), 154–85. Discussion of aristocratic patronage of tenth-century religious houses in general (with more detailed analysis of gifts made to six male congregations) may be found in J. M. Pope, 'Monks and nobles in the Anglo-Saxon monastic reform', *Anglo-Norman Studies*, 17 (1994), 165–80.

[64]   *Regularis concordia*, proem §§ 2–3 (ed. Symons, pp. 1–2); Æthelwold, 'An account', ed. Whitelock *et al.*, *Councils*, I, 151, no. 33.

[65]   Part II, *s.n.* Polesworth. The house at Bradford-on-Avon in Wiltshire has also not been included here. Although it has just sufficient claim to have housed a congregation of women in the early eleventh century to warrant a separate entry in the full survey of female congregations in part II, the act of royal patronage in its creation (and the consequent rich decoration of the stone church there) was made primarily in favour of Shaftesbury Abbey, whose cloistered women were given the new site as a refuge. Similarly, the five *domus familiarum* that King Edgar was supposed to have given, with Barking, to the nun Wulfhild (*Hamtunia*, Horton, Shaftesbury, Wareham, and Wilton) did not each thereby benefit from what was in effect a gift in Barking's favour: Goscelin, *Vita sanctae Wulfhildae*, ch. 4 (ed. Esposito, p. 17).

[66]   Others have also discussed the clustered distribution of reform nunneries: Meyer, 'Patronage', p. 334; D. A. Hinton, 'Amesbury and the early history of its abbey', *The Amesbury Millennium Lectures*, ed. John Chandler (Amesbury, 1979), pp. 20–31, pp. 22–3; see also the map in B. Yorke, *Wessex in the Early Middle Ages* (1995), p. 207, fig. 55.

richest pre-Conquest religious houses for women, but also those which succeeded in sustaining the longest history beyond the eleventh century.

Royal patronage would seem primarily to have been directed towards royal foundations, since all but one of these nine houses can lay some claim to have been founded by a member of the West Saxon royal house (even if that claim cannot be substantiated except by reference to texts dating from after the Norman Conquest). The only exception is Barking, the one house to trace its history back to the pre-Viking Age. Two of these nunneries were later held to have been founded by kings — Shaftesbury by King Alfred and Romsey by his son, Edward the Elder — and three were supposedly founded by queens (or dowagers): the Nunnaminster at Winchester by Ealhswith, King Alfred's widow, with the direct support of her son, Edward the Elder; and Amesbury and Wherwell by Ælfthryth, third wife of King Edgar, supposedly as a penitential act following her part in the murder of Edward the Martyr. Wilton is also frequently said to have been founded by King Alfred, but the evidence for his association with the house dates only from a fifteenth-century vernacular poem from Wilton and is not supported by any pre-Conquest source. As was made clear in the accounts of the evidence for their foundation given in the preceding section, the nunneries at Horton and Polesworth can be fitted only somewhat uneasily into this category; the grounds for including them are slight and depend on inferences drawn from post-Conquest hagiographical sources of less than secure reliability.

Returning to the nunneries more certainly connected with this family, royal patronage is most readily demonstrable by means of surviving charters recording grants of land in the nunneries' favour, examples of which survive for six of these houses; it is also known that the seventh too benefited in this way, although the document recording the gift is now lost.[67] Despite claiming royal foundation, none of these houses preserves a foundation charter with any claim to authenticity; the only extant foundation charter is in favour of Shaftesbury and cannot be accepted in the form in which it survives.[68] It is striking, as Julia Crick has noted, that none of nunneries founded by West Saxon kings is known to have received land from anyone other than a member of that dynasty, although it is conceivable that some of the charters in favour of laymen and women preserved in the cartularies of Barking, Shaftesbury and Wilton (the only ones of these houses for which cartularies survive) might relate to estates transferred to the nunnery by the lay recipient of the charter, or his or her heirs.[69]

Further links can be traced between the houses in this group. Amesbury and Wherwell (both founded by Ælfthryth) may at the start of the eleventh century both have been governed by one abbess, Heahflæd; Barking and Horton were at

---

[67]   Above, chapter 1; Amesbury is the house thought to have benefited from a charter of King Æthelred's that is now lost.

[68]   *Charters of Shaftesbury*, ed. Kelly, no. 7 (S 357).

[69]   Crick, 'The wealth', pp. 175–8.

different times ruled by Abbess Wulfhild; and St Edith's biographer alleged that she had control over three abbeys, Barking, the Nunnaminster at Winchester and a third that he did not name.[70] Several of the group were inhabited by close members of the royal family: the daughters of kings lived at the Nunnaminster in Winchester, Shaftesbury and Wilton, and Barking and Horton were both home to a former royal concubine.[71] Others served as guardians of the cults of the family's dead: Eadgifu, daughter of Edward the Elder, and his third wife, also named Eadgifu, were both buried at the Nunnaminster in Winchester;[72] the ætheling Edmund, as already mentioned, at Romsey.[73] Ælfgifu, first wife of King Edmund was buried at Shaftesbury, where the body of King Edward the Martyr also lay.[74] The second wife of Edward the Elder (Ælfflæd) together with two of her daughters (Eadflæd and Æthelhild) were buried at Wilton, and in 962 a kinsman (*mæg*) of the king from Devon was laid to rest in the same nunnery.[75]

West Saxon royal patronage in the tenth and eleventh centuries (beyond the blanket spiritual support acknowledged in the *Regularis concordia*) was directed exclusively towards those nunneries with which a recent member of the family had a direct association (in death or in life); that these are also the communities with the most substantial surviving archives and those to which medieval and modern historians have paid the closest attention is not coincidental.

(d) Short-lived and dissolved female congregations

Not all the houses known to have supported congregations of women at some time in the period beyond the accession of King Alfred survived as far as the Norman

---

[70]   H. P. R. Finberg, *The Early Charters of Wessex* (1964), p. 104; Goscelin, *Vita sanctae Wulfhildae*, chs. 4 and 9 (ed. Esposito, pp. 17 and 21); Goscelin, *Vita sanctae Edithe*, ch. 16 (ed. A. Wilmart, 'La légende de Ste Edithe en prose et vers par le moine Goscelin', *Analecta Bollandiana*, 56 [1938], 5–101 and 265–307, at p. 77).

[71]   Polesworth might also be added to this list, were Edith of Polesworth thought to have been royal.

[72]   William of Malmesbury, *GR*, II, 126 (ed. Mynors *et al.*, I, 200–1); Osbert, *Vita S. Edburge*, ch. 12 (ed. S. Ridyard, *The Royal Saints of Anglo-Saxon England* [1988], p. 284). King Alfred's widow, Ealhswith, was not buried at the Nunnaminster (*contra* J. C. Cox, 'Nunnaminster, or the abbey of St Mary Winchester', VCH Hampshire, II (1903), pp. 122–6, at p. 122), but rather at the New Minster. It is unlikely that the women's house was active as early as the time of Ealhswith's death in 903.

[73]   P. Stafford, *Queen Emma and Queen Edith* (1997), p. 91.

[74]   Æthelweard, *Chronicon*, IV.6 (ed. Campbell, p. 54); Anglo-Saxon Chronicle, *s.a.* 980 DE.

[75]   William of Malmesbury, *GR*, II, 126 (ed. Mynors *et al.*, I, 200–1); Anglo-Saxon Chronicle, 962 A. Pauline Stafford is mistaken in her suggestion that other royal men in the male line who never ruled were buried at Wilton: *Queen Emma and Queen Edith*, 90; see further part II, *s n.* Wilton.

Conquest. Did these ephemeral congregations share any common features that might have predisposed them to ultimate failure, or is it in fact appropriate to view them as unsuccessful? Some might have been intended to be ephemeral, if it could be shown that they had been created to satisfy particular spiritual aspirations within contexts that were always known to be temporary. It may equally be misleading to categorise as 'short-lived' communities that were active for a century or more but happen not to have sustained a female congregation right to the end of our period.

There is little in their geographical distribution to distinguish those congregations of religious women which either disappeared from the written record during our period or were deliberately suppressed. As is obvious from map 7 overleaf, the communities that fall into this category are relatively evenly spread across southern England. Whether any significance should be attached to the fact that the majority of these houses lay outside Greater Wessex is not clear, although that accident of geography did serve to remove most of these from the orbit of royal patronage in the tenth and eleventh centuries, a factor that we have already noted to be of prime importance both in the securing of an adequate endowment and in achieving lasting notice in the historical record. However, it was not necessarily the absence of royal patronage that doomed all of these particular establishments to failure. Horton and Southampton both apparently lay within King Edgar's gift, indicating some connection with royalty. An abortive attempt was made early in the eleventh century to institute a house for women at Ramsey was made with money supplied from the royal fisc by King Cnut;[76] the same king was further credited by Leland with foundation of a community for women at Coventry, although its members were supposedly expelled in 1043.[77] Dugdale offered in his history of Warwickshire a rather different account of this women's house, associating it with the shadowy saint Osburga and suggesting that it had been destroyed by Cnut in 1016.[78]

It might be argued that it was the gender of their occupants that determined the failure of these communities. Without undertaking a similarly rigorous survey of the evidence for male religious across the same period it is difficult to distinguish those eventualities which might have befallen all monastic communities from those which could be thought to be distinctive to the female experience in the post-Viking Age. Whether (other than during periods of war) female congregations did lead a more precarious existence than male ones in this period is not known. Antiquarian authorities argued for the violent destruction at the hands of the Danes of Boxwell, Castor, Warwick and Wareham; we have evidence to suggest that the last of these at least succeeded in sustaining a

[76]   For Horton and Southampton see Goscelin, *Vita S. Wulfhildae*, ch. 4 (ed. Esposito, p. 17); for Ramsey: *Chronicon Abbatiae Rameseiensis*, ed. Macray, p. 126.
[77]   Leland, *Collectanea*, I, 50; *Itinerary*, II, 107.
[78]   Dugdale, *The Antiquities*, p. 85.

religious congregation beyond the time of its supposed destruction (if not apparently to the end of the Anglo-Saxon period), but medieval sources with which to verify their statements have failed to survive in the other three cases.[79] In some of the instances discussed here, lack of evidence for the continuation of a previously attested nunnery has been taken — perhaps erroneously — to demonstrate its demise. The pre-Viking Age Mercian double houses of Wenlock and Winchcombe cannot be shown to have supported communities of women beyond the turn of the ninth century, nor are religious women known to have lived at Cheddar or at Bedwyn other than at the single moment when their presence was reported among the witnesses to, respectively, a land-conveyance and a manumission.[80] The early double minster at Wimborne also made only brief appearance within our period in the year 900 and not thereafter. The silence of the surviving sources does not, however, constitute evidence for the women's dispersal. The case of continuing double houses is particularly difficult in view of the attitude of monastics of later periods to the impropriety of such arrangements. Ramsey's twelfth-century chronicler expressed himself relieved at the failure of Cnut's project to establish a second, female, community at the abbey beside the pre-existing male monastery.[81] Similar disapproval of mixed-gender congregations might have informed Leland's assertion that *moniales* were ejected from Pershore by King Edgar to be replaced by monks, but it is equally possible that Leland erred in supposing that unreformed house to have been inhabited by female religious, an opinion which cannot be supported from other extant sources.[82]

It is once more from the silence of the historical record alone that Horton and Southampton are presumed to have ceased to function. Both first found mention as communities of female religious in Goscelin's *Life of St Wulfhild*, and Southampton was nowhere else so described, although an abbess of Horton was named in the *Liber Vitae* of Hyde Abbey, compiled *c.* 1021.[83] The nunnery of Reading was similarly attested in the early eleventh century via mention of its abbess in the *Liber Vitae* of Hyde Abbey, and may still have been active in 1066

---

[79] Above, §a.

[80] Cheddar, Wenlock and Winchcombe were all discussed above in §a, among the pre-Viking Age women's minsters. For the recording of the name of a *nunne* among the witnesses to a manumission preserved in a gospel book from Bedwyn (Bern, Burgerbibliothek, MS 671, fo 76v) see H. Merritt, 'Old English entries in a manuscript at Bern', *Journal of English and Germanic Philology*, 33 (1934), 343–51, pp. 346–7. This example is more appropriately catalogued in the next two sections which examine vowesses living under the shadow of male houses and single vowesses.

[81] *Chronicon Abbatiae Rameseiensis*, ed. Macray, p. 126.

[82] Leland, *Collectanea*, III, 160. Leland's statement was repeated by Tanner (*Notitia Monastica*, Worcestershire, xvii), but all medieval sources described Pershore as a male congregation.

[83] Goscelin, *Vita S. Wulfhildae*, ch. 4 (ed. Esposito, p. 17); *Liber Vitae* of Hyde Abbey (ed. Birch, p. 57).

Map 7   Ephemeral foundations, 871–1066

Map 7   Ephemeral foundations, 871–1066

i) short-lived new communities
   ?Abingdon [?vowesses at a male house]
   Coventry [antiquarian report]
   ?Exeter [post-Conquest source]
   Ramsey
   Reading
   ?Southampton [post-Conquest source]
   Standon

ii) older congregations dissolved or abandoned 871x1066
   Berkeley [pre-Viking Age house]
   Boxwell [pre-Viking Age; antiquarian]
   Castor [pre-Viking Age house]
   Folkestone [pre-Viking Age house]
   Cheddar [?pre-Viking Age house]
   Horton [new tenth-century foundation]
   Leominster [Domesday Book/pre-Viking Age house]
   Pershore [antiquarian report]
   Wareham [?pre-Viking Age]
   Warwick [pre-Viking Age house]
   Wenlock [pre-Viking Age house]
   Wimborne [pre-Viking Age house]
   Winchcombe [pre-Viking Age house]

when an abbess held a church at Reading from the king. That house was, however, no longer visible in 1086, by when it is generally thought to have been dissolved.[84] William of Malmesbury thought Reading's nunnery had decayed long before a Cluniac male house was created at the same site in the 1120s; he voiced a similar presumption about the time that had elapsed since Leominster in Herefordshire (whose estates were also used for the endowment of the new community at Reading) had last supported a female congregation.[85] The reason for Leominster's decay is, however, more readily surmised than is that for Reading: like the nuns of Berkeley, the Leominster community found itself victim of the rapacity of the Godwine family, which was said in both cases to have led directly to the nunnery's dissolution.[86] William of Malmesbury is our sole authority for a tale (accepted by a number of antiquaries, but doubted by many modern historians) that when Bishop Leofric relocated the see of Crediton to Exeter in 1050 he ejected a congregation of religious women from the church of St Peter in the town; nothing is known about the age, history or endowment of this supposed female house.[87]

No obvious relevance is attachable to differences between the periods at which these female communities were first established. Houses at Abingdon, Berkeley, Boxwell, Castor, Cheddar, Leominster, Pershore, Wenlock, Wimborne, Winchcombe (and conceivably Wareham and Warwick) supposedly predated the First Viking Age, although it is far from clear that all of these housed women in the earlier period. It is not known when the nunneries at Reading, Horton and Southampton might have been founded; if they were new creations of the tenth century their experience differed substantially from that of the other (mostly royal) foundations of Alfred's reign and beyond which were described above.[88]

There is no obvious single reason why these particular female congregations failed to sustain their communal existence throughout the period under investigation. This group of houses does, however, share certain features with other institutions explored here, notably a relatively insubstantial endowment and (possibly as a direct consequence of that economic insignificance) a paucity of surviving written evidence. That some women's houses had an ephemeral existence, sustaining communities for only one or two generations seems likely, and this would appear to have been true of a number of houses considered under other categories below. Whether it was the impermanence of their existence that

---

[84]   Ibid., p. 58; Domesday Book, I, fo 60ra (Berkshire, 15, 2). The abbess Leofrun who witnessed Robertson, *ASCharters*, no. 66, dateable to 990x992 (S 1454), is usually taken to have been abbess of Reading.

[85]   William of Malmesbury, *GP*, §§89 [Reading] and 86 [Leominster] (ed. Hamilton, pp. 193 and 188).

[86]   For Berkeley see Domesday Book, I, fo 164rb (Gloucestershire, 1, 63); for Leominster, Anglo-Saxon Chronicle *s.a.* 1046 C.

[87]   William of Malmesbury, *GP*, §94 (ed. Hamilton, p. 201).

[88]   Above §b.

led directly to their omission from the historical record must remain an open question. We should also consider the possibility that it is erroneous to associate impermanence with failure. The widow Æthelgifu gathered a community of *deuotae* around her on her principal estate at Standon after her husband died without ever envisaging that it would persist after her own death, for she made arrangements in her will to bequeath the Standon estate for two further lives before it was ultimately to revert to St Albans Abbey.[89] The absence of further record of vowesses at the site could be taken as a sign of the success of Æthelgifu's testamentary arrangements.[90] A similar interpretation might be made of the *nunne* (vowess) Æthelthryth who, together with the minster congregation from Bedwyn, witnessed a woman's manumission in the early tenth century that was recorded in Bedwyn's gospel-book;[91] that no other vowesses are known from Bedwyn may again suggest that this was a temporary arrangement made for one woman who had control over her own lands. We must, however, be cautious before developing too far an argument that is dependent on the silence of the written record.

That pious women were able in the later Anglo-Saxon period to acquire land (by gift or inheritance) on terms that enabled them to satisfy their personal spiritual aspirations in ways of their own choosing (and in a manner that left them free to enjoy whatever material benefits the land could offer as well as a good deal of personal independence) should be seen as a positive achievement. Despite the centralising and controlling ambitions of the tenth-century male monastic reformers (particularly Æthelwold of Winchester), diversity and independence of action in fact appear to have driven many devout women to make arrangements to suit their own and their families' convenience, arrangements in which the second generation of reformed clergy were at least willing to acquiesce, if not actively to support. A few of the congregations included within this category were abruptly terminated by external agents; some, having been designed to satisfy spiritual needs over several generations, may no longer have been thought to have been achieving those ends to the satisfaction of their benefactors or occupants; one at least was planned but never executed. Others categorised here may, however, be deemed successful, to have fulfilled for an intentionally short time the needs of a small group of women, who expressed their devotion to God (and to the memory of their kin) outside the framework of institutionalised monasticism, on their own, individually designed, terms.

---

[89]   *The Will of Æthelgifu*, ed. D. Whitelock *et al.* (1968) (S 1497).

[90]   On the other hand, the fact that the abbey of St Albans held at the Conquest only two of the estates that ought, according to the terms of this will, have come into its possession, would suggest otherwise; see Whitelock, *The Will of Æthelgifu*, p. 29.

[91]   Above, n. 80.

(e) Vowesses living beside male religious communities

There are several instances from the later Anglo-Saxon period of congregations of religious women which seem to have been loosely attached to, or to have lived in immediate proximity to regular constituted and better-endowed male communities. The evidence for these groups of women is often slight, sometimes little more than an allusion to their presence in Domesday Book, but a strong case has recently been made that women lived in such situations more commonly than has frequently been realised.[92] The advantage these arrangements presented to devout women unable to obtain their own independent landed provision from reluctant male relatives or lords is obvious: an established and well-endowed house for men could provide physical and economic security in the form of somewhere safe to stay and a regular supply of food and heating; its immediate environment would be at least in part separated from the outside world and its dangers as well as its exigencies; liturgical and sacramental services would be readily on hand at the monastic or cathedral church. Nor need such groups of women have been wholly parasitic on their male hosts. Their charitable services may have been valued by those communities such as St Albans and Bury St Edmunds that chose to house them in the almonry, devolving the monastic responsibility to care for the poor onto their shoulders. Since I am concerned with the evidence for congregations of religious women, there are listed here only those places where more than single religious women seem to have dwelt, or where modern authorities have sought to place congregations. Similar, perhaps less formalised, arrangements could equally have been made at the margins of other abbeys for single women with vocations, particularly widows, whose presence was too transitory to be recorded in the history of the parent house. It would be worth exploring further the personal histories of women who are found in the tenth and eleventh centuries as lifetime holders of estates destined ultimately to revert to the Church (as witnessed either by grants and leases made to particular women for up to three lives, or from the provisions of their own wills); especially if these beneficiaries were widows they could well have been using estates acquired in this fashion to support the pursuit of a religious lifestyle.[93] Some of the instances

---

92   Patricia Halpin ('Women', pp. 103–4) found evidence for the attachment of groups of nuns to male houses at Abingdon, Bury St Edmunds, Evesham, Glastonbury, Hereford, Peterborough, St Albans, St Pauls, Winchester and Worcester, although I am not convinced that all of these instances will admit of her interpretation. David Knowles (*The Monastic Order in England* [2nd edn, 1963], pp. 136–7, n. 2) provided a more modest list of 'monasteries who had among their dependants a small group of *moniales* who in some cases attended to the sick among the travellers, pilgrims and recipients of alms', namely those found at Bury St Edmunds, Evesham, Worcester and St Albans.

93   Attention was drawn to women who held land for their own lifetime only, and the frequency with which their tenure was granted on condition that they comemorate the souls of the

catalogued in the next section (single vowesses) may conceal unofficial associations of this sort. Since the co-habitation of cloistered women with members of the opposite sex was contrary to the revised Benedictine provisions imposed by the reforming council at Winchester late in Edgar's reign, it is more likely that all the women found living in these circumstances should be categorised as vowesses (*nunnan*) than as cloistered *mynecena*. Formal recognition of the status of these vowesses is found, as was argued in the last chapter, in the recommendations as to the behaviour of *nunnan* made in secular law-codes of the early eleventh century and in the prescriptive writings of Archbishop Wulfstan.

References to women religious with possible ties to male houses have been collected by Patricia Halpin, who has argued that the appeal of the sort of 'lay religious life' to which these women apparently aspired was in 'the fact that it allowed association with a foundation, yet freed these women, who were accustomed to a fair degree of power and autonomy, from complete submission to the authority of an abbess'.[94] Of the various instances which Halpin has collected, the one which most effectively supports her case is that of the noble matron Æthelflæda, who chose in widowhood to build herself a dwelling within sight of the church at Glastonbury where she lived a semi-secluded life until her death. She is known only from the account of her living arrangements and her spiritual prowess given in the earliest of the Lives of St Dunstan, which affords no evidence on which to test Halpin's supposition about the motives of such women,[95] these must on the available evidence remain unproven. Attempts that have been made to associate other *religiosae feminae* with Glastonbury Abbey are more problematical, depending as they do on the preservation in the abbey's archive of charters in these women's favour.[96] All those women might best be categorised as vowesses, record of their landed estates perhaps coming to the abbey as the ultimate recipient of reversionary grants; that these devout women could have availed themselves of such spiritual services as the abbey was able to offer seems more than likely, but does not in itself turn these *nunnan* into associates of the Benedictine house.

Of the various loose arrangements which can be shown to have existed between groups of women and more regularly constituted male houses, the most formal and also the most enduring seem to have been those pertaining at St Albans (if we can accept the testimony of the thirteenth-century historian of that house,

---

dead, in a paper given by Julia Crick to the fourth International Medieval Congress at the University of Leeds: 'Beyond the nunnery: Uncloistered religious women before the Conquest'.

[94] Halpin, 'Women', p. 104.

[95] 'B', *Vita S. Dunstani*, chs. 10–11 (ed. W. Stubbs, *Memorials of St Dunstan*, [1874], pp. 3–52, at pp. 17–20).

[96] *The Great Chartulary of Glastonbury*, ed. A. Watkin (3 vols., 1947–56), III, 670–1, no. 1235 (S 399); ibid., III, 608–10, no. 1133 (S 474); BCS 903 (S 563); Watkin, *Glastonbury Chartulary*, III, 642, no. 1195 (S 775).

Map 8   Vowesses beside communities of male religious

Map 8   Vowesses beside communities of male religious

Abbotsbury
Abingdon [short-lived new foundation]
Bedwyn
Bury St Edmunds [first recorded in Domesday Book]
Durham [first recorded in post-Conquest texts/dubious]
Ely
Evesham
Glastonbury
Hereford [first recorded in Domesday Book]
St Albans
St Paul's
Tamworth [first recorded in post-Conquest texts/dubious]
Westminster
Winchester, Old Minster
Worcester [first recorded in Domesday Book]

Matthew Paris). According to the *Gesta abbatum* of St Albans, women lived at the abbey as early as the tenth century, and instead of being ejected by an abbot keen to correct errors within the house's constitution, these *sanctimoniales semi-saeculares* were merely moved from the vicinity of the church to a dwelling in the almonry, where they still resided after the Conquest when further efforts were made to regulate their discipline.[97] The presence of women attached to the almonry is attested at other houses also; this was presumably the arrangement at Bury St Edmunds, where twenty-eight *nonnae* were specifically associated with a group of poor people in a statement in Domesday Book about the residents of the town,[98] and there may also have been women in the almonry at Evesham, even though that allusion dates in fact to beyond the period encompassed by this survey.[99] Ely's twelfth-century house history, the *Liber Eliensis*, referred to two unconnected late-tenth-century widows who appear to have adopted some sort of religious life after their husbands' deaths. The same text also appears to allude to a female community on one of its estates at Coveney in the eleventh century, but if this were a quasi-religious congregation, it was probably relatively short-lived.[100] These unrelated women are probably best to be taken to have been vowesses living in devotion on their own estates in the vicinity of, rather than under the direct shelter of, Ely Abbey.

Domesday Book provides further instances of groups of women associated with male houses (or at least living in their vicinity). Among the lands of the canons of the church of Hereford, two hides of the manor of Withington, which otherwise belonged to the canons, were said to have been held by the *moniales de Hereford*.[101] Similarly, four acres of land near the city of Canterbury were said to have been held by four *moniales* in alms from the abbot of St Augustine's abbey.[102] Separate valuations were not given for either the Herefordshire or Kentish estates; both were valued together with the more substantial holdings of the church on which the women were in some manner dependent. Two separate *moniales* were also mentioned in Domesday Book as holding estates connected with the church of Worcester: Eadgyth and Ælfeva.[103] The notion that there was a small female congregation here may be strengthened by the fact that the Life of

---

[97]   Matthew Paris, *Gesta Abbatum* (ed. H. T. Riley [3 vols., 1867–9], I, 11, 59).

[98]   Domesday Book, II, fo 372ra (Suffolk, 14, 167).

[99]   Dugdale, *Monasticon*, II, 37; see Knowles and Hadcock, *Medieval Religious Houses*, pp. 65 and 258.

[100]   Æthelflæd, widow of Æthelstan, was said to have lived the remainder of her life in chastity after Æthelstan died: *Liber Eliensis*, II, 64 (ed. Blake, pp. 136–7). Wulfflæd, widow of Siferth, made a bequest to the abbey at Ely on the day on which she took the vows of a nun: ibid., II, 10 (ed. Blake, p. 84). The congregation at Coveney, which was associated with another female benefactor of the house, Æthelswith, was described ibid., II, 88 (ed. Blake, pp. 157–8). Attention was drawn to these women by Whitelock, *The Will of Æthelgifu*, p. 34.

[101]   Domesday Book, I, fo 181vb (Hereford, 2, 17).

[102]   Domesday Book, I, fo 12rb (Kent, 7, 11).

[103]   Domesday Book, I, fo 173va–b (Worcestershire, 2, 54; 2, 67).

St Wulfstan of Worcester by William of Malmesbury reported that the saint's mother had taken the veil at Worcester (driven by fear of poverty in advancing age).[104] The vowesses from Worcester need, however, have had no relation one with another but each have satisfied her personal spiritual desires as a veiled woman living on her own lands. Other allusions to female religious in Domesday Book do not necessarily indicate a relationship between these women and the male houses in whose vicinity they lived.[105] Nor can single vowesses and *religiosae feminae* who received charters recording grants of land from tenth-century kings necessarily be linked with the male religious communities that claimed ownership of those estates at the time of the Domesday survey, or preserved the women's diplomas in their archives. On the basis of the charter evidence, Patricia Halpin has argued for the existence of an association between religious women and male houses at Abingdon, St Paul's in London, and at Winchester as well as further women who may have been linked with Glastonbury Abbey;[106] these instances are all discussed fully in the next section where they more properly belong.

One additional place, Abbotsbury, has been included under this category because a case was made by Marc Meyer for the presence of religious women there in the eleventh century, but as I argue in detail below, the evidence is too slight to support such an interpretation. There was at the Conquest a male, Benedictine abbey dedicated to St Peter at Abbotsbury, that traced its origins to a certain Orc (Urki, founder of the Abbotsbury guild) and his wife Tola; in widowhood the latter bequeathed her land and possessions to the abbey.[107] It is just possible, although Meyer did not suggest this, that Tola, who is not known to have remarried, lived as a *nunne* after her husband died, and that she may well have looked to St Peter's for spiritual succour, but if so, we should include her among the instances of single vowesses addressed in the next section. Bedwyn is likewise listed in this category because Barbara Yorke has suggested that it might have been the site of a mixed community of men and women in the tenth century; we have already seen, however, that the evidence for this supposition rests on the attestation of a single *nunne* in a manumission recorded in the Gospel Book from the male minster community, and it has been proposed that she be seen as a further

---

[104] William of Malmesbury, *Vita Wulfstani*, I, 2 (ed. Darlington, p. 7); E. Mason, *St Wulfstan of Worcester, c.1008–1095* (1990), pp. 41–2; Halpin, 'Women', p. 100. The possibility that Eadgyth had closer connections with the Worcester house is explored in detail in part II, *s.n.* Winchcombe and Worcester.

[105] The extent to which Halpin's list of houses with arrangements with women religious is dependent on references in Domesday Book is made clear in her footnotes: 'Women', p. 104, n. 31.

[106] Halpin, 'Women', p. 104. Abingdon: BCS 743 (S 448), BCS 778 (S 482); St Paul's: *Early Charters of the Cathedral Church of St Paul, London*, ed. M. Gibbs (1959), no. J 12 (S 1793); Winchester: BCS 734 (S 449), BCS 787 (S 487); Glastonbury: BCS 664 (S 399) and BCS 768 (S 474), BCS 903 (S 563).

[107] Harmer, *ASWrits*, no. 2 (S 1064); Domesday Book, I, fo 78rb–va (Dorset, 13); Tanner, *Notitia*, Dorset, i; Leland, *Collectanea*, IV.149.

instance of a single vowess living in the vicinity of, but without specific
attachment to, a male religious community.[108] In the same category falls the
instance of the *nunne*, Ælfwynn, reported to have been a tenant of Westminster
Abbey in the mid-eleventh century;[109] she also can better be seen as a single
vowess with no closer institutional link to the male house than that of the lessee
of land destined ultimately to return to the male house. Similarly, a certain
'Ecgfrida' (?Ecgfriðu), was reported in the late eleventh-century *De obsessione
Dunelmi* to have taken the veil at Durham on being repudiated by her second
husband;[110] this might provide evidence for a solitary vowess, living further north
than any of the others we have found. Tempting as it might seem, she cannot on
this evidence be made the focus of a female congregation. It is just conceivable
that a case could be made for associating another single devout woman, daughter
of Wulfric Spott the founder of Burton Abbey, with a male minster community,
this time at Tamworth;[111] since such an identification must remain highly
tentative, and the conclusion to which it tends is again that of a vowess living
alone, this example need not detain us here.

It can certainly be argued that insufficient attention has hitherto been paid
to the possibility that women in the later Anglo-Saxon period might have chosen
to live religious, or quasi-religious lives in the shadow of established male
communities (monasteries or cathedral churches), and that there may well be many
further instances of such arrangements record of which has not survived. Specific
male communities may, however, only be demonstrated to have made such
provision for women if their own records explicitly describe such a situation. That
a religious woman was once an abbey's tenant, that she bequeathed to a male
community land which she had formerly been granted in her own right, or enjoyed
the usufruct of an estate that one of her relatives had intended should ultimately
revert to that house, or even that she had deposited in a monastery's archive the
charter recording such her own title to her estates for safe-keeping, does not prove
that she ever lived on the church's margins or under its protection.

There is an entirely different way in which to view the whole question of
the links between vowed religious women and congregations of male monastics
or priests in the later pre-Conquest period, to which Steven Bassett has drawn my
attention. *Nunnan*, denied immediate access to the spiritual comforts more readily
available within a formally instituted Benedictine nunnery, may naturally have

---

[108]   Yorke, 'The Bonifacian mission', p. 169; Merritt, 'Old English entries', pp. 346–7.
[109]   Harmer, *ASWrits*, no.79 (S 1123).
[110]   *De obsessione Dunelmi*, ch. 3 (ed. T. Arnold, *Symeonis Monachi Opera Omnia* [2
vols., 1882–5), I, 215–20 at p. 217); C. Fell, *Women in Anglo-Saxon England* (1984), p. 140.
Patricia Halpin has read more into this story than I have been willing to do: 'Women', p. 106.
[111]   *Charters of Burton Abbey*, ed. P. H. Sawyer (1979), no. 29 (S 1536). By the terms
of Wulfric's will his daughter, described as *earm*, poor or wretched, was left a life-interest in two
estates at Elford and Oakley, both near Tamworth, which were ultimately to revert to Burton
Abbey.

gravitated towards congregations of secular priests able to supply them with sacramental solace (particularly via confession and the eucharist). Some widows could, like Æthelgifu have had a priest among their household (although whether there were many other enslaved priests in this period one might doubt),[112] but such a privilege was surely restricted to the richest of the devout women considered here. Many of the female religious communities listed under other categories in this survey are found in places where there are known to have been secular minster churches during the same period, for example Bedwyn, Berkeley, Chester, Tamworth, and Exeter. The proximity of houses of vowesses to such churches may well not have been accidental. We might indeed wonder whether vowesses would not have sought as much as possible to live within easy range of priestly services, in which case my category of 'religious women attached to male religious communities' would become otiose: the majority of non-Benedictine women's congregations might then be so described.

(f) Single vowesses

The original intention of this work was to gather and define the evidence for communities of female religious. But since we have found it necessary to distinguish clearly between cloistered women within enclosed nunneries (*mynecæna*) and devout vowesses (*nunnan*) living in the world on their own land, it is worth summarising here the evidence for solitary religious women. Wulfstan certainly anticipated that *nunnan* could be found within minsters, and one example has been given of a widow who had priests among her household and apparently gathered a congregation of pious women while living on land inherited from her husband that was destined ultimately for a male religious house (that of Æthelgifu). Instead of wondering how individual *religiosae feminae, moniales,* or *nunnan* might be fitted into the framework of organised monasticism by being linked with an established male or female community, it may be more appropriate to accept these women as being either, like Æthelgifu, the foci of small communities located on the estates for which the documentary sources provide proof of the woman's title, or as forerunners of the single 'worthy widow and *nunne*' described in the early eleventh-century writings of Wulfstan and Ælfric.[113]

These women are known mostly because of the survival of charters in their favour, where they were termed [*sancti*]*moniales, ancillae Dei* or *religiosae feminae*;[114] various individual *moniales* were also named in Domesday Book as

---

[112] *The Will of Æthelgifu*, ed. Whitelock (S 1497); and see above chapter 5, pp. 139–40.

[113] The quotation is from Ælfric's Glossary: *Ælfrics Grammatik und Glossar*, ed. J. Zupitza (Berlin, 1880), p. 299, lines 13–14: 'nonna: arwyrþe wydewe oððe nunne'.

[114] This group of charters in favour of religious women has been discussed by D. N. Dumville, *Wessex and England from Alfred to Edgar* (1992), pp. 177–8; N. Brooks, 'The career of St Dunstan', in *St Dunstan. His Life, Times and Cult*, ed. N. Ramsay *et al.* (1992), pp. 1–23, at

the holders of small pieces of land. While some of these are likely to have been solitary devout women,[115] it is of course also possible that others were in fact members of larger communities, houses which have been discussed elsewhere in this volume, where Benedictine ideals of collective not individual ownership of land were not being rigidly enforced.[116] A grant of land could equally have been made, in the first instance, for a named woman to hold in her own right with the ultimate intention that the estate would come to form the basis of a new foundation. The abortion of such ambitions, or the founder's failure to acquire additional lands by means of charter for the putative community, would ensure the absence of any further record of the establishment. Whether any of these possibilities were applicable to any particular individual named here cannot be determined on the basis of the evidence now extant.

Among the single women to whom mid-tenth-century charter draftsmen ascribed religious epithets are a few who are identifiable from other contexts; three (Eadburh, Ælfflæd and Eadgifu) may have had connections with the West Saxon royal house. Eadburh was King Æthelstan's sister, to whom in 939 the king gave an estate of seventeen hides at Droxford in Hampshire, describing her as being in a spiritual fellowship and under the holy veil of God.[117] Eadburh was the daughter of Edward the Elder and his third wife, Eadgifu, who supposedly chose the religious life at the age of three and became a nun at the Nunnaminster in Winchester, where she lived the rest of her life.[118] The Droxford estate does not, however, appear to have come to the Nunnaminster after Eadburh's death.[119]

---

p. 7; Halpin, 'Women', p. 103; and Venarde, *Women's Monasticism*, pp. 27–8. Each of these historians has given a slightly different list of diplomas of this type; in the discussion that follows I consider the evidence offered by one writ Harmer, *ASWrits*, no. 79 (S 1123) and the following eighteen charters: BCS 742–3 and 734 (S 446, 448–9), BCS 753 and 763 (S 464–5); Watkin, *Glastonbury Chartulary*, III, 608–10, no. 1133 (S 474); BCS 778 (S 482); Sawyer, *Charters of Burton*, no. 6 (S 484); Kelly, *Charters of Shaftesbury*, no. 13 (S 485); BCS 787 and 795 (S 487 and 493); C. Hart, *Charters of Barking Abbey* (forthcoming), nos. 6 and 7 (S 517b and 517a); Gibbs, *Early Charters of St Paul's*, no. J 12 (S 1793); Kelly, *Charters of Shaftesbury*, nos. 16–17 (S 534 and 562); BCS 869 (S 535); BCS 903 (S 563); Watkin, *Glastonbury Chartulary*, III, 642, no. 1195 (S 775).

[115] Compare Venarde, *Women's Monasticism*, p. 27: these women 'seem to have been unaffiliated with any monastery and living as anchorites or recluses'.

[116] Dumville, *Wessex*, p. 177.

[117] BCS 742 (S 446); Meyer, 'Patronage', p. 347; Venarde, *Women's Monasticism*, p. 24.

[118] William of Malmesbury, *GR*, II, 126 (ed. Mynors *et al.*, I, 200–1); Osbert of Clare, *Vita S. Edburge*, ch. 2 (ed. Ridyard, p. 265). Venarde appears to have included Eadburh with the other *religiosae feminae* whom he saw as anchorites or recluses: *Women's Monasticism*, p. 24.

[119] The charter of King Æthelstan's for Eadburh survives in the archive of the Old Minster Winchester, and a sixteen-hide estate at Droxford was listed in Domesday Book among those said to be for the supplies of the monks of the Old Minster (reduced to 14 hides by 1086): Domesday Book, I, fo 41va (Hampshire, 3, 9). The charter by which the Old Minster claimed to have been granted Droxford by King Ecgberht in 826 (BCS 393, S 276) is spurious. Twenty hides

Ælfflæd, the recipient of a grant of King Edmund's in 941 of fifteen hides at Buckland Newton and Plush in Dorset in which she was described as a *religiosa femina*,[120] was identified in the *De antiquitate ecclesie Glastonie* as the queen of Edward the Elder.[121] Marc Meyer has variously described Ælfflæd as having entered the Nunnaminster in Winchester after the dissolution of her marriage, and as being a 'nun dwelling at Wilton', where she and two of her daughters were said, on the authority of William of Malmesbury, to be buried.[122] Ælfflæd need, however, have had a formal association with neither community, but might have taken religious vows while remaining a laywoman, like other widows or discarded wives, and indeed her own daughter, Æthelhild.[123] King Eadred's mother, Eadgifu (third wife of Edward the Elder), was called *famula Dei* in one charter dated 953, by which her son gave her thirty hides of land at Felpham in Sussex; this document was preserved in the archive of Shaftesbury abbey, which held a twenty-one hide estate at Felpham at the Conquest.[124] Eadgifu may also have chosen a

---

at Droxford were granted to a noblewoman called Æthelhild by King Eadwig in 956: BCS 953 (S 600).

[120] Watkin, *Glastonbury Chartulary*, III, 608–10, no. 1133 (S 474); *De antiquitate*, §55 (ed. and trans. J. Scott, *The Early History of Glastonbury* [1981], p. 114). Ælfflæd was also said to have given an estate at Winterbourne to Glastonbury abbey (ibid., §54, p. 112); a charter survives by which she was granted Winterbourne by King Æthelstan, in which she is described as *amabilis femina*: Watkin, *Glastonbury Chartulary*, III, 670–1, no. 1235 (S 399). Halpin has argued ('Women', p. 104) that Ælfflæd was buried at Glastonbury, but I cannot find a source to support this assertion; she is generally held to be buried at Wilton (see below).

[121] The identification of Ælfflæd as Edward's queen was made in the *De antiquitate* attributed to William of Malmesbury, §§54 and 69 (ed. and trans. Scott, pp. 112 and 142) and is supported only by that author's *Gesta regum Anglorum*, §126 (ed. Stubbs, I, 136–7). See L. Abrams, *Anglo-Saxon Glastonbury* (1996), p. 64, n. 82, pp. 185–6 and n. 2, and p. 249, n. 43. Abrams has urged caution over the identification of Ælfflæd as Edward's queen, and noted that all the grants to Ælfflæd which were recorded at Glastonbury were not necessarily made to the same woman: *Anglo-Saxon Glastonbury*, p. 186, n. 2. For discussion of Edward's marriages and Ælfflæd's supposed interest in the reform movement see Meyer, 'Women', pp. 46–7 and 'The queen's "demesne" in later Anglo-Saxon England', in *The Culture of Christendom*, ed. M. A. Meyer (1993), pp. 75–113, at pp. 90–2.

[122] Meyer, 'Women', p. 47; 'The queen's "demesne"', p. 67. For her burial at Wilton see William of Malmesbury, *GR*, II, 126 (ed. Mynors *et al.*, I, 200–1).

[123] J. L. André, 'Widows and Vowesses', *Archaeological Journal*, 49 (1892), 69–82, at p. 76 (where the place of their burial is erroneously given as Winchester). The status of these three women was explored at length in chapter 5, p. 141.

[124] Kelly, *Charters of Shaftesbury*, no. 17 (S 562); Domesday Book, I, fo 17vb (Sussex, 8a, 1) . Meyer has added a further dimension to the discussion of the possible history of this estate by arguing (sadly without support) that the nunnery at Wilton also had an estate at Felpham, granted it by Edith, wife of Edward the Confessor. Meyer has tried to argue both that the dowager Eadgifu gave Felpham to Shaftesbury and that the estate remained in the queen's demesne for Edith to give it away in eleventh century: 'Patronage', p. 350, n. 2 and p. 356, n. 7. Dumville did not discuss this document with the other charters in favour of *religiosae feminae*: *Wessex*, pp. 177–8.

quasi-religious life in widowhood, but if she did, it did not prevent her from actively patronising the reforming activities of both Dunstan and Æthelwold;[125] such ecclesiastical patronage might on the contrary have been considered appropriate to a dowager queen whose mind was set more on heavenly than earthly life. Eadgifu can certainly not convincingly be shown to have been a member of the Shaftesbury congregation, any more than Ælfflæd can be located at Glastonbury or elsewhere. A more direct connection with Shaftesbury was argued in the case of the religious woman (*quaedam religiosa sanctae conuersacionis monialis femina*) Wynflæd, who received a grant from King Edmund in 942 also preserved in Shaftesbury's archive, and seems from her will to have had some direct association with the Shaftesbury community.[126] She was not, however, a cloistered nun and, it was suggested above, should probably rather be seen as a *nunne*, a woman who took vows in widowhood, leading a chaste life in nun's clothes and veil while remaining in the world.[127] It is impossible to determine whether or not a third woman, Ælfthryth, was ever a member of the Shaftesbury community. Although she was termed a *religiosa femina* in a diploma found in the abbey's archive recording her payment of sixty mancuses of purest gold to King Eadred in return for an eight-hide estate at Purbeck, and this land was held by Shaftesbury at the Conquest, her relationship with the nunnery was most likely equivalent to that of Eadwig's thegn, Wihtsige. A charter of King Eadwig for Wihtsige concerning an estate at Corfe and Balshenwell (adjacent to the Purbeck manor) is also found in the abbey's cartulary and his estate, with that originally granted to Ælfthryth, made up the nunnery's Domesday manor of Kingston.[128] Both these lay people appear to have held their estates in their own right before they (or their heirs) subsequently bequeathed them to the abbey.

Considerable caution must be exercised before attempting to postulate connections between any other religious women and the religious houses in whose archives their charters have been preserved. That single fact no more makes these women members of the institutions to which they (or their heirs) made bequests than it does all the other lay recipients of charters whose documents were copied into the later medieval cartularies of the larger monasteries of England. One possible exception to this rule is the case of Ælfswith, the widow of the Hampshire ealdorman Ælfheah; she was described as *vidua sanctimonialisque* in a diploma

---

[125] Meyer, 'The queen's "demesne"', pp. 93–4.

[126] Kelly, *Charters of Shaftesbury*, no. 13 (S 485); Wynflæd's will is Whitelock, *ASWills*, no. 3 (S 1539).

[127] For discussion of Wynflæd's status see Whitelock, *ASWills*, p. 109, G. R. Owen, 'Wynflæd's wardrobe', *Anglo-Saxon England*, 8 (1979), 195–222, at pp. 197–9 and 219; her case was also discussed above in chapter 5, pp. 136–9.

[128] Ælfthryth's charter is Kelly, *Charters of Shaftesbury*, no 16 (S 534); Wihtsige's is Kelly, *Charters of Shaftesbury*, no. 19 (S 632). Kelly has noted (ibid., pp. 82–3, no. 20) that *Charters of Shaftesbury*, no. 19 (S 573), which is a conflation of ibid., nos. 16 and 20 (S 534 and 632) is a later fabrication providing title to the combined estates.

in her favour from King Edgar dated 970, which was preserved in Glastonbury's archive and related to an estate at Idmiston, Wiltshire, where the abbey held land at the Conquest.[129] Ælfswith and her husband made several grants to the abbey, Ælfheah was buried there according to John of Worcester, and both were named in the list of obits from Glastonbury which survives in a thirteenth-century manuscript.[130] It has been argued that Ælfswith retired to the abbey on her husband's death; she may rather, like other women discussed under this heading rather have taken vows as a widow without formally leaving the world. She and her husband may always have intended that she should enjoy the profits of the Idmiston estate for the remainder of her own life before the land reverted ultimately to Glastonbury and the community's prayers would reward their munificence.

It is less likely that there was a direct association between Glastonbury and the cloistered woman from Wilton, Ælfgyth, even though a diploma of King Eadred's in her favour relating to Pennard Minster survives among the abbey's muniments;[131] the same woman was also beneficiary of a charter from King Edmund, found in Wilton's archive.[132] While Ælfgyth may indeed have elected, as was surmised in the *De antiquitate*, to bequeath her estate at Pennard to Glastonbury Abbey, this does not permit us to imagine that she had any closer a relationship with the male house than any other of its lay benefactors.[133] A more plausible case could be made for linking the vowess Ælfwynn with the male community at Westminster, on the basis of an allusion to her in a writ of King Edward's reporting that the king had given to Westminster some Hertfordshire estates 'as fully and completely as Ælfwynn the vowess (*Alwunn si nunne*) held them of the abbey and committed them to Abbot Edwin and the monks'.[134] It is

---

[129] Watkin, *Glastonbury Chartulary*, III, 642, no. 1195 (S 775); Domesday Book, I, fo 66vb (Wiltshire, 7, 14). There are other surviving charters relating to Idmiston — Watkin, *Glastonbury Chartulary*, III, 642–3, no. 1196 and pp. 643–8, no. 1197 (S 530 and 541) — and the text of a third has been lost: Finberg, *The Early Charters of Wessex*, no. 234 (S 1716). On this estate see Abrams, *Anglo-Saxon Glastonbury*, pp. 143–5.

[130] John of Worcester, *Chronicon, s.a.* 971 (ed. and trans. Darlington *et al.*, II, 420–1, and see p. 421, n. 6). See M. Blows, 'A Glastonbury obit-list', in *The Archaeology and History of Glastonbury Abbey*, ed. L. Abrams and J. P. Carley (1991), pp. 257–69, at pp. 265–6; Abrams, *Anglo-Saxon Glastonbury*, pp. 144 and 344–5, n. 129.

[131] BCS 903 (S 563); Eadred's grant was made to 'Ælfgyðe sancti moniali in Wiltunensi monasterio degenti', for her pleasing price of 120 *solidi* of gold. For discussion of this charter and the estate to which it relates see Abrams, *Anglo-Saxon Glastonbury*, pp. 195–8.

[132] BCS 795 (S 493). In the dispositive section of the charter Eadmund's grant is made to 'cuidam sancte conuersationis monialis femine'; in the Old English abstract preceeding the full text of the diploma in the Wilton cartulary the land is said to be booked to 'Ælfgyþe nunnan'.

[133] *De antiquitate*, §69 (ed. and trans. Scott, p. 144). For a contrary view see Halpin, 'Women', p. 104.

[134] Harmer, *ASWrits*, no. 79 (S 1123).

unnecessary to postulate any formal arrangement here beyond that of tenant and landlord.

The other religious women in whose favour contemporary (or supposedly contemporaneous) charters survive are otherwise unknown. Charters in favour of two *religiosae feminae* (Eadwulfu and Sæthryth) have been preserved in Abingdon's archive, but neither can be convincingly shown to have had any association with that male community.[135] The recently discovered Ilford Hospital charters from Barking's archive have provided texts of two Eadred charters in favour of *religiosae feminae* called Æthelgifu and Eawynne;[136] the latter is probably identifiable with the religious woman of the same name mentioned in a seventeenth-century excerpt from a lost St Paul's roll as the recipient of another grant from Eadred of land at Essex, later held by St Paul's.[137] Whether either woman was a member of the tenth-century community at Barking cannot be determined;[138] both might better be seen as vowesses living outside the cloister. Similarly, there are no obvious grounds for supposing that the two devout women who received separate grants of land in Kent in the 940s by means of charters whose originals have survived in the archive of Christ Church, Canterbury were in any sense linked to that cathedral church.[139] Nor need the three women whose charters found their way into the archives of the Old Minster at Winchester be thought to have been associates of that congregation.[140]

---

[135]   Eadwulfu received fifteen hides in Berkshire from King Æthelstan in 939: BCS 743 (S 448); and Sæthryth eleven hides in the same county from King Edmund in 942: BCS 778 (S 482). Stenton argued (*The Early History of the Abbey of Abingdon* [1913], p. 34) that Eadwulfu was probably a member of a monastic community, and Halpin ('Women', p. 104) tried to link both women to Abingdon, but neither argument is sustainable on the available evidence. The attempt made by Meyer to postulate the revival of a pre-Viking Age nunnery at Abingdon in the mid-tenth century (partly on the basis of these diplomas) is similarly unconvincing: 'Patronage', pp. 345–6.

[136]   Æthelgifu received a grant of four hides at *Tollesfuntum*: Hart, *Charters of Barking*, no. 7 (S 517a). Eawynne was recipient of nineteen hides at Hockley in Essex: ibid., no. 6 (S 517b).

[137]   Gibbs, *Early Charters of St Paul's*, no. J 12 (S 1763). The estate in question, twelve hides at Shopland, was not held by St Paul's in 1066 or in 1086, but it was among the manors of St Paul's listed in a document of *c*. 1000 which specified the contributions of men required from a series of estates for the manning of a ship: Robertson, *ASCharters*, no. 72. See part II, *s.n.* St Paul's.

[138]   See part II, *s.n.* Barking.

[139]   Æthelswith, *religiosa sancte monialis femina*, received ten hides at *Oswalding tune* (near Ashford) from King Edmund in 940: BCS 753 (S 464). A *religiosa femina*, Ælfwyn, paid two pounds of purest gold to King Eadred in return for six hides at Wickhambreux in Kent in 948: BCS 869 (S 535). The bounds of this charter refer to the community (*hired*) of St Mildrith; see part II, *s.n.* Canterbury and Minster-in-Thanet.

[140]   BCS 734 (S 449), a charter of King Æthelstan for Wulfswith, *ancilla Dei* of fifteen hides at East Overton, Wiltshire; BCS 763 (S 465), King Edmund to Æthelthryth 'cuidam religiose sanctae conuersationis monialis feminae' five hides at Poolhampton in Overton, Hampshire. In Domesday Book, I, fo 41va (Hampshire, 3, 10), Poolhampton was described in the time of King

Efforts to link these independent religious women with particular named monastic congregations (whether of males or females) serve only to confuse the issues raised by the survival of this group of seventeen charters from the mid-tenth century. The apparent desire retrospectively to force these women to conform to the standard pattern of communal religious observance (so pleasing to monastic legislators of all periods) serves to deny both the particularity of their own, individual experience, and to suppress evidence for what appears to be a contemporary acceptance of this form of religious expression, at least in the period before Æthelwold and his associates were able to impose compulsory uniformity of observance. The possibility that several of these women had taken vows as widows and were living quasi-monastic lives, wearing the veil and habit distinctive of their cloistered sisters, but remaining within the secular world and in control of their own property has also been suggested and has much to commend it.[141] The clustering of these grants within a relatively short chronological period (and one that happens coincidentally, not to afford much evidence for the existence of regularly constituted monastic houses for women) could be taken as a sign of the adoption by particularly fervent women of extraordinary strategies to enable them to satisfy their piety despite the absence of the regular communities to which they would in normal circumstances have turned.[142] Alternatively, the proliferation of royal diplomas for religious women in the 940s and 950s may reflect nothing more than the more general proliferation of diplomas in those years. However, the argument of the previous chapter tended towards the view that this is not a phenomenon particular to the years before Æthelwold restored the right order and cloistered women again received sufficient landed patronage to exercise their devotion collectively. On the contrary we saw that the *nunne* was as much a part of Wulfstan's church as of that of the immediate pre-reform generation, and furthermore that she continued to be seen later in the eleventh century.

The naming of ten single religious women as the holders of land in Domesday Book supports this suggestion that, although the extant charters in favour of single religious women are almost all restricted to the middle years of the tenth century, the phenomenon of the solitary nun did not die with the Benedictine reform.[143] Two religious women called Edith were mentioned in the survey; in Somerset Edith, *monialis*, held 12 acres of land in alms from the king

---

Edward as being for the supplies of the monks). Ælfswith, *religiosa femina*, received a grant of fifteen hides at Burghclere, Hampshire from King Edmund in 943: BCS 787 (S 487).

[141] André, 'Widows and vowesses'; Owen, 'Wynflæd's wardrobe', p. 198; Whitelock, *The Will of Æthelgifu*, p. 34

[142] Compare Dumville, *Wessex*, pp. 177–8.

[143] Nineteen documents were discussed in the above section; one of these is now lost but was attributed to the generosity of Eadred. All date from the mid-tenth century except for Edward's writ for Westminster, dated 1049.

in the lands of Curry.[144] The Worcestershire commissioners reported the history of an estate at Knightwick, one of the church of Worcester's three hides at Grimley which in 1086 was held by Robert the Bursar. This land was said to be for the household supplies of Worcester's monks and had previously been leased to a *monialis* called Eadgyth 'to have and give service for as long as the brothers wished and could do without it, but as their community grew TRW she gave it back'. Eadgyth herself was said to be alive and to be witness to this.[145] Also among the lands of the church of Worcester was one hide at Cudley in Worcestershire which had been held by Aelfeva, *monialis*, 'on the terms she could beg'; in 1086 this hide was held by a certain Urso.[146] In Lincolnshire a religious woman (*monialis*) Alswith was reported to have held some land within the borough of Grantham over which she had full jurisdiction, but she gave it to St Peter's of Peterborough, and at the time of the survey it was held by Kolgrimr, who had it with full jurisdiction.[147] In the same shire, Cwenthryth (*monacha*) had half a carucate of taxable land in Canwick, valued at 8s.[148] Another *monialis*, Cwenhild, held nine hides in Naunton in Gloucestershire from the king; she is listed among the king's thegns and her estate, of which four hides paid tax, was valued at £8 TRE, £5 at the time of the survey.[149] In the time of King Edward, a certain Edeva described as *monialis* held two hides in Pendley in Hertfordshire; she held this land of Engelric and was not able to grant it. In 1086 these two hides were held by the Count of Mortain, and were apparently among the 'seven hides which the count took in Tring'.[150] Leofeva *monialis* is twice mentioned as a land-holder in Warwickshire: she had two dwellings in the town of Warwick,[151] and held from the king in alms three hides formerly owned by Godiva, Earl Leofric's wife, at Salford Priors, valued formerly at 40s, but at £6 TRW.[152] A certain poor nun (*quaedam pauper monialis*) in Norfolk laid claim to four acres of land at

---

[144]   Domesday Book, I, 91va (Somerset, 16, 12). Several of these women have already been mentioned as part of the discussion of the language used of the religious life by the Domesday commissioners, above, chapter 4, pp. 103–4.

[145]   Domesday Book, I, fo 173vb (Worcester, 2, 67).

[146]   Ibid., I, fo 173va (Worcestershire, 2, 54). Halpin ('Women', p. 104) was presumably alluding to these two references in including Worcester among those male communities to which women were loosely attached.

[147]   Domesday Book, I, fo 337vb (Lincolnshire, 1, 9). I cannot agree with Patricia Halpin ('Women', p. 104) that Peterborough was a male house to which women were loosely attached if this Domesday reference is the sole evidence for that statement. This passage indicates nothing more than that Alswith was a benefactress of the male abbey; indeed the implication of this statement is that once the land was in Peterborough's possession Alswith was no longer connected with it.

[148]   Domesday Book, I, fo 370va (Lincolnshire, 67, 27).

[149]   Ibid., I, fo 170va (Gloucestershire, 78, 8).

[150]   Ibid., I, fo 136va (Hertfordshire, 15, 4).

[151]   Ibid., I, fo 238ra (Warwickshire, B, 2).

[152]   Ibid., I, fo 244rb (Warwickshire, 43, 1).

Seething, which she said she had held under Ralph both before and after he forfeited, to which the Hundred also testified, but this land was claimed by a certain Isaac as part of his holding from the king's gift.[153] Two women (*nonnae*) reported in the survey for Somerset to have held two-and-a-half virgates of land at *Honecote* in alms from the King at a value of 5s (10s when they acquired them) might also be mentioned at this point.[154] These might have been two vowesses who had chosen to combine their resources and live a devout life together (perhaps sisters sharing a parental inheritance, or a widowed mother and her unmarried daughter); if a larger community formed round the pair this can no longer be established.

Other than the two Worcestershire *moniales*, Eadgyth and Aelfeva, who might conceivably have had some association with the church of Worcester,[155] it is not possible to demonstrate that any of these religious women were directly linked with any known religious community (male or female). The failure to make such connections does not lead to the conclusion that these were necessarily all, or any of them, solitaries. As has already been suggested, they are best to be identified with the secular vowesses mentioned in the early eleventh century prescriptive literature, particularly that associated with Archbishop Wulfstan. A further example is provided by a story given in William of Malmesbury's Life of Wulfstan of Worcester, bishop of Worcester from 1062 to 1095. The bishop was said to have cured a young girl who lived at Evesham and was possessed by devils; on her restoration to health she took the veil and remained a religious for the rest of her life. She may have joined an established female community that William of Malmesbury failed to name, but she may also have lived as a solitary vowess, or with a small community around her.[156]

Bearing in mind the connections already established between *nunnan* and widows, it may be worth pondering whether any of the widows named in Domesday Book as holders of small estates could also be included within this category. In 1066 one-and-a-half hides at Drayton Beauchamp in Buckinghamshire had been held by 'a widow of Brictric's' who had the right to sell them; by 1086 the land belonged to William son of Nigel.[157] Half a yoke in Aloesbridge hundred in Kent was held by Robert of the bishop of Bayeux; a widow who paid 22

---

[153] Ibid., II, fo 264v (Norfolk, 47, 7).
[154] Ibid., I, fo 91va (Somerset, 16, 13).
[155] See part II, *s.n.* Winchcombe and Worcester. There it is suggested that Eadgyth might have been sister (or half-sister) to St Wulfstan of Worcester, whose mother would appear to have been married twice, receiving on the occasion of her second marriage to a man called Wulfric (1014x1016) a lease for three lives of land at Knightwick: Robertson, *ASCharters*, no. 76 (S 1459). Wulfstan's mother was also said to have taken the veil at Worcester in old age: *The Vita Wulfstani of William of Malmesbury*, I, 2, ed. R. R. Darlington (1928), p. 7.
[156] William of Malmesbury, *Vita sancti Wulfstani*, II, 4 (ed. Darlington, pp. 27–8).
[157] Domesday Book, I, fo 146rb (Buckinghamshire, 12, 14).

shillings a year lived there.[158] A certain Edeva (probably a widow) held one-and-a-half hides in Edmondsham in Dorset from Humphrey the Chamberlain.[159] Among the lands of the abbot of Abbotsbury, also in Dorset were mentioned two hides at *Atrim* which Bolle the priest and a widow held from the abbot, holders who could not be separated from the church with this land.[160] It may be unreasonable even to ask whether any of the women living on what are all small pieces of land might have taken vows of religion, although the association between widow and priest in the last example is at least suggestive. A vignette from the Surrey survey, however, offers a cautionary note. A widow was reported to hold one hide of land at Bramley of the bishop of Bayeux, and said to be able to 'go where she would';[161] she might also tentatively be placed among religiously-minded vowesses were it not for a note in the description of the burh of Guildford in the same shire. There is was said that in the town there was another house held by the reeve of the bishop of Bayeux from the manor of Bramley; 'Of this the men of the county state that he has no other right there, but that the reeve of the village [ie Bramley] took in marriage a widow whose house it was, and that therefore the bishop put the house into his manor; hitherto the king has lost its customary dues but the bishop has them'.[162] In the unlikely event that Bramley's widow had taken vows of continence, she had failed to keep them. It is most probable that it was by virtue of their social condition as *relictae* that these women were specifically marked out as *uiduae* by the commissioners; we might go further, and say that at the time of the survey none (except the Bramley widow) had remarried. As a group they hold strikingly small portions of land:[163] they might best be considered continent by default rather than by design and cannot contribute to our understanding of religious women in later Anglo-Saxon England.

---

[158]   Ibid., I, fo 11ra (Kent, 5, 181).

[159]   Ibid., I, fo 83rb (Dorset, 50, 2). The identification of Edeva as a widow was made by C. and F. Thorn *Domesday Book 7, Dorset* (1983) who suggested that she was probably the widow of the same name who held one hide from Humphrey the Chamberlain in the tax return for *Albretesburga* hundred.

[160]   Domesday Book, I, fo 78va (Dorset, 13, 8).

[161]   Ibid., I, fo 31rb (Surrey, 5, 1e).

[162]   Ibid., I, fo 30ra (Surrey, 1, 1d).

[163]   Compare the rather piteous statement in the survey for Gloucester where in the account of Hidcote, a three-hide estate belonging to the abbey of Evesham, it was reported 'the wives of four villagers lately dead have one plough': Domesday Book, I, fo 166ra (Gloucestershire, 12, 19). Only five per cent of the land assessed in Domesday Book was in female hands, and of that the greater part belonged to only eight women, relations of the great earls or of the royal house: P. Stafford, 'Women and the Norman Conquest', *TRHS*, 6th ser. 4 (1994), 221–49, at p. 226.

(g) Categories determined by the evidence

This typology has sought thus far to group congregations of religious women into categories designed to illustrate features of their common history, shared patterns of patronage or similarities in their composition. There is an equally important evidential typology that categorises communities according to the sources in which they are first represented, on which the separate entries in the second part of this study provide a commentary. That representational typology has therefore been situated in part II, since the whole of that volume concentrates on the problem of the sources for the study of these female religious communities.[164] It is nonetheless revealing to map these source-determined categories here, beside those determined by historical factors, since the picture they illustrate is so different. The following pages thus illustrate five further categories: groups of religious women recorded in contemporary (or supposedly contemporaneous) pre-Conquest texts; the women's religious houses whose existence was first reported in Domesday Book; congregations now known only from the report of post-Conquest, medieval writers (some of which may, of course, have been witnessed in pre-Conquest texts available to later medieval writers but since lost); and communities to whose existence only antiquaries have borne witness. One final group of houses where modern authorities have sought to locate female congregations on grounds open to challenge is discussed in part II but not mapped. The places concerned are Abbotsbury, Corbridge, Durham, Folkestone, Lyminge, Lyminster, Minster-in-Sheppey, St Osyth's at Chich, Tamworth, West Preston, Winchester, the Old Minster, and Woodchester.

Conclusion

The division of groups of houses into different categories based on similarities in their history or in the pattern of the evidence witnessing to their activities produces divergent conclusions. As is clear from the full list of places where female congregations have been attested, it has proved possible to identify many more places as home to religious women during this period than had been expected, yet the contrast between the eight or nine rich and prominent West Saxon royal houses and the impoverished, less visible majority is far starker than previously appreciated. The royal nunneries of Wessex have not just understandably, but appropriately dominated the historical literature: these were virtually the only 'nunneries' in later Anglo-Saxon England. Where the focus of much previous work has been misleading, however, has been in its implicit

---

[164]   The full range of sources testifying to the existence of communities of religious women active in the last two centuries before the Norman Conquest has already been explored above in chapter 1.

Map 9   Female religious communities mentioned in pre-Conquest
sources, 871–1066

Map 9   Female religious communities mentioned in pre-Conquest
              sources, 871–1066

Amesbury
Barking
Bedwyn
Berkeley
Bradford
Canterbury/Thanet
Cheddar
Glastonbury
Horton
Leominster
Minster-in-Sheppey
Reading
Romsey
Shaftesbury
Standon
?Tamworth
Wareham
Wenlock
Wherwell
Wilton
Wimborne
Winchcombe
Winchester, the Nunnaminster

○ Nunneries
+ Vowesses beside male abbeys

?Chester +

Chatteris ○

Leominster ○ Worcester
                  +
                              Bury +
Hereford +   St Edmunds

                              Barking ○

                              Canterbury +

            Wherwell
Amesbury ○   ○ Winchester
     Wilton ○   ○
Shaftesbury ○ Romsey ○

            Nonneminstre

0   50 miles

Map 10   Religious women in Domesday Book

Map 10   Religious women in Domesday Book

Bury St Edmunds [vowesses at a male house]
    Canterbury
    Chatteris
    ?Chester [post-Conquest sources/uncertain]
    Hereford [vowesses at a male house]
    Nonneminstre (in Sussex, either Lyminster, or West Preston)
    Worcester

Listed in Domesday Book also were the estates of:

    the royal nunneries:
        Amesbury, Barking, Romsey, Shaftesbury, Wherwell, Wilton,
        and Winchester, the Nunnaminster
    the abbess and nuns of Leominster [abandoned before 1066]
    a post-Conquest English foundation:
        St Mary Elstow
    French women's abbeys:
        Almenèsches, Holy Trinity, Caen, and Montivilliers

Map 11 Female religious communities first attested in post-Conquest medieval texts

Map 11   Female religious communities first attested in post-Conquest medieval
texts

Chester [Domesday Book?/dubious]
Chichester
Durham [vowess/dubious]
Ely
Evesham
Exeter
Polesworth
Ramsey
St Albans
Southampton [abandoned]
Tamworth [vowess/abandoned]

Map 12   Female religious communities attested only by antiquaries

Map 12   Female religious communities attested only by antiquaries

Bodmin
Boxwell [abandoned before 1066]
Castor [abandoned before 1066]
Coventry
Eltisley
Lincoln
Pershore [abandoned before 1066]
St Osyth's at Chich
Southwark
Stone
Warwick [abandoned before 1066
Woodchester [new foundation/dubious]

presumption that the enclosed, all female nunnery was the norm to which most congregations of women religious conformed, at least in the aftermath of the tenth-century monastic revolution. There were indeed many more female religious active in England during the tenth and eleventh centuries than the inmates of those few 'nunneries', but they were not 'nuns': the majority of women whose activites we have surveyed here (those living communally as well as the solitary) were secular vowesses.

The assigning of communities of female religious to typological groups according to the nature of the earliest source to witness to their existence, or by virtue of their possession of common characteristics (for example that the women lived in the immediate vicinity, perhaps under the shelter of, a male religious congregation) demonstrates to particular effect just how untypical were the royal houses of the most commonly found sorts of women's congregation. It could be argued that it was more usual for female religious not to acquire, or even not to seek to acquire, permanent landed endowments. The nunneries patronised by the royal family of Wessex were thus made exceptional by the manner of their foundation, quite apart from the fact that the mechanisms by which the lives of their inmates were governed were utterly alien to secular *nunnan*. The majority of the non-royal congregations of women religious appear, by contrast, to modern eyes to have been unsuccessful, by virtue of the brevity of their existence. This may be an inevitable consequence of the extent to which the surviving record has been determined by the preservation of record of land-ownership but, as has been argued, this is not an appropriate way in which to interpret the pattern of the surviving sources. Within the widely variable modes of female devout expression available, the permanently endowed institution for religious women is just one manifestation, made the more exceptional by its closely royal connections. Those royal ties are largely responsible for the unrepresentative geographical distribution of the nunneries within a confined area south of the Thames. Other sorts of women's religious house were more evenly distributed through England: although the attested examples all lie south of the Humber there are instances from Cheshire, the north midlands and Lincolnshire (areas far removed from the sphere of activity of the male Benedictine reformers); a couple of communities have even tentatively (and rather implausibly) been placed in Northumberland. We might just have accumulated sufficient examples of the individual and collective expression of spiritual devotion by women away from Wessex and western Mercia to suggest that the attention paid by Wulfstan, archbishop of York, in his normative writings to the activities of non-cloistered religious women and widows may have arisen in part from his direct experience of such *nunnan* in his northern province.

Chapter 7

Afterword

There hath bene monkes, then nunnys, then seculare prestes, then monkes agayn, and last canons regular in S. Petrokes chirch yn Bodmyn.

John Leland, *Itinerary in England and Wales*.[1]

It would hardly be reasonable to expect to find many precise notices of the very early religious foundation at Winchester, which in later days became so deservedly celebrated. Separated as its origin is by the long interval of a thousand years and more from the present time, the most one can hope to do is to rescue a few dim facts from the oblivion of the past, and to cast a few faint gleams of antiquarian light upon the pristine history of an institution which, however obscure its beginnings were, shone with effulgence unequalled by any similar institution in England before it became suddenly involved in the general proscription of all the religious houses in the land.

Walter de Gray Birch, *An Ancient Manuscript*.[2]

It remains to consider what might be the implications of the findings illustrated here (and demonstrated at length in part II). That women religious and the institutions in which they were housed are inadequately represented in the sources relating to England in the last two centuries before the Norman Conquest has long been recognised. That the nature of that evidence may have served to conceal the full extent to which women expressed spiritual devotion during this period has not always been so obvious: there are not only 'a lot of them about', but the means by which I have been able to identify so large a number of instances of religious women suggests that there may be many more to find. Little can, admittedly, be made of references such as that to the one-time presence of 'nunnys' at Bodmin made by Leland, but it is not necessary to abdicate from the application of critical skills to the dim relics of the past as Birch appears to have done in face of the inadequacy of the archive from the Nunnaminster at Winchester. This survey may not offer a definitive statement of female devotion during the later Anglo-Saxon period, but it does define new criteria within which more examples of veiled women can be sought as well as illuminating a context in which to situate them.

---

[1] The Itinerary of John Leland in or about the Years 1535–1543, ed. L. Toulmin Smith, 5 vols. (1964), I, 180.

[2] W. de Gray Birch, *An Ancient Manuscript of the Eighth or Ninth Century formerly belonging to St Mary's Abbey or Nunnaminster, Winchester* (1889), p. 3.

Whilst previous generations of monastic scholars allowed the weight of extant records to determine the emphases within their own explanations of the role of women in the late Anglo-Saxon Church (attributing the most importance to the small group of royal nunneries best witnessed in the historical record), of late more attention has been paid primarily to the devout women themselves, whose institutional affiliation has become an issue of secondary concern. Such recent studies have generally skirted round the question of categorising types, or classes, of religious women and hence around the related issue of the existence of more than one level of ecclesiastical site; they have not engaged directly with the potential for understanding the nature of the evidence afforded by the drawing of sharp distinctions in at least the normative sources between religious women of two sorts.[3] An answer to the evidential problem with which we began — how we should account for the apparent diminution in the evidence for female religious across the pre-Conquest period — can be posited if we recognise that the key to explanation lies in the language of the contemporary literature. The central argument defended here is couched in terms that acknowledge, and make use of, the linguistic clarity of the normative sources. Women who fulfilled their vocations within regularly constituted monasteries — *mynecena*, cloistered women — were contrasted in the vernacular literature with no less devout women who satisfied their spiritual aspirations while remaining in the world: *nunnan*, vowesses. The transparency of the texts on this matter points us to respond to the evidential difficulties by asking whether the surviving texts record instances of *nunnan* (who had formed the focus of designedly short-lived communities) rather than assuming that they must all relate to enclosed all-female religious congregations.

No originality can be claimed for this insight into the existence of parallel tracks for the expression of female devotion. Credit should in the first instance be paid to Felix Liebermann, who provided in his edition of the laws of the Anglo-Saxon kings analytical notes and a wide-ranging glossary that together explain the purport of the organisational distinction drawn first in Æthelred's fifth and sixth law-codes between cloistered *mynecena* and secular *nunnan*.[4] The historian who most effectively applied that legal material (supplemented by reference to contemporary hortatory and homiletic literature) to the situations of actual religious women in this period was Dorothy Whitelock. Her introduction to her edition of the will of Æthelgifu articulated for that one instance the central argument that has been defended here at length:[5]

---

[3]   Other than Roberta Gilchrist, *Gender and Material Culture* (1994), pp. 33–6; see further below.

[4]   F. Liebermann, ed., *Die Gesetze der Angelsachsen* (3 vols., Halle, 1903–16), II, 596–7 (*s v.* Nonne); III, 172 (*s v.* V Atr 4.1).

[5]   D. Whitelock *et al.*, *The Will of Æthelgifu* (1968), p. 34.

one suspects that [Æthelgifu] had followed the practice common
among widows of taking a vow not to remarry and living a religious
life at home without entering a nunnery.

Whitelock's remarks have not passed unnoticed; other historians have also
absorbed the significance of the existence of dual forms of female monastic
expression, or have at least drawn it to their readers' attention.[6] The greatest use
of this understanding has been made by Roberta Gilchrist, who has argued that,
since at least two classes of religious woman can be identified, corresponding
levels of ecclesiastical site may therefore be expected, formal communities of
moniales existing beside less formal congregations of *nunnan*.[7] It is, however,
possible to take this argument further than Gilchrist has done, and not solely by
establishing a fuller picture than hers of the distribution of late Anglo-Saxon
women's houses.[8]

Apply the understanding derived from the language of the sources to the
problem of the paucity of the evidence and, at one level, our answer is very
simple: there are fewer references in the sources to nunneries in England after the
First Viking Age than there are houses attested before *c.* 900 because there were
fewer nunneries in tenth- and eleventh-century England than there had been
previously (shall we say between 650 and 750). In other words, the evidence
reflects contemporary circumstances. The late Anglo-Saxon nunnery (a religious
house for cloistered women, *mynecena*) was generally a royal foundation,
permanently endowed with lands alienated from the royal demesne by means of
charter, occupied by the daughters and former wives of West Saxon kings and
playing a significant role in the commemoration of that family's dead. It lay in
central Wessex.[9] There were in the later period only nine or ten establishments
identifiable as nunneries by these criteria, precisely those that have dominated
both the contemporary sources and the secondary literature. The possession by
these nunneries of permanent landed endowments was, as we have seen, the most

---

6   B. Yorke, "'Sisters under the skin?' Anglo-Saxon nuns and nunneries in southern
England', in *Medieval Women in Southern England*, ed. K. Bate *et al.* (1989), pp. 95–117, p. 108;
M. Clayton, 'Ælfric's *Judith*: manipulative or manipulated?', *ASE*, 23 (1994), 215–27, at
pp. 225–7.

7   Gilchrist, *Gender*, p. 34. She has mapped 'Saxon nunneries' of four different types:
documented, supported by place-name evidence, cells at male houses, and informal communities
of religious women mentioned in Domesday Book: *Gender*, p. 27, figure 3, criteria that are
explained pp. 33–6. Gilchrist's argument has, to some extent, been adopted by B. Venarde,
Women's Monasticism and Medieval Society (Ithaca, New York and London, 1997), p. 47.

8   Compare map 1, with Gilchrist's map: *Gender*, p. 27, figure 3.

9   The only women's religious houses lying outside Wessex in this period that might
also be described as 'nunneries' in this restricted sense are Barking in Essex and Chatteris in
Cambridgeshire. The former had a number of connections with the West Saxon royal house, but
Chatteris is indeed exceptional as the only apparent 'nunnery' founded by a member of the
aristocracy rather than by the king or one of his close relatives during this period. See map 4,
chapter 4.

important single factor in ensuring their place within the historical record, but that is in itself a consequence of their royal associations. It was primarily royal patronage that ensured that these congregations achieved permanence in the historical record. Secondarily, the royal focus of much of the material has served to mask from view the variety of other forms of female religious expression available, for all that the evidence does tell us a good deal about the family politics of the West Saxon royal house in the tenth century, in which religious women played a crucial and visible role.

At one level, however, the sharpness of the contrast with the situation in the pre-Viking Age is illusory, for it depends on a tight and restrictive definition of what constitutes a nunnery that has no relevance to the earlier period. Indeed by the standards of the exponents of the tenth-century monastic revolution there were no nunneries in pre-Viking Age England, for there was not one house where adherence to the precepts of the Rule of St Benedict, claustration, or strict gender segregation was practised. There were *mynecena* nowhere in England before the tenth-century monastic revolution imposed the Benedictine ideal. The diversity of available forms of communal religious expression and the lack of a single model to which monastics should conform (or even aspire) during the first Christian centuries in England created a situation in which the criteria of later medieval monastic ideals had no relevance. We looked in an earlier chapter at the apparent fluidity of the composition of a number of early Anglo-Saxon minsters and wondered then how significant the distinction drawn — indeed invented — by modern historians between the 'double house' and the single-sex minster was to seventh- and eighth-century religious. Yet there are certain features of the female communal religious life that were constant across the pre-Conquest period. Double houses in particular were closely associated with the royal houses of the different English kingdoms; in its patronage of female monasticism the tenth-century West Saxon royal family was conforming to past practice. The marked difference in the geographical distribution of endowed religious houses for women before and after the First Viking Age is thus in part explained by the removal of the native royal lines of the other English kingdoms. The tenth-century West Saxon royal house endowed its devout females by alienating land from the family's own heartlands, not from territory it had acquired by conquest.

Early Anglo-Saxon religious houses for women, like their later counterparts, sustained close associations with the families, noble as well as royal, that had endowed them and were treated by their founders within broader dynastic and territorial strategies. There is every sign that early minsters continued to be perceived by the Anglo-Saxon aristocracy as family property for all that the charters by which they were founded purported to separate them from familial inheritance claims and free them in perpetuity for the service of God. The religious life afforded women in the pre-Viking Age the opportunity to control their own estates actively, retaining in large measure their aristocratic lifestyle while directing their prayerful devotion towards the commemoration of their kin. It offered a purposeful existence for widows and a potential solution to the problems inherent in the multiplication of heirs, by providing for unmarried daughters without permitting them to breed. A number of early foundations turned out ultimately — regardless of the intentions of their founders or first occupants — to have been ephemeral institutions, sustaining the religious life for only one or two generations before their lands were returned to secular use. Against this background the disappearance of the early Anglo-Saxon nun is chimerical. The concept of the cloistered woman we have shown to be an invention of tenth-century circumstances, arising from the novel imposition of Benedictine ideals, notably in this context the separation and claustration of women. The 'nun' did not disappear from England in the eighth or ninth century, she was not invented until the tenth. This is not, however, an adequate response to the evidential problems we have identified. There may have been no 'nuns' in England before the mid-tenth century, but there were large numbers of religious women who lived lives that were spiritually and economically active and successful, whose behaviour (both individually and collectively) was well-represented in the contemporary sources. The evidence from the later period is, by contrast, disproportionately skewed towards a small group of female monastic institutions distinguished by their royal associations and their probable adherence to at least the cloistered ideal, if not full Benedictine observance. Continuity before and after the ninth century lies in the expression of female devotion outside the confines of the cloister.

The late Anglo-Saxon noble *nunne* (*nonna*, or *religiosa femina*) satisfied her devotion outside the royal structure of the cloistered monastery, remaining within her own family nexus as a vowed, veiled woman and living on land which was either hers by inheritance or had been assigned to her use for her lifetime while still ultimately belonging to her male kin. Any congregation that accumulated itself around a *nunne* (whether of others of her female relations or women, perhaps with similar marital histories, from different families) was designedly impermanent. Its establishment satisfied the temporary spiritual needs of one woman, with or without companions, and provided materially for her devotion, and coincidentally for her economic support, without requiring that valuable land be permanently alienated from the family's demesne. The return to secular use of the estate(s) on which a widow or vowess had been supported should not be deemed to represent the failure of an aspiring community, but rather the natural death of an intentionally ephemeral arrangement. We ought, therefore to be wary before attempting to assign to any more formally constituted monastery, of men or of women, the single vowesses to whose spiritual desires the sources attest. Since the Church not only tolerated but legislated to control the activities of *nunnan*, those living singly as much as those in communities, it is more rational to place such women known to have had religious aspirations while retaining possession of their own landed estates outside the cloister, in their own homes.

It is here that we see the most clear continuity across the pre-Conquest period, for we know that there were *deo sacratae*, virgins and widows, living outside minsters on aristocratic family lands in the pre-Viking Age (even though they are not so clearly visible in England as in Merovingian Francia). The difference between the early and later periods lies in that since there were not before the tenth century such tight definitions as to what did and did not constitute a minster, many women who lived in this fashion may have been obscured from our view; their behaviour would not have fallen outside the norms of accepted devout practice. There is likely to have been no perceptible difference between the lifestyle followed by a group of women whose community was endowed on lands alienated permanently from the possession of a secular lord to the Church by means of charter, and women who occupied lands donated or bequeathed for just one or three lives, that would ultimately revert either to the kin of the first members or to a larger monastic or cathedral community. Where we encounter difference across the period is in the willingness of the Anglo-Saxon aristocracy to endow female congregations of the former type, those with independent landed possessions. Because it is primarily those institutions that were endowed by land booked by charter that have priority within the evidential record, the paucity of houses created as permanent establishments in the period after 900 (or in fact, from the late eighth century onwards) creates the disparity in the sources with which we have grappled throughout this study. The question we have failed to answer satisfactorily is why it was that patterns of female ecclesiastical endowment apparently changed such that only the West Saxon royal house continued to alienate land in perpetuity whereas the lay nobility (in Wessex and beyond) apparently preferred to support women's houses only temporarily. The temporary (and still more, the reversionary) grant gave bereaved and single women an element of economic security at minimal expense to their male relatives. Further, it provided for the commemoration of the wider kin group both in the short term (via the prayer and recitation of the psalter by these women in remembrance of their dead) and in the future, from the masses said by the ecclesiastical community to whom the land in question ultimately reverted. Less cynically, we should also allow for the possibility that the changes we appear to have witnessed in the patterns of endowment of the female religious life were, at least to some extent, driven by changes in women's own desires and aspirations. Women may have chosen deliberately not to enter the cloister but to satisfy their own material interests as much as their spiritual aspirations outside formally constituted monastic houses. The eternal rewards promised to both the virgin and the chaste widow were, after all, not conditional on her having submitted her will and her economic independence to the control of a monastic abbess.

Once again it may be observed that there was nothing remotely English about the female observance of devotion outside the confines of the cloister. The parallels between early Irish and Anglo-Saxon circumstances were explored in an earlier chapter where attention was drawn to the prevalence of veiled religious women in Ireland (virgins married to Christ and veiled penitents whose husbands were still alive as well as widows) who lacked institutional monastic affiliations.[10] Similarly, there were veiled, non cloistered *deo deuotae* in other parts of western Europe after the First Viking Age. Elisabeth Magnou-Nortier has explored the literature for such women particularly in southern France in the tenth and eleventh centuries and has found, as has Monteserrat Cabré y Pairet in relation to the Catalan regions, that while widows are well represented among women satisfying religious vocations in this manner, not all such women had previously been married.[11] Bruce Venarde has also collected examples of women who practised religious lives outside the coenobitic framework, citing the example of a crippled woman described in the mid-eleventh century *Miracula S Benedicti* as living in a little hut (*tuguriolum*) beside the gates of Fleury.[12] In a discussion of the charters preserved in the archive of the male Benedictine abbey of Gorze, John Nightingale has drawn attention to examples of women who retained the usufruct of estates that were ultimately to revert to the Church, and cited other examples of Lotharingian widows who held land in the same fashion;[13] some of these widows may have turned to the comforts of religion, particularly if they adhered to the Church's prohibition on remarriage. Plentiful examples can be cited from all over western Europe in this sphere, as in so many others, of the disjunction between ideal ecclesiastical prescription and actual lay practice. Patricia Skinner has illustrated this to particular effect in a discussion of widows in southern Italy in the tenth and eleventh centuries which she introduced by quoting from the life of a tenth-century saint, Nilus of Rossano. Nilus founded a convent dedicated to St Anastasia in his home city in Calabria, and urged the citizens of the town to look after these devout women: 'If any one of you dies and his widow wants to remain chaste for the rest of her life, if she has nowhere to seek refuge she will be forced to enter into a second marriage — and you will be to blame because you did not ensure that such an important city has a convent for women'.[14] However, as Skinner has demonstrated from the study of widows' wills from the region, bereaved women would often not refrain from remarriage and further those who

---

[10] Particularly helpful in this context is Máirín Ní Dhonnchadha's article, '*Caillech* and other terms for veiled women in medieval Irish texts', *Éigse*, 27 (1994–5), 71–96.

[11] E. Magnou-Nortier, Formes féminines de vie consacrée dans les pays du Midi jusqu'au début du XIIe siécle', in *La femme dans la vie religieuse du Languedoc (XIIIe–^{XIVe} s.)*, Cahiers de Fanjeaux, 23 (1988), 193–216, at pp. 206–7; M. Cabré y Pairet, '"Deodicatae" y "deovotae": La regulación de la religiosidad femenina en los condados catalanes, siglos IX–XI', in *Las mujeres en el cristianismo medieval. Imágenes teóricas y cauces de actuación religiosa*, ed. A. Muñoz Fernández (Madrid, 1989), pp. 169–82, at pp. 174–9.

[12] Venarde, *Women's Monasticism*, p. 47.

[13] J. Nightingale, 'Beyond the narrative sources: Gorze's charters 934–1000 AD', in *L'abbaye de Gorze au Xe siècle*, ed. M. Parisse and O. G. Oexle (Nancy, 1993), 91–104, at p. 103.

[14] *Vita di San Nilo*, trans. G. Giovanelli (Grottaferrata, 1966) VI, 46, trans. P. Skinner, 'Maintaining the widow in medieval southern Italy', in *Widowhood in Medieval and early Modern Europe*, ed. S. Cavallo and L. Warner (forthcoming).

did remain single and continent were as likely to fulfil those vows outside the cloister as within.[15]

The aim which first drove this study — that of identifying and cataloguing all the nunneries of later Anglo-Saxon England — has proved to be essentially misconceived through having been shaped around the wrong question. The 'nunneries' of the tenth and eleventh centuries are easily identifiable, and (within the constraints presented by the evidence) relatively readily catalogued and their sources described; they are the royal women's houses of Wessex, namely Amesbury, Horton, Romsey, Shaftesbury, Wherwell, Wilton, and the Nunnaminster at Winchester, the royally-patronised Essex house at Barking, together with the single aristocratic foundation at Chatteris in Cambridgeshire. The work of other scholars had already made it abundantly clear that there were many more places than this at which female religious had lived corporate lives of devotion, and further that there was a substantial, and until recently largely ignored, group of devout women who lived either as solitaries or in small communities, perhaps at the margins of male religious houses. Where I and others have erred was in framing questions about the larger group of female religious that were still conditioned by Benedictine notions of what constituted a nunnery, questions that focused on the paucity of evidence for all but that royal group of houses and sought explanation in the gender bias of the late Anglo-Saxon aristocratic patron or the Anglo-Saxon and later medieval historian. These veiled women did not, indeed, live in nunneries (enclosed, all female houses governed by a rule), they were not 'nuns' in the modern sense of the word, but neither did they live entirely outside the formal structures of the Church. Dynamic, flexible, inventive, independent they certainly were. Yet such women were not only recognised by the ecclesiastical establishment, their behaviour was controlled by legislation and hortatory literature was directed towards them as well as to their cloistered sisters.

Once we have fully understood the implications of the linguistic distinction drawn in vernacular texts between *mynecenu* and *nunne*, we have to rethink the questions around which our inquiry is framed. The aim of cataloguing all the congregations of veiled women active in England between the accession of Alfred and the Norman Conquest now seems unachievable. If women could use their own inheritance (whether acquired by marriage or from their blood kin) in order to support themselves individually or in small groups in religious devotion, their activities need have left no documented trail. It was only in the case of convents founded deliberately as permanent houses of God that it was necessary to acquire a written legal title to the estates from which the community was

---

[15]   Skinner, 'Maintaining the widow'. In the same article Skinner has noted that a woman's husband did not necessarily have to have died for her to be designated as a widow; she would be so described had her husband made himself 'dead to the world' by entering the cloister himself.

supported in order that their ecclesiastical use be clearly spelt out to future generations. Private arrangements on lands that never left the kin's possession but descended to a woman's own relatives according to the usual inheritance patterns had no need of written record. Only in situations where such claims were disputed (as for example, Æthelgifu struggled with her nephew over her right to inherit Standon[16]) did documentation become necessary; only when the ultimate beneficiary of the land was the Church might we otherwise expect to find surviving evidence, or the suggestion that written record had once existed. It is these, exceptional, circumstances that we have catalogued here. Those unmarried women and widows who quietly devoted their personal inheritance to religious use with the agreement of the rest of their kin, living and dying privately on family lands have found no place here, having left no written record of their devotion. Inevitably, therefore, this survey is incomplete. Despite my best efforts, there will be other vowesses and groups of *nunnan* for whom there is extant evidence that has escaped my notice. Local historians will be particularly well placed to point to any significant omissions. The possibility that more women than have been identified here chose to live as vowesses in the tenth and eleventh centuries could appropriately be considered by historians working on other aspects of the late Anglo-Saxon period, especially those concerned with patterns of aristocratic and female landholding, female inheritance, and women's testamentary arrangements. Parallel, but discrete, lines of further inquiry are suggested by the work Julia Crick has recently done both in sharpening perspectives of men and women left widowed through rigorous analysis of the literature in which they are described, but also in her important observations on the extra-ordinary status of women's testamentary statements.[17] There is a substantial body of vernacular literature that I have failed to explore which scholars of Old English might chose to reconsider in the light of my findings here.[18]

Centrally, however, my conclusions raise new questions about the Church in later Anglo-Saxon England, particularly the effect of the tenth-century monastic revolution on women's religious observance. Too long ignored by scholars of that movement, who have focused primarily on the male Benedictine houses connected with the three leading reformers, Æthelwold, Dunstan, and Oswald, and dealt with the West Saxon royal nunneries only in passing, reformed Englishwomen deserve greater attention, those living in the world as much as the cloistered. The need for further consideration of the liturgical evidence has already been mentioned; equally pressing are the questions of the education of religious women, and that of female book-ownership in this period. What might secular vowesses have read?

---

16   Whitelock, *et al.*, *The Will of Æthelgifu* (S 1497).
17   J. Crick, 'Men, women and widows: widowhood in pre-Conquest England', in *Widowhood in Medieval and early Modern Europe*, ed. S. Cavallo and L. Warner (1999), pp. 24–36.
18   This has to an extent already been begun by Mary Clayton, 'Ælfric's *Judith*: manipulative or manipulated?', *ASE*, 23 (1994), 215–27.

Was any devotional literature directed specifically at that audience? Continental comparisons also deserve further consideration; examples have been given of religious women living outside the cloister on family lands in Francia, Italy and Spain in the tenth and eleventh centuries and can be found a little later in Byzantine society also.[19]

Ultimately we can conclude that inquiry into the female religious experience in later Anglo-Saxon England must be made via the women themselves — with whose example this study began — before any attempt can be made to identify the sites where congregations of cloistered women or vowesses were found. It is not that contemporary and later medieval writers failed to bear witness to the existence of a substantial number of congregations of women religious active in the tenth and eleventh centuries. Rather, female religious devotion found communal expression more frequently in the later pre-Conquest period in forms other than that of the regularly constituted Benedictine nunnery, although that is the institutional model that once dominated the primary and secondary literature. Pious women, many of whom may have been widows, chose frequently not to leave their homes and join a distant, perhaps royally connected nunnery, but preferred instead to live as *deo deuotae* on their own estates. The 'nun' of the pre-Viking Age did not vanish during the ninth century, nor was her later Anglo-Saxon counterpart muffled deliberately by the authors of either contemporary or later medieval sources. It is not her gender that has hitherto made the veiled woman invisible, but an historical blindness to the language of the tenth-century religious life.

---

[19]   Lesley Brubaker, personal communication.

Bibliography

The evidence on which this study is based is not readily divisible into 'primary' and 'secondary' sources. Arguments about the activities of groups of religious women may rest as much on nineteenth- or twentieth-century authorities as on contemporary (or supposedly contemporaneous) witnesses to tenth- and eleventh-century events. This bibliography is therefore stratified by period. Continental and insular texts written before 1066 are listed in the first, pre-Conquest section; medieval texts date from 1066 to *c.* 1500 and early modern from *c.* 1500 to 1800. Modern authorities are those first published after 1800.

Pre-Conquest

Alcuin, *Epistolae* in *Epistolae Karolini Aevi, II*, ed. E. Dümmler, MGH, Epistolae IV (Berlin, 1895), 1–493.
Aldhelmi Opera Omnia, ed. R. Ehwald, MGH, Auctores Antiquissimi, XV (Berlin, 1919).
Aldhelm. The Prose Works, trans. M. Lapidge and M. Herren (1979).
Aldhelm. The Poetic Works, trans. M. Lapidge and J. Rosier (1985).
Die altenglische Version des Halitgar'schen Bussbuches, ed. J. Raith (Darmstadt, 1964).
Angelsächsische Homilien und Heiligenleben, ed. B. Assmann (Kassel, 1889, reprinted with a new introduction by P. Clemoes, Darmstadt, 1964).
The Anglo-Saxon Chronicle. A Collaborative Edition, ed. D. N. Dumville and S. Keynes, III, *MS A*, ed. J. M. Bately (1986).
Anglo-Saxon and Old English Vocabularies, ed. T. Wright, 2nd edn. ed. R. T. Wülcker (2 vols, 1884).
Anonymous, *Vita sancti Cuthberti*, ed. and trans. B. Colgrave, *Two Lives of Saint Cuthbert. A Life by an Anonymous Monk of Lindisfarne and Bede's Prose Life* (1940), pp. 60–139.
Anonymous, *Liber beatae Gregorii papae*, ed. and trans. B. Colgrave, *The Earliest Life of Gregory the Great* (1968).
Asser, *De rebus gestis Ælfredi*, ed. W. H. Stevenson, *Asser's Life of King Alfred together with the Annals of Saint Neots Erroneously Ascribed to Asser* (1904, reprinted with an introductory essay by D. Whitelock, 1959).
Ælfrics Grammatik und Glossar, ed. J. Zupitza (Berlin, 1880).
Ælfric's Lives of Saints. Being a set of Sermons on Saints' Days formerly observed by the English Church, ed. W. W. Skeat, 4 vols reprinted in 2, EETS o.s. 76, 82, 94, 114 (1881–1900, reprinted 1966).
Æthelwold, 'An account of King Edgar's establishment of monasteries', ed. and trans. Whitelock *et al.*, *Councils and Synods*, I, 142–54, no. 33.
'B', *Vita sancti Dunstani*, in *Memorials of St Dunstan*, ed. W Stubbs, Rolls Series 63 (1874), 3–52.
Bede, *Epistola ad Ecgbertum* in *Venerabilis Baedae Opera*, ed. C. Plummer (2 vols., 1896), I, 405–23.
— *Historia ecclesiastica gentis Anglorum*, in *Bede's Ecclesiastical History of the English People*, ed. and trans. B. Colgrave and R. A. B. Mynors (1969).

Baedae Homiliae evangelii, ed. D. Hurst, CCSL 122 (Turnhout, 1955), trans. L. T. Martin and
    D. Hurst, *Bede the Venerable. Homilies on the Gospels* (2 vols, Kalamazoo, Michigan,
    1991).
— *Venerabilis Baedae Opera Historica*, ed. C. Plummer (2 vols., 1896).
— *Vita santi Cuthberti*, ed. and trans. B. Colgrave, *Two Lives of Saint Cuthbert. A Life by an
    Anonymous Monk of Lindisfarne and Bede's Prose Life* (1940), pp. 142–307.
The Benedictional of Archbishop Robert, ed. H. Wilson (1903).
Boniface, *Epistolae*, ed. M. Tangl, *Die Briefe des Heiligen Bonifatius und Lullus*, MGH,
    Epistolae selectae I (Berlin, 1916).
Byrhtferth of Ramsey, *Vita sancti Oswaldi*, ed. J. Raine, *The Historians of the Church of York
    and its Archbishops*, Rolls Series 71 (3 vols., 1879–94), I, 399–475.
Capitularia regum Francorum, vol. I, ed. A. Boretius, vol. II ed. A. Boretius and V. Krause,
    MGH, Leges II, vols. 1–2 (Hannover, 1883 and 1897).
Charters of Barking Abbey, ed. C. R. Hart, Anglo-Saxon Charters (forthcoming).
Charters of Burton Abbey, ed. P. H. Sawyer, Anglo-Saxon Charters, II (1979).
Charters of St Augustine's Abbey, Canterbury and Minster-in Thanet, ed. S. E. Kelly, Anglo-
    Saxon Charters, IV (1995).
Charters of Selsey, ed. S. E. Kelly, Anglo-Saxon Charters, VI (1998).
Charters of Shaftesbury Abbey, ed. S. E. Kelly, Anglo-Saxon Charters, V (1996).
Charters of Sherborne, ed. M. A. O'Donovan, Anglo-Saxon Charters, III (1988).
The Chronicle of Æthelweard, ed. A. Campbell (London, 1962).
The Claudius Pontificals (from Cotton MS. Claudius A. iii in the British Museum), ed. D. H.
    Turner (1971).
Concilia Aevi Karolini, I, ed. A. Werminghoff, MGH, Leges III, Concilia II, 1 (Hannover and
    Leipzig, 1906).
Concilia Galliae A.314–A.506, ed. C. Munier, CCSL, 148 (Turnhout, 1963).
Concilia Galliae A.511–A.695, ed. C. de Clercq, CCSL, 148A (Turnhout, 1963).
The 'Constitutions' of Archbishop Oda, ed. Whitelock *et al.*, *Councils and Synods*, I, 67–74,
    no. 20.
Councils and Ecclesiastical Documents Relating to Great Britain and Ireland, ed. A. W.
    Haddan and W. Stubbs (3 vols., 1869–78).
*Die "Institutes of Polity, Civil and Ecclesiastical". Ein Werk Erzbischof Wulfstans von York
    herausgegeben von Karl Jost*, Schweizer Anglistische Arbeiten, 47 (Bern, 1959).
The Durham Collectar, ed. A. Corrêa (1992).
Early Charters of the Cathedral Church of St Paul, London, ed. M. Gibbs, Camden Society,
    3rd ser. 58 (1959).
Ex Wolfhardi Haserensis Miraculis sanctae Waldburgis Monheimensibus, ed. O. Holder-
    Egger, MGH, Scriptores, XV.I (Hannover, 1887), 535–55.
Felix, *Vita sancti Guthlaci*, ed. and trans. B. Colgrave, *Felix's Life of St Guthlac* (1956).
Die Gesetze der Angelsachsen, ed. F. Liebermann (3 vols., Halle, 1903–16).
The Great Chartulary of Glastonbury, ed. A. Watkin, 3 vols., Somerset Record Society, 59, 63,
    64 (1947, 1952, 1956).
Haddan, A. W., and W. Stubbs, ed., *Councils and Ecclesiastical Documents Relating to Great
    Britain and Ireland* (3 vols., 1869–78).
Die Heiligen Englands. Angelsächsisch und Lateinisch, ed. F. Liebermann (Hannover, 1889).
Die irische Kanonensammlung, ed. F. W. H. Wasserschleben (Giessen, 1874).
Judith. An Old English Epic Fragment, ed. and trans. A. S. Cook (Boston, Massachusetts,
    1888).
Die Konzilien der karolingischen Teilreiche, 843–859, ed. W. Hartmann, MGH, Leges III,
    Concilia III (Hannover, 1984).

Leges Langobardorum, ed. F. Bluhme, MGH, Leges, IV (Hannover, 1869); trans. K. F. Drew, *The Lombard Laws* (Philadelphia, PA, 1973).

The Leofric Missal as used in the Cathedral of Exeter during the Episcopate of its First Bishop, A.D. 1050–1072, ed. F. E. Warren (1883).

Lex Baiwariorum, ed. E. von Schwind, MGH, Leges, V, 2 (Hannover, 1926); trans. T. J. Rivers, *Laws of the Alemans and Bavarians* (Philadelphia, Pennsylvania, 1977).

Liber sacramentorum Gellonensis, ed. A. Dumas, CCSL 159 (Turnhout, 1981).

Liber Vitae ecclesiae Dunelmensis nec non obituaria duo ejusdem ecclesiae, ed. J. Stevenson, Surtees Society 8 (1841).

Liber Vitae ecclesiae Dunelmensis. A Collotype Facsimile of the Original Manuscript with Introductory Essays and Notes, ed. A. H. Thompson, Surtees Society 136 (1923).

The Liber Vitae of the New Minster and Hyde Abbey Winchester. British Library Stowe 944, together with Leaves from British Library Cotton Vespasian A. VIII and British Library Cotton Titus D. XXVII, ed. S. Keynes, Early English Manuscripts in Facsimile, 26 (Copenhagen, 1996).

Liber Vitae: Register and Martyrology of New Minster and Hyde Abbey, Winchester, ed. W. de G. Birch, Hampshire Record Society (1892).

The Old English Version of Bede's Ecclesiastical History of the English People, ed. & trans. T. Miller, 2 vols., EETS orig. ser. 95–6 and 110–11 (1890).

Le Pontifical romano-germanique du dixième siecle, ed. C. Vogel and R. Elze, 3 vols., Studi e Testi 226, 227 and 269 (Vatican City, 1963–72).

Pontificale Lanaletense (Bibliothèque de la Ville de Rouen A. 27. Cat. 368). A Pontifical formerly in Use at St. Germans, Cornwall, ed. G. H. Doble (1937).

Regularis Concordia. The Monastic Agreement of the Monks and Nuns of the English Nation, ed. T. Symons (1953).

Rudolf, *Vita Leobae abbatissae Biscofesheimensis*, ed. G. Waitz, MGH, Scriptores, XV.I (Hannover, 1887), 118–31.

Sancti Caesarii episcopi Arelatensis, Opera omnia nunc primum in unum collecta, ed. G. Morin, I: *Sermones* (Maredsous, 1937).

Sancti Eusebii Hieronymi Epistulae, ed. I. Hilberg (2 vols., Vienna, 1910).

Stephen, *Vita sancti Wilfridi*, ed. and trans. B. Colgrave, *The Life of Bishop Wilfrid by Eddius Stephanus* (1927).

Theodore, Penitential, ed. P. W. Finsterwalder, *Die Canones Theodori Cantuariensis und ihre Überlieferungsformen* (Weimar, 1929), pp. 285–334.

Two Anglo-Saxon Pontificals (the Egbert and Sidney Sussex Pontificals), ed. H. M. J. Banting, Henry Bradshaw Society, 104 (1989).

Vita Bertilae abbatissae Calensis, ed. W. Levison, MGH, Scriptores rerum Merovingicarum, VI (Hannover and Leipzig, 1913), 95–109.

Vita sanctae Monenne, ed. and trans. Ulster Society for Medieval Latin Studies, *Seanchas Ard Mhacha*, 9 (1979), 250–73 and 10 (1982), 117–41 and 426–54.

Warner of Rouen, Moriuht. A Norman Latin Poem from the Early Eleventh Century, ed. and trans. C. J. McDonough, Studies and Texts 121 (Toronto, Ontario, 1995).

The Will of Æthelgifu. A Tenth-Century Anglo-Saxon Manuscript, ed. D. Whitelock *et al.* (1968).

Wulfstan of Winchester, The Life of St Æthelwold, ed. and trans. M. Lapidge and M. Winterbottom (1991).

Wulfstan. Sammlung der ihm zugeschriebenen Homilien nebst Untersuchungen über ihre Echtheit, ed. A. Napier (Berlin, 1883).

Wulfstan, *Sermo Lupi ad Anglos*, ed. D. Whitelock (3rd edn, 1963).

Medieval

Chronicon Abbatiae Rameseiensis, ed. W. D. Macray, Rolls Series 83 (London, 1889).
De obsessione Dunelmi, ed. T. Arnold, *Symeonis monachi opera omnia* (2 vols., 1882–5), I, 215–20.
Goscelin, *Lecciones de sancta Hildelitha*, ed. M. L. Colker, 'Texts of Jocelyn of Canterbury which relate to the history of Barking Abbey', *Studia Monastica*, 7 (1965), 383–460, at pp. 455–8.
— *Libellus contra inanes s. uirginis Mildrethae usurpatores*, ed. M. L. Colker, 'A hagiographic polemic', *Mediaeval Studies*, 39 (1977), 60–108.
— *Liber confortatorius*, ed. C. H. Talbot, 'The *Liber confortatorius* of Goscelin of St Bertin', *Studia Anselmiana*, 37 (1955), 1–117.
— *Vita sanctae Edithae*, ed. A. Wilmart, 'La légende de Ste Edithe en prose et vers par le moine Goscelin', *Analecta Bollandiana*, 56 (1938), 5–101 and 265–307.
— *Vita sanctae Wulfhildae*, ed. M. Esposito, 'La vie de Sainte Vulfhilde par Goscelin de Cantorbéry', *Analecta Bollandiana*, 32 (1913), 10–26.
Historia Dunelmensis ecclesiae, ed. T. Arnold, *Symeonis monachi opera* (2 vols., 1882–5), I, 3–160.
Historia Regum, ed. T. Arnold, *Symeonis monachi opera* (2 vols., 1882–5), II, 2–283.
The Chronicle of Hugh Candidus, a Monk of Peterborough, ed. W. T. Mellows (1949).
Liber Eliensis, ed. E. O. Blake, Camden Society 3rd series, 92 (1962).
John of Worcester, *Chronicon: The Chronicle of John of Worcester, II The Annals from 450 to 1066*, ed. R. R. Darlington and P. McGurk, trans. J. Bray and P. McGurk (1995).
The Life of King Edward the Confessor, ed. and trans. F. Barlow (1962).
The Lombard Laws, trans. K. F. Drew (Philadelphia, Pennsylvania, 1973).
Osbert of Clare, *Vita sanctae Edburge*, ed. S. Ridyard, *The Royal Saints of Anglo-Saxon England* (1988), pp. 259–308.
Matthew Paris, *Gesta Abbatum*, ed. H. T. Riley, Rolls Series 28 (3 vols., 1867–9).
— *Chronica Majora*, ed. H. R. Luard, Rolls Series 57 (7 vols., 1872–80).
Nova Legenda Angliae, ed. C. Horstmann (2 vols., 1901).
Roger of Wendover, *Chronica, sive Flores Historiarum*, ed. H. O. Coxe (5 vols., 1841–4).
Sacrorum conciliorum nova et amplissima collectio, ed. J. D. Mansi *et al.* (Florence, 1759–98).
S Editha sive Chronicon Vilodunense, ed. C. Horstman (Heilbronn, 1883).
Symeonis monachi opera omnia, ed. T. Arnold, Rolls Series 75 (2 vols., 1882–5).
Vita sanctae Elfledae, ed. C. Horstman, *Nova Legenda Angliae* (2 vols., 1901), I, 379–81.
William of Malmesbury, *De antiquitate Glastonie ecclesie*, in *The Early History of Glastonbury. An Edition, Translation and Study of William of Malmesbury's De Antiquitate Glastonie Ecclesie*, ed. J. Scott (1981).
— *Gesta Regum Anglorum I*, ed. and trans. R. A. B. Mynors, R. M. Thomson and M. Winterbottom (1998).
— *De gestis pontificum Anglorum*, ed. N. E. S. A. Hamilton, Rolls Series 52 (1870).
— *Vita sancti Dunstani*, in *Memorials of St Dunstan*, ed. W Stubbs, Rolls Series 63 (1874), 250–324.
— *Vita sancti Wulfstani*, ed. R. R. Darlington, in *The Vita Wulfstani of William of Malmesbury*, Camden Society, 3rd series 40 (1928).

Early Modern

Camden's Britannia, ed. and trans. E. Gibson (1695).

Dugdale, W., *Monasticon Anglicanum: a History of the Abbies and Other Monasteries, Hospitals, Frieries and Cathedral and Collegiate Churches with their Dependencies in England and Wales*, 1655–73, new edn by J. Caley *et al.*, 6 vols. in 8 (1817–30).
—— *The Antiquities of Warwickshire* (1656, 2nd edn. 1730).
The Itinerary of John Leland in or about the Years 1535–1543, ed. L. Toulmin Smith, 5 vols. (1964).
Joannis Lelandi Antiquarii De Rebus Britannicis Collectanea, ed. T. Hearne (2nd edn, 6 vols., 1774).
Leland, J., *Commentarii de Scriptoribus Britannicis*, ed. A. Hall (1709).
Tanner, T., *Notitia Monastica or an Account of all the Abbies, Priories and Houses of Friers formerly in England and Wales* (1695, rev. edn J. Nasmith, 1787) [without pagination].

Modern

Abels, R. P., *Lordship and Military Obligation in Anglo-Saxon England* (Berkeley and Los Angeles, California, 1988).
—— *Alfred the Great. War, Kingship and Culture in Anglo-Saxon England* (1998).
Abrams, L., *Anglo-Saxon Glastonbury: Church and Endowment* (1996).
Allott, S., *Alcuin of York c. A. D. 732 to 804. His Life and Letters* (1974).
André, J. L., 'Widows and vowesses', *Archaeological Journal*, 49 (1892), 69–82.
Baker, D., ed., *Medieval Women. Studies Presented to Rosalind Hill*, Studies in Church History, Subsidia 1 (1978).
Baltrusch-Schneider, D., 'Klosterleben als alternative Lebensform zur Ehe?', in *Weibliche Lebensgestaltung im frühen Mittelalter*, ed. H.-W. Goetz (Cologne and Vienna, 1991), pp. 45–64.
Barlow, F., *The English Church 1000–1066* (2nd edn, 1979).
Barrow, J., 'English cathedral communities and reform in the late tenth and the eleventh centuries', in *Anglo-Norman Durham*, ed. D. Rollason, M. Harvey and M. Prestwich (1994), pp. 25–39.
Bateson, M., 'Rules for monks and secular canons after the revival under King Edgar', *EHR*, 9 (1894), 690–708.
Bethell, D., 'The Lives of St Osyth of Essex and St Osyth of Aylesbury', *Analecta Bollandiana*, 88 (1970), 75–127.
Bethurum, D., 'Archbishop Wulfstan's commonplace book', *Proceedings of the Modern Language Association*, 57 (1942), 916–29.
—— *The Homilies of Wulfstan* (1957).
Biddle, M. and B Kjølbye-Biddle, 'The Repton Stone', *ASE*, 14 (1985), 233–92.
—— 'Repton and the Vikings', *Antiquity*, 66 (1992), 36–51.
Birch, W. de Gray, *An Ancient Manuscript of the Eighth or Ninth Century formerly belonging to St Mary's Abbey or Nunnaminster, Winchester* (1889).
Bitel, L. M., 'Women's monastic enclosures in early Ireland', *Journal of Medieval History*, 12 (1986), 15–36.
Blair, J., 'Saint Frideswide reconsidered', *Oxoniensia*, 52 (1987), 71–127.
—— *Anglo-Saxon Oxfordshire* (1994).
—— 'Palaces or minsters? Northampton and Cheddar reconsidered', *ASE*, 25 (1996), 97–122.
Blows, M., 'A Glastonbury obit-list', in *The Archaeology and History of Glastonbury Abbey*, ed. L. Abrams and J. P. Carley (1991), pp. 257–69.
Bonner, G., D. Rollason, and C. Stancliffe, ed., *St Cuthbert, His Cult and His Community to AD 1200* (1989).

Boswell, John, '*Expositio* and *oblatio*: the abandonment of children and the ancient and medieval family', *American Historical Review*, 89 (1984), 10–33.

Boswell, J., *The Kindness of Strangers. The Abandonment of Children in Western Europe from Late Antiquity to the Renaissance* (1988).

Bremmer, J., 'Pauper or patroness: the widow in the early Christian Church', in *Between Poverty and the Pyre*, ed. J. Bremmer and L. van den Bosch (1995), pp. 31–57.

Bremmer, J. and L. van den Bosch, ed., *Between Poverty and the Pyre. Moments in the History of Widowhood* (1995).

Bremmer, R. H., 'Widows in Anglo-Saxon England', in *Between Poverty and the Pyre*, ed. J. Bremmer and L. van den Bosch (1995), pp. 58–88.

Brooks, N. P., 'The development of military obligations in eighth- and ninth-century England', in *England Before the Conquest. Studies in Primary Sources Presented to Dorothy Whitelock*, ed. P. Clemoes and K. Hughes (1971), pp. 69–84.

— 'England in the ninth century: the crucible of defeat', *TRHS*, 5 ser 29 (1979), 1–20.

— *The Early History of the Church of Canterbury. Christ Church from 597 to 1066* (1984).

— 'The career of St Dunstan', in *St Dunstan. His Life, Times and Cult*, ed. N. Ramsay *et al.* (1992), pp. 1–23.

Brooks, N. and C. Cubitt, ed., *St Oswald of Worcester. Life and Influence* (1996).

Brückmann, J., 'Latin manuscript pontificals and benedictionals in England and Wales', *Traditio*, 29 (1973), 391–458.

Brunner, K., *Altenglische Grammatik. Nach der Angelsächsischen Grammatik von Eduard Sievers* (3rd edn, Tübingen, 1965).

Byrne, Sister Mary of the Incarnation, of the Sisters of Divine Providence of Kentucky, *The Tradition of the Nun in Medieval England* (Washington, D.C., 1932).

Bullough, D., 'The continental background of the reform', in *Tenth-Century Studies*, ed. D. Parsons (1975), pp. 20–36.

Cabaniss, A., *Amalarius of Metz* (Amsterdam, 1954).

Cabré y Pairet, M., '"Deodicatae" y "deovotae": La regulación de la religiosidad femenina en los condados catalanes, siglos IX–XI', in *Las mujeres en el cristianismo medieval. Imágenes teóricas y cauces de actuación religiosa*, ed. A. Muñoz Fernández (Madrid, 1989), pp. 169–82.

Cambridge, E., 'Why did the community of St Cuthbert settle at Chester-le-Street?', in *St Cuthbert, His Cult and His Community*, ed. G. Bonner *et al.* (1989), pp. 367–86.

Campbell, A., *Old English Grammar* (1959, reprinted 1983).

Campbell, J., ed., *The Anglo-Saxons* (1982).

— *Essays in Anglo-Saxon History* (1986).

— 'Elements in the background to the life of St Cuthbert and his early cult', in *St Cuthbert, His Cult and His Community*, ed. G. Bonner *et al.*, (1989), pp. 3–19.

Chaplais, P., 'The authenticity of the royal Anglo-Saxon diplomas of Exeter', *Bulletin of the Institute of Historical Research*, 39 (1966), 1–34.

Charles-Edwards, T., 'Anglo-Saxon kinship revisited', in *The Anglo-Saxons from the Migration Period to the Eighth Century. An Ethnographic Perspective*, ed. J. Hines (1997), pp. 171–210.

Clayton, M., 'Ælfric's *Judith*: manipulative or manipulated?', *ASE*, 23 (1994), 215–27.

Clunies Ross, M., 'Concubinage in Anglo-Saxon England', *Past and Present*, 108 (1985), 3–34.

Coupland, S., 'The rod of God's wrath or the people of God's wrath? The Carolingians' theology of the Viking invasions', *Journal of Ecclesiastical History*, 42 (1991), 535–54.

Cox, J. C., 'Nunnaminster, or the abbey of St Mary Winchester', *VCH Hampshire*, II (1903), 122–6.

Craster, H. H. E., *Tynemouth Priory* (1907).
— 'Some Anglo-Saxon Records of the See of Durham', *Archaeologia Aeliana*, 4 ser 1 (1925), 189–98.
Crick, J., 'Men, women and widows: widowhood in pre-Conquest England', in *Widowhood in Medieval and Early Modern Europe*, ed. S. Cavallo and L. Warner (1999), pp. 24–36.
— 'The wealth, patronage, and connections of women's houses in late Anglo-Saxon England', *Revue bénédictine*, 109 (1999), 154–85.
— 'An eleventh-century prayerbook for women: the origins and history of the Galba prayerbook' (forthcoming).
Cubitt, C., *Anglo-Saxon Church Councils c. 650–c. 850* (1995).
— 'The tenth-century Benedictine reform in England', *Early Medieval Europe*, 6 (1997), 77–94.
— 'Universal and Local Saints in Anglo-Saxon England', in *Local Saints and Local Churches*, ed. R. Sharpe and A. Thacker (forthcoming).
Davies, W., 'Celtic women in the early middle ages', in *Images of Women in Antiquity*, ed. A. Cameron and A. Kuhrt (1993), pp. 145–66.
Dodgson, J. McN. and J. J. N. Palmer, *Domesday Book 37: Index of Persons* (1992).
Douglas, D., *The Domesday Monachorum of Christ Church, Canterbury* (1944).
Du Cange, C., *Glossarium mediae et infimae Latinitatis*, rev. edn. D. P. Carpenter and G. A. L. Henschel (10 vols. Niort, 1883–7).
Dumville, D. N., *Wessex and England from Alfred to Edgar. Six Essays on Political, Cultural and Ecclesiastical Revival* (1992).
— *Liturgy and the Ecclesiastical History of Late Anglo-Saxon England. Four Studies* (1992).
— *The Churches of North Britain in the First Viking Age*, Fifth Whithorn Lecture (1997).
Elkins, S., *Holy Women of Twelfth-Century England* (Chapel Hill, North Carolina, 1988).
Farmer, D. H., '*Regularis Concordia*: Millennium Conference', *Ampleforth Journal*, 76 (1971), 30–53.
— 'The progress of the monastic revival', in *Tenth-Century Studies*, ed. D. Parsons (1975), 10–19.
Fell, C., 'Hild, abbess of Streonæshalch', in *Hagiography and Medieval Literature. A Symposium*, ed. H. Bekker-Nielsen *et al.* (Odense, 1981), pp. 76–99.
Fell, C., with C. Clark and E. Williams, *Women in Anglo-Saxon England and the Impact of 1066* (1984).
Finberg, H. P. R., *The Early Charters of Wessex*, Studies in Early English History, 3 (1964).
— *The Early Charters of the West Midlands*, Studies in Early English History, 2 (2nd edn., 1972).
Fleming, R., 'Monastic lands and England's defence in the Viking Age', *EHR*, 100 (1985), 247–65.
Foot, S., 'Parochial ministry in early Anglo-Saxon England: the role of monastic communities', *Studies in Church History*, 26 (1989), 43–54.
— 'Violence against Christians? The Vikings and the Church in ninth-century England', *Medieval History*, 1 (1991), 3–16.
— '"By water in the Spirit": the administration of baptism in early Anglo-Saxon England', in *Pastoral Care Before the Parish*, ed. J. Blair and R. Sharpe (1992), pp. 171–92.
— 'Anglo-Saxon minsters: a review of terminology', in *Pastoral Care Before the Parish*, ed. J. Blair and R. Sharpe (1992), pp. 212–25.
— 'The role of the minster in earlier Anglo-Saxon society', in *Monasteries and Society in Medieval England*, Proceedings of the 1994 Harlaxton Symposium, ed. B. Thompson (Stamford, 1999), pp. 35–48.

— 'Language and method: the Dictionary of Old English and the historian', in *The Dictionary of Old English. Retrospects and Prospects*, ed. M. J. Toswell, Old English Newsletter, Subsidia 26 (1998), 73–87.

Foy, J. D., *Domesday Book 38: Index of Subjects* (1992).

Gibson, W. S., *The History of the Monastery founded at Tynemouth in the Diocese of Durham, to the Honour of God, under the Invocation of the Blessed Virgin Mary and S. Oswin, King and Martyr* (2 vols., 1846–7).

Gilchrist, R., *Gender and Material Culture. The Archaeology of Religious Women* (1994).

Godfrey, J., 'The place of the double monastery in the Anglo-Saxon minster system', in *Famulus Christi*, ed. G. Bonner (1976), pp. 344–50.

Golding, B., *Gilbert of Sempringham and the Gilbertine Order c. 1130–1300* (1995).

Gransden, A., 'Traditionalism and continuity during the last century of Anglo-Saxon monasticism', *Journal of Ecclesiastical History*, 40 (1989), 159–207.

Gryson, R., *The Ministry of Women in the Early Church*, trans. J. Laporte and M. L. Hall (Collegeville, Minnesota, 1976).

Halsall, G., 'Playing by whose rules? A further look at Viking atrocity in the ninth century', *Medieval History*, 2.2 (1992), 2–12.

Halpin, P., 'Women religious in late Anglo-Saxon England', *Haskins Society Journal*, 6 (1994), 97–110.

Hartmann, W., *Die Synoden der Karolingerzeit im Frankenreich und in Italien* (Paderborn, 1989).

— *Das Konzil von Worms, 868* (Göttingen, 1977).

Healey, A. diPaolo and R. L. Venezky, *A Microfiche Concordance to Old English* (Toronto, 1982).

Hilpisch, S., *Die Doppelklöster: Entstehung und Organisation*, Beiträge zur Geschichte des alten Mönchtums un des Benediktinerordens, 15 (Münster, 1928).

Hinton, D. A., 'Amesbury and the early history of its abbey', *The Amesbury Millennium Lectures*, ed. John Chandler (Amesbury, 1979), pp. 20–31.

Hohler, C., 'St Osyth and Aylesbury', *Records of Buckinghamshire*, 18 (1966), 61–72.

Hollis, S., *Anglo-Saxon Women and the Church: Sharing a Common Fate* (1992).

Horner, S., 'Spiritual truth and sexual violence: the Old English *Juliana*, Anglo-Saxon nuns and the discourse of female monastic enclosure', *Signs. Journal of Women in Culture and Society*, 19 (1994), 658–75.

Hughes, K., *Early Christian Ireland. Introduction to the Sources* (1972).

Hunter Blair, P., *The World of Bede* (1970).

— *Northumbria in the Days of Bede* (1976).

John, E., *Land Tenure in Early England. A Discussion of Some Problems* (2nd edn, 1964).

— *Reassessing Anglo-Saxon England* (1996).

Jong, M. de, *In Samuel's Image. Child Oblation in the Early Medieval West*, Brill Studies in Intellectual History, 12 (Leiden, 1996).

Jussen, B., 'On Church organisation and the definition of an estate: the idea of widowhood in late antique and early medieval Christianity', *Tel Aviver Jahrbuch für deutsche Geschichte*, 22 (1993), 25–42.

Ker, N. R., *Catalogue of Manuscripts Containing Anglo-Saxon* (Oxford, 1957, reissued 1990).

Keynes, S. and M. Lapidge, *Alfred the Great: Asser's 'Life of King Alfred' and Other Contemporary Sources* (1983).

King, P. D., *Charlemagne. Translated Sources* (1987).

Knowles, D., *The Monastic Order in England. A History of its Development from the Times of St Dunstan to the Fourth Lateran Council, 940–1216* (2nd edn., 1963).

Knowles, D. and R. N. Hadcock, *Medieval Religious Houses. England and Wales* (2nd edn. 1971).

Langefeld, B., '*Regula canonicorum* or *Regula monasterialis uitae*? The Rule of Chrodegang and Archbishop Wulfred's reforms at Canterbury', *ASE*, 25 (1996), 21–36.

Lapidge, M., *Anglo-Latin Literature, 600–899* (1996).

— 'Æthelwold as scholar and teacher', in *Bishop Æthelwold*, ed. B. Yorke (1988), pp. 89–117.

— 'The origin of CCCC 163', *Transactions of the Cambridge Bibliographical Society*, 8 (1981), 18–28.

— 'Ealdred of York and MS. Cotton Vitellius E. XII', *Yorkshire Archaeological Journal*, 55 (1983), 11–25.

Le Bourdellès, H., 'Les ministères féminins dans le haut moyen âge en Occident', in *La Femme au Moyen-Age*, ed. M. Rouche and J. Heuclin (Maubeuge, 1990), pp. 11–23.

Leroquais, V., *Les Pontificaux manuscrits des bibliothèques publiques de France* (4 vols., Paris, 1937).

Leyser, H., *Medieval Women. A Social History of Women in England, 450–1500* (1995).

Leyser, K. J., *Rule and Conflict in an Early Medieval Society* (1979).

MacGowan, K., 'Barking Abbey', *Current Archaeology*, 149 (1996), 172–8.

McKitterick, R., *The Frankish Church and the Carolingian Reforms, 789–895*, Royal Historical Society, Studies in History (1977).

McNeill, J. T. and H. M. Gamer, *Medieval Handbooks of Penance. A Translation of the Principal 'Libri Poenitentiales' and Selections from Related Documents*, Records of Western Civilization, 29 (New York, 1938, reprinted 1990).

Magnou-Nortier, E., 'Formes féminines de vie consacrée dans les pays du Midi jusqu'au début du XII siécle', in *La femme dans la vie religieuse du Languedoc (XIIIᵉ–XIVᵉ s.)*, Cahiers de Fanjeaux, 23 (1988), 193–216.

Martindale, J., 'The nun Immena and the foundation of the Abbey of Beaulieu: a woman's prospects in the Carolingian Church', in *Women in the Church*, Studies in Church History, 27, ed. W. J. Sheils and D. Wood (1990), 27–42.

Mason, E., *St Wulfstan of Worcester, c.1008–1095* (1990).

Mayr-Harting, H., *The Coming of Christianity to Anglo-Saxon England* (3rd edn, 1991).

Merritt, H., 'Old English entries in a manuscript at Bern', *Journal of English and Germanic Philology*, 33 (1934), 343–51.

Metz, R., 'Le statut de la femme en droit canonique médiéval', *Recueils de la Société Jean Bodin*, 12 (1962), 59–113.

— *La consécration des vièrges dans l'église romaine. Etude d'histoire de la liturgie*, Bibliothèque de l'institut de droit canonique de l'université de Strasbourg, 4 (Paris, 1954).

Meyer, M. A., 'Women and the tenth century English monastic reform', *Revue bénédictine*, 87 (1977), 34–61.

— 'Land charters and the legal position of Anglo-Saxon women', in *The Women of England from Anglo-Saxon Times to the Present*, ed. B. Kanner (1980), pp. 57–82.

— 'Patronage of West Saxon royal nunneries in late Anglo-Saxon England', *Revue bénédictine*, 91 (1981), 332–58.

— 'The queen's "demesne" in later Anglo-Saxon England', in *The Culture of Christendom. Essays in Medieval History in Commemoration of Denis L. T. Bethell*, ed. M. A. Meyer (1993), pp. 75–113.

— 'Queens, convents and conversion in early Anglo-Saxon England', *Revue bénédictine*, 109 (1999), 90–116.

Moreau, E. de, 'Les "monastères doubles": leur histoire surtout en Belgique', *Nouvelle Revue Théologique*, 66 (1939), 787–92.

Morrish, J., 'King Alfred's letter as a source on learning in England', in *Studies in Earlier Old English Prose*, ed. P. E. Szarmach (Kalamazoo, MI, 1986), pp. 87–107.

Muschiol, G., *Famula Dei. Zur Liturgie in merowingischen Frauenklöstern*, Beiträge zur Geschichte des alten Mönchtums und des Benediktinertums, 42 (Münster, 1994).

Nelson, J. L., 'Kommentar', in *Frauen in Spätantike und Frühmittelalter*, ed. W. Affeldt (Sigmarinen, 1990), pp. 325–32.

— 'Women and the word in the earlier middle ages', in *Women in the Church*, Studies in Church History, 27, ed. W. J. Sheils and D. Wood (1990), 53–78.

— 'The wary widow', in *Property and Power in the Early Middle Ages*, ed. W. Davies and P. Fouracre (1995), pp. 82–113.

Ní Dhonnchadha, M., '*Caillech* and other terms for veiled women in medieval Irish texts', *Éigse*, 27 (1994–5), 71–96.

Niermeyer, J. F., *Mediae Latinitatis Lexicon Minus* (Leiden, 1976).

Nichols, J. A. and L. T. Shank, *Medieval Religious Women I. Distant Echoes* (Kalamazoo, Michigan, 1984).

Nicholson, J., '*Feminae gloriosae*: Women in the age of Bede', in *Medieval Women*, ed. D. Baker (1978), pp. 15–29.

Nightingale, J., 'Beyond the narrative sources: Gorze's charters 934–1000 AD', in *L'abbaye de Gorze au Xe siècle*, ed. M. Parisse and O. G. Oexle (Nancy, 1993), pp. 91–104.

O'Brien, S., 'Terra incognita: the nun in nineteenth-century England', *Past and Present*, 121 (1988), 110–40.

Owen, G. R., 'Wynflæd's wardrobe', *ASE*, 8 (1979), 195–222.

Palazzo, E., 'Les formules de bénédiction et de consécration des veuves au cours du haut Moyen Age', in *Veuves et veuvage dans le haut Moyen Age*, ed. M. Parisse (Paris, 1993), pp. 31–6.

Parisse, M., 'Les chanoinesses dans l'empire germanique (ixe–xie siècles)', *Francia*, 6 (1978), 107–26.

— 'Der Anteil der Lothringischen Benediktinerinnen an der monastischen Bewegung des 10. und 11. Jahrhunderts', *Religiöse Frauenbewegung und mystische Frömmigkeit im Mittelalter*, ed. P. Dinzelbacher and D. R. Bauer (Cologne and Vienna, 1988), pp. 83–97.

— 'Des veuves au monastère', in *Veuves et veuvage dans le haut Moyen Age*, ed. M. Parisse (Paris, 1993), pp. 255–74.

— ed., *Veuves et veuvage dans le haut Moyen Age* (Paris, 1993).

Parsons, D., ed., *Tenth-Century Studies. Essays in Commemoration of the Millennium of the Council of Winchester and 'Regularis Concordia'* (1975).

Partner, N., 'Making up lost time: Writing on the writing of History', *Speculum*, 61 (1986), 90–117.

Pelteret, D. A. E., *Slavery in Early Mediaeval England from the Reign of Alfred until the Twelfth Century*, Studies in Anglo-Saxon History, 7 (1995).

Pontal, O., *Histoire des conciles mérovingiens* (Paris, 1989).

Pope, J. M., 'Monks and nobles in the Anglo-Saxon monastic reform', *Anglo-Norman Studies*, 17 (1994), 165–80.

Power, E. E., *Medieval English Nunneries* (1922).

Ramsay, N., M. Sparks and T. Tatton-Brown, *St Dunstan. His Life, Times and Cult* (1992).

Richards, M. P. and B. J. Stanfield, 'Concepts of Anglo-Saxon women in the laws', in *New Readings on Women in Old English Literature*, ed. H. Damico and A. H. Olsen (Bloomington and Indianapolis, Indiana, 1990), pp. 89–99.

Ridyard, S., *The Royal Saints of Anglo-Saxon England. A Study of West Saxon and East Anglian Cults* (1988).

Rigold, S. E., 'The "double minsters" of Kent and their analogies', *Journal of the British Archaeological Association*, 3rd ser. 31 (1961), 27–37.

Rivers, T. J., 'Widows' rights in Anglo-Saxon law', *American Journal of Legal History*, 19 (1975), 208–15.

Robertson, A. J., *The Laws of the Kings of England from Edmund to Henry I* (1925).

— *Laws of the Alemans and Bavarians* (Philadelphia, Pennsylvania, 1977).

Rollason, D. W., *The Mildrith Legend. A Study in Early Medieval Hagiography in England* (1982).

Rosenthal, J. T., 'Anglo-Saxon attitudes: Men's sources, women's history', in *Medieval Women and the Sources of Medieval History*, ed. J. T. Rosenthal (Athens, Georgia and London, 1990), pp. 259–84.

Sawyer, P. H., *The Age of the Vikings* (2nd edn, 1971).

Schneider, D. B., 'Anglo-Saxon women in the religious life: a study of the status and position of women in an early mediaeval society' (PhD thesis, University of Cambridge, 1985).

Schulenberg, J. T., 'Strict active enclosure and its effects on the female monastic experience (500–1100)', in *Medieval Religious Women I: Distant Echoes*, ed. J. A. Nichols and L. T. Shank (1984), pp. 51–86.

— 'The heroics of virginity: Brides of Christ and sacrificial mutilation', in *Women in the Middle Ages and the Renaissance. Literary and Historical Perspectives*, ed. M. B. Rose (Syracuse, New York, 1986), pp. 29–72.

— 'Female sanctity: Public and private roles, ca. 500–1100', in *Women and Power in the Middle Ages*, ed. M. Erler and M. Kowaleski (Athens, Georgia, 1988), pp. 102–25.

— 'Women's monastic communities, 500–1100: Patterns of expansion and decline', *Signs. Journal of Women in Culture and Society*, 14 (1989), 261–92.

Sims-Williams, P., *Religion and Literature in Western England, 600–800*, Cambridge Studies in Anglo-Saxon England, 3 (1990).

Sisam, K., *Studies in the History of Old English Literature* (1953).

Skinner, M., 'Benedictine life for women in central France, 850–1100: a feminist revival', in *Medieval Religious Women I: Distant Echoes*, ed. J. A. Nichols and L. T. Shank (1984), pp. 87–113.

Skinner, P., 'Maintaining the widow in medieval southern Italy', in *Widowhood in Medieval and early Modern Europe*, ed. S. Cavallo and L. Warner (forthcoming, 1999).

Smyth, A. P., *King Alfred the Great* (1997).

Spiegel, G., 'History, historicism and the social logic of the text', *Speculum*, 65 (1990), 59–86.

Stafford, P. 'Sons and mothers: Family politics in the early middle ages', in *Medieval Women*, ed. D. Baker (1978), pp. 79–100.

— 'The laws of Cnut and the history of Anglo-Saxon royal promises', *Anglo-Saxon England*, 10 (1982), 173–90.

— *Queens, Concubines and Dowagers. The King's Wife in the Early Middle Ages* (Athens, Georgia, 1983).

— 'Women and the Norman Conquest', *TRHS*, 6th ser. 4 (1994), 221–49.

— *Queen Emma and Queen Edith. Queenship and Women's Power in Eleventh-Century England* (1997).

— 'Queens, nunneries and reforming churchmen: Gender, religious status and reform in tenth- and eleventh-century England', *Past and Present*, 163 (1999), 3–35.

Stenton, F. M., *The Early History of the Abbey of Abingdon* (1913).

— *Anglo-Saxon England* (3rd edn, 1971).

Symons, T., '*Regularis concordia*: History and derivation', in *Tenth-Century Studies*, ed. D. Parsons (1975), pp. 37–59.

Swanton, M., *Anglo-Saxon Prose* (2nd edn, 1993).

Talbot, C. H., *The Anglo-Saxon Missionaries in Germany. Being the Lives of SS. Willibrord, Boniface, Sturm, Leoba and Lebuin, together with the 'Hodoeporicon' of St Willibald and a selection from the correspondence of St Boniface* (2nd edn, 1981).

Taylor, C. S., 'Berkeley minster', *Transactions of the Bristol and Gloucestershire Archaeological Society*, 19 (1894–5), 70–84.

Taylor, H. M. and J. Taylor, *Anglo-Saxon Architecture* (3 vols., 1965–78).

Thompson, S., 'Why English nunneries had no history: a study of the problems of the English nunneries founded after the Conquest', in *Distant Echoes*, ed. J. A. Nichols and L. T. Shank (Kalamazoo, Michigan, 1984), pp. 131–49.

— *Women Religious. The Founding of English Nunneries after the Norman Conquest* (1991).

Thorn, C. and F. Thorn, *Domesday Book 7: Dorset*, ed. J. Morris (1983).

Venarde, B. L., *Women's Monasticism and Medieval Society: Nunneries in France and England, 890–1215* (Ithaca, New York and London, 1997).

Verdon, J., 'Recherches sur les monastères féminins dans la France du Sud aux ixe–xie siècles', *Annales du Midi*, 88 (1976), 118–38.

— 'Recherches sur les monastères féminins dans la France du Nord aux ixe–xie siècles', *Revue Mabillon*, 59 (1976), 49–96.

Wallace-Hadrill, J. M., *Bede's Ecclesiastical History of the English People. A Historical Commentary* (1988).

Wemple, Suzanne, 'Female monasticism in Italy and its comparison with France and Germany from the ninth through the eleventh century', in *Frauen in Spätantike und Frühmittelalter. Lebensbedingungen — Lebensnormen — Lebensformen*, ed. W. Affeldt (Sigmaringen, 1990), pp. 291–310.

Wemple, S. F., *Women in Frankish Society. Marriage and the Cloister 500–900* (Philadelphia, Pennsylvania, 1981).

Whitelock, D., 'Archbishop Wulfstan: homilist and statesman', *TRHS*, 4th ser. 24 (1942), 25–45, reprinted in her *History, Law and Literature in 10th–11th Century England*, Variorum reprints (1981), no. XI.

— 'Wulfstan at York', in *Franciplegius. Medieval and Linguistic Studies in Honour of Francis Peabody Magoun Jnr*, ed. J. B. Bessinger and R. P. Creed (New York, 1965), pp. 214–31.

— 'The authorship of the account of King Edgar's establishment of monasteries', in *Philological Essays*, ed. J. L. Rosier (The Hague, 1970), pp. 125–36, reprinted in Whitelock, *History, Law and Literature in 10th–11th Century England*, Variorum reprints (1981), no. VII.

Wormald, P., 'Bede, "Beowulf" and the conversion of the Anglo-Saxon aristocracy', in *Bede and Anglo-Saxon England*, ed. R. T. Farrell, British Archaeological Reports, British series 46 (1978), 32–95.

— 'Æthelwold and his continental counterparts: Contact, comparison, contrast', in *Bishop Æthelwold*, ed. B. Yorke (1988), pp. 13–42.

— *How do we know so much about Anglo-Saxon Deerhurst?* Deerhurst Lecture 1991 (1993).

— 'St Hilda, saint and scholar (614–80)', in *The St Hilda's College Centenary Symposium. A Celebration of the Education of Women*, ed. J. Mellanby (1993), pp. 93–103.

Yorke, B., *Bishop Æthelwold: His Career and Influence* (1988).

— '"Sisters under the skin?" Anglo-Saxon nuns and nunneries in southern England', in *Medieval Women in Southern England*, ed. K. Bate *et al.* Reading Medieval Studies, 15 (1989), 95–117.

— *Wessex in the Early Middle Ages* (1995).

— 'The Bonifacian mission and female religious in Wessex', *Early Medieval Europe*, 7 (1998), 145–72.

Index

36, 152

East Dereham, Norfolk, 82

Eawynne, *religiosa femina*, 184

Ebchester, County Durham, 82

Ecgbert, archbishop of York, 22, 28–9, 45–6, 54

Ecfrida (Ecgfriðu), 135, 178

Edeva, widow, 188

Edgar, king of England, 2, 4, 6, 12, 14, 52, 60–1, 75, 85, 88, 91–2, 96–7, 101, 104, 122, 134, 136, 138, 140, 143, 154, 160–1, 163–4, 166–7, 173, 183

Edington, Wiltshire, 161

Edith, *monialis* in Somerset, 104, 185–6

Edith, sister of King Æthelstan, 157, 163

Edith, St, 2, 12, 94, 165

Edmund, king of Wessex, 136, 183

Edmund, martyr-king of East Anglia, 111, 135

Edmund, son of King Edgar, 161, 165, 182

Edward the Confessor, king, 183, 186

Edward the Elder, king, 2, 50, 86, 92, 97, 112, 141, 145, 154, 157, 160, 164–5

Edward, king and martyr, 76, 164–5

Edwin, abbot of Westminster, 183

Edwin, king of Northumbria, 35, 42, 45

Edwin, priest (slave) 1, 4, 139, 179

Elstow, St Mary's, Bedfordshire, 103, 193

Eltisley, Cambridgeshire, 16, 82, 197

Ely, Cambridgeshire, 23, 23, 41, 42, 44, 48, 55n, 72, 77, 82, 92, 140, 175, 176, 195

enclosure (monastic), 48, 51–2, 62, 67
   enclosed female communities, 5, 12, 97–8, 101, 104, 111, 179, 198, 200, 206

endowment (monastic), 2, 11–12, 16–17, 21, 25–6, 31, 33, 35, 43, 47–8, 54, 59, 64–6, 84, 92, 125, 142–4, 147–8, 152, 155–6, 160–2, 166, 170, 172, 198, 201–2, 204
   poverty of, 156, 170

entry to religion, 118

Eorcengota, 36

Eorcenwold, king of Kent, 54

Eormenhild, 42

Evesham, Worcestershire, 55n, 175, 176, 187, 195

Exeter, Devon, 8n, 16, 169, 170, 179, 195

family minsters, 42, 44–6, 52–3, 59–60, 64–5, 202–3

Faremoutiers-en-Brie, 36

fasting, 101, 116, 128

Fladbury, Worcestershire, 25

Flixborough, Lincolnshire, 51n

Folcburg, nun at Bath, 37

Folkestone, Kent, 25, 36, 44, 82, 151, 152, 169, 189

Francia, women religious in, 31, 36–7, 42–3, 46, 107, 113, 116, 119, 121, 204, 208

Frideswide, St, 23

Fulk, archbishop of Rheims, 74

gender, 9, 22, 32–4, 49, 51, 53, 63, 97, 143, 166, 202, 206, 208

Gilbert of Sempringham, 49

Glastonbury, Somerset, 12, 15, 55n, 62, 75, 85, 173, 175, 177, 181–3, 191

Gloucester, Gloucestershire, 25, 45, 80n

Godiva, wife of Earl Leofric, 186

Godwine, earl of Wessex, 157, 170

Goscelin of St Bertin, 12–14, 72n, 92n, 149, 161, 167

Guthlac, St, 23

Gytha, wife of Godwine, 157

Hackness, North Yorkshire, 82

Halitgar, Penitential, 123

Hamtunia, see Southampton

Hanbury, Worcestershire, 25, 82

Hartlepool, Durham, 36–7

Heahflæd, abbess of Amesbury and Wherwell, 164

Heiu, abbess of Hartlepool, 36–7

Hereford, Herefordshire, 55n, 103, 175, 176, 193

Hereswith, sister of Hild, 36–7

Hild, abbess of Whitby, 22, 25, 37, 40, 44

Hitchin, Hertfordshire, 138

Hoo, Kent, 25, 82

Horton, Dorset, 6, 11, 13, 92n, 159, 160–1, 164–7, 169, 170, 191

Hrothwaru, *religiosa femina*, 57

Hunrud, *deo deuota femina*, 57

Hyde Abbey, *Liber Vitae*, 13, 15, 23, 157, 167

Immena, 47, 68–9